NABOKOV'S OTHERWORLD

NABOKOV'S OTHERWORLD

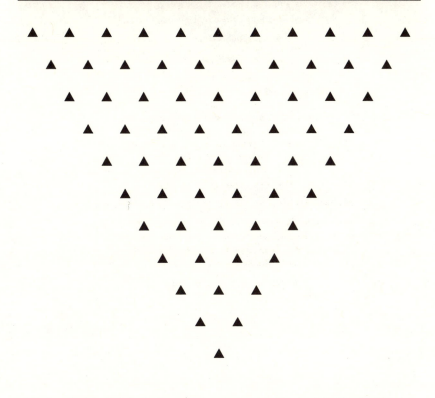

VLADIMIR E. ALEXANDROV

PRINCETON UNIVERSITY PRESS, PRINCETON, NEW JERSEY

Copyright © 1991 by Princeton University Press
Published by Princeton University Press, 41 William Street,
Princeton, New Jersey 08540
In the United Kingdom: Princeton University Press, Oxford

Library of Congress Cataloging-in-Publication Data

Alexandrov, Vladimir E.
Nabokov's otherworld / Vladimir E. Alexandrov.
p.   cm.
Includes bibliographical references and index.
ISBN 0-691-06866-6 (cloth : acid-free paper)
1. Nabokov, Vladimir Vladimirovich, 1899–1977—Criticism and
interpretation. I. Title.
PG3476.N3Z56   1991
813'.54—dc20   90-38555 CIP

This book has been composed in Linotron Sabon and Gill Sans

Princeton University Press books are printed on acid-free paper,
and meet the guidelines for permanence and durability of the
Committee on Production Guidelines for Book Longevity
of the Council on Library Resources

Printed in the United States of America by
Princeton University Press, Princeton, New Jersey

1   3   5   7   9   10   8   6   4   2

FOR NICHOLAS AND SOPHIA

Contents

Acknowledgments

I take pleasure in recording my gratitude to the
National Endowment of the Humanities for a Fellowship
for Independent Study and Research.

Excerpts from the works of Vladimir Nabokov (full
bibliographic data for which can be found in my list of
"Works Cited") are reprinted by arrangement with the
Estate of Vladimir Nabokov. All rights reserved.

A preliminary version of chapter 4 appeared as "The
'Otherworld' in Nabokov's *The Gift*," in *Studies in
Russian Literature in Honor of Vsevolod Setchkarev*,
edited by Julian W. Connolly and Sonia I. Ketchian,
Columbus, Ohio: Slavica, 1986, 15–33. Several pages of
chapter 1 and part of the Conclusion were published as
"Nabokov's Metaphysics of Artifice: Uspenskij's
'Fourth Dimension' and Evreinov's 'Theatrarch,' "
Rossiia/Russia 6, nos. 1 and 2 (1988):
131–43.

Note on Transliteration

A simplified version of the Library of Congress system
for transliterating the Russian alphabet is used throughout.
The only exceptions are Nabokov's own transliterations
of names from his works, several Russian names whose
spellings have become more or less fixed in English
(e.g., Tolstoy, Soloviev), and transliterations
in critical studies.

NABOKOV'S OTHERWORLD

. . . . . . Я счастлив, что совесть моя,
        сонных мыслей и умыслов сводня,
не затронула самого тайного. Я
        удивительно счастлив сегодня.
Эта тайна та-та, та-та-та-та, та-та,
        а точнее сказать я не вправе.
Оттого так смешна мне пустая мечта
        о читателе, теле и славе.
Я без тела разросся, без отзвука жив,
        и со мной моя тайна всечасно.
Что мне тление книг, если даже разрыв
        между мной и отчизною—частность?
Признаюсь, хорошо зашифрована ночь,
        но под звезды я буквы подставил
и в себе прочитал чем себя превозмочь,
        а точнее сказать, я не вправе.
Не доверясь соблазнам дороги большой
        или снам, освященным веками,
остаюсь я безбожником с вольной душой
        в этом мире, кишащем богами.
Но однажды, пласты разуменья дробя,
        углубляясь в свое ключевое,
я увидел, как в зеркале, мир, и себя,
        и другое, другое, другое.

(I'm happy that Conscience, the pimp / of my sleepy reflections and projects, / did not get at the critical secret. Today / I am really remarkably happy. / / That main secret tra-tá-ta tra-tá-ta tra-tá— / and I must not be overexplicit; / this is why I find laughable the empty dream / about readers, and body, and glory. / / Without body I've spread, without echo I thrive, / and with me all along is my secret. / A book's death can't affect me since even the break / between me and my land is a trifle. / / I admit that the night has been ciphered right well / but in place of the stars I put letters, / and I've read in myself how the self to transcend— / and I must not be overexplicit. / / Trusting not the enticements of the thoroughfare / or such dreams as the ages have hallowed, / I prefer to stay godless, with fetterless soul / in a world that is swarming with godheads. / / But one day while disrupting the strata of sense / and descending deep down to my wellspring / I saw mirrored, besides my own self and the world, / something else, something else, something else.)

Vladimir Nabokov, from "Fame," in *Poems and Problems*

Nabokov's Metaphysics, Ethics, and Aesthetics

THE AIM of this book is to dismantle the widespread critical view that Vladimir Nabokov (1899–1977) is first and foremost a metaliterary writer, and to suggest instead that an aesthetic rooted in his intuition of a transcendent realm is the basis of his art. From the time Nabokov began to rise to prominence within the Russian diaspora in Europe during the 1920s, to the present day, when he is regarded throughout the world as one of the leading novelists of the century, readers of the most different stripes have repeated that the ironic manipulation of the devices and forms of narrative fiction lies at the heart of his oeuvre.[1] This view persists no matter how Nabokov's penchant for self-conscious artifice is evaluated. A number of prominent Russian émigré critics wrote of the "un-Russianness" ("nerusskost' ") of his talent, by which they meant, in part, that he evinced no interest in the social, political, moral, or religio-philosophical themes (and attendant artistic forms) that characterized many of the most famous works of nineteenth-century Russian literature.[2] Thus from their perspective, the metaliterariness of Nabokov's fiction is reprehensible, albeit dazzling, frivolity, because by indulging in it he sidesteps the writer's obligation to address existing, "real" problems. At the opposite extreme are contemporary critics in the United States and Europe who see Nabokov's insistent artificiality as a laudable defense of the artist's free creativity in the face of a hostile, indifferent, chaotic, or valueless world.[3]

In my view, both facets of this approach are fundamental misreadings of Nabokov because they foreground only one major feature of his art and ignore its dependence on his central theme of the "otherworld." This term is my (not wholly satisfactory) translation of the Russian word *potustoronnost'*, a noun derived from an adjective denoting a quality or state that pertains to the "other side" of the boundary separating life and death; additional possible translations are "the hereafter" and "the beyond." The centrality of this concept for Nabokov's art was announced by his widow in her Foreword to the posthumous collection of his Russian poems published in 1979.[4] In her brief but seminal remarks, Vera Nabokov calls "potustoronnost' " Nabokov's "main theme," and stresses that although it "saturates everything he wrote," it does not appear to have been noted by anyone. She then names several poems from various periods of his life, and a passage from the novel *The Gift*, that express this theme with varying degrees of clarity. But she does not go beyond her husband's own veiled hints in these works about what "potustoronnost' " meant for him: it is "a mystery that he carries in his soul and that he neither may nor can betray"; it is what "gave him his imperturbable love of life ['zhizneradostnost' '] and lucidity even during life's most difficult trials." A fuller statement regarding Nabokov's otherworldly beliefs can be found in his lecture "The Art of Literature and Commonsense," which was published posthumously in 1980, and which is, among other remarkable things, a revealing expression of his sui generis faith in a transcendent realm.[5] Given that both the lecture and Vera Nabokov's Foreword have now been in print for a decade, and that they proclaim beliefs that fly in the face of trends that have dominated Nabokov criticism for some sixty years, it is surprising how few readers have attempted to engage these new ideas, or to consider their implications for a radical rereading of Nabokov's legacy, especially in view of the vast number of publications (reviews, articles, books) that have appeared.[6] Nevertheless, it is important to acknowledge that chronological pride of place for making significant claims regarding the centrality of metaphysics in Nabokov's art goes to a handful of earlier investigators.[7] It is, however, a source of puzzlement that these studies have also not had more of an effect on the reigning scholarly perceptions of Nabokov. Surely this is justification for a book-length study that investigates the otherworld in detail and places it at the center of Nabokov's entire oeuvre.

As far as I know, Vera Nabokov was the first to state that the central fact of both Nabokov's life and his art was something that could be characterized as an intuition about a transcendent realm of being (although occasional comments about aspects of Nabokov's metaphysical beliefs appeared earlier as well). At the same time, the form and substance of her valuable revelation underscore the pitfalls involved in talking about it. Because Nabokov believed that his "mystery" was ultimately incommunicable (which would have been a less convincing claim were he not an acknowledged master of three languages) he used only circumlocutions to describe it. For example, when an interviewer asked if he believed in God, Nabokov's famous response was: "I know more than I can express in words, and the little I can express would not have been expressed, had I not known more." In "The Art of Literature and Commonsense" he speaks of an aspect of his faith in the following terms: "That human life is but the first installment of the serial soul and that one's individual secret is not lost in the process of earthly dissolution, becomes something more than an optimistic conjecture, and even more than a matter of religious faith, when we remember that only commonsense rules immortality out."[8] It follows that any attempt to discuss this mysterious knowledge in terms other than the veiled ones he used, or in abstraction from the works in which he embodied it, is bound to betray it, at least to some extent. The risk is unavoidable, however, if one wishes to come to conscious awareness of the essence of his art. Moreover, there is a precedent for the endeavor, because the mystical and Romantic notion of the incommunicability of ultimate "religious" or "spiritual" experiences is widespread in many cultures (in Russia it received most famous expression in Fedor Tiutchev's poem "*Silentium*" [1833]: "Mysl' izrechennaia est' lozh'" ["An uttered thought is a lie"]). The practical consequence of Nabokov's reticence about what the "otherworld" means for him is that any attempt to fathom it has to be made on the ambiguous ground consisting of his veiled hints and the reader's inferences. For this reason, and because maximal precision in all things is an essential virtue that Nabokov imposes on his readers, it should be understood that the terms I use when discussing Nabokov's "otherworld" have only heuristic value; they are not items from Nabokov's own lexicon. This point is essential for understanding such apparent paradoxes as the appropriateness of calling Nabokov a metaphysical writer in *Invitation to a Beheading* or *Transparent Things*, while accepting his assertion that he was never interested in any organized systems of belief. But although the terms I use serve only as approximations to Nabokov's ideas, experiences, and practices their value is proven by the access they provide to the hidden mainsprings of his art.

"Otherworld" might seem to imply beliefs that are primarily metaphysical. However, Nabokov's writings show that his metaphysics are inseparable from his ethics and his aesthetics; indeed, all three are best understood as names for a single continuum of beliefs, not for separate categories of Nabokov's interests.[9] Nevertheless, for analytical purposes, it is necessary to formulate distinctions and definitions. By "metaphysics" I mean Nabokov's faith in the apparent existence of a transcendent, nonmaterial, timeless, and beneficent ordering and ordered realm of being that seems to provide for personal immortality, and that affects everything that exists in the mundane world. I say "apparent" and "seems to" because a cardinal tenet of Nabokov's faith is the irreducible alterity of this other realm from the vantage point of mortal experience: all one can have is intuitions of what it may be like; no certainty about it is possible. By "ethics" I mean Nabokov's belief in the existence of good and evil; his belief that both are absolutized by being inextricably linked to the transcendent otherworld; and that both are accessible to mankind, and especially to true artists, as universal criteria for guiding and judging man's behavior. Nabokov's "aesthetics" consist of two aspects: the first is the theme of the creation of art, which, as has long been noted by critics,

Nabokov embodies in his fictions in a variety of forms; the second is the characteristic shape and style of his works—the structures, devices, syntax, alliteration, narrative rhythm that are his signatures. The relationship among metaphysics, aesthetics, and ethics in Nabokov's works is so intimate that it might be visualized graphically as a ternary field with one of the terms labeling each of the apexes, and his works represented by points within the field. Thus, any work, or any aspect of a work, needs to be located in terms of metaphysical, ethical, and aesthetic criteria; and, conversely, any single criterion can be read in terms of the other two. By making this claim I do not mean to suggest that Nabokov is a grim figure concerned exclusively with deep and weighty issues. I join many of his admirers in seeing him as a comic genius; but he is also much more than that, because his conception of the otherworld underlies the comedy. Nabokov's description of Gogol's mature style is an apt characterization of his own later writing, especially in such works as *Pale Fire*, *Ada*, and *Look at the Harlequins!*: "It gives one the sensation of something ludicrous and at the same time stellar, lurking constantly around the corner— and one likes to recall that the difference between the comic side of things, and their cosmic side, depends on one sibilant."[10] Those who consider Nabokov merely a brilliant but shallow stylist and gamesman are simply unaware of the hidden depths in his works.

The thematic and formal unity of Nabokov's art can be illustrated by considering his intuition about the separation of the otherworld from mortal life: it necessitates an ironic (but decidedly not a nihilistic) attitude toward the possibility that man can know anything definite about the "other" realm. One of the ways Nabokov's conclusion pertaining to metaphysics merges into his aesthetic practice is through the multifarious forms of ambiguity and ironic undercutting that fill his works. For example, the reader who is persuaded by Fyodor's conclusion in *The Gift* that the fatidic patterning in his life is evidence of a beneficent otherworld is confronted near the novel's end with the fact that Fyodor is also the author of the work in which he appears, and thus may be responsible for creating the patterning he discovers. On the other hand, there is highly esoteric patterning in the text that seems to be beyond his ken. In this light, the reflexive structure of *The Gift* clearly has not only aesthetic but also metaphysical significance; or, in other words, the novel's form is a perfect mirror for its content.

The only way out of the charmed circles of Nabokov's fictions is to recognize the virtual identity of the characters' otherworldly intuitions with those in Nabokov's nonfictional writings, where they are not similarly undermined. Within a given novel or story, mutually exclusive readings frequently remain suspended, although usually not equally balanced, and, in any event, do not simply cancel each other. The net effect is a suggestive uncertainty, or irony about the role of the otherworld in human affairs. To put Nabokov's characteristic narrative tactic into proper perspective, however, it is necessary to realize that irony and faith need not be incompatible. Indeed, this blend was fundamental for the German Romantics, especially Friedrich Schlegel, and was widespread among the Symbolists, including Baudelaire, Mallarmé, Vladimir Soloviev, Aleksandr Blok, and Andrei Belyi.

Another link between Nabokov's metaphysics and aesthetics hinges on his seminal epiphanic experiences, which he describes at length in his memoir *Speak, Memory* and in "The Art of Literature and Commonsense." He also grants the experience to his favorite positive characters from novels spanning at least three decades, such as Cincinnatus in *Invitation to a Beheading*, Fyodor in *The Gift*, Krug in *Bend Sinister*, Pnin in the eponymous novel, and Shade in *Pale Fire*. The characteristic features of Nabokov's epiphanies are a sudden fusion of varied sensory data and memories, a feeling of timelessness, and intuitions of immortality. This perceptual, psychological, and spiritual experience is intimately connected with Nabokov's conception of artistic inspiration, and is thus a facet of his theme of the creation of art. But the experience is also structurally congruent with a characteristic *formal* feature of his narratives, in which details that are in fact connected are hidden within contexts that conceal the true relations among them. This narrative tactic puts the burden on the reader either to accumulate the components of a given series, or to discover the one detail that acts as the "key" for it; when this is achieved, the significance of the entire preceding concealed chain or network is retroactively illuminated. This process of decipherment that Nabokov imposes on his readers has far-reaching implications. Since the conclusion that the reader makes depends on his retaining details in his memory, he appears to have an atemporal insight into some aspect of the text's meaning; he is thus lifted out of the localized, linear, and temporally bound reading process in a manner resembling the way characters' epiphanies remove them from the quotidian flow of events within the world of the text.[11] The implication of this phenomenon is that the structure of Nabokov's texts is related to the structure of cognitive moments in life, at least as he conceived them. Even when the process of recognition is less spectacular than an epiphany, and entails the discovery of small-scale connections among a limited number of details in one of Nabokov's texts, "the mental operations of the reader," as Boyd has argued, are "akin to those of a person trying to appreciate his world."[12]

The way ethics merge into Nabokov's thematic and formal continuum is illustrated well by *Invitation to a Beheading*. Cincinnatus, the novel's protagonist, is morally superior to his jailers because of his visual acuity and perspicacity: for him the material world they inhabit and enjoy is a sham, and he understands or intuits things for which they do not even have concepts. Nabokov embodies this theme in the novel's form by intentionally including flaws in the narrative that *mimic* sloppy writing by a forgetful or careless author (there are additional facets to this device as well). This puts the reader into a position with regard to the novel's text that is exactly the same as Cincinnatus's with regard to the flawed material world within the novel. Thus, via the form of the narrative itself the reader becomes involved in what is, in the novel's own terms, an ethical enterprise—to differentiate between truth and falsehood together with Cincinnatus. The implication of this tactic, which Nabokov repeats with variations throughout his oeuvre, and which is buttressed by his discussions of ethics and aesthetics in his discursive writings, is that he may have seen the hermeneutics of experience and the hermeneutics of reading as being equivalents.[13] A necessary caveat regarding the transferability of interpretive strategies from life to art is that Nabokov clearly was not advocating a confusion of life with art. Pifer makes the essential point that the kind of artistic control Nabokov manifested in his works is punished when a character attempts to transfer it to life, as in the case of Axel Rex in *Laughter in the Dark*, Hermann in *Despair*, and Humbert in *Lolita*.[14] In this special sense as well, however, ethics remain attached to aesthetics because all three characters fall distinctly short of being true Nabokovian artists. Finally, because *Invitation to a Beheading* is underlain by a quasi-Gnostic, dualistic world view, Cincinnatus's and the reader's confronting flawed worlds on their respective textual levels also acquires metaphysical significance, and thereby adds metaphysics to the continuum between ethics and aesthetics.

I am of course aware of the irony inherent in claiming that a core of unvarying beliefs underlies Nabokov's variegated fictions, especially because he consistently celebrated unique details and condemned generalizations that obscured or ignored them. However, my claim about what the otherworld means in his art is not intended to belittle or deemphasize the atomistic details out of which he built his works (and which he captures with unequaled mastery), but rather to outline the laws that show how they are put together. Nabokov's own reading of other authors is predicated on these principles. As he illustrates in his book on Gogol, his focus on the distinctive stylistic details in "The Overcoat" leads him beyond mere formal considerations to the conclusion that the story contains "shadows linking our state of existence to those other states and modes which we dimly apprehend in our rare moments of irrational perception."[15]

Vera Nabokov's remarks about the thematic dominant of her husband's legacy were one of the catalysts for my attempt to approach Nabokov differently from the ways he had been read before. The other was my impression that no one had yet grasped something elusive at the core of his works, despite the significant, albeit partial insights made by several other readers. By acknowledging the origins of my investigation I realize some readers may conclude I have pursued a vicious circle, on the principle that the questions with which one begins cannot but shape what one finds. Although this is not the place to engage in a lengthy discussion of this complex topic and its long history in philosophy and literary theory, there are two responses that should be made. First, the conception of reading to which I subscribe posits that no one can take up a text without expectations of some sort—be they as general as what it means to read a novel, or as specific as what is meant by "fate," "consciousness," or "mimicry," to choose but three words that are central for Nabokov. Secondly, the literary work is not a pretext for the reader to project onto it anything he deems important: it will resist and deny irrelevant readings; conversely, it will affirm what a reader may believe to be untrue. A corollary of this view is that the accuracy of a reading can be validated, at least to some extent. The more facets and details in a text, or in an entire oeuvre, that an interpretation can identify, explain, and accommodate, the better it is. It certainly does not follow from this that all literary works necessarily have unique "solutions"; at the same time, there is no theoretical reason why some great works might not, at least with regard to some of their concerns. Neither is there any reason to see ambiguity as an absolute virtue or an inescapable fact of all aspects of all literary works (which is not a denial of the general importance of ambiguity in literature). For shorthand purposes, what I am describing is a three-dimensional expansion of Iser's essentially planar phenomenological model of reading. To his notion that "two people gazing at the night sky may both be looking at the same collection of stars, but one will see the image of a plough, and the other will make out a dipper,"[16] I would add that there will inevitably be additional arguments about whether the stars are stars and not, for example, planets or nebulae, and whether the lines are lines and not planes seen on edge. In other words, there will frequently be considerable agreement among different readers about which textual phenomena are especially noteworthy and need to be accommodated by an interpretation, even though there will be disagreements about the precise nature and meaning of these phenomena.[17] But the general point of Iser's model is still valid: a work's meaning emerges only as a result of an interaction between a reader and a text that consists of fixed structures and meanings as well as those that are not determined. Anyone familiar with the extensive critical literature about Nabokov will recognize very quickly that I build my arguments on the basis of many of the same passages and details in his works that others have analyzed before. These have obviously struck numerous readers as thematic and formal nodes of special significance.

The one method that has proven invaluable in delimiting possible interpretations of Nabokov's works is placing them within a context: that is, considering individual novels and stories in relation to his nonfictional writings, as well as to his entire fictional corpus. These contexts provide the external referents that allow one to resolve some, but not all of the important ironies and ambiguities contained in individual works. This is of course a familiar and widespread (although frequently unconscious) practice in contemporary criticism that is applicable to any author. But because it too might elicit objections, on the basis that it produces not only a vicious but a hermeneutic circle, I would like briefly to outline my rationale for employing it. Even if I cannot hope to preempt all objections, I can at least help to clarify my basic assumptions; at a minimum, this might obviate arguments about my specific conclusions that are in fact controlled by my points of departure. In looking for guidance to Nabokov's discursive writings—by which I mean all of the published works that are manifestly records of the historical Vladimir Nabokov, including his autobiography, interviews, articles, letters, and lectures—I am decidedly not committing the "intentional fallacy." Information about "what Nabokov wanted to say" is simply not available (at least in print) because he was unusually circumspect about the essence of his aims and beliefs when discussing his own works of art (*Lolita* is an exception). Nabokov's discursive writings are useful primarily in the way they foreground issues and views that he obviously found important and that parallel the themes of his fictions. The specific links between the discursive works and the fictions are certain key words and concepts to which Nabokov gives meanings that often bear no relation to those provided either by dictionaries or by other writers. In effect, his nonfictional writings are the highest linguistic authority to which we can turn in order to understand his belletristic works. (And because some of his novels treat the same important themes more openly than do others, they too function as expanded illustrations of central concepts. Needless to say, one should always be alert to the possibility of an author changing the meaning of a favorite term or concept over time.) An opposition between public and private meanings such as this has been made familiar by Saussure's distinction between "langue" and "parole," and is comparable to Todorov's between "language" (an abstract assemblage of lexical items and grammatical rules) and "discourse" (a "concrete manifestation of language" within a particular context). This opposition also has a venerable history in the West: it is at least as old as Cicero, can be found in Montaigne—who announced "I have my own private dictionary"—and, among others, in Alexander Pope.[18] Considering a given word of Nabokov's—or, by extension, a phrase, or an image—against the background of his discursive and belletristic writings is ultimately more important for understanding his fictions than is gauging them according to the world the reader knows (although the latter inevitably happens as well). The obvious reason for this is that Nabokov's world is not entirely that of any reader (or any other author). Indeed, it is the uniqueness of Nabokov's world, together with its exquisite detail and seductive complexity, that makes it desirable to appropriate it to one's own (and that provides the second reason for this book's title). The appeal of this kind of alterity is illustrated well by Nabokov's description of the effect that reading Gogol can have: "one's eyes may become gogolized and one is apt to see bits of his world in the most unexpected places."[19] Perhaps the most striking example of a familiar word that Nabokov redefines with far-reaching implications is "commonsense" (as he spells it in his above-mentioned lecture), which I will discuss in chapter 1. Other words to which Nabokov gives a unique, and frequently surprising meaning in his oeuvre (and which challenge the meanings the reader may bring with him to a text) are also neither minor nor peripheral: *reality, artifice, nature, good, evil.*

My conclusion that Nabokov's works lend themselves to analysis from the point of view of the unique meanings his words have is supported by his own pronouncements about the nature of language, and by his readings of other writers. In all of his discursive writings and lectures on Russian and foreign writers, and in his famous defense of strictly literal translation in connection with *Eugene Onegin,* he invariably stressed le mot juste. "The mysteries of the irrational as perceived through rational words" is how Nabokov defined "true poetry." Moreover, he obviously believed that maximally accurate communication between author and reader was possible: "True poetry of that kind provokes a radiant smile of perfect satisfaction, a purr of beatitude—and a writer may well be proud of himself if he can make his readers, or more exactly some of his readers, smile and purr that way."[20] It was a commitment to such communication, rather than self-indulgent eccentricity or pedantry, that motivated Nabokov's precise and at times esoteric lexicon: "The main favor I ask of a serious critic," he stated in an interview, "is sufficient perceptiveness to understand that whatever term or trope I use, my purpose is not to be facetiously flashy or grotesquely obscure but to express what I feel and think with the utmost truthfulness."[21] Given Nabokov's conception of writing, it is hardly surprising that his view of reading was similarly elitist and demanding. In his 1937 lecture on Pushkin he explained that "the only valid method of study is to read and ponder the work itself, to discuss it with yourself but not with others, for the best reader is still the egoist who savors his discovery unbeknownst to his neighbors. . . . The greater the number of readers, the less a book is understood, the

essence of its truth, as it spreads, seems to evaporate."[22] In sum, Nabokov's conception of language is antinihilistic in the sense that it is implicitly opposed to the view that all fixed meaning is inescapably elusive. On
the larger scale of entire literary works, Nabokov's style of reading other
writers indicates equally clearly that although he recognized ambiguity to
be inherent in art as in life, what he valued and recognized as artistic was
of course not loose accumulations of elusive, unframed and inherently
unframable details, which is now thought by some to be the sine qua non
of all art, but carefully fashioned wholes, where all elements contribute
to a total and intelligible (although certainly not fully rational) effect. I
agree, therefore, with Tammi's view that it is "precisely because of [Na-
bokov's] consistent emphasis on the superiority of the literary imagination [as when he draws a parallel between the artist and God as creators]
that one finds a little dubious the fashionable trend of placing [Nabokov]
directly in the camp of 'Postmodernists' [such as Barth, Borges, Beckett]
who, after all, base their enterprise on the ultimate *insufficiency* of all
fiction-making."[23] We cannot understand the quiddity of Nabokov's art
by ignoring his lexicon and conception of language in favor of someone
else's. On the other hand, with some effort, we can learn his language and
thus enter into his world.

Nabokov himself signals the necessity of using his fictional works as
contexts for each other by the simple expedient of alluding to earlier
works in later ones. For example, Pnin from the eponymous novel is resurrected in *Pale Fire*, which also contains a reference to "hurricane Lolita." Auto-allusions grow in frequency through time in Nabokov's oeuvre and become the dominant feature of *Look at the Harlequins!* Because
such textual echoes have obvious thematic functions, and are not merely
the author's private winks to himself, it follows that the works in which
they appear have to be read in terms of each other.[24]

On at least one occasion, in his postface to *Lolita*, Nabokov indicated
that it was necessary to read his Russian works in order to understand
those he wrote in English. He did not explain why, although it is likely
that his comment had something to do with the widespread misunderstanding of *Lolita* as a quasi-pornographic work, a charge against which
he was trying to defend himself. What a comparison of the two major
parts of Nabokov's legacy in fact shows is that his central themes are
somewhat more obvious in several of the Russian novels than in most of
his English ones. This is not to say that Nabokov was ever facile or transparent. But a broad change discernible in his oeuvre over time is an increase in the distance between the ostensible subjects of his works and
their actual meanings: his use of camouflage becomes more complicated,
as it were. (One can only speculate why this happened, especially given
the stability of the beliefs underlying the increasingly baroque intertextual

surfaces of the sequence of novels *Lolita, Pale Fire, Ada, Look at the Harlequins!* One possibility is that Nabokov indulged certain kinds of artifice more often in his late English works than in most of his Russian ones—there is, however, no simple, rectilinear development—because he may have been compensating for what he could not create on the subtler stylistic level of language. Although Nabokov's English style is absolutely dazzling, it never quite reaches the heights of genius that characterize his best Russian prose. Nabokov realized this himself, as he indicated in his postface to *Lolita* when he said that having to change from Russian to English was his "private tragedy".) Thus the utility of reading his oeuvre as a kind of macrotext is that this allows one to recognize congruences among works with widely differing surface features. Nabokov has himself admitted to the constancy of his preoccupations: "Derivative writers seem versatile because they imitate many others, past and present. Artistic originality has only its own self to copy."[25] In practice, structural and thematic repetitions are frequently the only guides to what Nabokov considers most important because he hardly ever calls explicit attention to what in fact dominates his art. On the contrary, one of the most striking, and often celebrated (or vilified) aspects of his art is that there is so much left hidden in it. Indeed, the fact of concealment and the necessity of discovery, for both the characters and as the reader, are themselves thematic and formal dominants of his fictional world, and are intimately connected with his conception of the otherworld.

The kinds of thematic paradigms that emerge from reading Nabokov's works as a macrotext include striking similarities in the way the consciousness of a certain positive type of character is structured; a necessary relationship between this and the topos of the material world seeming to be both patterned and insubstantial or transparent; characters in different works being ludicrous for the same reasons, and positive characters all loving and loathing the same things. Other paradigms that characterize Nabokov's works pertain to narrative strategies, alliterations, the use of recurrent imagery such as his famous butterflies, and various distinctive traits subsumed under the term *style*. For example, Lubin has identified a recurring syntactical feature in Nabokov that he terms "phrasal tmesis," and that embodies perfectly, on the molecular level of the text, what characterizes larger recurring elements in Nabokov's plots. Tmesis is defined by dictionaries as the separation of a compound word by the interposition of another word. But Lubin has found that Nabokov applies this principle to entire phrases, as in "I'm all enchantment and ears" and "the Arctic no longer vicious circle" (*Ada*), or "the Old and rotting World" and "an enchanted and very tight hunter" (*Lolita*). (In the latter case the phrase was originally defined by the novel itself—"The Enchanted Hunters" hotel—only to be separated later in the text.) Lubin's conclusion is that "phrasal tmesis" may be Nabokov's "greater deception writ small. The mind apprehends the terminal words which it expects to find juxtaposed, and then must accommodate the alien phonemes thrust between." The trope is thus analogous to the reader's discovery that Fyodor does not in fact hold conversations with Koncheyev in *The Gift*, or that Van does not shoot himself in *Ada*.[26] Deception through concealment is one of the most important constants on all levels of Nabokov's works.

Another paradigm that emerges from considering Nabokov's works in context could be called the hermeneutic imperative.[27] All his works consist of numerous, intimately interwoven strands of motifs (relating to physical objects, colors, shapes, states of mind, literary allusions, etc.), the component elements of which are often concealed by being placed in unrelated contexts, or by being alluded to in an understated and oblique manner. In their totality, the motifs invariably transcend the ken of even the most percipient of the characters, who at best see only a fraction of them. The motifs are not over the reader's head, however, even though it is unlikely that any one reader has ever apprehended all of them in a given work, together with all their multifarious connections (and I certainly do not pretend to have done so in the chapters that follow). Since the characters are involved in trying to make sense of some of the same details that confront the reader, and often dramatize what appear to be plausible conclusions about them, the reader is presented with a model for a hermeneutic strategy applicable to the work as a whole. (On occasion, as in *Despair*, the protagonist's misperception or projection of patterning serves as a *negative* example for the reader, who is thereby prompted to identify the correlations that the character missed.) A number of recent studies on reader-oriented approaches to literature have pointed out that the practice of including prods and guides to interpretation within works is far from rare.[28] In Nabokov's case, because connections among most categories of details have not been made by anyone in the text, every discovery the reader makes appears to be his own. Since this process reveals hidden meanings in the work, it is intrinsically satisfying; it is also seductive because it creates the illusion of verisimilitude by allowing the reader to function as if in "real life." And because the entire work is saturated with the net of motifs to the extent that these rival and often transcend the characters as bearers of the work's meanings, the text acquires the appearance of a fatidic web, which is also the way characters tend to see their lives.[29]

A uniquely Nabokovian feature of this kind of textual patterning is the tantalizing possibility that there is only one correct way in which details can be connected, and one unique, global meaning that emerges from them. This follows from the fact that Nabokov elevates the creation of extraordinarily cunning textual puzzles to a fundamental esthetic principle, and draws explicit parallels between this literary tactic, the phenomenon of mimicry in nature, and the composition of chess problems. Unique solutions are of course the rule in both of the latter, for it is a particular creature that camouflages its true nature in some specific way, and it is the one ideal solution to a chess problem that is concealed by false leads. Nabokov's artistic practice is in fact a good illustration of Uspensky's point that "the compositional structure of a literary work may specifically foresee some responses on the part of the reader, in such a way that the reader's reactions enter into the author's calculations, as if the author were programming those responses into the work."[30] The possibility that there may be only one correct way for the reader to put together some details in Nabokov's works does not mean, however, that all of the works' meanings are comparably narrowed or restricted. On the contrary, inherent ambiguities remain. For example, in the passages in *The Defense* dealing with Luzhin's apartment after he is married, the allusions to its labyrinthine floor plan, a small devil hanging from a lamp around which a fly circles with monotonous regularity, and the bust of Dante on a shelf clearly imply that the locus of Luzhin's seeming happiness is paradoxically closer to being the realm of evil. This conclusion is in agreement with other veiled details in the text that are derived from specific tenets of Gnosticism. But although such motifs suggest the necessity of adding a metaphysical explanation to psychological considerations, they do not resolve the meaning and nature of his suicide. As the novel ends, the choice between two alternative readings remains suspended: we may incline toward the view that Luzhin enters the otherworldly realm that has influenced his life from earliest childhood; but we cannot be sure that this happens. Nabokov's concretely defined conception of evil, and the specific role he gives it in Luzhin's life, thus do not necessarily shed any light on what happens to him when he dies.

As the example of Luzhin illustrates, one of the most important consequences of examining Nabokov's works in context is that this helps to determine the shape and location of his uncertainties. Although different works can be understood as explorations of different hypotheses regarding the nature of man's relation to the otherworld, the ambiguities that are part of Nabokov's faith remain constant throughout his oeuvre. It is rather like trying to discern a faint watermark on paper by taking other sheets from the same ream and holding them up to the light: the mark, as well as the blank areas within and outside it, becomes more visible.

It is of course possible, and frequently necessary, to go beyond the author's own words when seeking contexts to explicate his works. But with the exception of several forays in the conclusion of this study, I limit myself almost exclusively to what Nabokov wrote himself. The reasons for this are primarily practical. First of all, an attempt to include Nabokov in

a literary-historical, social, political, biographical, philosophical, psychological, or any other kind of milieu would far exceed the reasonable
length of a single volume whose aim is to explain several major works
from a point of view that has not received anything like the attention it
deserves. Secondly, Nabokov does not invite the creation of bridges between his works and the times and places in which he lived nearly as much
as many other great authors. There is of course "local color" in *The Gift*,
which describes and satirizes Russian émigré life and literary politics in
interwar Germany, as well as in *Lolita*, with its depictions of American
mores and vistas. But Nabokov's primary preoccupations—art, death,
love, fate, perception, blindness, beauty, truth—are hardly time-bound,
in the way that the problem of divorce in Russia in the 1870s is in *Anna
Karenina* for example.

The one major contextual category that Nabokov unequivocally implies is important for understanding him is literary allusions. His works
are filled with direct and concealed references to, and parodies of, Russian
and European literature, as well as various other cultural "monuments."
All of these can be seen readily as part of his expanded lexicon, and as
such would need to be analyzed exhaustively if one were to do full justice
to his art. But to do so would also exceed the limits of one book. Moreover, the complex of metaphysical, aesthetic and ethical issues that is my
focus is also the prism through which Nabokov's literary allusions are
refracted. He obviously did not simply insert details from other works
into his fictional worlds without incorporating them into the themes and
structures he created. And it is ultimately easier to understand the specific
paradigms governing Nabokov's art by temporarily suspending a consideration of how he utilizes disparate allusions to other works. I am not
arguing, however, for the absolute primacy of Nabokov's aesthetics or
philosophy over his allusive praxis. The two are intertwined much too
intimately for this kind of claim to be tenable. However, there is vindica-
tion for my approach in the fact that the "intertextual" readings have
inevitably buttressed the purely metaliterary view of Nabokov. A related
consideration is that, contrary to what some of his readers have claimed,
none of Nabokov's characters (or plots, settings, narrative stances) is
merely a collage of bits and pieces borrowed from other writers. I share
Pifer's conviction that his novels dramatize plausible and moving models
of human beings and "enduring humanistic values,"[31] albeit in a unique
way. As a consideration of his fictions within the context of his discursive
writings shows, Nabokov's ultimate source for much of what he wrote
was a series of questions or problems that preoccupied him throughout
his life (by which I do not mean that his fictions are simply autobiographical).[32] And even if Nabokov's preoccupations were partially the result of
what he had read, there is still a great difference between affirming that

he was concerned in his art with issues that touched on his own lived experience, and claiming that he actively shut out any such experience in favor of inhumanly reflexive aesthetic constructs.

Any reconsideration of Nabokov should address two fundamental questions pertaining to his critical legacy: Why have many readers missed his main theme for so long? And what is there in his novels and other fictions that allowed this to happen?

One of the two major facets of his art where a metaliterary and an "otherworldly" reading confront each other most directly is textual patterning.[33] The same "coincidences" of meaning and detail in a work can be interpreted in two different ways—either as a literary model of fate, or as the author's underscoring the artificiality of his text. Humbert's reading *Who's Who in the Limelight* is a case in point. The fact that he finds references in it to Quilty and to Lolita and a phrase she once uttered can be seen as either fateful coincidence, or as Nabokov's revealing his presence as authorial manipulator. The latter reading necessarily implies that coincidences of the sort we find throughout Nabokov's novels simply do not occur in "real life," and that by stressing them he is denying his texts' verisimilitude. The second facet of Nabokov's art that leads to the same confrontation between opposed readings is his Romantic irony—his characteristic practice of having the author intrude into his texts, both directly, as in the conclusion of *Bend Sinister*, and anagrammatically, as "Vivian Darkbloom" in *Lolita* (in *Who's Who in the Limelight* and elsewhere).[34] It is precisely in connection with these two characteristics of Nabokov's fiction that reading it in the context of his discursive writings is most illuminating. *Speak, Memory* is filled with Nabokov's detailed discussions of the patterning he found in his own life, and in the lives of his ancestors; furthermore, like the positive characters in his novels, Nabokov clearly implies that his existence bears the telltale marks of a transmundane agency. (The false patterns or coincidences that flawed characters like Hermann in *Despair* perceive are another matter entirely; these are in fact solipsistic projections rather than insights implying a higher reality. The reader's task in *Despair* is to sort out Hermann's delusions from the patterning concealed in the novel's world by its author-deity.) But Nabokov's related arguments and implications go even further. In interviews as well as in his autobiography Nabokov insists that the entire world of nature is also filled with patterning that implies it was fashioned by some higher consciousness: from mimicry among insects to "the popular enticements of procreation"—all is the product of ingenious, and, Nabokov stresses, nonutilitarian and deceptive craftsmanship.[35] In other words, Nabokov's nonfictional writings show that he completely redefines the terms *nature* and *artifice* into synonyms for each other. If any one idea can be considered to be "the key" to Nabokov's art, this is it. In light of this crucial redefinition, Nabokov's textual patterns and intrusions into his fictional texts emerge as imitations of the otherworld's formative role with regard to man and nature: the metaliterary is camouflage for, and a model of, the metaphysical. The remarkable resistance of some readers to even considering this possibility is illustrated well by Bader, who suggested substituting the word *art* for the term *hereafter* in the narrator's speculation about the nature of the realm beyond death on the penultimate page of *The Real Life of Sebastian Knight* (which reads, "The hereafter may be the full ability of consciously living in any chosen soul, in any number of souls"). Clearly, the kind of intuitive faith in an otherworld that Nabokov manifests in his writings has been perceived as unmodish in the context of "modern literature" and has, therefore, been dismissed as unacceptable by many of his readers. Another critic has approached Nabokov through an explicit, a priori opposition of "reality" to "fictionality" that betrays Nabokov's conception of the naturalness of artifice. Speaking of those novels by Nabokov that he considers weakest, Alter concludes that the "constructed fictional world [in them], however ingenious, is hardly allowed sufficient vitality to give the dialectic between fiction and 'reality' the vigorous to-and-fro energy which it requires: a play of competing ontologies cannot fully engage us when one of the competitors, the invented world of fiction, too often seems like intellectual contrivance."[36] Nabokov's point is of course precisely that the so-called natural world appears to have been "contrived" by some higher intelligence.

In most general terms, Nabokov's characteristic aesthetic practices resurrect the Romantic idea that the artist is God's rival, and that man's artistic creations are analogues to God's natural world. Nabokov was obviously aware of this conception, as he revealed when he stated in a lecture that "art is a divine game . . . because this is the element in which man comes nearest to God through becoming the true creator in his own right."[37] The importance of this remark is that it gives the lie to such unhappy critical notions as that he practiced "aggressive antinaturalism" in his fictions.[38] A more accurate formulation is that Nabokov's conception of what constitutes an appropriate formal embodiment for the "natural artifice" he saw in the world differs from the relatively shapeless or eclectic aesthetic—often anti-Classical in its origins and focus—that German Romantics and their followers called "organic form" (as, for example, Coleridge in his lectures on Shakespeare). Nabokov's form also seems "unnatural" because it differs from that found in much of the established, later-nineteenth- and twentieth-century literary canon (similarly produced under the influence of Romantic ideas), which is still often confused with "reality" and thus with what is "natural."[39] But this does not make his artificial form any less natural within his own world view.[40]

In connection with this misunderstanding of the relation between nature and artifice in Nabokov, it is worth digressing briefly to the way in which his public persona may have affected the way his works were read. I regret that I never had the pleasure of meeting Vladimir Vladimirovich Nabokov. But I have spoken with, and read accounts by a number of people who visited him in Montreux, where he lived during the last part of his life. Those who did not know him well frequently carried away the impression that he was aloof and eccentric; by contrast, his friends remember him as warm and kind. Inevitably, both groups linked their image of the man to the way they viewed his works, even though this was hardly fair in the case of visitors who knew him little. There are, after all, social and class backgrounds, forms of upbringing, and personal styles of behavior that quite reasonably balk at exhibiting undiscriminating familiarity or warmth toward a chance caller as readily as toward an old friend. In this context, putting one's feet up and launching into an uninhibited confessional exchange with a stranger, even one who has come a long way to speak with you, could be seen as vulgar pseudo-intimacy, and thus as a betrayal of one's values. Nevertheless, if one judges by the published criticism on Nabokov, the same kind of transference from life to text is often carried out by many readers of his interviews (especially those collected in *Strong Opinions*) and his prefaces to the English translations of his Russian novels; both sets of pronouncements are as close as most readers ever get to Vladimir Nabokov. What needs to be realized, however, is that these texts are not only expressions of Nabokov's strongly held views, but also of a carefully controlled public persona. "What I really like about the better kind of colloquy," he once explained in an interview, "is the opportunity it affords me to construct in the presence of my audience the semblance of what I hope is a plausible and not altogether displeasing personality."[41] Many readers have focused only on the aloof, self-confident and mocking side of the resulting personality, perhaps because it is the more prominent, and have neglected what is humane, witty, and noble in it. Inevitably, they have concluded that their partial reading of Nabokov's public face is related to his fictions, where it is manifested in his supposedly "antirealistic," metaliterary devices and practices. These seem to be elitist in their difficulty, and disdainful of common human concerns in their artificiality. Such a reading is of course unfair to Nabokov because he was a confirmed elitist only in the sense that he prized highly the difficulty and skill inherent in creating or grasping anything of value. As he explained in an interview, "I work hard, I work long, on a body of words until it grants me complete possession and pleasure. If the reader has to work in his turn—so much the better. Art is difficult. Easy art is what you see at modern exhibitions of things and doodles."[42] Whatever is easily accomplished or understood by all, whatever is popular, or a commonplace, automatically risks falsehood. This was for Nabokov a fundamental insight rooted in his experience of life. Given this, my inference is that the public persona Nabokov projected was in fact concerned with articulating and defending strongly held beliefs, correcting egregious misconceptions and misinterpretations, shaking off clichés and generalizations—and doing all of this in a way that would not betray through simplification what he was talking about. Coldness and aloofness are thus merely camouflage for opinions that are better described as passionately held. Anyone who doubts Nabokov's capacity for intense, and intensely moving emotion (outside of his fictions, which are filled with it) would do well to consider the passages dealing with love, friendship, and fatherhood in Speak, Memory, or his Russian correspondence with his sister, Perepiska s sestroi. Neither should Nabokov's elitism be seen as carrying with it any political overtones. Shortly after emigrating to the United States, he expressed in unequivocal terms his support for "the splendid paradox of democracy [which] is that while stress is laid on the rule of all and the equality of common rights, it is the individual that derives from it his special and uncommon benefit. Ethically, the members of a democracy are equals, spiritually, each has a right to be as different from his neighbors as he pleases. . . . Democracy is humanity at its best . . . because it is the natural condition of every man ever since the human mind became conscious not only of the world but of itself."[43]

Because of the importance of Nabokov's discursive writings for understanding his fictional works, the first chapter of this book is dedicated to inferring the paradigmatic relationship among his metaphysics, ethics, and aesthetics on the basis of Speak, Memory, interviews, lectures, and other comparable pronouncements. In addition to its intrinsic interest as one of the great memoirs of this century, Speak, Memory has special relevance for understanding Nabokov's novels because in its content it is scrupulously truthful about particular aspects of his life, while in its form it relies on techniques that carry over into his fictions. As he explained in an interview about Conclusive Evidence (an earlier version of Speak, Memory): "It is a memoir . . . and true. There is a good deal of selection in it, of course. What interested me is the thematic lines of my life that resemble fiction. The memoir became the meeting point of an impersonal art form and a very personal life story. . . . It is a literary approach to my own past. There is some precedent for it in the novel, in Proust say, but not in the memoir."[44] The use of Nabokov's discursive texts to explain fictions that, in some cases, were written decades earlier is justified by the congruence among their concerns and by the consistency of Nabokov's beliefs through time. The following chapters are dedicated to *The Defense, Invitation to a Beheading, The Gift, The Real Life of Sebastian Knight, Lolita,* and *Pale Fire*—a short list that constitutes an imperfect compromise among three criteria: my own favorites (I place *The Real Life* higher than do many of Nabokov's admirers), works that are widely acknowledged as Nabokov's best, and the constraints of reasonable length. What some might see as the conspicuous absence of *Ada* from this list is due largely to the existence of Boyd's highly insightful and convincing book about the novel that approaches it from many of the same vantage points I would have liked to use.[45] Where feasible, I allude briefly to Nabokov's other works and try to suggest how they fit the patterns of meaning I am discussing in his Russian and English novels. But I have chosen to keep this to a minimum because it is virtually impossible to do it succinctly. Nabokov's practice of hiding what is most important renders unusually ineffective generalizations about his texts that are not supported by extensive citations. The final chapter of this study is my only investigation of the important area of Nabokov's literary context, and constitutes an attempt to point out a few of his immediate antecedents in turn-of-the-century Russian culture—some of the possible sources for his most characteristic ideas and practices. I make no claim to having exhausted even this relatively narrow subject, and my connections are meant to be only illustrative. However, I felt it important to introduce the names Andrei Belyi, Aleksandr Blok, Nikolai Gumilev, Petr Uspenskii, and Nikolai Evreinov into the discussion of Nabokov's sympathies and debts because these are not sufficiently well-known to many of his readers outside the field of Russian literature.

The reader will notice that I make no secret of my admiration for Nabokov's art. In my opinion, he is one of the three greatest novelists that Russia has produced. However, I will refrain in the pages that follow from making additional evaluative comments about his works based on my analyses of them. I do not want to add to the kinds of circular arguments about Nabokov's merits or faults that fill critical writings about him (and that are familiar in much literary criticism in general). One inevitably finds that the subject of a given reader's analytical focus is correlated with Nabokov's supposed strengths and weaknesses. Thus if a critic believes that "self-consciousness" in the novel is an important feature in the history of the genre, he of course praises those authors, like Nabokov, who embody it in their works. This practice is equally prevalent in the writings of critics with whom I agree; and I am no different in believing that what I find in his works is what makes them great. But since the same characteristic features of Nabokov's art can be both praised and reviled, there seems little point in adding to what are in effect unprovable claims for excellence or weakness. Until a convincing connection between interpretation and evaluation is developed (and it may never be), one man's meat will remain another's poison.

Speak, Memory and Other
Discursive Writings

NABOKOV begins *Speak, Memory* (1966) with a discussion of death, life, time, and eternity that adumbrates themes he will develop at length throughout the work. But in keeping with his elevation of deception to a primary aesthetic principle, the seemingly straightforward remarks he makes are in fact misleading and conceal his true attitudes. Here as everywhere else in his oeuvre, Nabokov's method cannot be separated from his meaning.

The first sentence of the autobiography reads: "The cradle rocks above an abyss, and common sense tells us that our existence is but a brief crack of light between two eternities of darkness."[1] The key words here are "common sense," and they need to be examined within the context of Nabokov's own lexicon. Now, it is clear from everything he wrote that he valued precision and uniqueness most highly. Thus, anything that is widespread, thought of as given or "common" becomes suspect when he seems to be appealing to it. There is more specific evidence of Nabokov's distaste for the notion of "common sense" as well. In the Foreword to *Speak, Memory* (p. 10) he mentions that the autobiography's opening chapter was first published in 1950. (The same beginning lines appear in all book variants of the chapter—*Conclusive Evidence* [1951], the first version of the autobiography, and the revised Russian version *Drugie berega* [*Other Shores*, 1954].)[2] The date Nabokov provides suggests a general chronological connection with the lecture "The Art of Literature and Commonsense," which was delivered at about the same time as the first chapter of the autobiography.[3] In the lecture Nabokov quotes a standard dictionary definition of the term *commonsense*, and then goes on to redefine it with an unequivocally negative meaning: "Commonsense at its worst is sense made common, and so everything is comfortably cheapened by its touch"; "the biography of commonsense makes nasty reading"; "Commonsense has trampled down many a gentle genius whose eyes had delighted in a too early moonbeam of some too early truth. . . . commonsense has prompted ugly but strong nations to crush their fair but frail neighbors the moment a gap in history offered a chance that it would have been ridiculous not to exploit." By contrast, all the values

Nabokov advocates in the lecture stem from his conception of the unique and the "irrational," qualities that are manifested by various select individuals—"the meek prophet, the enchanter in his cave, the indignant artist, the nonconforming little schoolboy" (p. 372). When seen in Nabokov's own terms, therefore, the first sentence of *Speak, Memory* emerges as highly ironic, and suggests that the "commonsensical" view of life as being short ("a brief crack of light"), and without any issue into the realm of death ("between two eternities of darkness"), is simply wrong.

The next sentence, beginning "although the two [eternities of darkness] are identical twins," is also deceptive because the misleadingly authoritative "although" allows Nabokov to slip in a startling affirmation of something that he has not yet proven and that certainly cannot be taken for granted. Indeed, the remainder of the paragraph implies that the "abysses" preceding and following human life may not be quite as empty and foreboding as might seem. The primary vehicle for this oblique suggestion is the "young chronophobiac" whom Nabokov introduces and describes as being particularly unnerved by a home movie made several weeks before his birth because it shows a world from which he was absent. He is also upset by the baby carriage that appears in the film with the "encroaching air of a coffin"; it is empty, "as if, in the reverse course of events, [the chronophobiac's] very bones had disintegrated" (p. 19). Nabokov's deception in this passage lies in his concealing that the young man was mistaken to focus on the empty baby carriage and to regret that no one missed him prior to his birth. Obviously he had already existed in another form for some eight months before the film was made. Nabokov reinforces this idea by adding that the young man catches "a glimpse of his mother waving from an upstairs window" in the film, a significant detail that does not appear in either of the two earlier versions of the autobiography. Another inference suggested by this passage is that prenatal existence may not be exclusively physical in the familiar sense, because one is both present in the world and absent from it. And since we have been told that the abysses before and after life are "identical," we are left with the potential conclusion that just as man exists before birth, he may continue to exist in some form after death.

On the pages that follow, in a series of statements that can be, and have been readily misunderstood or dismissed as merely figurative language, Nabokov continues to intimate that a search for an escape from the "two black voids" is central to his life and works, and of primary importance for *Speak, Memory*. He admits that he repeatedly "made colossal efforts to distinguish the faintest of personal glimmers in the impersonal darkness on both sides of my life." And then he makes the surprising announcement that the "abysses" are illusory, which implies there is another existence after death: "That this darkness is caused merely by the walls of time separating me from the free world of timelessness is a belief I gladly share with the most gaudily painted savage" (p. 20). The surprise here lies in Nabokov's not explaining immediately the foundations of his belief. On the contrary, his affirmation of faith is seemingly undermined in the lines that follow because, although he describes the various methods he tried in order to reach the timeless realm, including occultism of a recognizably theosophical sort, he does not in fact acknowledge that he succeeded in doing so. Instead, he states that he saw "the prison of time" as "spherical and without exits." The deception in this case is that many pages of *Speak, Memory* deal precisely with the ways in which Nabokov succeeded in escaping from time's prison, even though the connections between these passages and the ones under discussion are never made explicit. (In fact, he later indicated in an interview that the reference to time as a prison in the autobiography "was only a stylistic device" with which he introduced the subject of time.)[4] One is thus forced to conclude that the view of time as a prison is more a reflection on the incorrect methods Nabokov had explored and rejected than his final word on this aspect of his metaphysics.

Nabokov's view of time as problematic is intimately connected with his conception of human consciousness. The mundane relationship between consciousness and time emerges from his recollection in *Speak, Memory* of how he first became aware of himself as a separate being when he discovered how old he was in relation to his parents. Because of this connection, Nabokov concludes that "the beginning of reflexive consciousness in the brain of our remotest ancestor must surely have coincided with the dawning of the sense of time" (p. 21). Moreover, deception is an inherent part of the process. Nabokov remembers that he associated the birth of his self-awareness with the image of his father wearing a splendid uniform, and that he did not realize until later that this must have been part of some "festive joke" on his father's part, who had in fact completed his military service many years earlier. This chance witnessing of a masquerade acquires "recapitulatory implications" for Nabokov that transcend its immediate significance because, as he concludes, "the first creatures on earth to become aware of time were also the first creatures to smile" (p. 22). In an interview Nabokov made similar connections among time, consciousness, and human evolution, and summarized them neatly as "time without consciousness—lower animal world; time with consciousness—man; consciousness without time—some still higher state."[5] The last formulation is especially important for understanding Nabokov's intuitions regarding the otherworld.

The paradoxical nature of time in Nabokov's view is underscored by the fact that although it comes into existence with consciousness, consciousness can also provide the means to escape it. The relation between

consciousness and the transcendence of time lies at the heart of Nabokov's probing discussion in *Speak, Memory* of the creation of art (and
thus throws a bridge between his metaphysics and his aesthetics). His
most revealing comments are prompted by his memory of how, in early
adolescence, he composed his first poem after seeing a raindrop run off a
leaf, which gave rise to the sequence of rhymes "tip, leaf, dip, relief."
Most significantly, he recalls that "the instant it all took to happen
seemed to me not so much a fraction of time as a *fissure* in it" (italics
added); and that the stanza of his nascent poem, although crude, "resembled the shock of wonder I had experienced when for a moment heart and
leaf had been one" (p. 217). Nabokov's image of a "fissure" in time obviously raises questions about its being a "spherical prison" with no exit.
Moreover, the poem emerges as stemming from a momentary fusion of
subject and object that is capable of being captured and communicated
by language. The implications of this are twofold: the work of art is underlain by a cognitive act, the form as well as the content of which can be
preserved in, or mimicked by, the artifact's verbal texture; and art has
truth value because it stems from specific phenomena illuminated by the
inner state of the observer. These inferences are supported by Nabokov's
admission in two interviews that philosophically he was an "indivisible
monist," which "implies a oneness of basic reality" and the impossibility
of separating "mind" and "matter." Similarly, in his book on Gogol, Nabokov insisted that phenomena cannot be conceived apart from the perceiver's mind: "bare facts do not exist in a state of nature, for they are
never really quite bare: the white trace of a wrist watch, a curled piece of
sticking plaster on a bruised heel, these cannot be discarded by the most
ardent nudist . . . I doubt whether you can even give your telephone number without giving something of yourself."[6]

Reflecting upon his youthful attempts to write poetry, Nabokov concludes that they were in fact primarily an expression of his beginning
sense of orientation in relation to the things and experiences constituting
his world. This thought leads him to the generalization that "all poetry is
positional," and to the seminal conclusion that "to try to express one's
position in regard to the universe embraced by consciousness, is an immemorial urge." Indeed, Nabokov raises this idea to a major principle of
his art, and thereby further intertwines his metaphysics with his aesthetics. Under the guise of quoting his "philosophical friend" Vivian Blood-
mark, whose name is of course an anagram of his own, Nabokov states
that "while the scientist sees everything that happens in one point of
space, the poet feels everything that happens in one point of time" (p.
218). He calls this experience "cosmic synchronization," a term that may
be somewhat tongue-in-cheek since it also derives from his anagrammatic
friend. But this does not detract from the significance of the concept, for

Nabokov says unequivocally that "a person hoping to become a poet must have the capacity of thinking of several things at a time." Neither does it reduce the utility of the concrete examples Nabokov gives of the experience itself, which can serve as paradigms for many of his novels: in works from his Russian and English periods "cosmic synchronization" appears as one of the characteristic traits of all of his positive characters, and as an aesthetic, cognitive, and moral touchstone against which negative characters are measured. As Nabokov stated in an interview, consciousness is *the* quintessential characteristic of man; when asked what distinguishes man from animals, he responded: "Being aware of being aware of being. In other words, if I not only know that I *am* but also know that I know it, then I belong to the human species. All the rest follows—the glory of thought, poetry, a vision of the universe."[7]

One especially beautiful illustration of Nabokov's thinking of "several things at a time" in *Speak, Memory* is his recollection of running into the village schoolmaster near his family's estate:

> While politely discussing with him my father's sudden journey to town, I registered simultaneously and with equal clarity not only his wilting flowers, his flowing tie and the blackheads on the fleshy volutes of his nostrils, but also the dull little voice of the cuckoo coming from afar, and the flash of a Queen of Spain settling on the road, and the remembered impression of the pictures (enlarged agricultural pests and bearded Russian writers) in the well-aerated classrooms of the village school which I had once or twice visited; and—to continue a tabulation that hardly does justice to the ethereal simplicity of the whole process—the throb of some utterly irrelevant recollection (a pedometer I had lost) was released from a neighboring brain cell, and the savor of the grass stalk I was chewing mingled with the cuckoo's note and the fritillary's takeoff, and all the while I was richly, serenely aware of my own manifold awareness. (Pp. 218–19)

The effect of such disparate details coming together is that they form "an instantaneous and transparent organism of events, of which the poet . . . is the nucleus" (p. 218). Because the essential feature of the experience is the individual's ability to apprehend connections among many phenomena that are not necessarily contiguous in terms of space, time, or causality, as well as between these phenomena and himself, the process might also be designated multidimensional metaphoric thinking or cognition. An additional way of conceiving of it is in terms of "epiphany," both in the sense of vatic, revelatory "moments" in time such as one finds in Romantic works like Wordsworth's *Prelude*, and in the sense usually associated with Joyce's *A Portrait of the Artist as a Young Man*, where it refers to the sudden "radiance" common objects can achieve.[8] In one of his lectures on literature, Nabokov himself indicates that the term *epiph-*

any could be applied to the famous incident of Marcel's memories being resurrected by the *madeleine* in Proust's *In Search of Lost Time*, an event that resembles "cosmic synchronization." Moreover, he quotes with apparent approval what Marcel says about the timeless truth of "reality" emerging only when sensations or memories are linked via metaphor, or, in other words, are embodied in art.[9] Sisson has shown that Nabokov's cosmic synchronization also resembles the holistic experiences related to the creation of poetry that Ezra Pound and T. S. Eliot described, as well as the kind of "universal noetic awareness" that William James posits as an essential characteristic of mystical experience in his *The Varieties of Religious Experience* (1902).[10] In his lecture "The Art of Literature and Commonsense," rather than speak of "cosmic synchronization" Nabokov uses the term "inspiration." However, the example he provides (pp. 377–78) shows that the experience behind this term is identical to the epiphanic moments he describes in *Speak, Memory*.[11] One of the most valuable and interesting aspects of the lecture is that it reveals exactly how the "spiritual thrill" of inspiration is connected with the creation of art. Nabokov explains that although many people who are not writers may be familiar with the instantaneous fusion of present phenomena and past memories, "the inspiration of genius adds a third ingredient: it is the past and the present *and* the future (your book) that come together in a sudden flash; thus the entire circle of time is perceived, which is another way of saying that time ceases to exist" (p. 378). The specific nature of the artist's epiphanic moment is, therefore, that it carries within it the germ of a future work of art. What this entails can be gleaned in turn from the fascinating details Nabokov provides in a late, important article entitled "Inspiration" (1972). Following an initial impression of a "prefatory glow," the "narrator forefeels what he is going to tell. The forefeeling can be defined as an instant vision turning into rapid speech. If some instrument were to render this rare and delightful phenomenon, the image would come as a shimmer of exact details, and the verbal part as a tumble of merging words." The writer takes this down, and in so doing "transforms what is little more than a running blur into gradually dawning sense, with epithets and sentence construction." Inspiration can then continue to serve the writer with additional jolts over time.[12] In "The Art of Literature and Commonsense" Nabokov also makes the important qualification that the initial seed of the future work may not be related to "a kind of glorified physical experience," such as in the case of sensory details suddenly jelling, but may be "an inspired combination of several abstract ideas without a definite physical background" (p. 379). This explanation is particularly germane for understanding how Nabokov dramatizes the origins of Fyodor's biography of Chernyshevski in *The Gift*, and why he could equate art and chess in *The Defense*. In any event, the writer can subsequently verify the flowering of his inspiration by examining the completed work, which will reveal that it is the "outcome of a definite plan contained in the initial shock" (p. 377), a conclusion that is identical to the one he reached in *Speak, Memory* with regard to his first poem. The continuity over time of Nabokov's aesthetic beliefs is suggested by the fact that as early as 1932 he had described the origins of his works in terms similar to those he used some four decades later in "Inspiration": "The plan of my novel comes to me suddenly, is born in a minute. . . . The first jolt is what is important."[13]

If one were to neglect for a moment the ecstatic character of Nabokov's descriptions of inspiration and cosmic synchronization, it might seem as if his claims about "forefeeling" future works are nothing more than figurative references to their origins in memory. But in fact Nabokov's expanded comments about these "prophetic" sensations suggest that the work literally derives from an otherworldly realm: "I am afraid to get mixed up with Plato, whom I do not care for, but I do think that in my case it is true that the entire book, before it is written, seems to be ready ideally in some other, now transparent, now dimming, dimension, and my job is to take down as much of it as I can make out and as precisely as I am humanly able to."[14] In a review of a book on philosophy, Nabokov even went so far as to suggest that the words of his works literally preexist his attempts to write them: the creative writer's "trying to set down his sentence in the best possible state—*of conservation rather than creation*—is but an effort to materialize the perfect something *which already exists in the somewhere* which [the philosopher in question] obligingly terms 'Nature' " (italics added).[15] The reason Nabokov brings up Plato at all in connection with the origin of art is presumably because of some resemblance between his own conception of the process and the Greek philosopher's metaphysics, in which terrestrial phenomena are but shadows of ideal forms in a noumenal realm. Indeed, it is clear from other comments by Nabokov that he found only Plato's politics distasteful. On one occasion he characterized Plato as "a fine artist-philosopher but a vicious sociologist," and on another concluded that he would not have survived "very long under [Plato's] Germanic regime of militarism and music."[16]

Another important link between Nabokov's aesthetics and his metaphysics is his conception of imagination. Because the creation of an artistic image "depends on the power of association, and association is supplied and prompted by memory," artistic imagination is actually "a form of memory." This is not, however, a retreat from a Neoplatonic aesthetic, because "when we speak of a vivid individual recollection we are paying a compliment not to our capacity of retention but to Mnemosyne's mysterious foresight in having stored up this or that element which creative imagination may want to use when combining it with later recollections and inventions."[17] Nabokov's references to memory in the guise of the mythical mother of the muses, and to the "mysterious" nature of memory, clearly imply that in his conception artistic imagination touches the transcendent, and is not just a process restricted to an individual's mind. ("Voobrazhenie—mladshaia sestra iasnovideniia" is the way the Russian writer Mikhail Kuzmin phrased the same idea: "imagination [is] the younger sister of clairvoyance".)[18] This inference is supported by a remark Nabokov makes in *Speak, Memory*, where he says that memory's "supreme achievement" is "the masterly use it makes of *innate* harmonies when gathering to its fold the suspended and wandering tonalities of the past" (italics added, p. 170). As one can infer from the context, by "harmonies" Nabokov obviously means patterns in human life, which, together with mimicry in nature, constitute one of his major forms of evidence for the existence of a transcendent otherworld. Thus it is possible to conclude that memory's remarkable ability to correlate data from different times is due not to an individual's projecting order onto the world around him, but to the fact that memory operates in some mysteriously harmonious way with the patterns "imprinted" by an otherworld onto life and nature themselves.

Nabokov's conviction that art derives at least in part from a transcendent dimension suggests an explanation for his descriptions in interviews of how he would write a work by putting down onto index cards random passages from various parts of the completed whole, which was fixed in its entirety in his mind, rather than by writing out the text from beginning to end. In "The Art of Literature and Commonsense" he states that "time and sequence cannot exist in the author's mind because no time element and no space element had ruled the initial vision" that constitutes the germ of the future work (pp. 379–80).[19] Thus, although the reader may have to confront a temporal dimension when reading a novel, the author does not when it is first born in his mind. The reason is presumably that the work derives from the same timeless realm the author is vouchsafed to touch during moments of highest consciousness or inspiration. This suggests that Nabokov's characteristic practice of filling his fictions with epiphanic *structures*—with networks of concealed details, the connections among which emerge suddenly—is an aesthetic embodiment of a metaphysical experience.

The lexicon Nabokov uses when speaking of inspiration in "The Art of Literature and Commonsense" further implies that his aesthetics are part of a continuum that includes his metaphysics. He describes the moment when the artist feels that time has ceased to exist as "a combined sensation of having the whole universe entering you and of yourself wholly dissolving in the universe surrounding you. It is the prison wall of the ego suddenly crumbling away with the nonego rushing in from the outside to save the prisoner—who is already dancing in the open" (p. 378). This is the unabashed language of mystical exaltation, which in Nabokov's fiction becomes translated into both the structure of imagery and the experiences of characters. The sentence about the "prison wall . . . suddenly crumbling" and the "prisoner . . . dancing in the open" is an especially good illustration of the latter, since it is an obvious echo of the concluding scene of *Invitation to a Beheading*.

Despite the metaphysical implications of cosmic synchronization, it is important to understand that the experience does not resemble a trance or a dream; on the contrary, it is a state of highly enhanced wakefulness. Nabokov makes this point in *Speak, Memory* together with one of his most candid admissions about faith in a transcendent when he discusses the nature of dreams in which the dead appear:

> It is certainly not then—not in dreams—but when one is wide awake, at moments of robust joy and achievement, *on the highest terrace of consciousness, that mortality has a chance to peer beyond its own limits*, from the mast, from the past and its castle tower. And although nothing much can be seen through the mist, there is somehow the blissful feeling that one is looking in the right direction. (Italics added; p. 50)

The image of "mortality . . . peer[ing] beyond its own limits" recalls the (illusory) spherical prison of time that is fissured or transcended by the experience of cosmic synchronization. One is also tempted to infer that the value Nabokov places on consciousness explains why he dwells at length in his autobiography on his lifelong loathing of sleep (pp. 108–9).

Artistic inspiration is not the only experience that grants Nabokov the peak moments of his existence. His passion for butterflies, which is necessarily based on a high level of scientific awareness, does as well: "the highest enjoyment of timelessness—in a landscape selected at random—is when I stand among rare butterflies and their food plants. This is ecstasy, and behind the ecstasy is something else, which is hard to explain. It is like a momentary vacuum into which rushes all that I love. A sense of oneness with sun and stone" (p. 139).[20] Like cosmic synchronization, this experience awakens in Nabokov a very strong intuition about a transcendent otherworld: "A thrill of gratitude to whom it may concern—to the contrapuntal genius of human fate or to the tender ghosts humoring a lucky mortal." Elsewhere, Nabokov makes an overt connection between the experience of cosmic synchronization and the recognition of mimetic behavior in nature when he describes the birth of a poem "that hurtles from heights unknown" in terms of how "the tangle of sounds, the leopards of words, / the leaflike insects, the eye-spotted birds / fuse and form a silent, intense, / mimetic pattern of perfect sense."[21]

Love is the third kind of experience that has similar metaphysical implications for Nabokov, and that is associated with a sensation identical
to "cosmic synchronization." In *Speak, Memory*, he states that whenever
he thinks of his love for his wife and child he is impelled by an urge to
orient himself in relation to them, and to immediately draw "radii" from
his love, "from my heart, from the tender nucleus of a personal matter—
to monstrously remote points of the universe." The experience might best
be termed mystical, for it overwhelms Nabokov with "the sense of something much vaster, much more enduring and powerful than the accumulation of matter or energy in any imaginable cosmos." The reason why
"all space and all time" have to participate in Nabokov's "mortal love"
is, as he puts it, "so that the edge of its mortality is taken off." This helps
him "to fight the utter degradation, ridicule, and horror of having developed an infinity of sensation and thought within a finite existence" (pp.
296–97). It emerges therefore that Nabokov posits an automatic causal
connection between his intense experience of love and his intuition of a
transcendent cosmos.

One of the widespread misconceptions in the critical literature is that
Nabokov's art bears no relation to the "real" world.[22] It is hard to understand how anyone could have gotten this impression, and any familiarity with his discursive writings would have underscored its erroneous-
ness. The cardinal experience of cosmic synchronization demonstrates the
extent to which the artist depends on a precise observation of the surrounding world during the initial stage of the complex creative process.
Moreover, a number of Nabokov's aphoristic formulations about the
connections between art and science show how the importance of data
from the external world extends beyond the moment of inspiration directly into the work of art itself: "there is no science without fancy, and
no art without facts"; "a spurt of genius" can be found "in the paper of
a naturalist"; "a creative writer must study carefully the works of his
rivals, including the Almighty . . . the artist should *know* the given world.
Imagination without knowledge leads no farther than the back yard of
primitive art."[23] Although remarks such as these should clearly not be
taken to imply that Nabokov was interested in holding up a mirror to
"reality," they do indicate that he was concerned with creating plausible
simulacra of the phenomenal world.

The idea that facts about the external world are not an end in themselves in art, and serve ultimately as a springboard toward the otherworldly, is one to which Nabokov returns in the most varied writings. In
a review of a book on butterflies he asks if "there does not exist a high
ridge where the mountainside of 'scientific' knowledge joins the opposite
slope of 'artistic' imagination."[24] He answers this rhetorical question in
Speak, Memory when he postulates that "there is, it would seem, in the

dimensional scale of the world a kind of delicate meeting place between imagination and knowledge, a point, arrived at by diminishing large things and enlarging small ones, that is *intrinsically* artistic" (italics added; pp. 166–67). The key word in both passages is "imagination," which, as we have seen, implies the transcendent in Nabokov's metaphysical aesthetics. Especially fascinating is his idea that close scrutiny of the material world must end at some point in a transition to imagination, and, therefore, in grazing the edges of the perceiver's intimations about the otherworld. Nabokov's description of the limitations of scientific modes of inquiry suggests how this view might have been founded in his own studies of butterflies. He concludes that reality "is a very subjective affair" and can be defined "as a kind of gradual accumulation of information; and as a specialization." Any natural object, such as a particular flower, will be more real to a naturalist than to a layman; it will be even more real to a botanist, and more real still to one specializing in the particular flower. The result is that one can only get "nearer and nearer" to reality, which is "an infinite succession of steps, levels of perception, false bottoms, and hence unquenchable, unattainable." The things that surround man are therefore "more or less ghostly."[25] But the kind of close scrutiny of which Nabokov speaks here recalls what he describes as triggering the burst of inspiration leading to his first poem, as well as all his other examples of cosmic synchronization. Thus it would seem that the impossibility of seizing material things in all their uniqueness and fullness may be compensated for by the insights epiphanic moments yield. Nabokov himself implied this in an interview when he said that he tended "more and more to regard the objective existence of *all* events as a form of *impure imagination* [italics added]. . . . Whatever the mind grasps, it does so with the assistance of creative fancy, that drop of water on a glass slide which gives distinctness and relief to the observed organism." This view explains why Nabokov always insisted on placing quotation marks around the word *reality*—to stress its absolute dependence on the unique mind of each perceiving individual (without abandoning, of course, his resolutely hierarchical view of the different capacities that individuals have for insight and perspicacity). The distinction between "impure" and "pure" forms of imagination that Nabokov also makes in this interview underscores that he has not altered his view of the link between imagination and the otherworld. Whereas the former is manifested automatically during mundane perceptions and consciousness, the latter, in its unadulterated form as it were, is awakened during moments of peak consciousness: Nabokov explains that "pure imagination" must come into play when the individual tries to apprehend the events constituting cosmic synchronization, because it is physically impossible "to reproduce those events optically within the frame of one screen." And only if it were possible to reproduce their simultaneity would cosmic synchronization conform to "reality."[26] Given the context of Nabokov's other discursive writings, this connection between imagination and cosmic synchronization necessarily links the former to the otherworld. In its strongest formulation, Nabokov's conception of the relation between creative imagination and the world of phenomena comes close to giving priority to the former: "Average reality begins to rot and stink as soon as the act of individual creation ceases to animate a subjectively perceived texture." Elsewhere he explained that although "the material of this world may be real enough (as far as reality goes) . . . it does not exist at all as an accepted entirety: it is chaos, and to this chaos the author says 'go!' allowing the world to flicker and fuse. It is now recombined in its very atoms— not merely in its visible and superficial parts. The writer is the first man to map it and name the natural objects it contains."[27] Nabokov takes a similarly radical approach toward the possibility of knowing another human being. In his 1937 lecture on Pushkin, he concludes that the truth of another's life may be inaccessible, because thought cannot help distorting whatever it tries to encompass. Nevertheless, the intuitions and conjectures of a fictionalized biography that are motivated by love for its subject yield a "plausible" life that approaches in some mysterious way the "poet's work, if not the poet himself."[28] Although in this case Nabokov is speaking about another's life in terms of its being an inaccessible object, rather than about phenomena that have no apparent existence at all outside of mind, he still conceives of the imagination as that which warrants ontological validity, and that which touches, however tentatively, what might otherwise have seemed to be absolutely unknowable.

All aspects of this complex of Nabokov's beliefs are highly relevant for his works of fiction. It would not be an exaggeration to say that the shifting boundary between "imagination" and "fact," as he conceived of them, is the central issue in virtually his entire fictional corpus. Variants of this problem include the protagonists' insights regarding otherworldly patterning in their lives in *The Defense*, *Invitation to a Beheading*, and *The Gift*, the relative balance between solipsism and insight in *The Real Life of Sebastian Knight*, *Lolita*, and *Pale Fire*, and the "ghostliness" of matter in contrast to a higher reality in *The Defense*, *Invitation to a Beheading*, *The Gift*, *Pnin*, and *Transparent Things*. It is essential to realize, however, that although the relation of "fact" to "imagination" is in a sense the enduring concern of all art (and of the novel since Cervantes), and therefore might seem to be the province of any exegetical scheme, it would be misleading to consider this issue outside the context of Nabokov's highly developed aesthetic, metaphysical, and ethical system that defines the terms in question in a specific way.

Although it is clear that Nabokov's metaphysical beliefs may be partially congruent with a variety of religious experiences or philosophical systems, ultimately they are sui generis. This raises an important terminological point. Nabokov repeated a number of times that he was not interested in "religion." Indeed, he stated it never meant anything to him "beyond literary stylization," and once recalled with some pride the annoyance he had caused an émigré critic by his "utter indifference to organized mysticism, to religion, to the church—any church."[29] The key to understanding remarks of this sort is to realize that Nabokov always objected to having himself or his works identified with ideas or systems of belief that were not his own, and that therefore could not do justice to his insights and intuitions. This, and not a denial of any form of belief in another world is the implication of the above remark, and of the comment in *Speak, Memory* that "in my metaphysics, I am a confirmed non-unionist and have no use for organized tours through anthropomorphic paradises" (p. 297).

In the continuation of this passage Nabokov suggests instead that his own experiences, and those of close family members, have been the sole sources of his world view. This subject is part of the much broader, and highly important theme of the persistence of psychological traits and fate through time and generations in the Nabokov family. Although Nabokov frequently calls attention to such repetitions in his own and his ancestors' lives, there are numerous instances in which he leaves the parallels unarticulated, thereby inviting the reader to draw them instead. One major example is his description of his mother's beliefs, which sounds very much like what he could have written about himself, and what he did imply throughout his works:

> Her intense and pure religiousness took the form of her having equal faith in the existence of another world and in the impossibility of comprehending it in terms of earthly life. All one could do was to glimpse, amid the haze and the chimeras, something real ahead, just as persons endowed with an unusual persistence of diurnal cerebration are able to perceive in their deepest sleep, somewhere beyond the throes of an entangled and inept nightmare, the ordered reality of the waking hour. (P. 39)

The implicit denigration of sleep in this passage recalls Nabokov's avowed distaste for it because of its incommensurability with the high states of consciousness he values. In fact, the implicit analogies in this passage between sleep and earthly life on the one hand, and wakefulness and a transcendent world on the other, is a Gnostic topos found in many of Nabokov's works, including *The Defense, Invitation to a Beheading, The Gift*, "Perfection," "Ultima Thule," *Bend Sinister*, and *Transparent Things*.

There are also spiritual analogies between Nabokov and his mother, which suggests that in his view the otherworldliness touching her survived in him. He recalls how during his boyhood he would mention "this or that unusual sensation" to her, only to have her begin to discuss with "a somewhat eerie ingenuousness" various related, occult experiences that she had had (p. 39).[30] In turn, Nabokov implies that a similar parallel exists between himself and his son, suggesting thereby that the sensitivity to the otherworldly has been passed on to yet another generation. During his son's infancy, Nabokov sees in his eyes something like preserved reflections of the Edenic land where "man's mind had been born," and characterizes the baby's hand and eye coordination as his "first journey into the next dimension." The context makes it clear that this is not merely Nabokov's figurative description of the wonders of human consciousness. He openly dismisses the explanations of behavioral psychologists, and suggests instead that the "closest reproduction of the mind's birth obtainable" is "the precise moment when, gazing at a tangle of twigs and leaves, one suddenly realizes that what had seemed a natural component of that tangle is a marvelously disguised insect or bird" (p. 298). Although this might seem to be a frivolous or eccentric comment, within Nabokov's hierarchy of values in *Speak, Memory* mimicry and disguise in nature are essential evidence for a transcendent otherworld. Thus, the parallel he draws between a child's cognitive development and the grasping of a mimetic phenomenon implies the involvement of a transcendent agency at the basis of an infant's, and therefore, of human consciousness. Furthermore, the incremental leap in consciousness implied by the idea of the child reaching for "the next dimension" resembles Nabokov's description of the expansion of consciousness during "cosmic synchronization," and thus also points to the transcendent. Finally, the passages about Nabokov's son cast retroactive light on the opening pages of the autobiography and the "chronophobiac" who did not understand that he may have existed prior to his birth in more ways than one.

Because of the extraordinary value Nabokov places on consciousness, and because consciousness is dependent on the visual discovery of interrelations among phenomena, it is not surprising that he would have wanted to nurture this skill in his son. The one major example in the autobiography of how Nabokov did this is of particular interest because it also suggests the reason why he chose to structure his narrative in such a way that connections among highly important details are not made explicit, and are left for the reader to discover. All narratives contain devices to draw the reader into developing the meaning of the text, and this is a process that is essential for the pleasure of reading. But in addition to identifying the devices in question, it is most enlightening to try to understand in what specific aspects of the text the author may want the reader to become involved. The last lines of *Speak, Memory* suggest what this goal may have been for Nabokov. He describes how he, his wife, and son were approaching the harbor where the ship that was to take them to the United States was docked. The parents saw the ship first through various buildings and clotheslines that lay between them and the dock (obstacles to which Nabokov typically refers as "all sorts of stratagems"), but intentionally chose not to call their son's attention to it. The reason was that they wanted to "enjoy in full the blissful shock, the enchantment and glee he would experience" on discovering for himself the "ungenuinely gigantic and unrealistically real" prototype of all the toy boats he had ever played with (p. 309). Nabokov likens the experience of grasping the ship's presence to the game "Find What the Sailor Has Hidden" in a picture that has been scrambled. Because this is also a good description of the task the reader must carry out with *Speak, Memory*, one concludes that an important specific function of the puzzle-like aspect of Nabokov's narrative technique in general is to provide the reader with an opportunity to make a perceptual and cognitive leap that mimics a sudden expansion in consciousness. An inevitable corollary is that because Nabokov places a very high value on this ability, anyone who lacks it automatically emerges as tainted by blindness. Although this theme is not developed to any great extent in the autobiography, it is one of the major constants in virtually all of Nabokov's fiction.

The inference that Nabokov may have wanted his readers to relive without mediation the same seminal experiences that underlie his works is supported by his response to an interviewer's question about what were the pleasures of writing: "the felicity of a phrase is shared by writer and reader: by the satisfied writer and the grateful reader, or—which is the same thing—by the artist grateful to the unknown force in his mind that has suggested a combination of images and by the artistic reader whom this combination satisfies."[31] The implication is clearly that the ideal relation between the reader and the work is like that between the author and the otherworld, which, through the agency of "mysterious" memory, participates in the writer's aesthetic consciousness.[32] In a lecture, Nabokov described the act of reading as capable of providing a full apprehension of the original work: "its rare flavor will be appreciated at its true worth and the broken and crushed parts will again come together in your mind and disclose the beauty of a unity to which you have contributed something of your own blood."[33] And in his book on Gogol, Nabokov argues that this kind of privileged communication between writer and reader is not accidental, but a manifestation of artistic skill: "Even in his worst writings Gogol was always good at creating his reader, which is the privilege of great writers."[34]

Chess, and specifically chess problems—the fourth subject that elicits

Nabokov's greatest passion in *Speak, Memory*—provide analogous parallels.[35] When the solver of a chess problem finally arrives at "the simple key move," he experiences "a *synthesis* of poignant *artistic* delight" (italics added; p. 292).[36] Particularly intriguing is that in his comments about chess problems Nabokov underscores the value of deception as a general aesthetic criterion, which has an obvious bearing on the puzzle-like dimension of his literary works: "Deceit, to the point of diabolism, and originality, verging on the grotesque, were my notions of strategy" (p. 289). The parallels between chess and art, which are found throughout Nabokov's ọeuvre, are most clearly drawn in his chess novel, *The Defense*, and the collection *Poems and Problems* (1970). The latter is especially revealing of his attitude because it openly places the chess problems he composed on the same footing with his poems; as Nabokov put it in the Introduction, "chess problems demand from the composer the same virtues that characterize all worthwhile art: originality, invention, conciseness, harmony, complexity, and splendid insincerity."[37]

As we have seen, moments of "cosmic synchronization" provide Nabokov an escape from time. But it is still necessary to determine what specific meaning timelessness had for him, and how this experience articulates with his fictions. In *Speak, Memory*, Nabokov describes timelessness not only as oblivion to time, but also in terms of accompanying translations from situations in what would normally have been called "the past" to their analogues in the atemporal "present," and vice versa. For example, in describing his "trancelike state" when he was laboring to complete his first poem, Nabokov recalls how he was hardly surprised to find himself lying first on a couch in the manor house with his arm dangling over a floral carpet, then on a wharf with his arm extended toward water lilies, and finally on a bench in the park with his arm dipping into colored shadows (pp. 222–23). He concludes that "ordinary measures of existence" were so insignificant in his state that he "would not have been surprised to come out of its tunnel right into the park of Versailles, or the Tiergarten, or Sequoia National Forest." These three locales are of course allusions to Nabokov's long wanderings as an émigré, first in Europe, and then in the United States. But his including them in a description of a burst of inspiration that he had experienced decades earlier in Russia devalues the ontological weight of the voyaging implied by his emigration in comparison with the exalted (albeit intermittent) creative state. The disappearance of time and the concomitant slippages in space persist when Nabokov shifts to his creative endeavors during the narrative present: "when the old trance occurs nowadays, I am quite prepared to find myself, when I awaken from it, high up in a certain tree, above the dappled bench of my boyhood, my belly pressed against a thick, comfortable branch and one arm hanging down among the leaves upon which the shadows of other leaves move" (p. 223). In this passage, the seeming movement is in the opposite direction—from the narrator's present to what would conventionally be called the past; but there is no difference for the individual in the throes of artistic creation because time has ceased to exist. The immediacy and reality of this experience are rendered by Nabokov with special beauty when he shifts from his memories of a snowbound landscape in Russia to the one in which he is standing in New England in the 1950s: "All is still, spellbound, enthralled by the moon, fancy's rear-vision mirror. The snow is real, though, and as I bend to it and scoop up a handful, sixty years crumble to glittering frost-dust between my fingers" (pp. 99–100). The force of memory, which is for Nabokov a facet of privileged consciousness, thus negates the specificity of both New England and Russia as spatiotemporal realities because with the disappearance of time one's location in space emerges as a function of one's heightened consciousness. The Russian space of Nabokov's youth is thus not really lost to him after decades of emigration, even though it is accessible only during privileged moments that lift him out of mundane experience. This is a conception of time and consciousness that has remained inaccessible to some of Nabokov's readers. One critic actually inverts Nabokov's meaning in the passage about sixty years crumbling to frost-dust, and enlists it in support of Nabokov's supposed conviction "that the past must never be confused with the present, the imaginatively recreated memory with the event itself." This misreading is, however, in keeping with the critic's overall view that Nabokov saw "death as that which finally cannot be transcended."[38]

Nabokov's passages in *Speak, Memory* about translations through space during timeless moments also reveal an additional important facet of heightened consciousness. Not only does time disappear during epiphanic moments, but, because events from the past are automatically evoked by analogous experiences in the present, life emerges as patterned with repetitions. When the privileged moments pass, time reasserts itself as a seeming fact of existence, but without vitiating the repetitions. This raises a question about how the repetitions are related to time, and how time is "shaped." Nabokov's answer appears to be the image of his life as a "colored spiral in a small ball of glass." "The spiral," as he puts it, "is a spiritualized circle. In the spiral form, the circle, uncoiled, unwound, has ceased to be vicious; it has been set free. . . . Hegel's triadic series . . . expressed merely the essential spirality of all things in their relation to time" (p. 275). The spiral is thus a form that reconciles repetitions with change through time: repetitions are implied by the fact that whorls follow each other even as they describe new arcs, and time is symbolized by the imaginary axis around which the whorls are arranged.[39] Nabokov's image of a glass ball containing a colored spiral of course evokes a child's marble. But it also recalls the (deceptive) idea of time as a spherical prison he introduces in the beginning of *Speak, Memory*. Given that Nabokov did find ways to escape from time, it is tempting to infer that the image of the marble is meant to represent only a segment of a life spiral that in fact extends in some spiritualized form beyond the temporal sphere in which it appears to be enclosed. This is what Nabokov himself seems to hypothesize later in the autobiography when he speculates about "the spiral unwinding of things" in general: "if . . . space warps into something akin to time, and time, in its turn, warps into something akin to thought, then, surely, another dimension follows—a special Space maybe, not the old one, we trust, unless spirals become vicious circles once again" (p. 301).

In addition to providing discursive or analytical examples of timelessness in *Speak, Memory*, Nabokov also incorporates passages in the text that function as concrete and unsignaled embodiments of such moments. Some of these are dazzlingly deceptive, and thus provide additional illustrations of a fundamental aspect of his narrative technique. They also confront the reader with having to pay attention to the text as closely as Nabokov indicates is necessary in order to achieve the level of consciousness that underlies timelessness. Among the recollections of Nabokov's boyhood is a butterfly hunt he undertook in a bog near the family estate. After describing his captures, he continues: "At last I saw I had come to the end of the marsh. The rising ground beyond was a paradise of lupines, columbines, and pentstemons. Mariposa lilies bloomed under Ponderosa pines." Thus, without any warning or transition, at the end of the second sentence Nabokov shifts from the flora of his pre-Revolutionary boyhood in northern Russia to an herb, a flower and a tree from the American West, where he hunted butterflies only after emigrating to the United States from Europe in 1940. The final sentence of this paragraph confirms that we have moved to the United States: "In the distance, fleeting cloud shadows dappled the dull green slopes above the timber line, and the gray and white of Longs Peak" (pp. 138–39; a similar example appears on p. 120). The fact that Nabokov does not explain what he has done in this passage naturally puts the burden on the reader to interpret it on his own. In addition to the quantum leap in understanding this entails, the nature of the transition between the two sentences captures the collapse of time the author experienced, and gives the reader a taste of the experience himself, in the way an analytical summary could not.

Nabokov characterizes this syntactical and stylistic trick as his liking "to fold my magic carpet, after use, in such a way as to superimpose one part of the pattern upon another," and concludes with the flourish "let visitors trip."[40] If the pattern in question was overt when he was composing his poem (his repeated prone positions with dangling arm), this time it is less obvious. In fact, some of Nabokov's comments imply it was not simply his reference to two butterfly hunts that constitutes a pattern, but that he saw butterflies in the American West that were identical, or related to those he had pursued in northern Russia.[41] This suggests that the metaphor of "folding" a "magic carpet" could be a reference to the creative process underlying both the discovery of significant patterning in one's life, and the achievement of timelessness—that is, the resurrection of memories of the earlier butterfly hunt during the later one, under the stimulus of a resemblance between the species being pursued. The metaphor may also be seen as referring to the style of Nabokov's autobiography, in which the theme of timelessness is reflected in the unmarked transition between contiguous sentences referring to experiences on different continents. All these readings of the metaphor in *Speak, Memory* are buttressed by a poem that Nabokov wrote in Russian in 1943: "In this life, rich in patterns . . . no better joy would I choose than to fold / its magnificent carpet in such a fashion / as to make the design of today coincide / with the past, with a former pattern, / in order to visit again—oh, not / commonplaces of those inclinations, / not the map of Russia, and not a lot / of nostalgic equivocations—/ but, by finding congruences with the remote, / to revisit my fountainhead, / to bend and discover in my own childhood / the end of the tangled-up thread."[42] Thus one can draw the inference from the metaphor of the folded carpet that the formal aspects of Nabokov's art are based, at least to some degree, on the way he perceives, remembers, arranges, and ranks phenomena. This is the same conclusion that is suggested by the parallels between Nabokov's descriptions of "cosmic synchronization" and the structure of his works. Additional support for this conclusion can be found in Nabokov's lecture on Proust's *In Search of Lost Time*, in which he approves Marcel's discovery that lost time can be recovered when a present sensation combines with memories of "the sensuous past," and concludes that "the illumination is . . . completed when the narrator realizes that a work of art is our only means of thus recapturing the past." Nabokov also quotes approvingly Marcel's realization that re-creating past impressions through memory—plumbing them "to their depths," and transforming them into "intellectual equivalents"—is one of the "prerequisites, almost the very essence of a work of art such as I conceived."[43]

Perhaps the single most important manifestation of the otherworld for Nabokov is patterning in life, nature, and art. In Nabokov's own life patterning takes the form of fate, which raises the vexing question of the relation between determinism and free will in his world view. He once admitted that fate may indeed be his "muse," and acknowledged that "in common with Pushkin, I am fascinated by fatidic dates."[44] However, he also expressed a belief in free will on a number of occasions, as when he stated that "the highest achievements in poetry, prose, painting, showmanship are characterized by the irrational and the illogical, by that spirit of free will that snaps its rainbow fingers in the face of smug causality"; and "I doubt that any strict line can be drawn between the tragic and the burlesque, fatality and chance, causal subjection and the caprice of free will." By contrast, in speaking of writing for the stage, he found a middle ground and hypothesized that "a writer of genius" could "without suggesting anything like the iron laws of tragic fatality" still "express certain definite combinations that occur in life."[45] Nabokov's conception of inspiration also implies that the artist is happily constrained in his creativity by the otherworld from which his works appear to derive, at least in part. If one judges by Nabokov's fictional writings, it is difficult to find any room at all for free will amid the fatidic patterning that ensnares every positive and negative character. Because there does not appear to be any way of resolving this paradoxical range of views on the possibility of freedom, it might be best to conclude that either the issue was never resolved unequivocally in Nabokov's mind, or that he conceived of free will and determinism as capable of functioning in different aspects of life.

In keeping with the subtle way in which the otherworld operates in Nabokov's view, as well as with his abhorrence of the automatic associations that accompany such loaded words as *fate*, he avoids using the term itself in *Speak, Memory* when he describes his attempts to understand his life: "Neither in environment nor in heredity can I find the exact instrument that fashioned me, the anonymous roller that pressed upon my life a certain intricate watermark whose unique design becomes visible when the lamp of art is made to shine through life's foolscap" (p. 25). However, if neither heredity nor environment can explain Nabokov's unique traits, then, presumably, the only agency that remains is a realm transcending the earthly. This is, in fact, precisely what Nabokov proclaimed in an early Russian poem utilizing the same image of the watermark. The lyric persona imagines that when his soul is lifted out of earthly darkness and held up to the light like a letter, "prosiiaet to, chto sonno / v sebe ia chuiu i taiu, / znak ne stiraemyi, iskonnyi, / uzor, pridumannyi v raiu" ("there will shine through that which / I sleepily sense and keep secret within me, / an indelible, immemorial mark, / a design devised in paradise").[46]

The first example Nabokov gives in *Speak, Memory* of a fatidic repetition illustrates well the great significance he ascribes to seemingly minor events in his life. He recalls how he was once introduced to General Kuropatkin, a friend of the family, who, in order to amuse him, performed a simple trick with matches. Moments later he was called away because he had been given command of the Russian Army in the war with Japan. Fifteen years later this incident had "a special sequel," as Nabokov puts it. While his father was escaping from the Bolsheviks in St. Petersburg, he chanced to be stopped by a peasant who asked him for a light. It turned out to be the general in disguise. "What pleases me," Nabokov explains, "is the evolution of the match theme: those magic ones he had shown me had been trifled with and mislaid, and his armies had also vanished, and everything had fallen through." (Typically for Nabokov, together with the repetition to which he calls attention, the passages in question contain a series of references to bodies of water and trains falling through ice [pp. 26, 27]—veiled repetitions that are left for the reader to discover.) Nabokov's conclusion is that "the following of such thematic designs through one's life should be . . . the true purpose of autobiography" (pp. 26–27). The fact that he phrases this in terms applicable to literary analysis recalls his other parallels between literary form and consciousness.

The general pattern of the fateful repetitions to which Nabokov calls attention in *Speak, Memory* follows that of the incident with the matches: seemingly insignificant details emerge as implying major events or thematic dominants in his life. For example, his first conscious return to Russia from a trip abroad while a child becomes, "sixty years later, a rehearsal—not of the grand homecoming that will never take place, but of its constant dream in my long years of exile" (p. 97). The name "Tamara," which he assigns to the great love of his youth, "kept cropping up (with the feigned naiveté so typical of Fate, when meaning business)" for some time before he actually met her, "as if Mother Nature were giving me mysterious advance notices of Tamara's existence" (p. 229). In speaking of the beginnings of what was to become his lifelong passion for butterflies, Nabokov refers to his "guiding angel" in this pursuit (p. 120), and to how his "imagination" planned "the most distant events of my destiny" with regard to the mark he would eventually make in the world of lepidoptery (p. 136). That Nabokov is indeed talking about fate in this passage, and not merely about congruences between his hopes and their fulfillment, can be inferred from his conception of "imagination" as a "form of memory" that is dependent on a mysterious connection to the otherworld.

Nabokov's approach to the lives of family members is also strongly colored by his awareness of fate. He notes that his jurist father wrote "rather prophetically in a certain odd sense" of "little girls [in London] . . . from eight to twelve . . . being sacrificed to lechers" (p. 178), thus prefiguring his son's *Lolita*. He juxtaposes his sense of relief when a duel his father almost fights in St. Petersburg is called off with his father's murder in Berlin years later, and comments that "no shadow was cast by that future event upon the bright stairs of our St. Petersburg house . . . and several lines of play in a difficult chess composition were not blended yet on the board" (p. 193). The use of chess terminology as a metaphor for fate of course also recalls the central complex of images in *The Defense*.

Other examples of telling, cross-generational patterning in *Speak, Memory* reach even further back in time. The incident of Kerensky's aide asking Nabokov's father for a car the premier might use to escape from the Bolsheviks in 1917 is "an amusing thematic echo" of his ancestor Christina von Korff's lending her new carriage to Louis XVI and his family when they tried to escape from revolutionary Paris to Varennes in 1791 (p. 183; Nabokov does not call attention to the fact that even the two dates are linked "anagrammatically").

The parallel between the artist's creative activities and those of the memoirist (and, one might add, the "fatalist" concerned with discerning patterns in his and ancestors' lives) is underscored by Nabokov in *Speak, Memory* when he describes his little son's finding a piece of pottery on the beach in Mentone. He says he does not doubt that the shard "fitted exactly" the one he had found on the same shore in 1903, nor that both "tallied with" a third his mother had found in the same place in 1882, and with a fourth found by his grandmother a century earlier, and so on. All the missing fragments could be put together to form the complete bowl "broken by some Italian child, God knows where and when," which, Nabokov stresses, is "now mended by *these* rivets of bronze" (pp. 308–9). Even if these remarks are not literally true, they can be seen as an expression of Nabokov's belief in memory's ability to retrieve patterns from human lives extending over long stretches of the past, and to fix them in language. In his view the two activities of recollecting the past and fashioning a work of art are inevitably linked because of the inherently artistic nature of memory. In the short essay "Personal Past," he explains that because the individual cannot retain all he has experienced, the best he can do is try to recollect the most vivid or significant events—the "patches of rainbow light flitting through memory." This process of partial retention, however, "is the act of art, artistic selection, artistic blending, artistic re-combination of actual events." When Nabokov was asked if he was worried by the unavoidable distortion of detail inherent in remembering, he answered "not at all." The reason is that "the distortion of a remembered image may not only enhance its beauty with an added refraction, but provide informative links with earlier or later patches of the past."[47] Thus, instead of solipsism, the imprint of the mind on data from the past yields evidence of a pattern in human existence that transcends the will of the individual.[48] Nabokov's subject in these remarks is of course only artistic autobiography and not art in general, in the sense of fiction. But elsewhere he addresses the latter as well, and speaks explicitly about the continuity between the "pure satisfaction" to be found in "an inspired and precise work of art" and the "comfort one feels when one realizes that for all its blunders and boners the inner texture of life is also a matter of inspiration and precision."[49] There is again, therefore, a parallel between artistic form and the process of selection inherent in memory. Both entail the creation of patterned wholes out of disparate elements, and both have a structure comparable to cosmic synchronization.

Nabokov's conception of his life as filled with patterning extends to his view of the world of nature as "made." His description of natural phenomena in terms of artifice in *Speak, Memory* and elsewhere thus implies not merely that they have been transformed by being incorporated into an autobiography or other text, but that they too were fashioned by an occult agent transcending the material world of heredity and environment. As a result, even though Nabokov never does more than hint about higher forces at work in human existence, it is possible to infer on the basis of his autobiographical writings that man and nature may have been fashioned by the same otherworldly agency.

In *Speak, Memory* Nabokov occasionally describes scenes as if they were theatrical stage sets (a device he also uses extensively throughout *Invitation to a Beheading*, as well as *The Gift, Bend Sinister* and other works, in order to render the artificiality of the physical world in comparison to a spiritual one). For example, in recalling scenes from his youth he says that snowflakes "passed and repassed with a graceful, almost deliberately slackened motion, as if to show how the trick was done and how simple it was" (p. 89). When seasons change, he describes a "berimed tree and a high snowdrift with its xanthic hole" as being "removed by a silent property man" (p. 105).

However, Nabokov reserves the most extensive and far-reaching comments about artifice in nature for mimicry among butterflies. He adduces a number of extraordinary examples—spots on a butterfly's wing that imitate bubbles of poison to the extent they seem to refract underlying structures, a caterpillar capable of imitating simultaneously a larva and an ant attacking it, and butterflies imitating leaves down to the detail of seeming to show holes bored by grubs. On an abstract level, mimicry or camouflage is a form of patterning because it involves one creature reproducing the shapes and colors of another. The reason such "mysteries" fascinated Nabokov is that they "showed an artistic perfection usually associated with man-wrought things" (pp. 124–25). In order to account for this phenomenon, he explicitly rejects the traditional, and one should add, materialistic explanations of natural history in favor of intuitions of the otherworldly:

"Natural selection," in the Darwinian sense, could not explain the miracu-
lous coincidence of imitative aspect and imitative behavior, nor could one
appeal to the theory of "struggle for life" when a protective device was carried to a point of mimetic subtlety, exuberance, and luxury *far in excess of a
predator's powers of appreciation*. I discovered in nature the nonutilitarian
delights that I sought in art. Both were a form of magic, both were a game of
intricate enchantment and deception. (Italics added; p. 124)

Nabokov returns to this idea in several of his interviews (and also treats
it at length in *The Gift*). "All art is deception and so is nature," he explains in one—"all is deception in that good cheat, from the insect that
mimics a leaf to the popular enticements of procreation." On another
occasion, he was asked the following question: "Magic, sleight-of-hand,
and other tricks have played quite a role in your fiction. Are they for
amusement or do they serve yet another purpose?" Nabokov's response
was that "deception is practiced even more beautifully by that other
V. N., Visible Nature. A useful purpose is assigned by science to animal
mimicry, protective patterns and shapes, yet their refinement transcends
the crude purpose of mere survival. . . . A grateful spectator is content to
applaud the grace with which the masked performer melts into Nature's
background."[50] The last sentence can be read as Nabokov's suggestion
that his characteristic practice of filling his works with puzzles, patterns,
anagrams, veiled allusions, false leads, deceptive narrators, doubles, and
the like—in other words, all of the characteristics of his art that are ad-
duced in discussions of its self-conscious artifice, might best be understood as Nabokov's imitation of the fundamental principle he discerned
in nature. This, in turn, implies that the reader of Nabokov's texts can be
seen as occupying a position with regard to them that is analogous to that
which Nabokov assumes with regard to his real world.

Although Nabokov calls *Speak, Memory* "strictly autobiographic,"[51] he
utilizes devices in it that one normally associates with works of fiction.
Their most general characteristic is oblique, rather than direct communication with the reader, and, as a result, they require an effort to be apprehended and understood. Nabokov's primary method of achieving
obliqueness is to apply the structure of cosmic synchronization to his narrative form: to present several major themes and subjects not in continuous narrative passages, as one might expect from a straightforward memoir, but in fragments embedded in different contexts, which not only
separates the pieces one from another, but camouflages their true import
as well. If all the components are borne in mind as they are encountered,
a point in the text is reached when a final detail is learned that "explains"
everything coming before it, and that gives the reader insight into some-

thing major and fundamental in Nabokov's life. Because the moment when fragments coalesce transcends the linear dimension of time inherent in the act of reading, the reader has the impression of being lifted out of time. The pleasure a reader receives from recognizing hidden meanings in the work is an obvious consequence of this narrative tactic as well, and thus constitutes an additional parallel with the epiphanic moments with which it is congruent. This translation of cosmic synchronization into the texture of a narrative resembles what Frank called "spatial form" in modern literature.[52] The significance he ascribes to it is that it implies discomfort with temporality. Given Nabokov's well-documented distaste for time, this explanation is clearly relevant for his works as well.

One especially moving example of a hidden pattern in *Speak, Memory* is the death of Nabokov's father.[53] The subject is first broached in connection with a description of how he was tossed into the air three times by peasants grateful for a favor he has granted them. The final toss is the highest, and Nabokov preserves in his memory an image of his father

> reclining, as if for good, against the cobalt blue of the summer noon like one of those paradisiac personages who comfortably soar, with such a wealth of folds in their garments, on the vaulted ceiling of a church while below, one by one, the wax tapers in mortal hands light up to make a swarm of minute flames in the mist of incense, and the priest chants of eternal repose, and funeral lilies conceal the face of whoever lies there, among the swimming lights, in the open coffin. (Pp. 31–32)

The fact that this may be a description of Nabokov's father in his coffin does not become clear to the reader who knows nothing about his life until later details retroactively illuminate the scene. At the same time, because of the reference to "mortal hands," which contrasts with "paradisiac personage" and "eternal repose," the description is colored by a hint of an opposition between body and spirit. And when, upon rereading, one realizes that the face in the coffin concealed by lilies may be the same one that is "reclining" in the sky, one is left with at least an intimation of immortality.

The pattern of oblique references to the father's death develops when Nabokov describes an evening in Berlin that he was spending with his mother. He gives the precise date, 28 March 1922, and remembers how a remark his mother was making was interrupted by the telephone ringing. But he provides no indication of the significance of the call, and immediately changes to another topic (p. 49). Ten pages later, however, he reveals indirectly that the telephone call must have been about his father's murder when he mentions that his grandfather died on 28 March 1904, or "exactly eighteen years, day for day, before my father" (p. 59). This detail of course also contributes to another pattern in the life of Nabokov's family, and functions as part of a network in the text that the reader has to perceive. Nabokov finally speaks openly of his father's death at the beginning of the chapter dealing with his biography (p. 173), and describes how it actually occurred at the chapter's end (p. 193).

One of the facets of cosmic synchronization is that it provides Nabokov with a sense of transcending the mundane conditions of existence. Thus quite apart from the imagery connected with the scene of his father's coffin in church, Nabokov's application of a narrative structure based on cosmic synchronization to the subject of his father's murder also implies that his death might not have been final. This is in fact supported by what he once wrote about his father in a letter to his mother: "We shall again see him, in an unexpected but completely natural paradise, in a country where everything is radiance and fineness. He will walk towards us in our common bright eternity. . . . Everything will return. In the way that in a certain time the hands of the clock come together again."[54] Nabokov expressed a similar attitude toward the death of another individual he esteemed very highly, the poet Vladislav Khodasevich. In his 1939 obituary, Nabokov wrote that Khodasevich "left for the region from where, perhaps, a faint something reaches the ears of good poets, penetrating our being with the beyond's ['potustoronnei'] fresh breath and conferring upon art that mystery which more than anything characterizes its essence."[55] As has been shown by Tammi, Nabokov conceived of poetic art as linked to "potustoronnost' " ("the otherworld" or "the hereafter") as early as 1922.[56]

Other concealed structures in *Speak, Memory* include Nabokov's presentation of how his much admired cousin, Yuri, died in a cavalry charge against a Red machine-gun nest during the Civil War. This is adumbrated by references to the toy soldiers the cousin collected, including one "with bandy legs still compressing an invisible charger" (pp. 196, 197, 200). In similar fashion, the seemingly humble detail of a "dead horsefly" lying in a pavilion, among other, more charming details (p. 216), anticipates "Tamara," the great love of Nabokov's youth. His first meeting with her follows soon after she is described as slapping a horsefly dead (p. 230). In this case, the reader participates with Nabokov, as it were, in discovering retroactively evidence of fate's having arranged their romance. On another textual level, Nabokov addresses an unnamed "you" a number of times in *Speak, Memory* before it finally emerges in the Index (which contains other concealed patterns as well) that these are references to his wife (pp. 129, 195, 258, 281, 292, 295, 298, etc.; a related device appears in *The Gift*).[57]

Finally, trains appear as one of the most insistent of the many leitmotifs in the autobiography (pp. 28, 48, 66, 91, 93, 102, 136, 141, 288, 300). To be sure, the motif derives in part from the importance of trains as a means of transportation during the first decades of this century, and from Nabokov's fondness for them. But the crowning passage in this sequence goes beyond historical verisimilitude and shows the kind of intricate "braiding" of strands of motifs that characterizes Nabokov's art, where one connects with another, which branches into others, and so on. This is Nabokov's description of his son's fondness for trains, which leads him to posit surprising parallels between velocity in all its manifestations and the physiological and psychological processes constituting life itself:

> Rapid growth, quantum-quick thought, the roller coaster of the circulatory system—all forms of vitality are forms of velocity, and no wonder a growing child desires to out-Nature Nature by filling a minimum stretch of time with a maximum of spatial enjoyment. Innermost in man is the spiritual pleasure derivable from the possibilities of outtugging and outrunning gravity, of overcoming or re-enacting the earth's pull. (P. 301)

In Nabokov's view, therefore, the child's love of speed is a result of the rapidity with which his psychophysical organism develops and functions; and this personal experience of velocity underlies the child's wish to control the kind of time he experiences in the world by vicariously or directly partaking of as much rapid motion as possible. What this basically means is that the child—and by extension man in general—automatically seeks correlates for internal experiences in the external world. There is a process of selection implied in this that makes the individual's consciousness the organizing principle of the world in which that individual exists—an idea that recurs in different contexts in Nabokov. In other words, the experience of time emerges as a human projection onto the world, rather than a feature inherent in it. (There is an obvious parallel here with Kant's conception of time as an a priori condition of experience.) And the child's fascination with speed can be read as a figure for inevitable human delusion about the world.

Thus, via the implications of one aspect of the autobiography's train imagery, we can conclude that in Nabokov's conception there is a parallel between artistic inspiration and the child's predilection for velocity. This follows because as velocity increases, the traveler approaches the theoretical limit of omnipresence in a moment of time. Nabokov himself suggests an equation in *Speak, Memory* between omnipresence and the omniscience implied by cosmic synchronization when he discusses the development of hand and eye coordination in a child, and characterizes the child's acquisition of the ability to reach for something as a "first journey into the next dimension" (p. 298). The first intentional act of grasping is, therefore, a manifestation of what Nabokov calls in *Speak, Memory* "an immemorial [human] urge": "to try to express one's position in regard to the universe embraced by consciousness" (p. 218).

This complex of views is clearly filled with paradoxes: the child's passion for fast travel is a vector pointing toward a transcendence of the laws of nature, of time and of this world; the artist can perceive time both as a given of life and as an illusion. What reconciles these paradoxes is Nabokov's world view: the transcendent and timeless otherworld is the true reality, while the time-bound world of phenomena is an alluring illusion. And since time is a function of motion and change in this world, from the vantage point of the transcendent any voyage is illusory, which is the same conclusion that was suggested by Nabokov's descriptions of his timeless translations through space.[58]

Nabokov also implies links among trains, velocity, consciousness, and metaphysics in a deceptive passage that includes a quotation from an unnamed, and most likely invented critic. The remarks are too perceptive about Nabokov's Russian novels, and too intimately connected with the rest of *Speak, Memory* in their style and lexicon, to have been written by anyone but Nabokov himself. The subject is the reaction of certain Russian émigrés to a writer named "Sirin," which also constitutes a (mild) deception because Nabokov does not reveal here that this was his own pseudonym during his first European period, although of course the fact is well known. He states that readers in the emigration were "impressed by the fact that the real life of his books flowed in his figures of speech, which one critic has compared to 'windows giving upon a contiguous world . . . a rolling corollary, the shadow of a train of thought' " (p. 288). This passage is replete with echoes of Nabokov's most seminal ideas. The view that a "contiguous world" is implied in the language of his works sounds much like a reference to the otherworld. The notion of another world being a "shadow of a train of thought" recalls the tentativeness of Nabokov's intuitions about the transcendent, and suggests a link between particular states of consciousness and higher states of being. The connection between "a train of thought" and another world also echoes Nabokov's speculations about thought possibly warping into "another dimension" (p. 301). Finally, it is relevant that Nabokov used a related image to characterize what he felt was most essential about Gogol's art: "It appeals to that secret depth of the human soul where the shadows of other worlds pass like the shadows of nameless and soundless ships."[59]

Nabokov's occasional expressions of seeming indifference to ethical questions have misled many of his readers in the past, and continue to contribute to his image of being an aloof aesthete. However, if these remarks are considered in the context of his frequent, strongly ethical judgments, they turn out to mean something quite different from the way they are usually taken. Take, for example, what he said about his most famous novel: "No, it is not *my* sense of the immorality of the Humbert Humbert-Lolita relationship that is strong; it is Humbert's sense. *He* cares, I do not. *I* do not give a damn for public morals, in America or elsewhere."[60] This statement should be understood as his repugnance at the thought of being associated with generalizations based on too simple an identification of author and character (or narrator), and on the author being implicitly ascribed a nonliterary motivation that has no personal relation to him, such as "public morals." On the other hand, Nabokov's claim that he does not care about what Humbert has done with Lolita flies in the face of the novel itself, and is probably motivated by a polemical desire to make a point about art's independence from vulgar demands for social or ethical commitment. This inference is supported by the fact that on another occasion, when he was not confronted with a generalization that the interviewer tried to ascribe to him, Nabokov described Humbert as one of his "villains" who is "frustrated." And, by contrast, he referred to his "favorite creatures" and "resplendent characters" in the *The Gift, Invitation to a Beheading, Ada,* and *Glory* as "victors in the long run." Rather than being evidence of Nabokov's inconsistency with regard to ethical questions, these remarks should be taken as mutually supportive, and as addressing the same problem on different occasions, and in specifically different contexts. Nabokov's own view of how he would be seen in the future buttresses this conclusion: "I believe that one day a reappraiser will come and declare that, far from having been a frivolous firebird, I was a rigid moralist kicking sin, cuffing stupidity, ridiculing the vulgar and cruel—and assigning sovereign power to tenderness, talent, and pride."[61]

The relation between Nabokov and his characters is also more intimate, albeit in a highly ironic way, than remarks such as those about *Lolita* might suggest. When asked about the "strain of perversity amounting to cruelty" in his novels, Nabokov responded that he did not care about his "beastly" characters because "they are outside my inner self like the mournful monsters of a cathedral facade—demons placed there merely to show that they have been booted out."[62] This remark recalls Nabokov's characterization of his own chess problems and literary works as founded on "[d]eceit, to the point of diabolism, and originality, verging upon the grotesque," or, in other words, on a deceptive division between misleading surface and true inner meaning. Nabokov's attitude toward the fictional characters of other authors is similarly judgmental. In his lecture on *Ulysses* he states that Bloom "indulges in acts and dreams that are definitely subnormal in the zoological, evolutionary sense." Although Nabokov criticizes this as a flaw in Joyce's method of characterization, his formulation suggests that the ethical dimension of the phenomenon was still important for him. Similarly, one of the dominant themes in Nabokov's lectures on *Don Quixote* is the "cruelty" and "brutality" that fill the novel.[63]

Other comments Nabokov made show that ethics were as much a concern for him outside fiction as they were within it. In a letter to his mother from 1924, he wrote that he has "reached the original conclusion that if one performs at least one good act per day (even if it is nothing more than giving one's place to an elderly person on the tram) life becomes exceedingly more pleasant. In the final analysis everything in the world is very simple and founded upon two or three not very complicated truths."[64] On the first page of *Strong Opinions* (thereby setting the tone for the entire collection, as it were) he affirms first his absolute independence from any grouping whatsoever, and then his "simple" "loathings" for "stupidity, oppression, crime, cruelty, soft music."[65] The last entry in this short list may seem merely facetious; but in fact it recalls Nabokov's famous, elaborate, and scathing definitions of *poshlost'*—a mean-spiritedness, "philistinism in all its phases," or self-satisfied vulgarity—which affects many aspects of all modern (and past) cultures.[66] On numerous occasions Nabokov expressed his unequivocal loathing for the tyrants Lenin, Stalin, and Hitler. Speaking of the notorious American criminal Charles Manson, Nabokov admitted that "it would have interested me greatly to look for one spark of remorse in that moronic monster and his moronic beast girls."[67] But he was also capable of making moral distinctions about real people who were not known primarily as villains, as when he spoke of the "destinies" of Oscar Wilde and Lewis Carroll: "one flaunting a flamboyant perversion and getting caught, and the other hiding his humble but much more evil little secret."[68] This statement is particularly telling because Nabokov's implicit condemnation of pedophilia coincides with the widespread view that the victimization of children is especially reprehensible within the negative hierarchy of vice.

Nabokov's famous attacks on Freud, which began as early as 1931, and which reached a crescendo in interviews and in the prefaces to English translations of his novels, are, incredibly, still often taken as a form of arch playfulness on his part, or even as examples of reluctant or unwitting admissions of complex influence (i.e., Nabokov "protests too much").[69] In fact, they are authentic instances of repugnance based on a loathing for facile generalizations, which, moreover, are unrelated to his own experiences. It should also be stressed that Nabokov's expressions of distaste for Freud and psychoanalysis, rather than being mere superciliousness or pedantic love for precision, are founded on moral grounds. Nabokov complained to an interviewer that the "Freudian faith leads to dangerous ethical consequences, such as when a filthy murderer with the brain of a tapeworm is given a lighter sentence because his mother spanked him too much or too little—it works both ways."[70] Thus in all their varied manifestations, Nabokov's ethics are hardly eccentric, in the sense of lying outside the familiar codes of free Western societies, even though they may derive exclusively from his own principles and beliefs.

That art and ethics were linked in Nabokov's mind is clear from all his fictions, and from comments such as the following about the Soviet Futurist poet Vladimir Mayakovsky: although "endowed with a certain brilliance and bite, [he was] fatally corrupted by the regime he faithfully served."[71] But *why* should a sense of morality be connected with aesthetics and with metaphysics? Nabokov provides the clearest answer to this question that can be found in any of his published writings in "The Art of Literature and Commonsense." To the totally negative concept "commonsense," which typifies all that is gray, tepid, and banal, he opposes the unusual, the eccentric, and the irrational. Commonsense can be "defeated" by anyone whose "mind is proud enough not to breed true." Indeed, it is "freakishness" understood in this way that may have been the true force behind human evolution in Nabokov's view: "the ape would perhaps never have become man had not a freak appeared in the family." The way a writer defeats commonsense is by following the "secret connections" among his figures of speech, rather than accepted, conventional, and therefore stultifying literary prescriptions. Nabokov's remarkable conclusion about the consequences of following personal inspiration is that "the irrational belief in the goodness of man (to which those farcical and fraudulent characters called Facts are so solemnly opposed) becomes something much more than the wobbly basis of idealistic philosophies. It becomes a solid and iridescent truth."[72] Nabokov's ethics thus emerge as absolutist, not relativistic, and as intimately connected to his conception of artistic inspiration.

It is surprising that a belief in man's innate goodness could have been advocated by an individual who had been brushed by the worst horrors of the twentieth century. Nabokov and his family had to escape from the Bolsheviks in Russia, his father was murdered in Berlin by political assassins, one of his brothers perished in a Nazi concentration camp, and Nabokov and his wife (who is Jewish) risked the same by staying in Germany until 1937. When he delivered "The Art of Literature and Commonsense" around 1951, Nabokov anticipated the objection that it might seem "mildly speaking, illogical to applaud the supremacy of good at a time when something called the police state, or communism, is trying to turn the globe into five million square miles of terror, stupidity, and barbed wire" (p. 373; a similar formulation appears in the 1941 version). However, he insisted that such facts cannot disprove his fundamental conclusion. The contemporary horrors are "unreal" for him not because he is now physically far removed from them and living safely in the United States,

but because I cannot imagine (and that is saying a good deal) such circumstances as might impinge upon the lovely and lovable world which quietly
persists, whereas I can very well imagine that my fellow dreamers, thousands
of whom roam the earth, keep to these same irrational and divine standards
during the darkest and most dazzling hours of physical danger, pain, dust,
and death. (P. 373)

Nabokov's reference to the "divine standards" of those who inhabit this
"home for the spirit" recalls the metaphysical implications of his conception of artistic inspiration. Moreover, his claim for the primacy of imagination over physically horrific "reality" supports the inference that he
saw imagination as putting the earth-bound artist into contact with a
more real, transcendent realm. Thus, Nabokov's ethical system is
founded on his faith in a benevolent otherworld that manifests itself in
man's material world.

The specific connection that Nabokov makes in the lecture between
aesthetics and ethics can be inferred from his description of what "irrational standards" mean for him and his "fellow dreamers": "the supremacy
of the detail over the general, of the part that is more alive than the whole,
of the little thing which a man observes and greets with a friendly nod of
the spirit while the crowd around him is being driven by some common
impulse to some common goal" (p. 373). The two essential features in
this characterization are familiar from Nabokov's hierarchy of values—
the individual recognizing something others would miss, and then grasping a tie between it and himself. Nabokov's "irrational standards" thus
turn out to be a form of maximally enhanced consciousness, with all the
associations this concept has in *Speak, Memory*. And it is precisely during
such mental states, he concludes, "in this childishly speculative state of
mind, so different from commonsense and logic, that we know the world
to be good" (p. 374). Nabokov does not in fact go on to reveal what
exactly it is about moments of highest consciousness that leads him to
conclude man and the world are good. However, on the basis of *Speak,
Memory*, in which he describes a number of moments of privileged consciousness, it is possible to infer that they provided him with intuitions of
a benevolent otherworld. This conclusion suggests that Nabokov may
have been motivated by more than a supercilious sense of humor when
he said in a lecture that "every artist is a manner of saint," and that this
is something he felt "very clearly" himself.[73]

Nabokov's discussion of "inspiration" in the lecture (p. 377) provides
the final link between his ethics and aesthetics. The "spiritual thrill" of
inspiration, which contains the germ of the future work of art, entails
primarily a mental reorientation from a "dissociative stage to the associ-
ative one" (p. 377). Now, an artist's ability to note the "metaphoric"

relations among disparate phenomena of course depends on his acute awareness of details as well as a vivid memory. In other words, the artist must first be able to dismember the given world into specifically observed components before he can begin "to build" a new one. And he cannot begin to put one together unless he establishes cognitive links between himself and phenomena. But this is precisely what Nabokov said lies at the core of the "irrational standards" distinguishing him and his "fellow dreamers." Thus, the "irrational standards" are actually a proto-artistic faculty. Recognizing individual details must precede the apprehension of details in the totality that constitutes cosmic synchronization (and that provides intuitive insight into a benevolent otherworld).

The other side of the connection between Nabokov's aesthetics and his metaphysically determined ethics is his conception of evil. If highest consciousness is a state during which the ultimate goodness of man and the world can be apprehended, then evil would necessarily have to be connected with blindness. Thus it comes as no surprise that Nabokov's description of evil in "The Art of Literature and Commonsense" should resemble St. Augustine's view of it as an absence of good rather than as a presence of an independent negative force: " 'badness' is a stranger to our inner world; it eludes our grasp; 'badness' is in fact the lack of something rather than a noxious presence; and thus being abstract and bodiless it occupies no real space in our inner world. Criminals are usually people lacking imagination" (pp. 375–76). According to Nabokov, even a very primitive imagination would prevent someone from committing a crime simply "by disclosing to their mental eye a woodcut depicting handcuffs." Once again, therefore, because the individual appears to be determined by his imaginative and perceptual faculties, Nabokov's ethics emerge as absolutist. The ultimate implication of his view of good and evil is that a true artist of the highest caliber would be incapable of crime. The crucial consequence this has for Nabokov's fiction is that the worlds conceived by his flawed artists, or criminal characters and narrators (such as Hermann in *Despair*, Humbert in *Lolita*, or Van in *Ada*) are inevitably shallow or skewed in comparison to the worlds of his positive characters and narrators. This is not to say that the flawed artists or criminal personae cannot be fascinating, charming, or even eccentrically insightful. And it is rare that their flaws or perceptual distortions are primitive or obvious (which would make the works much too simple). But Nabokov's novels do embody definite hierarchies of consciousness that manifest themselves in distinct networks of imagery. As a result, the reader necessarily has to make sense of them, and this involves inferring the degree of error or insight shown by the fictional personae. The highest benchmark is of course consciousness on the level of cosmic synchronization.

In "The Art of Literature and Commonsense" Nabokov also stresses a

point he makes repeatedly in interviews and prefaces to the English translations of his novels—that a true writer can never be concerned with public morality. Instead, a moral component will arise as an automatic consequence whenever an artist pursues his proper task and uses the
"pointless trifles" that commonsense would condemn "in such a fashion
as to make iniquity absurd" (p. 376). Nabokov suggests that a writer in
effect punishes evil by means of the understated, gleeful skill with which
he captures the details of his target's appearance. For example, a "twin-
kle" appears in his eye as he "notes the imbecile drooping of a murderer's
underlip, or watches the stumpy forefinger of a professional tyrant ex-
ploring a profitable nostril in the solitude of his sumptuous bedroom" (p.
376). Nabokov extends this principle beyond literary characterization as
well, and claims that "there is nothing dictators hate so much as that
unassailable, eternally elusive, eternally provoking gleam." Thus, in his
view, the reason for the murder of the poet Nikolai Gumilev under Lenin
was that during the entire ordeal of arrest, torture, and transportation to
the place of execution "the poet kept smiling" (p. 377). The implication
is, of course, that Gumilev was one of Nabokov's "fellow dreamers" and
that he smiled because he was aware of his ability to see the world in ways
that his destroyers could not. Nabokov returns to this image of Gumilev,
which functions as the reification of all his values in the lecture, in a number of his best-known works, including *The Gift* and *Pale Fire*.

Although a survey of Nabokov's oeuvre does not suggest that his deep-
est convictions varied much, if at all, over time, it is important to note
that the fate of a number of other Russian writers in the Soviet Union led
him to admit in an interview that art was, after all, incapable of doing
justice to their extraordinary sufferings. He continued to insist that tyrants would never succeed in hiding their ludicrousness from perceptive
artists; however, he added that "contemptuous laughter is all right, but it
is not enough in the way of moral relief. And when I read Mandelshtam's
poems composed under the accursed rule of those beasts, I feel a kind of
helpless shame, being so free to live and think and write and speak in the
free part of the world."[74] He also had no illusions about the brute power
of evil: "Morally, democracy is invincible. Physically, that side will win
which has the better guns."[75]

Overt metaphysical speculation is another major concern of Nabokov's
remarkable lecture. There is one statement in it that not only provides a
foundation for all he has said about good, evil, and artistic insight, but
that is also one of the most candid avowals of his belief in the otherworld
that can be found in any of his published writings:

> That human life is but a first installment of the serial soul and that one's
> individual secret is not lost in the process of earthly dissolution, becomes

something more than an optimistic conjecture, and even more than a matter of religious faith, when we remember that only commonsense rules immortality out. A creative writer, creative in the particular sense I am attempting to convey, cannot help feeling that in his rejecting the world of the matter-of-fact, in his taking sides with the irrational, the illogical, the inexplicable, and the fundamentally good, he is performing something similar in a rudimentary way to what [*two pages missing*] under the cloudy skies of gray Venus. (Sic! p. 377)

The first sentence is self-explanatory, as is the sentiment expressed in this paragraph as a whole. However, the second sentence appears to contain an editorial error. Nothing in the critical apparatus of *Lectures on Literature* explains the surprising hiatus in this crucial passage. In fact, it seems rather unlikely that two pages would actually be missing because the gap appears in lieu of the second half of an analogy that was prepared in the first part of this sentence and that is resolved in its final phrase. The problem is easily cleared up by comparing the paragraph in question to its original in the 1941 version of the lecture. Its conclusion, which cements aesthetics, ethics, and metaphysics, is surely what Nabokov intended in 1951 as well: "in his taking sides with the irrational, the illogical, the inexplicable and the fundamentally good, [the true artist] is performing something similar in a rudimentary way *to what the spirit may be expected to perform, when the time comes, on a vaster and more satisfactory scale*" (italics added).[76]

The Defense

ON THE SURFACE, *The Defense* (*Zashchita Luzhina*, 1930)[1] is the story of Grandmaster Aleksandr Ivanovich Luzhin, a Russian chess genius who confuses his game with his life, goes mad, and commits suicide. In fact, however, the novel is Nabokov's celebration of the tragic incommensurability of matter and spirit, and of the literally transcendent nature of the art of chess.[2]

Nabokov's view of chess as a form of high art is well documented. In *Speak, Memory*, for example, he speaks openly of parallels between "the ecstatic core of the process" of composing chess problems and "other, more overt and fruitful, operations of the creative mind."[3] He also explains that "inspiration of a quasi-musical, quasi-poetical, or to be quite exact, poetico-mathematical type, attends the process of thinking up a chess composition" (p. 288). And in an interview he acknowledged that although he had "no ear for music," he found "a queer substitute for music in chess—more exactly, in the composing of chess problems."[4]

A similar view of chess as being related to music constitutes a major theme in *The Defense*, and is one of several important strands of motifs that leads to the novel's hidden meaning. Nabokov introduces the connection for the first time in his often deceptive Foreword to the English translation of the novel, in which he mentions an American publisher who expressed interest in the work in the late 1930s, but wanted chess to be replaced by music and Luzhin to be "a demented violinist" (8: 18). The reason this is probably a typical instance of Nabokov's pulling the unwary reader's leg—and surreptitiously planting a hint about the novel at the same time—is that a linked motif of chess and music in fact appears throughout the text: Luzhin's father dreams that his son is a Wunderkind playing a piano (25: 33; a related example appears on 78: 86); a violinist who had just performed compositions by Luzhin's grandfather comments that chess combinations are "like melodies" (43: 51); and Luzhin looks for chess games in old magazines in his grandfather's study under the gaze of a statue of a boy with a violin (54: 62). Similarly, the Luzhin family's country doctor remarks that the great chess player Philidor was also "an accomplished musician" (68: 75); when reminiscing about his years as a child chess prodigy Luzhin bends his head "as if listening to distant music" (72: 79); the anonymous young woman who will become Luzhin's wife thinks he looks like a musician even after she has been told that he is a great chess player (85: 94); and acquaintances who see her with him at an émigré ball think he is "an unsuccessful musician, or something of that sort" (196: 207). The omniscient narrator reinforces these associations between chess and a recognized form of high art when he comments that Luzhin feels "the keen delight of being a chess player, and pride, and relief, and that physiological sensation of harmony which is so well known to artists" (213: 224). The crowning example of chess being linked with music is the description of the great match between Luzhin and Turati, his most important opponent: "The weightiest elements on the board called to one another with trumpet voices. . . . a kind of musical tempest overwhelmed the board and Luzhin searched stubbornly in it for the tiny, clear note that he needed in order in his turn to swell it out into a thunderous harmony" (137–38: 147; a similar "translation" of chess into music appears on 57: 65).

In addition to reflecting his own experience of the game, Nabokov's linking of chess and music in *The Defense* may also have been motivated by a desire to exploit the view of music as the highest of the arts that has been widespread since at least the Romantics, and thus perhaps to induce the reader to see chess in a nobler light than he might otherwise. Luzhin's entire existence supports the implication that he is pursuing an activity congruent with Nabokov's conception of art, rather than a complicated but ultimately frivolous game. As a result, chess is transformed into something that is readily capable of supporting the metaphysical and ethical themes that Nabokov develops in the novel. Like music, but unlike Nabokov's conception of literary art, chess is of course not representational. Implicitly absent from it is any necessity, or possibility, of incorporating aspects of the external world, which are an essential part of cosmic synchronization, and thus of artistic creation. (Indeed, this is the unique characteristic that distinguishes chess from the other three experiences that Nabokov describes in *Speak, Memory* as providing him with the peak moments of existence.) It should be remembered, however, that in "The Art of Literature and Commonsense" Nabokov acknowledges that abstract ideas could also initiate inspiration, which obviously fits the case of chess. Such considerations "redeem" Luzhin and militate against interpreting his blindness to the realia of the external world as a certain sign of Nabokov's condemnation.

A second insistent leitmotif in the novel that broadens the significance of chess is its link with love, in both its sensual and platonic forms. In *Speak, Memory* Nabokov creates a comparable association when he places his love for his wife, child, and other members of his family on a level with the three pursuits he valued most in life—artistic creation, lepidoptery, and chess. The effect of the association of chess and love in *The*

Defense, when added to that of chess and music, is that the board on which Luzhin plays emerges as a surprisingly variegated world (or as a model for the world at large) rather than a confined arena for a seemingly sterile pastime.

A slight but definite erotic association marks little Luzhin's introduction to chess by the violinist who briefly describes the marvels of the game to him after concluding a flirtatious telephone conversation with an unidentified woman (42: 50). The boy is actually shown how to play the game for the first time by his "aunt" (actually a "second cousin to his mother") who has been having, or is about to begin, an affair with his father. In Nabokov's world it is also no mere chance that this crucial lesson takes place when the aunt has to seek refuge from a family storm that she has precipitated in the very same study in which the violinist had spoken to Luzhin about chess on the previous evening. The special, nurturing role that the aunt plays with regard to Luzhin's chess prowess is underscored by the narrator's references to her as "sweet," and by his observation that she is the only person "in whose presence [little Luzhin] did not feel constrained" (44, 45: 52, 53). The boy begins to develop his abilities at his aunt's apartment by playing with another of her admirers (55: 63). Luzhin's father becomes aware of his son's great gift—which leads to the boy's being able to show it openly—after returning home from an illicit tryst with the aunt (65: 73). The aunt surfaces again in Luzhin's life when she joins him and his father at a German spa, soon after Luzhin's mother leaves it to return to Russia. The aunt's appearance at this point acquires additional significance because Luzhin's father had hoped to retard his son's growing immersion in chess, whereas the spa turns out to be the site of a major tournament and one of Luzhin's first great successes abroad (74: 81–82).

The association of chess and eros up to this point in the novel is based only on what might be termed fatidic contiguity: every important step in Luzhin's development as a child prodigy is marked by the aunt's influence or presence nearby. The motif of chess and eros continues to develop, and becomes more intimately or directly attached to Luzhin, with the appearance of Valentinov, Luzhin's chess trainer and agent. A cynical and ultimately malevolent figure, Valentinov keeps Luzhin away from women because he believes that Luzhin's chess prowess is linked to the development of his sexual urge (94: 103). The banal theory of "sublimation" underlying this view is undoubtedly an instance of Nabokov's irony at Valentinov's (and, covertly, Freud's) expense because Valentinov is in fact totally unaware of the peculiar but important role that the father's and aunt's affair actually played in Luzhin's life. (Similarly, Valentinov never realizes how great a role Luzhin's love for his fiancée will have in returning brilliance to his play in the tournament with Turati.) Valentinov's theory clearly derives from popular psychologizing, which, because it is based on generalizations, rather than on precise observation of unique phenomena, cannot be anything but automatically erroneous in Nabokov's view. The description of how Valentinov behaves toward Luzhin when he decides to abandon him implies that in the context of the novel's linked chess and love motif Valentinov is responsible for the variant of jaded eros: "he made a gift to Luzhin of some money, the way one does to a mistress one has tired of"; "he dropped out of Luzhin's world, which for Luzhin was a relief, the odd kind of relief you get in resolving an unhappy love affair" (93: 102–3). Later in the novel, Valentinov's philistine linking of eros and chess reappears in the form of his attempt to involve Luzhin in a tawdry film about a protagonist who sexually assaults a young woman, only to eventually become a great chess player (247–48: 259).

An entirely new tone is struck in the novel when Luzhin meets the young Russian woman who will eventually marry him. She is the only person for whom Luzhin feels anything that resembles romantic love, and his involvement with her has a direct effect on his chess and life. Indeed, the subject of their love leads directly to the theme of the irreconcilability of the flesh and the spirit that lies at the center of the novel. The young woman's importance is further signaled by the fact that the narrator grants her the kind of perspicacity with regard to aspects of the physical world that often distinguishes Nabokov's positive characters:

> what was most captivating about her . . . was the mysterious ability of her soul . . . to seek out the amusing and the touching; to feel constantly an intolerable, tender pity for the creature whose life is helpless and unhappy; to feel across hundreds of miles that somewhere in Sicily a thin-legged little donkey with a shaggy belly is being brutally beaten . . . it seemed that if at once, at once, she did not help, did not cut short another's torture (the existence of which it was absolutely impossible to explain in a world so conducive to happiness), her heart would not stand it and she would die. (105–6: 115)

The young woman's ability to feel a strong emotional link to real or imagined events that may be very far from her in space if not time seems congruent with the type of metaphoric linkages that underlie Nabokov's cosmic synchronization in *Speak, Memory*. Similarly, her attitude toward suffering and evil, and her view of the ultimate goodness of existence, recall Nabokov's views in "The Art of Literature and Commonsense." It would be going too far, however, to say that the young woman is an embodiment of all the virtues that Nabokov is capable of granting the characters he favors. Indeed, her role in Luzhin's life will be almost tragically ironic.

When Luzhin first notices her, the narrator implies that this event is somehow linked with everything that had been important in his life heretofore, presumably including chess: she is both "unexpected" and "familiar," and speaks "with a voice that seemed to have been sounding mutely all his life and now had suddenly burst through the usual murk" (98–99: 108). Because there is no mundane explanation in the novel for Luzhin's a priori sense of familiarity, an occult explanation is indicated (one, moreover, that is also implied by other details in the text). Luzhin's moment of recognition is in fact similar to situations that recur in the writings of metaphysically inclined Romantics and Symbolists, and that can ultimately be traced to the allegedly Platonic conception of the primal union of male and female souls in an ideal realm. The suggestion that there is a spiritual link between Luzhin and the young woman is confirmed by what she hears in his clumsy speech: a "mysterious intonation hinting at some other kind of words, which were living and charged with subtle meaning, but which he could not utter." Nabokov has his narrator confirm this impression by noting that "Luzhin harbored within him a barely perceptible vibration, the shadow of sounds that he had once heard" (168: 178–79). In addition to hinting at an otherworldly source for the sounds, this passage also recalls the Romantic idea of the inexpressibility of profound spiritual truth.

At the same time, the young woman is openly associated with Luzhin's somnolent eros. Trying to account for Luzhin's sense that she was somehow familiar, the narrator says that he "recalled quite irrelevantly but with stunning clarity the face of a bare-shouldered, black-stockinged young prostitute" he had once seen, albeit with the difference that Luzhin's young woman was "primly dressed and less pretty" (99: 108). Given the motif of the aunt in Luzhin's life, the narrator's reference to Luzhin's "irrelevant" erotic association may be an ironic deception intended to help conceal the motif from the reader. However, it may also be Nabokov's foreshadowing of the change that Luzhin's attraction to the young woman will undergo. Although in the early stages of his "infatuation" he makes repeated blundering attempts to embrace her, she limits and resists his advances very easily. He does not persist, and seems to stop his attempts altogether after they are married. The fundamentally platonic, nonerotic basis of their love is revealed most openly in the description of their wedding night: the young woman prepares for bed with some nervousness only to find that Luzhin has fallen asleep across it (183: 194). There are indications later as well that they find fulfillment, or as much as Luzhin is capable of achieving outside chess, without actually consummating their marriage (although the narrator mentions that Luzhin reads with a mixture of interest and embarrassment "all sorts of frivolous French novels" that his wife brings to divert him [167: 178]).

Despite the change in the tenor of the love now directly associated with

Luzhin in the novel, the connection of love and chess persists. Luzhin begins "his own peculiar declaration of love" to the young woman "with a series of quiet moves" (99: 109), and later she notices in his eyes "that forlorn devotion . . . that mysterious light that had illumined him when he bent over the chessboard" (124: 134). An even more striking link between chess and Luzhin's love is the effect that the young woman has on his game. After displaying great brilliance as a youth, and although still venerated as an international grandmaster, Luzhin enters into a period of stagnation upon achieving adulthood. His "plight," as the narrator puts it, is that of "a writer or composer" who finds that others have "left him behind in the very devices where he recently led the way" (97: 107). But Luzhin's falling in love with the young woman leads to a turning point in his career. During the tournament for the championship of the world that follows, Luzhin suddenly transcends all his previous limitations and plays games that "had been even then termed immortal by connoisseurs" (134: 144). And whereas Luzhin's previous encounter with Turati, his most serious opponent, had ended in defeat, this time no one can decide who would have won had Luzhin been able to complete the game (154: 164). The young woman emerges as something like Luzhin's muse, although, ironically, she will reappear later as an abettor of his destruction as well.

It is most interesting to note that it is precisely nonphysical love that seems to be associated with Luzhin's brilliant play during this crucial tournament. When he notices the young woman's presence at his games, he is troubled by it, as he is by the "crackling and rustling, and smelly human warmth" of the other spectators whenever he does not "retreat too deeply into the abysses of chess" (122: 132). Indeed, Luzhin has to ask the young woman to stop coming to his matches (125: 135), which suggests that even platonic earthly love is incommensurable with chess.

This tension also appears from the start of the novel. Despite the fact that his parents love and care for him, Luzhin is strikingly alienated from them and nearly everyone else as well. It is telling that many years later in the emigration Luzhin's father plans to write a novella about a chess prodigy who is obviously modeled on his son, but with the difference that the boy is adopted (75: 83). This emphasis on Luzhin's loneliness combined with genius reminds one of Nabokov's celebration of the unique individual in "The Art of Literature and Commonsense," and his own claim in *Speak, Memory* that he could not find the pattern of character that had been imprinted on him either in his environment or in heredity.

Luzhin emerges from the first pages of *The Defense* not only as a little boy with a difficult personality, but as a human vessel waiting to be filled with some as yet unspecified content. Before he encounters chess he already has a predilection for solving various kinds of problems and dealing with subtle spatial relations that anticipate the game. He finds a "mysterious sweetness in the fact that a long number, arrived at with difficulty, would at the decisive moment, after many adventures, be divided by nineteen without any remainder" (17: 25); similarly, he becomes engrossed in a collection of problems and puzzles entitled "Merry Mathematics," and memorizes cab numbers (36: 44; 50: 58). He also likes the "crafty and accurate way" magic tricks come out, although he is irritated by their "complicated [physical] accessories," and longs instead for "harmonious simplicity" (36: 44). The young aunt surfaces with a fateful role in this phase of Luzhin's existence as well. She gives him *The Adventures of Sherlock Holmes*, and *Around the World in Eighty Days*, two books with which he falls "in love for his whole life." Both clearly prefigure his passion for chess because what attracts him to them is the "exact and relentlessly unfolding pattern" each describes (33–34: 41–42). One of the few other things little Luzhin enjoys is jigsaw puzzles, and it is no mere chance that some of the more complicated ones—those that inspire him to try "to determine by scarcely perceptible signs the essence of the picture in advance"—were given to him by his aunt as well (38: 45–46).

A related feature of Luzhin's personality is a fine sensitivity to foci of danger or lines of force. For example, he insists on never varying the itinerary of his daily walks with his governess, during which he always tries to be as far away as possible from the cannon fired at noon from the Saints Peter and Paul Fortress in St. Petersburg (21: 29). (A connection between this sensitivity and chess is suggested by Luzhin's suddenly ceasing to be afraid of the midday gun on the morning after he hears the violinist speak about the game for the first time [43: 52].) His avoidance of the cannon prefigures his later attempts "to find a point equidistant" from three boys he fears most during recesses at school (29: 37); the maneuvers also foreshadow the "imperceptible stages" by which he makes his way to his father's study—where he will first hear of chess—when trying to avoid guests (40: 48).

Considered individually, the events that constitute the history of Luzhin's involvement with chess itself appear to be chance occurrences. But when examined retrospectively they emerge as links in a chain attaching him irrevocably to the game. The understanding of Luzhin's predicament that the reader achieves (which parallels Luzhin's own attempts to decipher the patterns in his life) resembles the retroactive examination of the past that Nabokov described in *Speak, Memory*. And as in Nabokov's case, concatenations of seemingly chance events in Luzhin's life suggest that an otherworldly fate operates in it. The tension between Luzhin's life and art thus ultimately derives from an otherworldly force that controls his existence.

When Luzhin wakes up on the morning after he hears the violinist describe the splendors of chess, he is filled with an "incomprehensible excitement" (43: 51). Later, when he is with his aunt in the study, the narrator says the house seems filled with "a kind of expectation of something," a description that clearly implies more than his parents' marital scandal that is erupting into the open that day. Given the fact that Luzhin's feeling turns out to be a prophetic anticipation of his lifelong attachment to chess, one is reminded of Nabokov's own remarks about being able to "forefeel" his future works, which appear to preexist him in another dimension. The narrator comments that "for some reason" little Luzhin "remembered that day with unusual brightness, the way you remember the day preceding a long journey" (44: 52). This remark reinforces the prophetic character of Luzhin's feelings because it echoes the later description of Luzhin's recovery from his collapse after the game with Turati as a return from a "long journey" through mysterious realms with an entirely alien form of time (159–60: 169–71). When little Luzhin is in the study with his aunt, he refuses to play anything but chess even though he has heard of the game only once before (45: 53). And immediately after being shown how the pieces move, he recognizes, with a striking precocity that implies some mysterious form of prior knowledge, that "the Queen is the most mobile." He also manifests his concern for spatial relations by positioning the piece more exactly in the center of its square (46: 54).[5] Because of the brewing marital scandal in the Luzhin household this first lesson is short-lived. But approximately "a week or so later" seeming chance provides Luzhin with a free period in school, and the opportunity to witness two classmates play the game. In keeping with his unique predilection for chess, he watches them with the paradoxical feeling that "in some way or other he understood the game better than these two, although he was completely ignorant of how it should be conducted" (49: 57). Following this tantalizing experience, Luzhin begins to miss school in order to play with his aunt, but she proves to be inept at the game. Then fate intervenes again, this time to provide him with the partner he needs—the aunt's admirer, an old man who "played divinely." He would usually arrive "just right"—in terms of Luzhin's needs—or "a few minutes after Luzhin's aunt left" in her constant attempt to avoid him (55: 63). Luzhin achieves his first draw against this opponent, and the narrator signals the significance of this step in the boy's life by using imagery pertaining to vision in order to describe his sensations: "Luzhin perceived something, something was set free within him, something cleared up, and the mental myopia that had been painfully beclouding his chess vision disappeared" (56: 64).

This description is especially noteworthy because it has a direct bearing on the central issue of Luzhin's blindness with regard to the physical world around him. Given the value Nabokov placed on visual acuity, Luzhin's egregious inattention to the precise details of what surrounds him would seem to tarnish, if not condemn him in his creator's eyes. But by describing Luzhin's sudden insight into the world of chess in terms of the sense of sight, Nabokov implicitly validates chess as a supremely noble pursuit, which the associations of chess with music and with love also suggest. This is not to say that in *The Defense* Nabokov changes his mind about the values and rewards of perception directed at the external world. The narrator's description of the fiancée's long-range sympathies, and his richly detailed (and typically Nabokovian) rendering of settings and characters in the world of the novel constitute a striking contrast with Luzhin's myopia. But rather than emerge as an irresolvable tension in the work, this contrast suggests the multiplicity of valid pursuits in Nabokov's world. As *Speak, Memory* demonstrates, art, chess, love, and butterflies are at the top of Nabokov's hierarchy of values. And butterflies alone are missing from the halo of associations surrounding Luzhin's chess. (By contrast, a monomaniacal fixation on butterflies to the exclusion of everything else in life characterizes the eponymous protagonist in Nabokov's short story "Pil'gram" [1931; translated as "The Aurelian"], and his passion is clearly sanctioned by the story's omniscient narrator.)[6]

Fateful coincidences continue to conspire to keep Luzhin attached to the world of chess even when other individuals try to prevent it. In a manner recalling how Luzhin lands in the middle of a tournament at the German spa to which his father takes him in the hope of distracting him from the game (73: 80–81), Luzhin's wife does her best to keep him from thinking about the game after his nervous collapse. But a former acquaintance of hers arrives from the Soviet Union precisely, as the narrator stresses, at the time when Luzhin is again starting to sink into the world of chess, with the result that the wife's vigilance is frustrated (209, 215: 220, 226). The game's hold on Luzhin is consolidated by his finally discovering the pocket chess set that had been lost in the lining of his jacket for several months (218: 229), and by the various small chores and delays that prevent his going on a trip abroad, which his wife plans in order to entertain and distract him (234: 245).

For Nabokov in *Speak, Memory* immersion in chess, like the experience of cosmic synchronization and writing poetry, stops time. Recalling a period of intense work on composing a chess problem, he describes his watch as "a brooklet of time in comparison to [the] *frozen* lake on the chessboard" (italics added; p. 292). Since temporality is an unavoidable dimension of physical existence, the achievement of timelessness implies transcendence. Chess thus emerges as an additional means of escape from the prison of temporally bound earthly life that Nabokov introduces in the opening pages of his autobiography.

Chess and timelessness are similarly linked in *The Defense*. The narrator says that the day on which Luzhin discovers chess "froze forever, while somewhere else the movement of seasons, the city spring, the country summer, continued in a different plane—dim currents which barely affected him" (39: 47). Near the conclusion of the novel Luzhin begins actively to seek timelessness. In his search for a way to escape the chess-like combinations that he discerns in his life, he yearns "to stop the clock of life, to suspend the game for good, to freeze" (214: 226); at one point he wishes he could "arrest time at midnight" (235: 247). In this context, Luzhin's suicide, or "sui-mate" as Nabokov called it, can be understood not as a wish for extinction of the self, but as an unconscious and desperate attempt to achieve timelessness, or, in the context of the novel's hidden meaning, to transcend the physical world and move into another dimension of being.

One of the most striking aspects of timelessness that Nabokov describes in *Speak, Memory* is the privileged moment of artistic or mnemonic inspiration that results in a timeless translation of the individual through space. Luzhin experiences something like this in *The Defense* as well. On the day of his game with Turati, following a period of very intense play, he wakes up in his hotel room fully dressed, and not knowing where he had slept; neither his bed nor his couch appears to have been touched. "The only thing he knew for sure," the narrator explains, "was that from time immemorial he had been playing chess," and he is surprised to see a corridor rather than the chess hall outside the room (135: 145–46). This passage can of course be read as an instance of Luzhin's forgetfulness, of his simply having passed the night asleep in a chair. But given his fateful predisposition for the game from boyhood, the remark that he had been playing "from time immemorial" implies that he may in fact exist on two different temporal planes, one related to the physical side of his being, and the other to the timeless and transcendent world of chess. As a result, his bewildered awakening could also be seen as resulting from his return to earthly existence from the timeless dimension he enters or touches during his games.

There is another way that chess appears to put Luzhin in contact with a realm transcending the mundane. His ability to perceive receding series of branching combinations of moves in a moment of time, including those from past games, occupies a place in his consciousness comparable to that of timeless moments of cosmic synchronization for Nabokov in *Speak, Memory*. The structural analogy between the two is additional, albeit indirect, confirmation that Luzhin's pursuit is valid in Nabokov's eyes. It is worth noting that Nabokov also provides Luzhin with a proto-epiphanic moment that serves as a bridge between pure chess patterns and the kind of sensory perceptions that constitute cosmic synchronization when he falls into a reverie on the very day he will finally be able to reveal his skill at chess to his father: the various "limpid sounds" he hears "were strangely transformed . . . and assumed the shape of bright intricate patterns on a dark background; and in trying to unravel them he fell asleep" (60: 68). Luzhin's falling asleep is a major difference between his experience and Nabokov's, which is invariably a moment of maximally heightened consciousness. But the blending of sounds, an effect strongly augmented by rich sound repetitions in the Russian original, creates the impression of Luzhin being at the center of a short-lived unity that bears some resemblance to Nabokov's descriptions of cosmic synchronization. Another difference is the absence of memories of past events from Luzhin's experience, which, in Nabokov's descriptions, meld with sensory impressions to yield a timeless moment. On the other hand, Luzhin's synesthetic "vision" of sounds "transformed" into "bright intricate patterns on a dark background" clearly foreshadows both his immersion in chess and how he will come to see his life in chess terms. And this is very like Nabokov's descriptions of the way in which inspiration mysteriously yields, as in a seed, the entire future work of art. Moreover, since Nabokov implies that the work ultimately derives from some otherworldly realm in which it preexists its earthly "creation," Luzhin's vision might be understood as a brief and imperfect, but still significant insight into the transcendent dimension of his world, which appears to be chesslike (and which reappears in a similar guise a second before his death). Luzhin is granted a related insight in the scene describing his recovery from childhood illness (71: 78).

That chess provides a link to the otherworld is also implied by the motif of parallel lines in *The Defense*. Luzhin is described as "experiencing bliss and horror" when he contemplates a geometrical drawing in *Merry Mathematics* of "an inclined line" sliding "upwards along another, vertical one [thus] illustrating the mysteries of parallelism." The problem Luzhin sees in this is that the point of intersection of the two lines "together with his soul, glided upwards along an endless path," never achieving the parallelism they promised. Luzhin's solution is simple: "with the aid of a ruler he forced [the lines] to unlock: he simply redrew them, parallel to one another, and this gave him the feeling that out there, *in infinity*, where he had forced the inclined line *to jump off*, an unthinkable *catastrophe* had taken place, an inexplicable *miracle*, and he lingered long in those *heavens* where *earthly lines go out of their mind*" (italics added; 37: 45). This rich passage implies that in geometry there may be an otherworldly dimension fundamentally opposed to the earthly one, and that the two function according to irreconcilable laws. The passage can also be read as a prophecy of Luzhin's ultimate fate. The inclined line's "jumping off" clearly anticipates his method of suicide, which, in the human realm, is as radical an act as his redrawing parallel lines in the world of geometry. And what may appear to be an "unthinkable catastrophe," or sheer madness from a purblind earthly perspective, may also be the "inexplicable miracle" of transcendence from an otherworldly point of view.

These implications are resurrected in the seemingly casual remark made by the old man against whom Luzhin achieves his first draw: "You'll go far if you continue on the same lines [esli budete prodolzhat' v tom zhe dukhe]. Never saw anything like it before. . . . Yes, you'll go very, very far . . ." (56: 64). It is possible that the translation of the original Russian phrase "in the same spirit" into the English "on the same lines" was motivated by Nabokov's wish to augment the parallel line motif. The motif may also be implied when the narrator stresses how long Luzhin had to climb the stairs to his apartment after escaping from Valentinov: "his ascent continued for some time; he seemed to be climbing a skyscraper" (250: 261; a related movement is described on 125: 136). And after he reaches his apartment, Luzhin climbs even higher onto a chest, and then onto a chair, in order to reach the window out of which he will finally let himself fall (255: 266–67).

Because chess in *The Defense* abuts the otherworld, much of the novel's imagery dramatizes a dualistic conception of existence. We find repeated oppositions between spirit and matter, as well as their analogues—chess life versus mundane life, madness versus normality, reality versus unreality, waking versus sleep. Nabokov first hints at the existence of this dualism in the Foreword when he says: "there is something in [Luzhin] that transcends [chto vozvyshaetsia nad] both the coarseness of his gray flesh and the sterility of his recondite [zagadochnogo] genius" (10: 21). In the novel proper, this statement is echoed by the narrator's explanation that Luzhin deeply enjoyed playing blindfolded because he "did not have to deal with visible, audible, palpable pieces whose . . . materiality always . . . seemed to him but the crude mortal shell of exquisite, invisible chess forces" (91: 101; a similar example is "an incorporeal force" becoming a "heavy, yellow Pawn" when Luzhin removes it from a board, 137: 148). Putting it even more overtly, the narrator states that Luzhin actually played his games "in a celestial dimension" ("v nezemnom izmerenii," 92: 101). Indeed, after the adjournment of the game with Turati, Luzhin appears to transcend materiality altogether and enter the world of chess via the board: "it was as if he were becoming flatter and flatter, and then he soundlessly dissipated" (143: 153).

From the time he discovers the game, chess for Luzhin is infinitely more attractive and compelling than the mundane world of physical existence. But it is only after he begins his intensive play in the tournament with Turati that the chess world he enters actually becomes more real than the so-called "real" world. This transvaluation persists between games as well. The first question he asks his fiancée when she comes to visit him in his hotel room is "are you real?" (130: 142). After he wakes up from the nap into which he drifts following her visit, he remembers her as "a delightful dream he had dreamed" (132: 142; he sees her parents' apartment and guests in the same way, 133: 143). Thus only "chess life" is "real life" for Luzhin (134: 144).

Another aspect of Luzhin's dualistic existence is that after he adjourns his game with Turati the division of the novel's world between spirit and matter also becomes the difference between good and evil. The long description of Luzhin's laborious and confused progress out of the hall where he had played resembles nothing so much as a nightmarish journey through hell. Phantoms, shades, ghosts, and shadows are mentioned some dozen times in two pages. Darkness, blackness, smoke, murk, and fog obscure his sight; "thick, cotton-wool air" deadens his hearing; and what he does glimpse is monstrous: "a drum . . . being beaten by an arched, thick-maned chess Knight" (140–41: 150–51). Luzhin's escape acquires additional mythical resonance when he reaches a river and a bridge on which "great female figures [golye velikanshi]" appear, which recall the fatidic motif of eros, and the so-called guardians of thresholds that heroes in many mythological systems must confront in order to complete their quests (142: 153).[7] More specifically, the entire ominous realm through which Luzhin passes after the game recalls the Gnostic view of the world of matter as fallen: it resembles a prison, a dream, or a world of the dead, it deadens the senses, and it is dark, in contrast to the transcendent, light-filled world of spirit.[8] Nabokov's utilization of topoi congruent with Gnostic myth in this scene confirms the impression that Luzhin's life outside the world of chess is falling under the sway of evil.

The question of good and evil reappears later in the novel as well, but in an entirely different and surprising context. After Luzhin returns to mundane consciousness following his collapse, his fiancée decides to take care of him. On the one hand, she does everything she can to keep his mind off chess, and to distract him with what could be called normal, but frivolous, hobbies. On the other, she takes it upon herself to make his life increasingly physical (something in which he had never been interested [95: 105]). She begins by taking him to a tailor, but, as the narrator puts it, "the renovation of Luzhin's *envelope* did not stop here" (italics added; 170: 181). A new room is also found for him in her parents' building; and then the reader is given an unexpectedly long and detailed description of the apartment, including the floor plan, in which Luzhin and his fiancée will live when married (172–74: 183–85). Because this accretion of new matter around Luzhin is complemented by his fiancée's efforts to make him forget chess, the overall effect is that the spiritual side of his existence is muted and physically obscured, as it were. And since Luzhin's chess genius crowns the hierarchy of values Nabokov embodies in *The Defense*, the young woman's loving attempts to arrange for Luzhin's physical well-being emerge, ironically, as negative. (The irony is doubled and made even more poignant when we recall that her appearance in Luzhin's life seems correlated with the renaissance of his genius.) Gnostic beliefs support this interpretation because garments and physical dwellings are widespread symbols for the matter entrapping the divine soul of the individual who is mired in the fallen physical world.[9]

Even without being aware of Gnostic symbolism, one could not but conclude that Luzhin's young woman, no matter how well-intentioned and attractive because of her sensitivity and kindliness, has a deleterious effect on him. Despite his vague anticipation of the pleasures of married life in "this world of ours," as the narrator phrases it, prior to the wedding Luzhin also experiences moments of "strange emptiness" (177: 187–88). Afterward, his wife tries to prevent him from playing chess and indulges his lethargy and somnolence: he gains weight steadily, thereby literally augmenting his body at the expense of his spirit (233: 244). When he oversleeps, she comments approvingly, but without realizing the irony in her words, "that way you could sleep your whole life away" (236: 247). And finally, in a phrase that is especially touching and, in the context of the novel's Gnostic theme, horrible at the same time, she encourages him to "stay in bed a while longer, it's good for you, you're fat" (239: 250).

Luzhin's fiancée admires his genius without understanding it. She is ultimately blind to the significance chess has for him; neither can she accept that it is his true life. While cleaning out his hotel room following his collapse she packs his chess set, magazines, notes, and diagrams thinking "he did not need this now" (152: 162). The error, and thus the (inadvertent) evil associated with her stems therefore from the same general sort of failure of the imagination that Nabokov describes in "The Art of Literature and Commonsense." This is of course not to say that she is as negative as Valentinov in *The Defense*, or as patently or ludicrously evil as the villains in Nabokov's other works, such as Axel Rex in *Laughter in the Dark*, and Paduk in *Bend Sinister*; she does not, after all, seek to do harm—quite the opposite. But she is caught in the extremely poignant situation of having to deny the most important side of her husband's being, of being unable to choose Luzhin's chess over his life—all after inadvertently inspiring him to new heights in the game—which is a reflection of the novel's overarching theme of the ultimate incommensurability of art and life.

In addition to evoking Gnostic topoi in *The Defense*, Nabokov plants a number of other subtle details to suggest that the concept of evil is relevant to the novel and, moreover, that it has metaphysical implications.

The most significant of these are associated with Luzhin's marriage, but what might be termed more neutrally "occult" signals also mark an earlier stage in his life. After witnessing his son's chess prowess for the first time, Luzhin's father remarks that "he's not just amusing himself with chess, he's performing a sacred rite." Immediately thereafter Nabokov has his narrator report the following: "A fat-bodied, fluffy moth with glowing eyes fell on the table after colliding with the lamp. A breeze stirred lightly through the garden. The clock in the drawing room started to chime daintily and struck twelve" (66: 73–74). All three details confirm the father's remark: butterflies (and, by extension, moths) are frequently used by Nabokov as a private symbol for fateful recurrence in *Speak, Memory* as well as in the novels; the light breeze could be taken as Nabokov's parodic evocation of a device used in (frequently naive) works by Symbolists, such as Maeterlinck's *L'Intruse* or Belyi's *The First Symphony*, to signal the presence of otherworldly phenomena; and a clock striking midnight is a widespread and worn-out device for signaling a fatidic turning point in life. The parodic dimension of two of these details might mislead the reader into believing that the possible role of the occult in Luzhin's life is being undermined through irony by the implied author. But the third detail militates against this interpretation and suggests that the occult may be a real force in Luzhin's world.

At least one face of this force is revealed via several details in the apartment Luzhin comes to share with his wife. In describing the dining room, the narrator casually mentions that "above the table a lone, fluffy, little toy devil was hanging from the low lamp" ("nad stolom odinokii pushistyi chortik povisal s nizkoi lampy," 173: 184). No explanation of this bizarre object or entity is given; neither Luzhin nor his fiancée appears to notice it; and the narrator quickly turns to more familiar sorts of furnishings. Later, however, on the wedding night, Luzhin places a plush dog he happened to pick up somewhere in the apartment onto the dining room table, upon which "a fluffy imp hanging from the lamp immediately came down like a spider" ("i srazu k nei [sobake] spustilsia, kak pauk, pushistyi chortik, povisshii s lampy," 181: 192). Once again, this odd incident passes without any comment from the narrator or notice by the characters. The reader, however, cannot help but register the repetition and conclude that it is significant. A few lines further on this impression is augmented by the description of the bizarre, trancelike state that Luzhin's wife assumes in the bedroom: "she smiled and for a long time watched a big, sluggish fly that circled around the Mauretanian lamp, buzzing hopelessly, and then disappeared" (181: 192). Because one of the biblical names for Satan is Beelzebub, which means "Lord of the Flies," a possible diabolical presence or influence may be implied in this scene as well.[10] Moreover, a lamp is again associated with a symbol of evil, as it was earlier. It is tempting to connect the two, and to suggest that together they evoke the Gnostic idea that the light of the fallen world of matter is false (and evil because it fosters attachment to matter) in comparison to the true light of the world of the spirit.[11] (Perhaps the sequence of connections is Mauretania = Africa = blackness.) Thus the apartment, which is a synecdoche for Luzhin's marriage and earthly existence, and as such should imply a haven and personal fulfillment, emerges instead as a trap. This implication may also lie behind the lengthy description of the apartment's labyrinthine layout. The prolonged circling of the fly, and its association with the wife's drowsiness, suggest a dulling repetitiveness that impedes spiritual effort and achievement. This is in fact an accurate foreshadowing of the pall that falls over Luzhin's life in the apartment.

Nabokov reinforces the impression that through his marriage Luzhin is condemned to a sort of hell by adding a casual reference to a literary work containing a famous depiction of its torments: a bookcase in the apartment's study is "crowned with a broad-shouldered, sharp-faced Dante in a bathing cap" (173: 184). The humorous reference to the close-fitting headgear the poet is usually depicted as wearing may be an instance of the author's attempt to mislead the reader into not taking the allusion seriously. But even if the reader should miss this reference, it is repeated later when Luzhin, in a vain attempt to entertain the visiting Soviet woman's little boy, refers to "the author of a certain divine comedy," and points to "the bust of Dante" (216: 227–28). In this context, Luzhin's escape from the apartment by means of suicide seems less the act of a madman than an attempt to transcend an evil realm by releasing the soul from the fetters of the body.

The fact that Luzhin's wife attempts, but fails to make him forget chess establishes a connection between the game and the apartment, which is the primary locus of her efforts. But is there any suggestion that evil is associated with Luzhin's pursuit of the game itself? A significant detail implying that this is not the case, one that also illustrates the remarkable cohesion of the novel down to an "atomic" level, is the resemblance between the narrator's description of Dante's bust and of Turati at the tournament. The Italian grandmaster is also "broad-shouldered," and although he is of course not wearing a "bathing cap," his head is covered with something that looks very similar: he has "short-cropped hair [that] seemed to have been closely fitted to his head and came down onto his forehead in a small peak" (124–25: 134–35). The difference between this allusion to Dante and the overt references to him and his epic poem in connection with Luzhin's apartment is that now a brilliant practitioner of chess is implicitly crowned with a resemblance to a literary genius. One can infer, therefore, that Nabokov wanted to place his invented Italian grandmaster's chess genius on a level with Dante's, and since Luzhin seems to be a match for Turati ("no one could find the key to indisputable victory" in the adjourned game between them [154: 164]), we return to the conclusion that he is in the same exalted company of artists. The different uses to which Dante appears to have been put in the novel are actually less circular than may seem when one recalls that Dante was both the poet and the protagonist of his epic journey.

The presence of diabolical symbolism in *The Defense* is of course Nabokov's device for implying the presence of evil in his fictional world, and should not be taken as an expression of his personal belief in metaphysical evil. Indeed, the "sins" of the negative characters are blindness and a limited imagination, and are thus a form of absence rather than a "noxious presence," as Nabokov described it in "The Art of Literature and Commonsense." Valentinov is the primary villain because he heartlessly uses Luzhin's chess prowess to advance his own financial interests and neglects the human side of Luzhin's nature. The narrator stigmatizes Valentinov as a selfish parasite by giving him vampiric traits: he "pursed his wet, red lips and tenderly narrowed his eyes" when he finally meets Luzhin, who, in the traditional cinematic response to a vampire's hypnotic gaze, immediately surrenders his will (244: 256; Luzhin's wife perspicaciously imagines Valentinov as a "slippery, repulsively wriggling" creature, 240: 251). Another negative character, who is merely absurd rather than malevolent, is the psychiatrist overseeing Luzhin's recuperation. Nabokov's contempt for presumptuous generalizations underlies the fun he makes of the professor's attempts to fathom Luzhin by delving into his childhood. The result is farcical because the "analysis" is obviously motivated by preconceived theories, rather than attention to actual details in the patient's life: " 'Let me imagine your house,' " the psychiatrist says to Luzhin, "'Ancient trees all around . . . the house large and bright. Your father returns from the hunt . . .' Luzhin recalled that his father had once found a fat, nasty little fledgling in a ditch. 'Yes,' replied Luzhin uncertainly" (163: 174). The psychiatrist is undermined even more by his view of Dostoevsky as a mirror for the troubled modern age (167: 178). Given Nabokov's oft-professed distaste for Dostoevsky, this view is the author's way of settling scores with clichés, facile generalizations, and sociological interpretations of literature—all in one.

Although there is no suggestion that Luzhin's mania for chess is tainted in any way by error or evil, the game does appear frightening to him when he has to adjourn his match with Turati: "he had seen something unbearably awesome, the full horror of the abysmal depths of chess . . . his brain wilted from unprecedented weariness. . . . There was horror in this but in this also was the sole harmony, for what else exists in the world besides chess? Fog, the unknown, non-being" (139: 149–50). Why would there be two sides to Luzhin's reaction to chess? The answer may lie in the fact that his physical and spiritual sides are nurtured very differently. It would not be too great an oversimplification to say that what is good for one is bad for the other. But because chess in its essence transcends the material world, in Luzhin we have the situation of a human being, possessing both a body and a soul, confronting a purely spiritual realm. This incongruity lies at the heart of the novel's problematics. The bliss and harmony of chess can be seen as a reflection of the transcendent nature of the game. But the horror is due to Luzhin's corporeality, to the incommensurability of his body and spirit. It is noteworthy that he glimpses the terrifying depths of chess during a moment of pain caused by the match that burns down to his fingers and interrupts his meditation on the game—in other words, when his body asserts itself and he looks at the board from the point of view of a physical being. But despite this, Luzhin never really returns to a "normal" earthly existence after the game is adjourned. His seeing the material world around him as spectral implies that he is still in the higher, chess world, into which he had "crossed" during the game. The idea that Luzhin passed from this world to another, but did not succeed in fully returning even when the game was stopped, is implied in the description of his return to mundane consciousness days later in the psychiatric sanatorium: "upon the expiry of many dark centuries—a single earthly night—the light again came into being" (159: 169). Thus in contrast to the flow of time on earth, the realm from which Luzhin returns approaches timelessness. The whole character of his life on the eve of his wedding and following it also suggests that some major part of his psyche is absorbed elsewhere.

What strikes many readers as clear evidence of Luzhin's being simply insane is that as the novel progresses he sees his life increasingly in chess terms—as a frightful "combination" that he thinks is developing against him. Luzhin's situation seems so alien and implausible that many readers have been tempted to dismiss it as an obvious example of Nabokov's perverse fondness for playing with the destinies of eccentric characters.

However, Luzhin's preoccupation with evidence that his everyday existence is part of some vast game or conspiracy is at most only an artistic exaggeration of Nabokov's own perfectly sane and serious search for patterns in his own life. He argues in *Speak, Memory* that the point of autobiography should be "the following of . . . thematic designs through one's life" (p. 27), a practice that, as he demonstrates, reveals patterning that implies the workings of fate. In fact, Nabokov himself uses chess imagery in the autobiography when describing how his father was spared the necessity of fighting a duel—an event that, in his view, foreshadows his father's murder years later (p. 193). As Johnson has noted, the linked motif of chess and threats to the father's life continues to develop in *Speak,*

Memory when Nabokov's father disguises himself in order to elude Bolshevik death squads, which is likened to a "simple and elegant" move (p. 245), and when Nabokov and his father play chess while the ship on which they escape from the Crimea is under Bolshevik fire.[12] There is of course a difference between a handful of images in an autobiography and a dominant theme in a novel, but Luzhin's ability to recognize repetitions of events in his life is analogous to Nabokov's, and is actually a sign of his perspicacity with regard to the mainsprings of his existence. (Although his reaction to what he discovers is tinged by fear rather than the wonder and happiness we find in Nabokov, this "revaluation" is not unlike what we see in *Invitation to a Beheading*, where Cincinnatus perceives the artifice of his world as distinctly negative in contrast to Nabokov's reveling in the madeness of his world.)

The fact that Luzhin begins to see mundane phenomena in terms of chess is also not simply a madman's paranoia, and needs to be understood in the light of the laws that underlie this particular novel's fictional world. Because chess is at the pinnacle of the hierarchy of values in *The Defense*, and appears to transcend the physical realm, it is appropriate for a player with vatic gifts to see the things of this world in terms of the true, higher reality that holds sway over matter (even if this makes him into a madman in mundane terms).

To make sense of the novel it is essential to realize that Luzhin's life *is* filled with patterns, and that they are not simply delusions he projects onto an indifferent world. In addition to the developing "combination" he notices, there are many repetitions of which he is unaware even though they bear on his life. Because these occur both before and after he becomes immersed in chess, the two parts of his physical existence emerge as linked and chess is eliminated as the sole cause of his "madness" and suicide. For example, his fear toward the end of his life that a plot is developing against him is foreshadowed as early as the first page of the novel in the plot that his parents hatch: they plan to tell him that they have decided to send him to school (but do not actually do it for several pages, thus keeping the reader also in the dark about their specific intentions) and, in preparation for this unpleasant revelation, move "around him in apprehensively narrowing circles" all summer long (15: 23). This move to the city that will enable Luzhin to attend school will of course also initiate the sequence of events leading to his discovery of chess. In like manner, the threat Luzhin fears at the end of his life is a series of reminders of his past chess genius, which, if he submits to them, will lead to his sinking again into the horrifying but compelling abysses of the game. Another example of a childhood experience that is repeated in later life is Luzhin's running away from his parents at the country train station because he is afraid of being sent to school (21: 28). This prefigures his attempt to run away from home after his chess gift blossoms and his parents try to force him to continue with school (70: 77); much later, he flees from the chess café after the adjournment of his match with Turati (141: 151). Even Luzhin's climbing into the country house through a window after running away from his parents at the station (22–23: 30) is recapitulated in a different key when he commits suicide through "defenestration," as Nabokov once called it (255: 267). In both instances, Luzhin is escaping pursuers and returning to what he believes is his only safe haven. Because of the tightness of Nabokov's fictional weave it is hardly possible to stop tracing a particular thematic strand at any given point. One leads to another, reaching forward and backward through the text, with the result that a tug in one place moves the whole fabric of the work. A final instance of patterning related to Luzhin's childhood escape is worth mentioning, however, because of its significance for interpreting the novel's conclusion. When Luzhin returns to consciousness in the sanatorium, he is struck at first by the physical resemblance between the psychiatrist who is treating him and the peasant who had been recruited by his parents to bring him bodily down from the attic in the country house to which he had fled from the train station (160: 171). Understandably, this peasant became the "future inhabitant of [Luzhin's] future nightmares" (24: 32). In addition to the "coincidence" that the two men look alike, the repetition in this case lies in the fact that the psychiatrist can also be understood as having brought Luzhin back from an escape into another realm (the narrator describes Luzhin as coming back "from a long journey" [160: 171]). And if this parallel holds, then the "real" world to which Luzhin returns following his collapse is also like a nightmare because it is the habitation of the peasant's physical analogue—the psychiatrist. This conclusion is in keeping with the view of the "real," material world as fallen that emerges from a consideration of the Gnostic, and other, related dualities in the novel. An additional conclusion is that the world to which Luzhin had escaped during his chess-induced collapse is the antithesis of a nightmare—or is, in other words, the true waking state. And since this other world seems to be something like a transcendent dimension into which Luzhin had crossed, one can infer that according to the novel's logic the otherworld is preferable to this world. In this light, Luzhin's suicide is a return to a realm to which he had journeyed temporarily during his unconsciousness. Perhaps this is the reason the narrator describes Luzhin as looking like "a flabbier Napoleon" when he is recuperating in the sanatorium (163: 173). Whatever else this may say about his physical appearance, his past, or his gifts, it also implies that he might be viewed as an exile from a happier place and time after he returns to mundane consciousness.

The "horizontal" network of repetitions in The Defense that ties together different periods in Luzhin's life coexists with a "vertical" multi-plicity of levels of patterning. This can be illustrated readily in the scenes dealing with two instances of familial discord. When Luzhin's mother leaves the dining room table because of his father's gaiety after what was obviously a tryst with the "aunt" in the city, Luzhin, who remembers the earlier scandal, realizes "that all this had happened once before" (62: 70). What he cannot yet understand of course is the full prophetic significance of the recurrence. If the first scandal resulted in his learning some of the rudiments of chess from the aunt in his father's study, the second one will lead to the father's offer to teach him chess openly because he had learned of the boy's interest in the game from the aunt (66: 74). Luzhin does not realize that his father's offer was prompted by the aunt's "betraying" his secret passion for chess, and Nabokov uses this as a pretext to have his narrator make a tantalizing digression about insight and blindness: "the most obvious explanation did not occur to him, just as sometimes in solving a problem its key turns out to be a move that seemed barred, impossible, excluded [vypadaiushchim] quite naturally from the range of possible moves" (63: 71). This remark operates on a sufficiently abstract level to be relevant for chess and many other things. But given its general tone, as well as the fact that Nabokov originally used a Russian word for "excluded" that derives from the verb for "to fall out," the remark may be a veiled hint about the novel's conclusion and the "impossible" move Luzhin makes to solve his problems. The chess set the father will use to teach Luzhin (63: 71) represents yet another instance of significant patterning that Luzhin notices but does not fully comprehend, because the board is the same one that the boy's gaze had unwittingly taken in, but not recorded, when he hid in the attic after running away from the train station (23: 31). There is, however, a third and even more subtle level of repetition between the two scandals. The first time Luzhin's mother makes a scene at table is when the aunt is flirting with Luzhin's father and manages to toss a crumb into his mouth (44: 52). On the second occasion, after Luzhin's mother leaves the table, the boy notices "a crumb on his father's beard" (62:70). Given the importance of the first crumb, it is unlikely that the second one is merely a gratuitous "realistic" detail. Nabokov's tactic of concealing subtle patterns within more obvious ones can also be found throughout *Speak, Memory*, as well as all his other works of fiction.

The most interesting patterns in *The Defense* are those that Luzhin does not notice at all, and that are left by Nabokov for the reader to discover. These are very numerous, and because they were obviously concealed in the text with great skill and subtlety, it is clear that the device carries considerable weight in terms of the work's overall meaning. Although describing all the instances of patterning that emerge in *The De-*

fense would take too much space, it will be useful to point out a number of examples in order to suggest the scope and significance of the phenomenon.

No character is around to notice that the pose Luzhin's father assumes when he is an aging émigré sitting in a Berlin café—"a finger pressed to his temple" (76: 84)—is the same as had been captured years before in a photograph that his son chances to glimpse at his aunt's in St. Petersburg (51: 59). No one but the reader (except for the narrator, who is largely mute about such matters) is in a position to recognize the similarity between the plan Luzhin's father has to write a novel about a child prodigy based on his son, whom he unwittingly endows with the clichéd traits of a musical genius (78: 86), and his fantasies years earlier about discovering that little Luzhin is a Wunderkind "playing on an enormous, black piano" (25: 33; the picture reappears in the apartment Luzhin occupies after his wedding [174: 185]). No explanation is given of the reason why, after guests have left his apartment, Luzhin sits looking at a "black match tip, writhing in pain after having just gone out in his fingers" (233: 245). His wife is puzzled and upset by his seeming lethargy, and it is up to the reader to infer that Luzhin was lost in recollections of his game with Turati, which was adjourned moments after a match he had forgotten to raise to a cigarette burned down to his hand (139: 149). In short, we conclude that he was contemplating another sign of the combination that is developing against him, and threatening to reimmerse him in the abysses of chess he both fears and loves.

Luzhin feels most threatened by the return of events from various periods in his past, including his schooldays. His coincidental encounter with Petrishchev, a former classmate, at an émigré ball in Berlin is part of such a pattern, as he himself realizes (200: 212). But Nabokov leaves concealed a much subtler form of patterning that would probably have seemed far more sinister to Luzhin had he been able to grasp it. It turns out that the young woman Luzhin will marry in Berlin had known at least one of his classmates in St. Petersburg—a "shy and retiring" boy who subsequently lost an arm in the Civil War (90: 99, 31: 39). But such links between Luzhin and his fiancée, which predate their meeting by some two decades, do not stop there. It also emerges that although they went to different schools, they probably had the same geography teacher. The narrator states that the young woman's teacher also taught at a boys' school. She recalls the man as suffering from tuberculosis, being surrounded by a romantic aura, and having an impulsive manner of noisily running into his classroom (88–89: 98). The last detail grows in significance when Luzhin has his highly unpleasant encounter with his old classmate at the émigré ball, because the latter recalls how their "geographer" would "fly like a hurricane into the classroom" (198: 209; a trait that the narrator confirms [48: 55]). It is interesting that in the English translation of the novel, Petrishchev no longer remembers the teacher's name and patronymic, "Valentin Ivanych." Perhaps Nabokov deleted this detail to avoid an additional echo of "Valentinov" in a scene that is already laden with recurrences. As it happens, the role of the geography teacher is fateful in Luzhin's life even without an evocation of his cynical chess agent. For it is this teacher's unexpected absence due to a cold that leads to a free hour in school and Luzhin's witnessing the beginning of a game between two boys (47–48: 55–56). The morning after, Luzhin makes his "unprecedented decision" to skip school and visit his aunt in order to learn to play the game. On the way to her apartment, another multi-leveled coincidence occurs. Luzhin runs into the geography teacher, "who with enormous strides . . . was rushing in the direction of the school, blowing his nose and expectorating phlegm as he went" (the reference to what may be a chronic cold of course recalls the schoolgirl's perhaps romanticized notion of the teacher's consumption). To avoid being seen by him, Luzhin turns abruptly and feigns looking into a hairdresser's window, which causes the chess set in his satchel to rattle (50: 58). Thus the teacher is again associated with chess, as well as with the young woman who will become Luzhin's wife, and therefore with his entire later life. But even this does not exhaust the coincidences. When facing the display window, Luzhin sees "the frizzled heads of three waxen ladies with pink nostrils . . . staring directly at him." This scene returns years later at a moment in Luzhin's life when he is especially vulnerable to patterning. He has recently concluded that everything he does, and everything that happens to him, is part of a mysterious opponent's design because it is all tinged with a sense of déjà vu. The tactic with which he hopes to counter this is an unmotivated act that he hopes will confuse "the sequence of moves planned by his opponent" (242: 255). While out shopping with his wife and mother-in-law, Luzhin suddenly feigns having to see a dentist, and after a short taxi ride sets off for home. To his dismay, he recognizes that he had done even all this before (during his repeated attempts to "escape"), and goes into the first store he sees, "deciding to outsmart his opponent with a new surprise." The store turns out to be a lady's hairdresser, and, in what Luzhin thinks is "an unexpected move, a magnificent move," he offers to buy a wax bust. But as he realizes, without saying exactly where and how he had seen it already (which the reader can do), "the wax lady's look, her pink nostrils—this also had happened before." The crowning event in this sequence, which recapitulates childhood incidents that led to Luzhin's immersion in chess, is that shortly after leaving the hairdresser's he is hailed by Valentinov and falls into his clutches (243–44: 254–55). The similarity between this character's surname and the geography teacher's first name makes it seem as if Luzhin were somehow "found out" years after he decided to skip school. The association between chess and the teacher that was established in Luzhin's childhood also blossoms with the reappearance of Valentinov, of course, because he was not only Luzhin's agent but also his chess teacher of sorts.

Thus far, the repetitions examined have all occurred in Luzhin's life. There is another type of patterning in the novel, however, that consists of details anticipating his end, such as the still from a film showing a man hanging from a ledge (247:258).[13] The primary difference between these repetitions and those in Luzhin's life is that his own memory can illuminate the latter. But the details foreshadowing Luzhin's death are beyond his or any other character's ken, which is what has led some readers to take them as instances of Nabokov's intrusive presence in the text—an interpretation that is valid only so long as Nabokov is understood to be impersonating an otherworldly fate. For example, the drawings Luzhin makes after his marriage include a train on a bridge spanning a chasm, and a skull on a telephone book (208: 219). The first clearly implies a potential for catastrophe should the bridge collapse or the train fall, as does the "memento mori" aspect of the second. The telephone book may serve as an adumbration of the important use to which Valentinov will put the telephone when attempting to reach Luzhin in order to inveigle him into taking part in a film, an action that contributes greatly to Luzhin's sense of entrapment later in the novel; the telephone is also linked with Luzhin's first hearing of chess from the violinist. In a similar fashion, the largely ridiculous newspaper articles that Luzhin's wife reads to him as a distraction contain a number of phrases that comment on his existence or anticipate his death: "The whole activity comes down to a fundamental transformation and augmentation, which are designed to insure" (which sounds like an allusion to the change in Luzhin's life that she wants to effect), and "disaster is not far away" (224: 234–35). Since Luzhin is only feigning attention in this scene, and is actually engrossed in solving a chess problem in his mind, the phrases the wife reads and Luzhin's intercalated thoughts take on the appearance of a dialogue, but only for the reader.

Luzhin's transfer of a chess mentality to his life—his desire to anticipate and forestall what will happen to him—is in effect an attempt to read his own future. This may be possible on a chess board, where extrapolations from a given position can anticipate future positions, but is it possible in life? As Nabokov insisted in interviews, he did not believe that a future of this sort exists.[14] In *Speak, Memory* he makes it clear that evidence of fate's workings can be gleaned only from one's past life by means of memory. Nonetheless, it appears that Nabokov does allow Luzhin partial insight into his future, or into one possible future. This is suggested by Luzhin's reaction to Valentinov after he is snatched up by him and taken to the film studio with the obviously ironic name "Veritas." Multitudes of beautiful chess memories flash through Luzhin's mind, and the narrator lends his voice to Luzhin's recognition that "everything was wonderful, all the shades of love, all the convolutions and mysterious paths it had chosen. And this love was fatal. . . . The key was found. The aim of the attack was plain. By an implacable repetition of moves it was leading once more to that same passion which would destroy the dream of life. Devastation, horror, madness" (246: 258). This passage is rich in meanings. Luzhin finally understands that he is being inexorably drawn back into the world of chess. However, he cannot rise to the perspective that would allow him to recognize that he has been fated to this from childhood. In terms of the dominant duality reigning over the novel, it is most revealing that, after an initial ecstatic recapitulation of a thousand games he had played in the past, Luzhin shifts to the destructive nature of this passion. This double attitude embraces both sides of his being—the spiritual and the physical. Luzhin's horror is the expression of the physical being's shrinking away from the extinction of the self that is the price for total immersion in the world of chess. The reference to "the dream of life" ("zhiznennyi son"), a phrase betraying the presence of the implied author in this passage of free indirect discourse, recalls the Gnostic themes evoked earlier in the novel, and indicates that the quotidian physical existence Luzhin seems to cherish at this moment is a delusion, and that real life is elsewhere. Similarly, the references to "love" in relation to Luzhin's past crown the complex series of associations between his development as a player and the themes of sensual and platonic love. This is a level of meaning about the hidden springs in the world of the novel that also betrays the presence of an implied author.

Luzhin decides to commit suicide in order to escape from what the reader can see as his destiny from early childhood. But does his suicide indicate that Luzhin has in fact succeeded in asserting his free will and thwarting fate? Probably not. There is a possibility that his seemingly freely willed death is yet another, consummately ironic manifestation of predestination. When Luzhin looks down from the window out of which he will let himself fall, the narrator states that "the whole chasm was seen to divide into dark and pale squares." This image is usually read as the final instance of Luzhin's deluded projection of chess-related images onto the world around him. But because there is much evidence in the novel implying that Nabokov transvalued earthly madness into otherworldly sense, it may also be argued that the chessboard pattern he briefly glimpses is in fact the image of the true eternity that awaits him. In other words, if through death Luzhin enters the same world he touched during the peak moments of his games, then even suicide does not allow him to escape from the chess that is his fate. The passive construction in the phrase about the chessboardlike squares he sees from the window ("was seen to divide"; the Russian original is reflexive: "vsia bezdna raspadalas'," which means literally "the entire abyss was falling into parts") implies that the pattern of light and dark squares is not necessarily a function of Luzhin's creative perception (or projection). Such a reading of the phrase allows one to connect the chessboard pattern that Luzhin sees with the "eternity" that the narrator says "was obligingly and inexorably spread out before him," but without further identifying its nature. It would obviously be a mistake to claim that the novel concludes with more than a hint that Luzhin may be entering another mode of existence. But it is important to note that Nabokov once implied this possibility himself when he said: "As I approached the conclusion of the novel I suddenly realized that the book doesn't end."[15]

Invitation to a Beheading

NVITATION to a Beheading (Priglashenie na kazn', 1938) resembles an allegory more than any of Nabokov's other novels.[1] On the surface, it is the story of the final weeks and execution of a prisoner in a banal future tyranny. But unlike such familiar dystopias as Evgenii Zamiatin's *We*, Aldous Huxley's *Brave New World*, and George Orwell's *1984*, which are concerned primarily with questions of political and social organization and with their psychological and ethical implications, Nabokov's novel focuses on the individual's relation to a metaphysical reality. Indeed, as Moynahan suggested, and as Davydov demonstrated in detail, much in the life of the protagonist Cincinnatus C. is modeled on major Gnostic topoi.[2] Nabokov in effect hinted at this himself when he changed the definition of Cincinnatus's crime from the general "gnoseologicheskaia gnusnost' " ("gnoseological turpitude") in the original Russian to the much more specific "gnostical turpitude" in the English translation (72: 80). This is not to claim, of course, that the novel is evidence for Nabokov's having embraced a resurrected Gnosticism as a faith. But the appearance of Gnostic motifs in many of his works suggests that he must have found some (albeit not all) aspects of this ancient world view congruent with his own.

It may have been the dominance of metaphysical issues in *Invitation to a Beheading*—and their inevitable extension into aesthetics and ethics— that led Nabokov, in his "Preface" to the English translation of the novel, to dismiss the possibility that the Bolshevik and Nazi regimes served as prototypes for it, or that Kafka influenced it (pp. 5–6). In marked contrast to the latter's works, and despite Nabokov's great admiration for "The Metamorphosis," *Invitation to a Beheading* is characterized by a strong faith in an otherworldly dimension, in the light of which the seemingly purposeless sufferings of the protagonist in his apparently absurdist world are transformed into a recapitulation of Gnosticism's cosmic drama of redemption. Contrary to what most critics have claimed, therefore, there is much more to the novel than Nabokov's condemnation of political oppression, or his celebration of Cincinnatus's purely imaginative freedom in the face of death. The novel simply cannot be understood without placing the otherworld at the center of its concerns.[3]

Among the numerous evocations of Gnosticism that Davydov has identified and explained in his perceptive reading of the novel is the central image of Cincinnatus as a prisoner in a labyrinthine stone fortress: this recalls the Gnostic ideas that man is trapped in an evil material world, and that his physical body is the prison of his soul. Even such details as the snakelike appearance of the road leading to the fortress, and the dog masks the prison guards wear are borrowed from Gnostic symbology of evil. The incident of Cincinnatus walking on air during his childhood, which is one of the radical differences between him and those around him, and which leads eventually to his imprisonment and death sentence, is modeled on the Gnostic division of mankind into spiritual and fleshly individuals, and on the myth of the original fall of divine spirit into material entrapment. Related to this are such complexes of details as the opposition between Cincinnatus's ethereal appearance and the gross physicality of his wife and his executioner, the image of Cincinnatus stripping off parts of his body as if they were articles of clothing, and his conception of his essential self being like a pearl embedded in a shark's fat—all of which have parallels in Gnostic texts. The Gnostic belief that a savior or a message from the positive, spiritual realm of light can awaken the soul of the chosen individual from its slumberlike state in the darkness of earthly life appears in the novel in such images as the celestial beam that Cincinnatus inexplicably sees piercing a prison corridor, and in the cryptic message that his mother brings him about his mysterious, unknown father. Cincinnatus's oft-repeated but practically incommunicable intuition that he knows something of utmost importance, and his growing recognition that death is to be welcomed as liberation from the earthly prison, reflect the Gnostic idea that salvation is achieved through knowledge of the ultimate truths ("gnosis"). Finally, as Davydov stresses, the destruction of the physical world that follows Cincinnatus's execution and entry into another dimension is a dramatization of the Gnostic belief that upon the return of all spiritual essences to their source in God the material cosmos will be destroyed.[4] Implicit also throughout the novel is the elitism of Gnosticism, according to which Cincinnatus is one of the elect few, and thus certainly not the Everyman that some readers take him to be.[5] In fact, his portrait is congruent with the image of the "anti-commonsensical" poet, eccentric, or hero that we find throughout Nabokov's oeuvre.

An awareness of the novel's dependence on Gnostic motifs, only some of which can be summarized here, buttresses strongly a "metaphysical" reading of it, and points up the surprisingly esoteric character of some of Nabokov's religio-philosophical affinities. However, despite the high density of Gnostic details in the novel (which is not exceeded in any of Nabokov's other works, although, perhaps, it is matched in the short story "Sovershenstvo" ["Perfection," 1932]), *Invitation to a Beheading* is clearly concerned with the same issues we find throughout Nabokov's oeuvre. This is signaled as early as the novel's epigraph, "Comme un fou se croit Dieu, nous nous croyons mortels" ("As a madman believes himself to be God, we believe ourselves to be mortal"), which is drawn from Pierre Delalande's *Discours sur les ombres*. When unraveled, Delalande's formulation indicates that we are as mistaken to think of ourselves as being mortal as is a madman who thinks he is God—a conclusion that has a clear bearing on Cincinnatus's end as well as on the title of the novel. The pointed nature of Nabokov's choice of an epigraph is underscored by the fact that he invented its author, as he admits in the Preface to the English translation of the novel (p. 6), and by his readiness to quote from him again, and at much greater length, in an important passage in *The Gift* that also deals with survival after death.

The relevance of the epigraph to the novel is borne out by Cincinnatus's final moments, during which he appears to transcend his mortal being following his decapitation (222–23: 217–18). Nabokov produces this impression through a masterful description of two overlapping series of actions dealing with two Cincinnatuses. The first keeps counting to ten, as the headsman, M'sieur Pierre, instructs him. The second hears the sound of the "unnecessary count" receding after the axe begins to fall, and suddenly experiences a new, joyous insight into his true situation that allows him to get up from the chopping block. The fact that Cincinnatus's mortal self was indeed decapitated during this process is implied by the description of one of the witnesses as sitting "doubled up, vomiting" at the sight. By contrast, the nonphysical nature of the second Cincinnatus is underscored by the ironic and (in the context) humorous indication that after the axe falls he not only stands up from the block but also *looks* around. This implied duality of body and soul is given an unequivocal ethical coloration when the seemingly "real" setting around the scaffold disintegrates and collapses like a badly constructed stage set. Finally, the novel's concluding phrases, which describe how Cincinnatus "made his way in that direction where, to judge by the voices, stood beings akin to him," imply that he not only survives death but enters a preexisting, and for him, intelligible and familiar transcendent realm.

The dualistic world view underlying these concluding scenes is repeatedly foreshadowed from the novel's first pages, and explains many passages that have either puzzled readers or prompted elaborate, purely metaliterary exegeses (even among those who recognize that the novel's conclusion is couched in imagery implying that Cincinnatus's soul is immortal). For example, we encounter a suggestion that there may be two sides to Cincinnatus when he fails to make a coherent response to the prison director and the narrator reports that an "additional Cincinnatus" rearranges the words "Kind. You. Very" into the commonplace polite phrase "You are very kind" (15: 29; related examples appear on pp. 69: 76, 198: 194, 211: 206). The spiritual nature of Cincinnatus's "second" self also emerges from the narrator's remarks about "the double" ("prizrak," or "specter" in the original Russian) that he says accompanies everyone—Cincinnatus, himself, and the reader. The narrator's inclusion of himself and the reader in this series is startling because it implicitly makes the remark relevant for the world outside the novel. But the explanation that follows reveals how the narrator's claim fits into Nabokov's world view. The "double" 's distinguishing and highly telling characteristic is that it does "what we would like to do at that very moment, but cannot" (25: 37). From this it follows that the second Cincinnatus's leaving the executioner's scaffold after his decapitation is the fullest manifestation of his spiritual being. Moreover, assuming that the "double" is something like a soul that has its true home in a transcendent—which is implied by the second Cincinnatus's going toward "beings akin to him"—imagination can be understood as a function of man's otherworldly nature. Thus in the novel's own terms the "double" is clearly much more than a mere reification of a standard, psychological conception of imagination. This inference is entirely in keeping with what Nabokov implies about the otherworldly dimensions of imagination and inspiration in his discursive writings, and recalls what he says in "The Art of Literature and Commonsense" about the anticommonsensical traits of the artistic sensibility.

The opposition between Cincinnatus's body and spirit also resembles Nabokov's depiction of Luzhin's quandaries. Both characters are attached to a transcendent reality that is beyond the ken of others, and that is infinitely more alluring than the frequently sordid world of matter. Although both protagonists appear clumsy and inept in the mundane world, they transcend it by virtue of their ability to touch or intuit spiritual reality. Moreover, Luzhin via his suicide, like Cincinnatus via his execution, appears to return to the spiritual homeland to which he had been attached throughout his life. The ambivalent attitude of Cincinnatus to his impending execution also recalls Luzhin's ambivalence toward chess, which is the source of both bliss and horror. Just as Luzhin knows that total immersion in chess (which leads to madness in earthly terms) is the vehicle to an alluring nonmaterial world, Cincinnatus realizes that death will liberate him from the fetters of the flesh. But since both characters straddle matter and spirit, they cannot help fearing losing a part of themselves by moving entirely to the otherworldly side of being.

Additional confirmation for the view that the double is a metaphysical entity in *Invitation to a Beheading* is provided by the narrator's extended digression about the "fleshy incompleteness" of Cincinnatus. There is something about him that makes it appear "as if one side of his being slid into another dimension"; it also "seemed as though at any moment . . . Cincinnatus would step in such a way as to slip naturally and effortlessly through some chink of the air into its unknown coulisses to disappear there" (120–21: 122–24). Earlier in the novel, the narrator describes something like Cincinnatus's spiritual essence dissolving in the air and immersing itself in its mysterious native medium after he temporarily sheds his physical body (32: 44–45). These descriptions, which imply there is a nonmaterial aspect to Cincinnatus's being, interdict interpretations of his "double" as simple wish fulfillment, or as fantasy without foundation in reality. A related feature of the narrator's attempt to characterize Cincinnatus's evanescent nature is his description of him as an unfinished drawing by a "master of masters," which is an impression that Cincinnatus shares (21–22: 35). Considered outside the context of Nabokov's discursive writings, this passage might appear to warrant a purely metaliterary interpretation of *Invitation to a Beheading*. But as we have seen, conceiving of a human being as an artifact is an inevitable consequence of a dualistic world view in which the transcendent authors the mundane world.

This conclusion is especially important because it underscores the necessity of understanding the novel in the light of Nabokov's "Neoplatonic" beliefs rather than in exclusively Gnostic terms. The view that spiritual reality rules over matter cannot be reconciled with Gnosticism's radical dualism, according to which the world of matter is irredeemably evil and separate from the transcendent world of spirit. As a result, one could not liken the implied author of the novel to the hidden, positive god of light in Gnosticism, and see Cincinnatus as his incomplete material creation, because according to Gnostic beliefs the hidden god is not manifested in the material realm in any way other than through the divine spark contained in some select individuals' souls. Cincinnatus's "unfinished" material being would have to be the product of the "demiurge" who rules over the world of fallen matter. In terms of literary fiction, one could imagine this as being the narrator, which could make for an interesting narrative form. But the narrator is of course best understood as one of the complexes of devices employed by the implied author—a relationship that is not gainsaid by Nabokov in *Invitation to a Beheading*—and is thus his agent rather than his opponent in the familiar phenomenology of writing. This conclusion again leads to a contradiction with Gnosticism's fundamental dualism, although it approaches one of the possible ways of seeing evil's role in Christianity (or Neoplatonism). In the final analysis, we have to return to the obvious point that although Nabokov may have used Gnostic motifs when it suited him, he did not follow an archaic religious doctrine slavishly.

In the context of the narrator's description of the "double," Cincinnatus's leaving the scaffold after his execution can be seen as the culmination of several earlier flights of the imagination that were incapable of changing his situation permanently. In the second chapter, for example, he drags a table to a window, lifts a chair onto it, and tries unsuccessfully to see out of his cell. Then the jailer appears, and the narrator begins what subsequently turns out to be a deceptive description of how Cincinnatus's double steps on the jailer's face while Cincinnatus himself is getting down from the chair (28–29: 40–41). This act is of course a manifestation of Cincinnatus's revulsion at his captivity. More important, however, is the implication that since the jailer is unaware of the full extent of what Cincinnatus' double has done (he sees Cincinnatus climb up, but not step on him), the jailer is somehow lacking a "double," or a spiritual faculty with which to register the offense fully. On the other hand, the fact that the jailer can see part of the action carried out by Cincinnatus's double underscores the ontological weight of spiritual reality in the world of the novel (especially for the reader, who is the other witness of Cincinnatus's climb). (Elsewhere in the novel Cincinnatus comes to the conclusion that the jailer and most of the other characters are merely "specters" [36: 47; 70: 77], by which he means that they are entirely unreal. It is possible that Nabokov chose to substitute the word "double" for the original Russian "specter" in order to distinguish more clearly between the real spiritual entity that is a part of select human beings like Cincinnatus, and Cincinnatus's and the reader's perceptions of most other characters as soulless puppets.) The deception in the narrator's description of how Cincinnatus's double behaves is signaled by the continuation of the scene. On the following page we find the statement that Cincinnatus "tried—for the hundredth time—to move the table" but could not because "the legs had been bolted down for ages" (30: 42). Thus, in light of what we have been told about the nature of the double, the entire incident with Cincinnatus moving the table turns out to be a failed attempt by his spirit to escape its physical confines, against which the corporeal Cincinnatus is also totally impotent. Without this explanation, the narrator's two descriptions of Cincinnatus and the table would appear to be in fundamental contradiction with each other. Thus the novel's metaphysical superstructure preempts any necessity of trying to understand the contradiction in terms of either absurdist or metaliterary criteria. There is, however, a second level of deception implicated here that stems precisely from the fact that there is only a seeming contradiction in the descriptions of Cincinnatus and the table. Invitation to a Beheading has built into it several major "flaws" on the level of the narrator's descriptions of events that function as reflections of the novel's central theme, which could be characterized as the imperfection of the material world in comparison to a transcendent prototype. Thus, because the remarks about the table can be reconciled in the novel's own terms, the pseudocontradiction between them can be understood as the narrator's deceptive and elusive strategy of having one device mimic another—a false narrative flaw mimics a real one—which is of course a practice entirely in harmony with the value Nabokov placed on mimicry and deception, as well as with the demands he placed on his readers.

In general, there is a hierarchical arrangement of levels of artifice in the novel, ranging from the fictional world within the text to the reader's interaction with it. The most widespread and obvious form of artifice is based on an extensive elaboration of the metaphor that all the world is a stage. Few readers have failed to notice that Cincinnatus sees himself as being caught in a theatrical performance that does not quite come off even though it supposedly constitutes his real life. For example, the prison director wears a "perfect toupee," has a face "selected without love," and cheeks with a "somewhat obsolete system of wrinkles." He is thus presented as a dated and rather carelessly fashioned simulacrum of a human being. That he is part of a charade being played out for Cincinnatus's benefit can be inferred from his vanishing and "dissolving into the air" upon entering Cincinnatus's cell, and then coming in through the door again a minute later (14–15: 28). In contrast to Cincinnatus's dissolving after divesting himself of his body, an act that the narrator indicates is a function of his spiritual essence, the prison director behaves like a puppet with whose first entrance an invisible handler was dissatisfied. All of the other prison personnel are also systematically described in terms of wearing makeup or costumes, or of acting, and frequently overacting, their roles (21: 34, 29: 42, 37: 48, 38: 50, 68: 76, 71: 78, 78: 85, 130: 131, 152: 152, 207: 202, 210: 205).[6]

A somewhat higher level of artifice within the general theatrical motif is defined by flaws in the actual "script" of the "play" being acted out before Cincinnatus. (That he is literally witnessing a play is clearly suggested by the fact that most of the characters who visit him consult crib sheets when they appear to forget their lines.) At one point, M'sieur Pierre tries to entertain Cincinnatus with a trick that involves guessing which card the prison director drew from a deck (84: 90). The problem is that Cincinnatus is not included in the "trick," which was ostensibly staged for his benefit, and that no provision was made for verifying that the executioner in fact guessed the correct card. The impression this produces is of a small but significant flaw in the composition or text of the scene, an impression that is confirmed two pages later when M'sieur Pierre tries to repeat the trick but makes a mistake that renders it meaningless (86: 93). A joke he attempts to tell about an old woman who goes to a doctor to complain of an illness—and which, from the reader's point of view is literally meaningless and not funny—has a similar function (84: 90–91;

184: 181). The same kind of discrepancy between action and words on the part of M'sieur Pierre and the director characterizes their exchange regarding Cincinnatus's age and his resemblance to his mother (82: 88). Under more traditional narrative circumstances, details such as these could be interpreted as simple misunderstandings between the characters. But given the narrator's emphasis on their frequent reliance on crib sheets and the like, the onus for the slips in logic and coherence must fall on the script they continue to follow mechanically without adjusting what they say when their prescribed situations change.

Cincinnatus is well aware that the world surrounding him is a flawed, artificial construct (69–70: 77, 91: 96). However, just as Luzhin does not perceive every aspect of the fatidic chess "combination" that is developing throughout his life, Cincinnatus does not notice all the defects in his world. This is left for the reader to discover, who, if he goes along, is thus made to enact something that is as important in terms appropriate to *Invitation to a Beheading* as discerning the workings of fate is for *The Defense*. The category of flaws that escapes Cincinnatus's notice transcends the relatively untalented acting of the characters around him, as well as the insufficiently polished script they follow, both of which are readily subsumed by the implied consciousness of the text's crafty narrator. This cannot be claimed, however, for the inconsistencies in the novel that simulate flaws on the level of the narrative itself. They are beyond both Cincinnatus's and the narrator's awareness, and are thus evidence of the distance between the novel's narrator and its implied author.

A sequence of concealed substitutions of one character for another, which produce the impression that the narrator is forgetting which characters he is dealing with, begins with Cincinnatus's lawyer, Roman Vissarionovich, entering his cell. Next, the prison director, Rodrig Ivanovich, comes in. The two engage in dialogue, until suddenly and without any indication from the narrator that anything is awry, instead of the director, the jailer Rodion appears as the lawyer's interlocutor. This substitution is both marked and masked by the narrator's reference to the interlocutor at one point by the ambiguous term "the former" ("tot" [39: 50]) rather than by name. The fact that we are now dealing with Rodion is revealed gradually—first by the reference to his keys, then by his stylized, folksy chatter, and finally by his being addressed by name. An even more elusive instance of the narrator's "forgetfulness" appears in the continuation of this scene, when the lawyer, the jailer, and Cincinnatus go for a walk to a platform at the top of the prison fortress's, tower. Cincinnatus stands transfixed by the view, while the lawyer is described as having inadvertently soiled his back with chalk, and the jailer sweeps the terrace with a broom he found (43: 54). But at the conclusion of the scene the jailer has disappeared, and we read that it is the director, Rodrig Ivanovich, who

suddenly tosses away a broom, announces it is time to return inside, and
has chalk stains on the back of his coat (44: 55).

These shifts are of course a carefully contrived device on Nabokov's
part and not real slips of the pen. But invoking narrative error is not the
only way of interpreting its significance. Later in the novel the narrator
acknowledges openly that the director and lawyer look identical without
their makeup (207: 202). One concludes that the other characters surrounding Cincinnatus may also be interchangeable, which is in fact implied by M'sieur Pierre's ordering the director around in the end of the
novel as if he were the jailer (210: 205).[7] The reason characters should be
interchangeable is explained by the novel's metaphysics: if Cincinnatus
stands out from among everyone else because of his soul, it follows that
the identity of different characters is most likely due to their not having
souls. Cincinnatus seems generally aware of this fact, which is why he
refers to those around him as "specters, werewolves, parodies" (40: 51).
However, he does not give any sign that he has noticed the specific metamorphosis of the director into the jailer, or vice versa. It is possible, of
course, that one character replacing another is a given of the physical
world in *Invitation to a Beheading*, and that the narrator is simply going
along with it in the scenes in question. But at the same time, he is flouting
a basic fictional convention; moreover, he does so surreptitiously. Thus
the absence of any indication in the text that either the narrator or Cincinnatus is aware of the substitutions is what makes it possible to interpret them as narrative "errors." Reading them in this way is appealing
because the reader is placed in the position of discerning flaws in the text
that are analogous to the flaws Cincinnatus perceives in his physical
world.[8] Another way of saying this is that Nabokov's simulation of a
narrator losing track of characters in his tale—a strikingly original aspect
of the novel's aesthetics—is modeled on the novel's metaphysics.

Within the context of Nabokov's metaphysical aesthetics there are also
Platonic implications to a narrative that is flawed. As Nabokov implied
in several of his discursive writings, he apparently believed that the works
he created preexisted him in a transcendent realm, and that his, or by
implication, any true author's job was actually to transcribe what he
writes as best he can. In *Invitation to a Beheading* a similar connection
between language and the otherworld is implied by the passage in which
the narrator stumbles over his words in a manner recalling Cincinnatus's
inability to respond coherently to the director before his second, spiritual
self rearranges the words. This appears in the description of the lawyer's
search for a lost cufflink in Cincinnatus's cell: "It was plain that he was
upset by the loss of that precious object. It was plain. The loss of the
object upset him. The object was precious. He was upset by the loss of
the object" (36: 47). The redundancy may be read as a sign of the narra-

tor's momentary entrapment in the dulling world of material concerns. But as the narrator admits, he is like Cincinnatus in having a spiritual "double," from which we can infer that this double may be responsible for the narrator's not only coherent but often poetic prose. Narrative stumbling is thus like narrative forgetfulness in implying the existence of a higher consciousness that is the locus of the ideal version of the narrative, and that incorporates seeming imperfections into a larger artistic design. In literary terms this is like saying that the narrator is subsumed by the implied author, or that the narrator's double may *be* the implied author. This connection between the two is another reason for not seeing the former as the demiurge and the latter as the hidden god of Gnosticism. (Indeed, if anyone in the novel might be considered to rule over the physical world it is M'sieur Pierre. This is suggested by the deference he is accorded by every character except Cincinnatus, and by his increasingly obvious control over events as the novel draws to a close—to the extent of acting like a stage director on the scaffold when he asks for an adjustment in the lighting [221: 216].)

Other than the implications of narrative "flaws," the most evident link between Nabokov's metaphysical aesthetics and *Invitation to a Beheading* is that Cincinnatus has the gift of cosmic synchronization. When he tries to define what makes him unique, one of the things he writes in his journal is

> I am not an ordinary—I am the one among you who is alive—Not only are my eyes different, and my hearing, and my sense of taste—not only is my sense of smell like a deer's, my sense of touch like a bat's—but, most important, I have the capacity to conjoin all of this in one point—No, the secret is not revealed yet—even this is but the flint—and I have not even begun to speak of the kindling, of the fire itself. (52: 62)

Cincinnatus's reference to his ability to "conjoin" multifarious sensory impressions "in one point" is what sounds most like the epiphanic experience Nabokov knew himself and gave to his favorite characters. Especially telling is that Cincinnatus describes this ability in terms of its being the necessary prerequisite ("the flint") for something much more grand and important ("the fire itself"). One can infer what this is from the context of the passage, which is Cincinnatus's attempt to assuage his anguish over not knowing when he will be executed, and of his inability to express himself fully in writing (which inextricably links his aesthetic program to his metaphysical quandary). It is vitally important for Cincinnatus to be able to communicate a clarity and immediacy of perception that are like those underlying cosmic synchronization, to make his reader "suddenly feel just as if he had awakened for the first time in a strange country. What I mean to say is that I would make him suddenly burst into tears of joy, his eyes would melt, and, after he experiences this, the world will seem to him cleaner, fresher" (51–52: 62). The mention of "awakening" of course resurrects the entire motif of mundane life as sleep and the transcendent as a true waking state that is developed at length in the novel (e.g., 26: 39, 36: 47, 92: 97). A variant of this is the passage dealing with a large, beautiful and powerful moth—an obvious symbol of the soul[9]—which perceives earthly light in Gnostic terms as a darkness in which it can only "slumber" (203–4: 198–99). The view of life in this world as sleep leads readily to Cincinnatus's conclusion that what surrounds him is largely dreamlike and illusory (what he sees during his actual dreams, however, is glimmers of the otherworldly realm [93: 99]). It is thus inevitable that he would see the awakening that death brings in terms of a cosmic synchronization-like leap in consciousness.

But why would Cincinnatus think that writing will mitigate his metaphysical despair? The answer that *Invitation to a Beheading* provides is a variation of Nabokov's metaphysical aesthetics in *Speak, Memory* and "The Art of Literature and Commonsense." Cincinnatus states that he needs to express himself verbally in order to know the otherworldly reality that fills his intuitions; in other words, poetic language is a guide to, and an expression of, metaphysical reality. This connection is confirmed by Cincinnatus's description of the style he would like to master, which echoes the fire imagery he invokes when speaking of his cosmic synchronization-like gift: "Not knowing how to write, but sensing with my criminal intuition how words are combined, what one must do *for a commonplace word to come alive and to share its neighbor's sheen, heat, shadow. . . .* I am nevertheless unable to achieve it, yet that is what is indispensable to me for my task, *a task of not now and not here*" (italics added; 93: 98). Fire imagery also recurs in Cincinnatus's memories of his prenatal origins, an association that establishes yet another link between the otherworld and writing: "I issue from such burning blackness, I spin like a top, with such propelling force, such tongues of flame [pylom, 'heat' in the original Russian], that to this day I occasionally feel (sometimes during sleep, sometimes while immersing myself in very hot water) that primordial palpitation of mine, that first branding contact, the mainspring of my 'I' " (90: 95). Thus we can infer that the fire imagery associated with Cincinnatus's cosmic synchronization–like sensory acuity, which also underlies his conception of ideally expressive language, is ultimately a reflection of his origins in a cosmic realm. His desire to write is, therefore, a means of touching that realm through its manifestation in language; and it is the existence of that realm that is comforting in the face of physical death. Nabokov traces virtually the same associations among cosmic synchronization, artistic inspiration, and survival after death in "The Art of Literature and Commonsense" when he concludes his characterization of the "inspiration of genius" with the image of the "ego" being liberated from its imprisonment in the world of time and space.[10]

In order to grasp fully the conception of writing that Nabokov embodies in the novel, it is important to realize that there is a major discrepancy between Cincinnatus's idea of what constitutes ideally expressive language and how he feels he writes himself. Immediately after saying he regrets that he cannot cause his words to share their "sheen, heat, shadow," which he needs, as he puts it in a key phrase, for "netutoshnei moei zadachi" ("my task, a task of not now and not here"—the English translation preserves the *t* alliteration of the Russian), he writes: "Ne tut! Tupoe 'tut,' podpertoe i zapertoe chetoiu 'tverdo,' temnaia tiur'ma, v kotoruiu zakliuchen neuemno voiushchii uzhas, derzhit menia i tesnit" ("Not here! The horrible 'here,' the dark dungeon, in which a relentlessly howling heart is encarcerated, this 'here' holds and constricts me"; 93: 98–99). The consonance and assonance in the Russian (especially *t*, but also *o*, *u*, *iu*, *p*, *zh*, and other sounds) are more prominent than in the English translation, and are augmented by the rythmic organization of the passage. Furthermore, the repetitions of *t* on the one hand (particularly stressed in the Russian by the phrase "podpertoe i zapertoe chetoiu 'tverdo,' " which is absent altogether from the English, and means literally "propped up and locked in by a couple of 'tverdo,' " which is the old Russian name for the letter *t*), and the word *tut* ("here") on the other, acquire additional semantic significance by virtue of their alliterative link to the oft-mentioned "Tamara Gardens" for which Cincinnatus yearns. "Tam" means "there" in Russian, which in the context of the novel's oppositions implies not only the freedom of a sylvan setting but also the otherworldly realm that glimmers in Cincinnatus's consciousness and memory.[11] The significance of all these sound repetitions and their associations is that they produce nothing less than an effect *exactly* like that which Cincinnatus holds up as the desirable ideal: each word "reflect[s] itself in its neighbor and renew[s] the neighboring word in the process, so that the whole line is live iridescence" (93: 98). Now, the interdependence of sound and meaning is an obvious fact of poetic language. Part of the beauty of Nabokov's Russian and English works stems from the extent to which he exploits sound repetitions. Thus there can be no doubt that the goal for which Cincinnatus strives, and which he achieves unwittingly, has Nabokov's full sanction. But if Cincinnatus is not consciously responsible for what he writes, who is? Could it be his "double," or some other transcendent agency, that guides his hand when he writes beautifully orchestrated prose? One reason this is in fact the most likely explanation is the pressure of the novel's Gnostic context, which makes Cincinnatus's whole existence into an intimate part of a cosmic process. The discrepancy is not just a matter of his being out of touch with his own abilities, therefore, because the novel's metaphysical superstructure provides an explicit, otherworldly explanation for the workings of the "wishful" imagination.

Another reason for invoking an occult force to explain Cincinnatus's writing is that this is the only plausible explanation for an unusual transition that occurs between the narrator's and Cincinnatus's texts, specifically his letter to Marthe, in which he tries to convince her that both it and his suffering are real:

> it is I, Cincinnatus, who am writing, it is I, Cincinnatus, who am weeping; and who was, in fact, walking around the table, and then, when Rodion brought his dinner, said:
>
> "This letter. This letter I shall ask you to . . . Here is the address . . ."
>
> "You'd do better to learn to knit like everybody else," grumbled Rodion. . . .
>
> "I shall try to ask you anyway," said Cincinnatus, "are there, besides me and the rather obtrusive Pierre, any other prisoners here?"
>
> Rodion flushed but remained silent.
>
> "And the headsman hasn't arrived yet?" asked Cincinnatus.
>
> Rodion was about to furiously slam the already screeching door. . . . (143: 143)

The exchanges between Cincinnatus and the jailer continue until M'sieur Pierre arrives, after which the chapter runs on to its end without any explanation of the continuity between Cincinnatus's letter and the narrator's text. This event briefly but significantly changes Cincinnatus's role with regard to the narrator that had been maintained from the start of the novel. After being in a position of relative ignorance, dependence, and passivity in relation to his situation and surroundings, Cincinnatus seems to be suddenly elevated to the privileged position of (relative) omniscience, which is the opposite of the common novelistic practice of having the third-person narrator descend into the more restricted consciousness of a character via free indirect discourse. One way of reconciling the original relation between the two with the apparent change in Cincinnatus's status would be to see him as the narrator's *amanuensis*, both here and by implication elsewhere in the novel. In other words, if one takes the narrator to be something like an occult entity with regard to the characters, then he could be seen as inducing Cincinnatus's thoughts and guiding his writing hand. This could be explained in the novel's own terms by invoking Cincinnatus's "double," which is the side of him that appears attached to a spiritual reality. It would not be reading too much into the text to interpret Cincinnatus's double as occupying the same metaphysical space as the narrator: in a sense, both are free to imagine events that are impossible in "reality." The general agreement between Cincinnatus and the narrator regarding such subjects as the unreality of matter, and the narrator's support for Cincinnatus's nagging intuitions of his spiritual homeland, buttresses the resemblance between them. Moreover, given the narrator's definition of the double, and the fact that Cincinnatus wants to express himself fully in his letter to his wife but feels he does not have the verbal skills necessary to do so, it is appropriate in the novel's terms for his double to try to fulfill this desire. (Another way of saying this is that what Gnosticism would call the "hidden god" manifests himself through Cincinnatus's writing.)

The possibility that Cincinnatus's double is indeed a concealed author of his memoir is suggested by the fact that the last entry in it is the crossed out word *death*. This (superficially) "deconstructive" sign is an unequivocal and literally graphic denial of the word's meaning. However, the narrator's description of Cincinnatus's behavior implies that he was not fully conscious of what he had written: he muses briefly about how better to verbalize what he wants to say, which implies that part of him is unaware of how well he has already expressed an intuition that will always remain beyond words, and then abruptly leaves the "blank sheet with only the one solitary word on it, and that one crossed out" to look for the symbolic moth that is hiding in his cell (206: 201).

These far-reaching implications of the continuity between Cincinnatus's and the narrator's texts can be reconciled with the "flaws" on the level of the latter by assuming that the narrator "forgot" to indicate a transition from Cincinnatus's letter to his own narrative in the same way that he occasionally "forgets" which characters he is dealing with. It is also possible that from the implied otherworldly perspective of the narrator Cincinnatus and his world are as alike as the characters who surround him, at least while he is still in his mortal state. In the end, however, all of the narrator's "errors" emerge as covert communications to the properly attuned reader from the highest consciousness ruling over the world in the text.

If we do not accept the unmarked transition between the narrator's and Cincinnatus's texts as evidence for an occult influence on him, we have to assume that Cincinnatus is in fact the concealed author of the entire novel. The narrative in which he exists would thus be dependent on his consciousness in the same way that his physical world is shown at the novel's conclusion to depend on his mortal existence. Nabokov in fact toys with a similar situation in his short novel *The Eye* (*Sogliadatai*, 1930), where a character's thoughts seem to generate his reality. But such an interpretation of *Invitation to a Beheading* is most implausible because there is hardly any evidence, beyond that already mentioned, to support it.

Another form of continuity between the narrator's and Cincinnatus's texts that also implies his writing is literally inspired by an otherworldly agency is, as Davydov argues, that some of his words appear to have been suggested to him directly by the narrator.[12] When Cincinnatus asks to see the catalogue of the prison library, the narrator commiserates about the varieties of "anguish" he must endure (48: 58), a word he repeats several more times with a curious insistence (49–50: 59–60). Finally, Cincinnatus starts setting down his thoughts, upon which he immediately picks up the word *anguish* and uses it, with the same exclamatory intonation as the narrator, two times near the beginning and two times at the end of his jottings (51: 61). It is worth noting that the passage in question includes his description of his sensory acuity, with its implied connection to cosmic synchronization and his awareness of the transcendent. The entire sequence of remarks is thus saturated with intimations of links between Cincinnatus and the otherworld, on the level of his self-consciousness, as well as of his lexicon. A related detail in the novel is that Cincinnatus recalls the day he walks on air, which is one of the earliest and most obvious manifestations of his divinely ordained status, with having just learned how to write (96: 101).

Nabokov also creates an oblique link between writing and the otherworld by means of a network of details implying that human life is like a book authored by a transcendent realm. This begins on the second page of *Invitation to a Beheading* when the narrator first compares the waning of Cincinnatus's life to the decreasing thickness of a volume one is reading, and then describes a pencil that is "as long as the life of any man except Cincinnatus" (12: 26; by the novel's end, when Cincinnatus's life is almost over, the pencil is worn down to a stub [206: 201]). The obvious and conventional interpretation of the narrator's remarks is that they are Nabokov's way of calling attention to Cincinnatus's undeniable fictionality. There is, however, a second and more important meaning behind this one. Because the narrator is not merely the teller of Cincinnatus's story but can also be construed as a spiritual entity, his "metaliterary" remarks revaluate Cincinnatus's existence by implying that it is dependent on utterances deriving from the transcendent. What the narrator says is thus doubly deceptive with regard to what he means: not only does Cincinnatus's significance in the novel transcend narrowly metaliterary themes, but because his dualistic nature extends beyond the finitude of earthly life, a book about him that one has finished reading is not an adequate image for the totality of his existence. The implication is that Cincinnatus will continue to exist in some new form after death, just as a character continues to "live" in the mind of the reader long after the book in which he appears, and in which he may perish, is set aside. This implicit analogy between text and earthly life on the one hand, and imagination and the transcendent on the other, which can be found throughout Nabokov's oeuvre (see especially the deitylike author who induces Krug's saving madness in the conclusion of *Bend Sinister*), is also articulated openly by Cincinnatus when he expresses envy for poets who are able to "speed along a page and, right from the page, where only a shadow continues to run, to take off into the blue" (194: 190; a similar formulation appears on p. 26: 38). The image of a shadow that continues to move while the object casting it has suddenly soared away is a clear adumbration of Cincinnatus's transcending the chopping block at the end of the novel. And if we translate the novel's conclusion back into the terms of Cincinnatus's comments about poetic language, his transcending earthly life puts him into the realm in which imagination rules, which, as the narrator's remarks about the "double" suggest, is akin to a spiritual reality. The result of these implications and thematic associations is that the reader, into whose imagination Cincinnatus enters via the act of reading, is placed into the position of an otherworldly witness to Cincinnatus's crossing over into a new form of being. Perhaps one of the meanings of the novel's last phrase about Cincinnatus joining "beings akin to him" is not that he moves into a totally imponderable realm, but that his experiences are also the reader's (even if the latter may not have been aware of it). Indeed, part of Nabokov's point in exploiting parallels between elements of fiction and metaphysical beliefs may have been the appeal of confronting the reader with a unique conception of existence by reconceiving the seemingly accessible and familiar act of reading.

Cincinnatus imitates the narrator by giving language ontological weight as well, albeit without consciously linking it to the transcendent. As we have seen, from the novel's start he places the greatest importance on being able to verbalize his innermost essence, as if this were the only thing that defines him: "I have no desires, save the desire to express myself" (91: 96). Moreover, he cannot be satisfied unless he thinks he will have a reader (194: 190), and his final request before being taken to his execution is to be allowed to finish writing down his thoughts (209: 204). As he implies in his letter to Marthe, his purpose is in part didactic: he hopes that by expressing himself to her, she will acquire his world view; in other words, gnosis is carried by language (142: 43). Cincinnatus also goes so far as to imply an equation between words and being by concluding that there is not a "single human" in his world because "there is in the world not a single human who can speak my language" (95: 100). (Furthermore, because all that happens around Cincinnatus emerges as having been the function of a flawed script, the widespread references to acting, costumes, and other theatrical effects constitute a variant of the idea that language carries ontological weight, although obviously to differing degrees, and depending on how and by whom it is used.) Cincinnatus's emphasis on defining himself through language is thus in harmony with the narrator's ostensibly "metaliterary" remarks about him, which suggests that Cincinnatus's self-conception, and, by extension, his other thoughts, both written and not, derive from the otherworld and are enactments of a divinely ordained plan.

The associations among being, language, and the transcendent culminate in the passages about the novel *Quercus*, a "biography" of an oak tree. The narrator describes the work as tracing all the historical events that occur near the tree during its six-century life span, and as including various scientific and popular descriptions of the tree itself. In order to make sense of this invented novel's thematic function in *Invitation to a Beheading*, it is obviously important to note that the narrator speaks favorably about it, and that it has traits recalling Nabokov's own works and values. The description of different individuals who pass near the tree over time, and the unusual narrative point of view around which the novel is structured—"as though the author were sitting with his camera somewhere among the topmost branches of the Quercus, spying out and catching his prey" (123: 125)—recall the otherworldly narrator's easy "sinking" through layers of time when cataloguing what has happened in the same place in *Transparent Things* (1972). In both works, the collocation of movement through time with immobility in space is a reflection of Nabokov's conception of time as illusory, an idea that is also prominent in *The Gift* and in *Speak, Memory*. The scientific and other technical descriptions of the tree are reflections of Nabokov's insistence on precise knowledge and acute observation.

The relevance of *Quercus* for Cincinnatus's quandary is also indicated by the fact that we first encounter the novel when he has read "a good third of it, or about a thousand pages" (122: 125). The statement about how much he has finished recalls the analogy the narrator drew earlier between Cincinnatus's life and the thickness of an unread text. Indeed, Cincinnatus goes on to read, or perhaps better to say, misread *Quercus* precisely in terms of the surface meaning of the narrator's analogy. The novel induces "melancholy" and "distress" in him because he sees it as deceitful and dead, because he knows that he will die, and because, as he believes, "the only real, genuinely unquestionable thing here was only death itself, the inevitability of the author's physical death" (123–24: 126). "Physical" is of course the key word in this remark, and signals an instance of authorial irony at Cincinnatus's expense: it is clear that his repeated inklings of a transmundane existence have been temporarily eclipsed by the weakness of his corporeal self. Cincinnatus's mistaken despair increases until he asks out loud if anyone will save him, which leads to the following remarkable passage: "The draft became a leafy breeze. From the dense shadows above there fell and bounced on the blanket a large dummy acorn, twice as large as life, splendidly painted a glossy buff, and fitting its cork cup as snugly as an egg" (126: 128). This acorn appears like a deus ex machina, and is obviously meant as an answer to Cincinnatus's despairing question. But rather than being merely an instance of the author's heavy-handed intrusion into the text via a flagrantly artificial model of a natural object, the novel's Gnostic context suggests that the acorn can be seen as a coded sign or a "call" sent by the hidden deity to a select individual to awaken in him the desire to escape the earthly prison. By appearing in Cincinnatus's cell the acorn establishes a bridge between his physical world and the imaginary world of fiction represented by the novel *Quercus*, thereby granting equal reality to the latter as well as to the powers of imagination and consciousness that underlie it (which are, in turn, intertwined with the otherworldly). The materiality of the acorn thus disproves Cincinnatus's view of the novel as deceitful fiction, as well as his related belief that the only thing to be said about it is that its author must die. If the acorn falls on Cincinnatus's bed, then Cincinnatus's world can be said to be included in the vantage point of *Quercus*'s author, and to be part of its timeless perspective on earthly things. The artificiality of the acorn does not deny its relative reality in the novel's fictional world, where everything else is also "made." Indeed, the skill with which it was painted elevates it above the level of most material things surrounding Cincinnatus. And if the acorn is a sign from a transcendent realm, then the true author of *Quercus* was not a mortal man.

Although Cincinnatus appears to be attached to an otherworld, little can be gleaned about it except that it is radically different from earthly life. As we have seen, this is a fundamental aspect of Nabokov's own world view. It is also entirely in keeping with the radical dualism of Gnosticism, which prohibits easy contact, or even transmission of information between the material and spiritual realms. One of the most important illustrations of this theme in the novel is the discussion of the bizarre objects called "*nonnons*" by Cecilia C., Cincinnatus's mother. She recalls them from her childhood, and is prompted to describe them to him during a visit to his cell after he makes a disparaging remark about the clumsy artificiality of his physical world. She tells him that they appeared shapeless and absurd to normal vision, and came with special distorting mirrors in which reflections of everyday objects also made no sense to the eye. But when placed in front of their mirrors, the "*nonnons*" suddenly revealed perfectly intelligible images. Cincinnatus is understandably puzzled why his mother would tell him all this, until suddenly, for a brief instant, he sees in her eyes evidence that she knows "that ultimate, secure, all-explaining and from-all-protecting spark that he knew how to discern in himself also. . . . the spark proclaimed such a tumult of truth that Cincinnatus's soul could not help leaping for joy" (135–36: 136–38). This is clearly the same divine spark that constitutes both Cincinnatus's soul and his link to the transcendent. The "*nonnons*" thus appear to be models that Cecilia C. invokes (or invents) for the purpose of hinting to Cincinnatus that the absurdities and suffering that surround him in prison, which prefigure his impending execution, will show their actual, illusory nature when they are seen in the proper context of the world of spirit. Another way of phrasing this would be to say that one cannot imagine the true shape of the experiences one may have on the other side of the division between this world and the next. The connection of the "*nonnons*" with the transcendent is further implied by the imagery Cincinnatus employs during his earlier rhapsody about the possible nature of the otherworld, which includes a mirror that shines "*there*" and that "now and then sends a chance reflection here" (94: 100).

Although the otherworld may be ultimately unfathomable, Cincinnatus's experience of time constitutes another nexus of themes and images that sheds light on the relation between the material and spiritual planes of being. On the one hand, he describes how he once saw a man move away from a wall while his shadow seemed briefly to remain behind: "between his movement and the movement of the laggard shadow—that second, that syncope—there is the rare kind of time in which I live" (53: 63). And in the next sentence, Cincinnatus goes on to intimate that he is attached by an "invisible umbilical cord" to a mysterious otherworldly realm. The two remarks support each other by implying that Cincinnatus's proper environment, or, more exactly, that of his double, is both timeless and spiritual. On the other hand, he is also a physical being, which is why his mundane life is characterized not by timelessness, but by a dulling, repetitive cyclicity that is a function of a prison's inevitable routine. This is reinforced by such details as his discovering that a prison corridor circles back to his cell (77: 84), and that the tunnel M'sieur Pierre had dug leads to the prison director's quarters (166: 165). Cincinnatus's attempt to characterize the atemporal "moment" in which he lives anticipates the imagery Van Veen will use in his discussion of time in *Ada*, which, in turn, reflects Nabokov's own beliefs.[13] Cincinnatus also anticipates Nabokov's deceptive description in *Speak, Memory* of time as a spherical prison when he says that "the sphere of my own self still limits and eclipses my being [*soboiu oblo ogranichen i zatmen*]" (89–90: 95). There is a resemblance as well between the ways Cincinnatus and Nabokov escape these prisons. After he leaves the scaffold Cincinnatus is described as being "overtaken by Roman, who was now many times smaller" (222–23: 217), which suggests that Cincinnatus has grown, or expanded beyond the limits of his old, corporeal self. A radically expanded consciousness that appears to be capable of embracing all existence is also part of Nabokov's repertoire of images in *Speak, Memory* when he describes the timeless moment of cosmic synchronization.

Time is inevitably central to Cincinnatus's ceaseless attempts to determine when he will be executed (which resemble Luzhin's febrile search for clues regarding the directions in which the "combination" he feels is developing against him will move). The fact that he consistently fails to guess the answer or to cajole it from various visitors to his cell may be a reflection of Nabokov's idea that one's future is unknowable, or that it does not exist because it is not fixed, at least for mortal consciousness. The latter qualification needs to be added because of a detail in the scene between Cincinnatus and his mother. Immediately after he notices the spark in her gaze that causes his heart to leap for joy, the narrator describes Cecilia C. as making an "incredible little gesture": she "hold[s] her hands apart with index fingers extended, as if indicating size—the length, say, of a babe" (136: 138). Although the narrator underscores the significance of the mother's cryptic gesture, he leaves it to the reader to interpret it. The sequence of events in this scene suggests that, on one level, the gesture may be the mother's indication of how little time her son has left to live; on another level, however, it can be interpreted as indicating that he has to wait only a little while longer before all mysteries are revealed. The latter is implied by the narrator's reference to a "babe," which, from the context, emerges as a veiled hint about death as a rebirth. Cincinnatus does not seem even to notice his mother's gesture, much less try to understand it, which suggests it is his double, rather than his not fully conscious mortal self that rejoices at recognizing the spark. But his relative purblindness does not negate the evidence that Cecilia C.'s role in the novel is that of a Gnostic more "advanced" than he is. She not only possesses the divine spark, but seems able to reveal it at will; she knows that Cincinnatus's father was also a "pneumatic" or spiritual being; and by describing the "*nonnons*" she implies that she understands the ultimate mysteries of existence, such as the irreconcilable difference between the Gnostic worlds of matter and spirit. One concludes, therefore, that from her superior vantage point Cincinnatus's future may not be a secret. As a result, Cincinnatus emerges as being wrong to accuse her of being a "parody" (132: 133), a point that Nabokov implied himself in an interview when he said that Cincinnatus's accusation was not quite fair.[14]

The hierarchical relationship between Cincinnatus and his mother may be related to the veiled motif of travel by water that accompanies him throughout the novel, and that also has a bearing on the issue of his experience of time. The narrator describes his cell as having a "peephole like a leak in a boat" (12: 25), and his jailer as peering through it "with a skipper's stern attention. . . . at the horizon, now rising, now falling"

(13: 26; related imagery also appears on 57: 66, 64: 73, 65: 73). Boat
and water imagery are also associated with the description of Cincinnatus's "feasting" on books in his youth (27: 39), and, because of the narrator's references to the "coolness" Cincinnatus experiences following his
"immersion," to the scene in which he dismembers himself and then dis-
solves in his "secret medium" (32: 44–45). Since both passages are central to the novel's concern with the relation between the transcendent and
terrestrial realms, one concludes that Nabokov may have wanted to exploit the mythical significance of water and voyaging as symbols for rebirth and enlightenment. The unidirectional movement this implies suggests that there is a rectilinear component to Cincinnatus's experience of
time, and that he approaches gnosis and transcendence gradually. These
associations may explain why the narrator mentions twice on one page
that Cecilia C. wears a raincoat when she comes to visit her son, and
underscores her "waterproof hat with lowered brim (giving it something
of the appearance of a sou'wester)" (130: 131). Although she complains
about the stormy weather she encountered on her way to the prison, the
narrator's comment about her hat links her to the motif of voyaging by
water, which, given her apparent possession of "gnosis," further attaches
the motif to progressive enlightenment. Cecilia C.'s garb also provides an
opportunity for Cincinnatus to demonstrate the occasional blindness that
punctuates his general insightfulness. In keeping with his mistaken view
of his mother as another instance of imperfect theatrical invention, he
fastens on the fact that her shoes are dry whereas her raincoat is wet, and
characterizes it as an instance of "carelessness" on the part of the "prop
man" (132: 133). Cecilia C. retorts that she wore rubbers and had taken
them off (a rare instance in the novel of seeming artifice being explained).
But what seems most important about the scene is that the entire discussion allows another resurrection of the motif of travel by water, together
with all its associations. Cincinnatus's mother thus also becomes colored
by an implied unidirectional physical movement that suggests movement
through time. The significance of this is that time is validated as a means
of attaining the desired end. In sum, there is a bridge of sorts (it need not
be imagined as continuous) between earthly life and the otherworld, despite the gulf between them. This is really another way of saying that the
experiences of this world are the necessary preconditions for transcending
it, which, although alien to the radical dualism of Gnosticism, is of course
a dominant idea throughout Nabokov's oeuvre.

The links among Cincinnatus's perceptions, his verbal creation, and his
otherworldly origins point up a major difference between Gnosticism's
dualism and Nabokov's beliefs. Cincinnatus resembles his creator in that
his sensory acuity bespeaks an attraction to, and an understanding of the
things of this world. Even though Cincinnatus sees through the shabby

artifice that characterizes the man-made and human realms around him, he still loves his shallow, grossly physical, and cruelly unfaithful wife (60: 69), yearns for the Tamara Gardens through which he used to roam (27–28: 40), and even longs for scenes of street life in town (73–75: 80–82). In other words, his attitude toward aspects of the physical world is not consistently negative, as Gnosticism would require. One could argue that Cincinnatus overcomes these feelings by the end of the novel, when his spiritual side manages to gain greater ascendancy over the physical. He suggests as much himself when he writes that he has reached "the dead end of this life, and I should not have sought salvation within its confines" (205: 200). But just before M'sieur Pierre finally arrives to convey Cincinnatus to the place of execution, we are presented with the second extended description of the moth that had escaped from the jailer. The passage is thus located at a crucial juncture in the text. It is typically Nabokovian not only by virtue of its subject matter but also in the way the moth's physical attributes are described in great detail, and in the general tone of admiration that surrounds the insect's combined beauty and power. The moth's traditional significance as a symbol of the soul is overt, and the eye-spots on its wings evoke one of Nabokov's favorite images for the all-embracing consciousness that man may achieve after death (in *The Gift*, Delalande will speculate that after death man will become an "all-seeing eye"). In his enchantment Cincinnatus strokes the moth's large wings, which prompts the narrator to exclaim "what gentle firmness! what unyielding gentleness!" The importance of this characterization is that it reminds the reader of the implausibility of the jailer's plan to feed the moth to the spider, which is an equally obvious symbol of death. (The spider's emergence as artificial [78: 85, 210: 205] is of course yet another suggestion that death is illusory.) Because the passage is narrated in free indirect discourse, Cincinnatus is implicated in the entire loving description of the magnificent insect, which is a point of view at odds not only with his own general denigration of the physical world but with Gnosticism's attitude toward it. (Similarly, Nabokov grants Cincinnatus another of his favorite gifts—skill at chess [144: 146].) The possibility that Cincinnatus's involuntary attraction to the moth is a reflection of Nabokov's disagreement with Gnosticism—and therefore his way of correcting the overly spiritualized view that his protagonist developed—is also suggested by Cincinnatus's error regarding his mother in the passage preceding the description of the moth. He had included "a mother's moist gaze" in the list of "theatrical, pathetic" things that had "duped" him and that motivated his conviction that "salvation" must not be sought on earth. Cincinnatus thus appears to have forgotten his own (or not registered his double's) exultant recognition of the truth of what she told him and of the spiritual spark both share. Nabokov's ability to capture sensuous details, which is one of the most striking and oft-celebrated features of his writing from both his Russian and English periods, did not prevent him from being able to transcend matter via matter, as it were, in his conception of cosmic synchronization, and in his views on mimicry and artifice in nature. The difference between Nabokov's views and Cincinnatus's partially Gnostic attitudes toward matter could thus be described as relative—one of degree and tone—not substantive.

The connection between ethics and metaphysics in *Invitation to a Beheading* is one of the most obvious and straightforward in Nabokov's oeuvre. Good is firmly attached to Cincinnatus because he is the only character (except for his mother) who has intimations of, and spiritual links to, a transcendent realm; this insight is what allows him to see the physical world for what it is. The other characters are totally ignorant of this higher realm; as a result, they are mired in a shallow physical world, and are consistently presented as foolish, absurd, and irredeemably vulgar. M'sieur Pierre is an especially perfect embodiment of that petty evil or self-satisfied vulgarity called *poshlost'* in Russian, to which Nabokov gave famous definition in his book on Gogol. Cincinnatus's platonic love for Marthe is in stark contrast to her grossly carnal sexuality, which Nabokov renders with striking mastery (141: 142). The failing of these and other characters is pointed up by Cincinnatus's overwhelming desire to make them understand his plight, something of which they are constitutionally incapable. There is, however, no horrible, or Satanic evil in the novel, which reflects Nabokov's own view of evil as absence, and which thus constitutes an additional departure from Gnostic dualism.

The dominant theatrical metaphor that Cincinnatus and the narrator use in describing the world in the novel adds aesthetics to the continuum between ethics and metaphysics. Both have grasped that matter is an imperfect copy, or a lesser image of a spiritual reality (a belief that is also at odds with Gnosticism). But since gnosis is the province of the few, the values embodied in *Invitation to a Beheading*, as in all of Nabokov's other works, emerge as inflexibly elitist. The only character who will be saved is Cincinnatus (and perhaps his mother: the ambiguous image in the novel's final paragraph of "a woman in a black shawl, carrying the tiny executioner like a larva in her arms" may be Cecilia C.; she appears dressed in black earlier in the novel, and her size relative to the executioner suggests an expansion comparable to the one Cincinnatus apparently undergoes; it is unclear, however, why she should be carrying the executioner, unless it is to suggest her new power over death). All the other characters are automata for whom even the category of salvation is irrelevant (with the possible exception of the prison librarian, who seems associated with Cincinnatus's nascent gnosis). In connection with this it is interesting that Cincinnatus implies that children have the potential to develop into something better than what most adults become in his fallen world, and that he was closer to the transcendent himself when he was a child (95: 100–101). This anticipates Nabokov's own conception of his son's childhood in *Speak, Memory*, which is characterized by hints of links to transmundane modes of being, and echoes Romantic and Symbolist topoi embodied in such works as Wordsworth's ode "Intimations of Immortality from Recollections of Early Childhood," or Andrei Belyi's novel *Kotik Letaev*.[15] Fedor Sologub expressed well a related view in his famous Symbolist novel *The Petty Demon* (*Melkii bes*, 1907), which contains a number of interesting parallels to *Invitation to a Beheading*: "Only the children, those eternal, tireless vessels of God's joy in the earth, were alive, and ran, and played. But sluggishness was beginning to weigh even upon them, and some faceless and invisible monster, nestling behind their shoulders, peered from time to time with eyes full of menace into their faces, which suddenly went dull."[16]

CHAPTER FOUR

The Gift

T HE GIFT (*Dar*, 1937–38; 1952) occupies a special place in Nabokov's oeuvre because he called it his favorite and best Russian novel.¹ Although in his Foreword to the English translation Nabokov warns against naive biographical readings of the work, Fyodor Godunov-Cherdyntsev, the young Russian émigré writer living in Berlin in the 1920s who is both the novel's protagonist and its ostensible author, shares with his creator virtually identical views on a number of important topics—the origins and significance of literary art, the relations among birth, death, time, and a transcendent dimension of existence, the beneficent artistry to be found in nature and in human fate, and the banality of error, moral failing, and evil.² Nabokov's widow also provides indirect confirmation of a deep link between what lies at the novel's core and her husband's spiritual makeup when she refers to Fyodor's description of a mysterious aura surrounding his father as a good illustration of what *potustoronnost'* ("the otherworld") meant for Nabokov. Similarly, Nabokov's son acknowledged that Fyodor's description of his father was an accurate portrait of an essential aspect of Nabokov himself.³ Additional evidence implying that some of the novel's central themes are Nabokov's own was his decision to omit from the Russian version of his autobiography (*Drugie berega*) the eleventh chapter of *Conclusive Evidence*, which describes the birth of his first poem, "because of the psychological difficulty of replaying a theme elaborated in my *Dar* (*The Gift*)."⁴ (He reinstated this chapter in the second English version of his autobiography *Speak, Memory*.) What distinguishes *The Gift* from Nabokov's other major Russian novels, as well as from the works he would write in English, is the relative congruence between the surface appearance of the work and its hidden meanings. This is not to say that *The Gift* is simple or transparent, but it is in many respects Nabokov's most candid fictional treatment of themes that are also paramount in his autobiographical and discursive writings.

Nabokov signals the importance of metaphysical questions in *The Gift* a dozen lines into the novel's first paragraph by having Fyodor describe lettering on the side of a moving van as having been shaded in "a dishonest attempt to climb into the next dimension" (15: 9). On one level this minute touch is of course a fresh description of a conventional means of creating the illusion of three dimensions on a flat surface. On another, however, it raises the question of whether or not there are "honest" attempts to move into another dimension. It thus adumbrates the entire complex of passages about Alexander Chernyshevski's problematic relationship with the ghostly realm into which he believes his son, Yasha, has passed after committing suicide, as well as Fyodor's thoughts and dreams about encountering his dead father, and Fyodor's and Delalande's discussions of life after death. Hundreds of other details such as these, beautifully camouflaged by the casualness with which they are introduced, are scattered throughout *The Gift,* and add immeasurably to the resonance of a theme that will be the subject of extensive overt deliberation in the text.

One of the most important motifs in the novel touching on the possibility that some individuals are vouchsafed glimpses of an otherworldly dimension is childhood illness. Fyodor remembers how he once experienced a state of extraordinary "lucidity" when he was recovering from a very severe case of pneumonia. Ironically, he states it was then that "he attained the highest limit of human health: my mind had been dipped and rinsed only recently in a dangerous, supernaturally clean blackness" (35: 29). The startling consequence is that he has an authentically clairvoyant experience: he sees his mother going to a shop, buying him a pencil, and starting off for home with it. He even glimpses an uncle whom his mother does not notice. Moments later, she enters his sickroom carrying the pencil, a "display giant" that had once aroused his "whimsical greed." Thus, the only mistake in what he had foreseen about the entire event was the pencil's size. This incident is especially noteworthy because, as Nabokov reveals in *Speak, Memory,* he had virtually the same experience when a boy (pp. 37–38).

It is typical of the great density of significant details in Nabokov's style that Fyodor's error with regard to the pencil's size foreshadows his later discussion of the incommensurability of this world and the next, which he says cannot be imagined because it cannot be compared to anything. Lest this seem an instance of stretching the evidence, it is worth noting that near the conclusion of the passage about his clairvoyant experience, Fyodor describes his return to health in terms of "plug[ging] up certain chinks with bread" (36: 30). This image remains enigmatic until one connects it with a passage some three hundred pages later in which Delalande (the author of the epigraph to *Invitation to a Beheading*) describes life as a house, and death as the unknown and unknowable landscape surrounding it, but from which "air comes in through the cracks" (322: 347). The imagery of breezes and permeable barriers also appears in the passages about Alexander Chernyshevski and his dead son's ghost.

Fyodor describes his sister's childhood illness in terms suggesting that she too was touched by something like a spiritual plane of being: "I saw her lying in bed with an air of remoteness about her as if she had turned toward the other world [k potustoronnemu], with only the limp lining of her being toward me!" (33: 27). The same associations among childhood, illness, and another world appear in Fyodor's descriptions of his attempts to probe his prenatal origins. If one has a dualistic world view, the idea that illness distances one from matter and brings one closer to spirit can be understood as following naturally. This is what enters into Fyodor's speculations about the similarities he perceives between the state out of which one passes at birth and that into which one moves at death. His conclusion is an intimation of immortality, which he presents in an inverted form like that of Delalande's epigraph to *Invitation to a Beheading*. When he strains his memory in order to "taste" the prenatal "darkness," he fails "to see at the verge of this dying-in-reverse anything that would correspond to the boundless terror that even a centenarian is said to experience when he faces the positive end" (23: 17). The inference one draws from Fyodor's observation is that he does not fear death because it does not seem to be a "positive end." The importance of this insight for Nabokov is attested by its appearance on the opening pages of *Speak, Memory*, in his description of human existence as "a brief crack of light between two eternities of darkness" that are "identical twins," and in the image of the baby carriage as a coffin. Moreover, Nabokov's conclusion that this darkness is ultimately not real, and that it "is caused merely by the walls of time separating me . . . from the free world of timelessness," is borne out by his revelation that he can transcend time, which he interweaves throughout the autobiography in a manner directly comparable to that in *The Gift*.

One such example in the novel is a subtle and complex network of motifs linked to water imagery that arises out of Fyodor's clairvoyant experience and that clearly implies that death is not final. Associations among water, death, and rebirth are of course traditional in many mythological systems and literary works. Fyodor uses water imagery extensively to suggest the alien nature of the realm that he had touched during his illness. In his description of how he waited for his mother to return from her shopping trip, he likens the "incredible lucidity" that he developed to the ability to discern in the sky "the cape and shallows of God knows what far-off islands—and it seems that if you release your volatile glance [legkoe oko, literally—"lightweight eye"] just a little further you will discern a shining boat drawn up on the damp sand and *receding footsteps filled with bright water*" (italics added; 34–35: 29). The perfectly colloquial turn of phrase referring to a transcendent being in this passage is deceptive and telling in the context, as is the reference to a far-reaching gaze, both of which anticipate the complex theme of transcendent vision in the novel. By virtue of an association with the sky, there is also a hint of otherworldliness attached to the image of the boat and the footsteps leading away from it. Because these images are introduced in connection with a clairvoyant event that is linked to the theme of immortality, the possibility is raised that Fyodor's vision of the boat and footsteps may be prophetic or symbolic of survival after death.

Precisely this seemingly far-fetched possibility is realized in Fyodor's first imaginary dialogue with Koncheyev at the end of chapter 1, which includes the following lines from, and fragmentary discussion of a poem Fyodor is composing: "slow black ferry . . . Lethean weather . . . with *this* I'll step upon the shore some day. . . . That river is not the Lethe but rather the Styx . . . a crooked bough looms near the ferry, and Charon with his boathook, in the dark, reaches for it, and catches it" (87: 86–87). These details obviously evoke the Greek myth of Hades, and as such allude to survival after death. Fyodor's elimination of Lethe—the river of forgetfulness—from the poem, which implies that his lyric persona's soul will not drink from it, is significant because memory is a cornerstone for his earthly intuitions of the otherworld, as it was also for Nabokov; it is inconceivable that either would have imagined imbibing oblivion. The fact that this passage follows immediately after Fyodor's complaint that his new shoes pinch underscores the liberating effect of the step that he imagines he will make as a disembodied spirit onto the other shore of the Styx. Moreover, the opposition implied between physically confining shoes and the free step anticipates the cluster of motifs later in the novel that opposes life, a house, and an eye socket, to life after death, a landscape beyond the house, and an all-seeing eye free of any constraints.

The next appearance of what might be termed the "footstep motif" is a page later, at the beginning of chapter 2. Fyodor remembers a rainbow that once appeared "with the elusive suddenness of an angel" on his family's country estate in Russia, which elicits a rhapsodic recollection from him: "My darling! Pattern of Elysian hues! Once in Ordos my father, climbing a hill after a storm, inadvertently entered the base of a rainbow—the rarest occurrence!—and found himself in colored air, in a play of light as if in paradise. He took one more step—and left paradise" (89: 89).[5] The reference to Elysium—the realm in which the souls of the good abide after judgment in Hades—recalls the theme of survival after death in the poem with Charon, as does the father's stepping into and out of "paradise." The father's absence from Fyodor's life, and his probable death during, or on the return from, a scientific expedition in Central Asia is a major theme in *The Gift*, but this passage plants a hint that his physical death may not have been a "positive end." Fyodor reassociates himself with the footstep motif less than a page later, and hints again that the physical absence of an individual may not mean that the individual has ceased to exist. He describes how he "jumped a puddle" left after the rain that produced the rainbow "and printed his sole on the edge of the road: a highly significant footprint, *ever looking upward* and *ever seeing him* who had vanished" (italics added; 90: 90). The association of sight and eternity in this passage is an echo of all the associations that the footstep motif has accumulated up to this point in the novel, and foreshadows the central image of the all-seeing eye that Fyodor quotes from Delalande in order to suggest the nature of the insight that the soul will acquire after death. (It may be worth recalling in this context that Nabokov himself believed that his father had survived death, and that they would meet in another form of existence, as he indicated in his letter to his mother following his father's murder.[6] Moreover, the references to "paradise," "radiance" and brightness in the letter recall the imagery in *The Gift* associated with the footstep motif.) A link between rain and life after death similar to the one in the passage about the rainbow will also reappear later in the novel, albeit in a parodic form, in the description of Alexander Chernyshevski on his death bed.

Two more instances of the footstep motif appear near the novel's end, the first when Fyodor is swimming in a lake in the Grunewald: "he swam for a long time, half an hour, five hours, twenty-four, a week, another. Finally, on the twenty-eighth of June around three P.M., he came out [vyshel] on the other shore" (348: 377).[7] A footstep as such is not mentioned in this passage, although it is obviously implied. Water continues to be associated with a nonquotidian realm of existence by virtue of its being ruled over by another form of time: what had presumably been a swim of some normal duration for the mundane Fyodor appears to be weeks long from another point of view. (The association between water and a form of time that in its elasticity can be said to approach eternity recalls the vastly different scale of time experienced by Luzhin in *The Defense* when he is in the sanatorium recovering from his collapse, and the timeless moment that Cincinnatus considers to be his proper milieu.) It is of course no mere coincidence in Nabokov's world that the shore onto which Fyodor steps is near the ravine where Yasha Chernyshevski had committed suicide, and Fyodor notes that he always feels drawn to the place whenever he is near it (349: 377). The association between crossing bodies of water and surviving death that has been established in the novel heretofore raises the possibility that Yasha's death may also not have been final. The denouement for the entire footstep motif appears in Fyodor's dream about his father's return—he hears doors opening, "a familiar tread," and then "a light broke through, and his father with confident joy spread out his arms" (366–67: 398).

Because Fyodor is a writer, the process of literary creation inevitably occupies a central place in his consciousness and in the novel. The most striking comments he makes are about how his works originate, and everything he says implies that they derive in some fundamental way from an otherworldly source. Indeed, although Fyodor claims that his childhood illness was the only time he ever experienced clairvoyance, his description of how his works arise resembles an ability to foresee the future: "It's queer," he comments to his fiancée Zina at one point, "I seem to remember my future works, although I don't even know what they will be about. I'll recall them completely and write them" (206: 218). The implication of this remark is that the works exist in some realm that transcends the time-bound world, and all Fyodor, or, by implication, any writer does is to transcribe them. As Nabokov amply reveals in *Strong Opinions* (pp. 31, 40, 69, 78), this is one of the fundamental aspects of his own conception of art.

These parallels between Fyodor and Nabokov are crucial for understanding *The Gift* because they point to a way out of its circular narrative structure.[8] Near the end of the novel, Fyodor tells Zina that he will write a fictionalized treatment of their lives that sounds much like *The Gift* itself (376: 409). He also makes the specific remark that "every creator is a plotter; and all the pieces impersonating his ideas on the board were here as conspirators and sorcerers. Only in the final instant was their secret spectacularly revealed" (184: 193). Although he is speaking about chess, what he says is clearly also applicable to a literary text. Fyodor's pronouncements thus leave open the possibility that everything in the text (and at a minimum, an important dimension of it) is an aspect of his artistic design, rather than his record of actual, lived experience. His forefeeling "future works" could thus be taken as his granting his fictionalized self intuitions regarding his later, authorial self, presumably for the sake of underscoring the metaliterary nature of his interests. By the same token, all forms of patterning in the text could also be read as Fyodor's artistic design meant to underscore the fictionality of his story. What militates against both of these interpretations, however, and in favor of the view that Fyodor has quasi-Platonic intuitions regarding his art and life, is precisely that Nabokov does as well.

Fyodor reiterates his impression that his works preexist him at the start of practically every new literary endeavor he undertakes. Referring to himself in the third person after surveying his first collection of poetry, he says that "a special intuition forewarned the young author" that he would one day want to write about his famous father in an entirely different style than he wrote his poems about childhood (27: 21). To his mother Fyodor confesses that he occasionally feels his book about his father "has already been written by me" (150: 156). Fyodor's failure to finish writing this book can thus be read as his inability to transcribe it fully from its ideal state. *The Gift* itself suggests the relevance of such an interpretation: for example, in speaking of his poems, Fyodor remarks that "some of them did not materialize in final form [ne dotiagivali do polnogo voploshcheniia], dissolving instead" (73: 71). The literal meaning of the Russian phrase is closer to "did not make it to full incarnation," which underscores the implied otherworldly origins of the poems more strongly than the English translation. Elsewhere, Fyodor explains his error during early attempts at writing as his thinking that he had "embarked" on "creation," whereas it was actually "expression" (165: 172), which again implies that a text preexists his attempt to write it.

Another way in which Fyodor describes his dependence as an artist on the transcendent is by saying that he has to seek out the one "genuine voice" from among "a thousand interlocutors" when he is trying to compose a poem. The "concentration and ardor" this requires are, as he phrases it, "dangerous to life"—a formulation that recalls the theme of childhood illness and the contact with the otherworld it provides. Thus, despite the passion and effort Fyodor must expend in composing the poem, he concurrently and paradoxically remains a passive recipient of something from outside himself, and it is only after he finishes the poem that he realizes it "contained a certain meaning" (68: 65–66). The same impression is conveyed by his description of how "somebody within him, on his behalf, independently from him" had "absorbed," "recorded," and "filed . . . away" details that he thinks he would like to use to start the novel that becomes *The Gift* (16: 10).

The complement of the artist's relative passivity is the subtly intrusive character of what turn out to be the germs of future works. Prior to even thinking of writing the biography of Nikolai Chernyshevski—the famous nineteenth-century Russian radical—Fyodor keeps noticing his face in the Soviet chess magazine he chances to buy, and even refers to being "glared at by a butting N. G. Ch." (185, 187: 195, 196). The fact that Chernyshevski is associated with chess is already sufficient in Nabokov's world for it to be no mere coincidence that Fyodor would have bought the magazine. At first, however, the prospect of writing about Chernyshevski seems so alien to Fyodor that he can refer to it only jokingly. But even after he solves all the problems in the magazine and seems to have put it aside for good, the insistent theme manages to catch his attention. Finally, several days later "he happened to come across" the magazine again, and gets so interested in the excerpt from Chernyshevski's diary that he goes on to borrow his collected works from the library (206: 218).

Like Nabokov, Fyodor sees chess, and especially chess problems, as a high form of art. Not unexpectedly, Fyodor's conception of the process by which chess problems arise is entirely analogous to his view of literary creation. He refers to "an inner impulse which was indistinguishable from poetic inspiration" that provides him with the seed for a future problem. Moreover, only a faith that is capable of overriding reason allows him to pursue the task of capturing the problem: "If he had not been certain (as he also was in the case of literary creation) that the realization ['voploshchenie,' literally 'incarnation'] of the scheme already existed in some other world, from which he transferred it into this one, then the complex and prolonged work on the board would have been an intolerable burden to the mind ['razuma,' literally 'reason'], since it would have to concede, together with the possibility of realization, the possibility of impossibility" (183: 192). This view of chess obviously recalls *The Defense*.

The dependence of art on an otherworldly realm explains why Nabokov has Fyodor experience the "real," temporal world as *unreal* when he is in the throes of inspiration. Like Luzhin following the adjournment of his match with Turati, Fyodor transcends habitual "reality" and seems to shift into another existence altogether when a new poem is born in him: "He was somnambulistically talking to himself as he paced a nonexistent sidewalk; his feet were guided by local consciousness, while the principal Fyodor Konstantinovich, and in fact the only Fyodor Konstantinovich that mattered, was already peering into the next shadowy strophe, which was swinging some yards away and which was destined to resolve itself in a yet-unknown but specifically promised harmony" (67: 64). Although this state (which also recalls Cincinnatus's "double") does not last long, Fyodor reexperiences something like it when he spends an entire morning in bed composing poems. After he concludes, the "real" world and the one he enters during moments of creation are transvalued: "he got up and passed immediately from a world of many interesting dimensions into one that was cramped and demanding" (169–70: 177). Although not illusory in this case, the realm of quotidian existence is less compelling than the otherworld of art.

Fyodor also includes a variant of this transvaluation topos in his rendering of Alexander Chernyshevski's perceptions of his dead son. Imagining how the father may see the young man's ghost, Fyodor remarks: "how much more substantial [the son] was than all those sitting in the room! The sofa could be seen through Vasiliev and the pale girl!" (47: 42). Fyodor's practice of identifying very intimately with the inner lives of interlocutors (see other examples on pp. 41: 36, 47: 43, 48: 44) is a facet of the Nabokovian cognitive stance that includes cosmic synchronization. (Such identification reappears in other works, and reaches its fullest development in the conclusion of *The Real Life of Sebastian Knight*, where the narrator achieves what he believes is a spiritual union with his dead half brother by means of total imaginative sympathy with him.) In contrast to Alexander Chernyshevski, however, Fyodor does not believe that contact with the otherworld is possible to the extent that seeing a ghost would imply. This is an essential accompaniment of Fyodor's often agonizing thoughts about his absent father. Despite these differences between Fyodor and his characters, Yasha's relation to the guests in his parents' apartment is still colored by Fyodor's sense of the relation between higher and mundane reality. The scene can thus be construed as an illustration of the parodic relationship, as Fyodor later calls it, between his own existence, which includes his grief for his father, and Alexander Chernyshevski's grief-induced madness.

The higher reality Fyodor touches during artistic creation is shown in the novel to be capable of coloring an individual for life. In her discussion of the "otherworld" in her husband's works, Vera Nabokov calls attention to Fyodor's description of his father in *The Gift* as providing a "more exact" sense of what this concept entails: "In and around him" Fyodor sees "something difficult to convey in words, a haze, a mystery, an enigmatic reserve. . . . It was as if this genuine, very genuine man possessed an aura of something still unknown but which was perhaps the most genuine of all." Fyodor's emphasis on the word "genuine" in this context recalls the "genuine" voice that he strives to hear when composing his poem, which is linked to the "genuine" artistic gift he carries "like a burden" within himself (106: 107–8); the word thus connects the father's aura to his own artistic creativity. In both cases "genuine" also evokes the transvaluation of conventional reality. Fyodor goes on to explain that the father's aura did not seem to have any direct connection with the other members of the family, or even with butterflies, which are "the closest of all to him." (Since Fyodor discusses butterflies largely in the context of mimetic behavior that implies a transcendent maker, the father's special association with them implies some link to the otherworld as well.) Nevertheless, Fyodor later acknowledges that his family was "imbued with a magic unknown in other families," and that he borrows his own artistic "wings" from this atmosphere (127: 131). In the end, he cannot find a name for his father's mysterious aura, and concludes by citing the opinion of an old family servant (whom he shrouds in an amusingly Gothic atmosphere—"a crooked old man who had twice been singed by night lightning") that "father knew a thing or two that nobody else knew" (126–27: 130–31). Fyodor's description of his father thus echoes several major motifs in the novel, and strongly implies that he had a privileged knowledge of, and position with regard to, the otherworld.

Fyodor's name for cosmic synchronization is "multi-level thinking" ("mnogoplannost' myshleniia"; 175: 183), and his description of the experience, as well as the significance he ascribes to it, is identical to what we find in Nabokov's discursive writings. Fyodor introduces the concept when he complains about having to waste time giving language lessons in order to make a living. What he should be teaching instead is this "mysterious and refined thing" that he alone knows, perhaps out of "a million men." The major example he provides is especially close to Nabokov's in *Speak, Memory* in terms of both the kinds of images it includes and the structural relationship among them:

> you look at a person and you see him as clearly as if he were fashioned of glass and you were the glass blower, while at the same time without in the least impinging upon that clarity you notice some trifle on the side—such as the similarity of the telephone receiver's shadow to a huge, slightly crushed ant, and (all of this simultaneously) the convergence is joined by a third thought—the memory of a sunny evening at a Russian small railway station; i. e., images having no rational connection with the conversation you are carrying on while your mind runs around the outside of your own words and along the inside of those of your interlocutor. (175–76: 183–84)

A number of descriptive passages in *The Gift* are underlain by a consciousness such as the one implied in this example. Moreover, like Nabokov, Fyodor links the experience to the genesis of his art. He indirectly reveals the role that multi-level thinking may have played in his composing the poems about childhood when he decides to review them in his mind. The image he uses for resurrecting all the remembered details out of which they developed stresses the gathering of multifarious phenomena and memories in one point and in one consciousness: he "reconstructed everything . . . as a returning traveler sees in an orphan's eyes not only the smile of its mother, whom he had known in his youth, but also an avenue ending in a burst of yellow light and that auburn leaf on the bench, and everything, everything" (21–22: 16). The same kind of experience underlies the inception of Fyodor's novel that will become *The Gift* when he and Zina are in a restaurant:

> he finally found a certain thread, a hidden spirit, a chess idea for his as yet hardly planned "novel." . . . It was of this that he spoke now, spoke in such a way as if it were really the best and most normal expression of his happiness—which was also expressed in a more accessible edition by such things as the velvetiness of the air, three emerald lime leaves that had got into the lamplight, the icy cold beer, the lunar volcanoes of mashed potato, vague voices, footfalls, the stars among the ruins of clouds. . . .
> "Here's what I'd like to do," he said. (375: 407)

The actual sequence of a perception leading to cosmic synchronization and then to the birth of a poem is dramatized in the scene of Fyodor's walk along a street at night during which mundane reality is transvalued. His constant, painstaking attention to the world around him results in his noticing a circle of light cast by a swinging street lamp. Although at first apparently unrelated to him in any way, it "nevertheless nudged something off the brink of his soul," which turns out to be the beginning of a new poem (66: 64). Fyodor's state in this scene differs from a fully developed moment of multi-level thinking only in the way that the disparate details jell: their unification for Fyodor—and the reader—is signaled and effected via the rich sound repetitions in the original Russian of the passage. Thus, not only does the poem appear to be born out of the acoustically charged nocturnal scene, but the sound repetitions link the verbal components of the description in a way that is analogous to the "metaphoric" links in cosmic synchronization. The following Russian example—in which some of the consonance is indicated by capitalization (assonance is also present but not underscored)—is of course much richer than the English translation: "i uZHe Ne PReZHNiM oTDaleNNyM PRiZyvoM, a PolNyM BliZKiM RoKoToM PRoKatilos' 'BlaGoDaRiu TeBia, oTchiZna'."

Fyodor also resembles Nabokov in *Speak, Memory* when he describes his epiphanic apprehension of the complex life of butterflies in a meadow. He perceives everything "in a flash," and remarks that the truth of the scene could be probed best "by knowledge-amplified love: by its 'wide-open orbs'—to paraphrase Pushkin" (144–45: 150–51). The Russian original refers to "otverstye zenitsy," which, as many commentators have noted, is an allusion to the line "Otverzlis' veshchie zenitsy" ("The vatic orbs opened") from Pushkin's famous poem "Prorok" (1826, "The Prophet"). The relevance of this association for the scene Fyodor is describing is that it echoes the theme of an all-seeing eye in *The Gift*, and underscores again the metaphysical implications of Fyodor's perception.

The relation between Fyodor's father and the ideal form of perspicacity that Nabokov describes in "The Art of Literature and Commonsense" is perhaps the closest in his entire fictional oeuvre. In the lecture, when describing the superiority of the "real writer" to whatever banal evil he confronts, Nabokov evokes the image of the poet Gumilev being led to his execution under Lenin in 1921. This is virtually identical to the scene Fyodor conjures up when trying to imagine how his father might have died if he had been captured by the Reds:

> Did they shoot him in the ladies' room of some godforsaken station (broken looking glass, tattered plush), or did they lead him out into some kitchen garden one dark night and wait for the moon to peep out? How did he wait with them in the dark? With a smile of disdain? And if a whitish moth had hovered among the shadowy burdocks he would, even at that moment, I *know*, have followed it with the same glance of encouragement with which,

on occasion, after evening tea, smoking his pipe in our Leshino garden, he used to greet the pink hawks sampling our lilacs. (149: 155)

But the parallels between the son and the father go even deeper. In *Speak, Memory*, and several of his interviews and articles, Nabokov stresses the necessarily close link that must exist between facts and imagination in both real art and science. In addition to the way this connection is manifested in Fyodor's multi-level thinking and related perceptions, it also appears throughout *The Gift* as a motif that describes Fyodor's artistic imagination in terms of travel imagery, which is of course his father's domain. He remarks, for example, that "much cigarette ash would have to fall under the arm chair" in which he will sit and muse or compose "before it would become suitable for traveling" (20: 14). Later, Fyodor anticipates reaching "the mountain pass to a kind of happiness . . . with pen in hand" (37: 32; other examples appear on pp. 28: 23, 48: 44, 127: 131, 156: 163). This motif takes on a new form in Fyodor's description of a unified or collated, imaginary version of his father's expeditions. Although he begins with such turns of phrase as "I see the caravan" (128: 132), he then shifts to "our caravan" (131: 136), and finally, when especially exotic marvels begin to accumulate, changes exclusively to the first-person singular (134: 139). Since Fyodor's point of view in these passages is merged with what he imagines his father's would have been, the travel descriptions constitute an extreme case of his practice of "sitting inside" someone. Moreover, because Fyodor's dream of his father's return implies that he has transcended death (367: 398), the possibility also exists that Fyodor's imagined identification with his father during the latter's expeditions may have been due to his father's otherworldly influence. This inference is entirely in keeping with the otherworldly provenance of the impulses that underlie artistic creation in Fyodor's and Nabokov's aesthetics.

There are occasions when Fyodor's attention to the world of phenomena does not lead to his experiencing "esthetic bliss." His snarling description of the physically and morally repulsive Berliners in the Grunewald on a warm day (348: 376–77) is a striking contrast to his epiphanic moments. But by including elements he finds odious in his narrative, Fyodor demonstrates that he can rise above the sort of prejudice embodied in his descriptions of Berliners. Although he does not transform them during the act of perception, he does resurrect them in a different light when he incorporates them into his story, in which they are no longer isolated instances of ugliness, but parts of a complex and beautiful artistic weave. For example, Fyodor's references to the Germans' hideous feet and legs in the context of his description of their spiritual poverty cannot but evoke parodic associations with the footstep motif and all that it implies.

The proto-epiphanic connections among seemingly unrelated details in this case occur on the level of Fyodor as author (and his narrative) rather than Fyodor as character (and his lived experiences). And this implies that the reader's and a character's experiences may be comparable because the authorial Fyodor creates a structure similar to what he experiences as a character. Fyodor's incorporation into his art of what he found offensive is also important because it demonstrates the extent to which individual perceptions control the ratio of beauty to ugliness in the world.

In "The Art of Literature and Commonsense," Nabokov explains that not all novels begin with "a kind of glorified physical experience" deriving from sensory details, and that abstract ideas can also be the stimuli for an artist's inspiration (p. 379). Fyodor's response to the excerpt from Chernyshevski's diary that prompts him to write the radical's biography illustrates the analogous role that the printed word can have. Similarly, Fyodor's reading of Pushkin's nonfictional prose triggers "a sweet, strong stab from somewhere" that results in his decision to write a biography of his father (107: 108, 108: 109). An important implication of such deeply personal cognitive relationships that Fyodor can establish with both verbal and natural phenomena is that "reality" is relative—a point Nabokov makes openly in several of his discursive writings. But in addition to embodying this epistemic stance in the behavior of positive characters like Fyodor, Nabokov also affirms it by means of negative examples, such as in the chapter on Chernyshevski in *The Gift*, and in the associated discussions of other radicals including Lenin. Indeed, one of the purposes of these parts of the novel is to provide Fyodor with the opportunity to ridicule materialism and the belief that reality is independent of the perception (255: 273).

It is especially significant for understanding *The Gift* that Fyodor's "multi-level thinking" also provides him with a hint of immortality, or, as he phrases it, "the constant feeling that our days here are only pocket money, farthings clinking in the dark, and that somewhere is stocked the real wealth." The metaphysical implication of this passage is augmented by Fyodor's reference in the next sentence to the (invented?) book *Travels of the Spirit* by a certain "Parker," which sounds like something from the occult or theosophical camp. Fyodor mentions it in support of "the very rare and painful" experience he has had—also apparently a function of "multi-level thinking"—the "so-called 'sense of the starry sky' " (176: 184). His invoking an obscure and possibly apocryphal treatise in support of his experience may be an act of Nabokovian misdirection. Jonas has explained that the image of "the starry sky" was widespread in antiquity from Plato to the Stoics, and symbolized "the purest embodiment of reason in the cosmic hierarchy, the paradigm of intelligibility and therefore of the divine aspect of the sensible realm."⁹ If one deemphasizes the idea of certainty in this description, it comes very close to fitting Fyodor's (and Nabokov's) sense of the relation between this and the other world.

Nabokov also links multi-level thinking to Fyodor's dominant image for the understanding man will achieve after death. Fyodor says he admires the author Delalande (376: 409), and quotes from his *Discours sur les ombres*:

> For our stay-at-home senses the most accessible image of our future comprehension of those surroundings which are due to be revealed to us with the disintegration of the body is the liberation of the soul from the eyesockets of the flesh and our transformation into one complete and free eye, which can simultaneously see in all directions, or to put it differently: a supersensory [sverkhchuvstvennoe] insight into the world accompanied by our inner participation (322: 347).

If realized in practice, a cognitive stance such as this would lead to a state of permanent cosmic synchronization, of limitless consciousness.¹⁰ Fyodor's comment immediately following the quotation, "that this is only symbols—symbols which become a burden to the mind as soon as it takes a close look at them," should not be understood as a dismissal of Delalande's idea, but as an acknowledgment of the difficulty for an earthbound being to grasp the otherworldly.¹¹ (The misleading reference to Delalande as an "elegant atheist" in the passage that follows, together with the other ruminations, clearly belong to the deluded, and dying, Alexander Chernyshevski, not Fyodor [324: 349].) Earlier, Fyodor had made the same point when he expressed his conviction "that extraordinary surprises await us" after death, even though it is a pity that "one can't imagine what one can't compare to anything" (205: 217; this is also the meaning of Fyodor's description of a shuffled fence [188: 198], which anticipates a passage in *Speak, Memory* [p. 221]). Delalande is also the source of a variant of this idea that is linked to the major "house-room-door-key" motif in the novel. Through free indirect discourse, Fyodor implicitly lends his authority to Delalande's view that it is erroneous to see life as a journey because "the other world ['zagrobnoe,' literally 'that which is beyond the coffin'] surrounds us always and is not at all at the end of some pilgrimage." (Fyodor provides a typically Nabokovian, small-scale parodic echo of the erroneous, viatical view of life as a progress toward death and its revelations in his comparison of a mortician's window model of a crematorium to a "Pullman model" that Cook's exhibits [324: 349].) Instead, Fyodor uses a static, and implicitly timeless, metaphor for his sense of the relation between this world and the next: earthly life is a house in which the windows are replaced by mirrors and the door is closed, even though (as Fyodor's experiences amply confirm) intimations of what lies beyond can occur (i.e., "air comes in through the cracks"). Moreover, death—the passageway out of life—bears no relation to whatever other form of existence there is, in the same way that a door is not connected with the topography surrounding a house (321–22: 346–47).

The sense of division between incommensurable realms, albeit with the possibility of occasional, partial, and inconclusive permeability that this imagery conveys, also informs the ghost motif associated with both Alexander Chernyshevski and Fyodor. The major difference between the two is that for the former the "partition dividing the room temperature of reason from the ugly, cold, ghostly world into which Yasha had passed suddenly crumpled." Fyodor echoes Delalande's house imagery when he speaks of the irreparability of the resultant gap, the necessity of draping it, the "stirring folds" one tries not to look at, and the "other world" ("nezemnoe," literally "the unearthly") that seeps into Chernyshevski's life (61: 58–59). By contrast, when Fyodor thinks of meeting his dead father he is "seized . . . by a sickening terror" that yields to "harmony [only] when he removed this meeting beyond the boundary of earthly life" (100: 101). In addition to the parodic relationship between Fyodor and Alexander Chernyshevski that this contrast suggests, the form of the latter's "occult" experience militates against its being creditable in Delalande's (and Fyodor's or Nabokov's) terms. Thus, Chernyshevski's madness is negative and not heaven's sense. In this regard it differs from Luzhin's in *The Defense*, which is never undermined by strong opposing views.

Chernyshevski's behavior in the psychiatric hospital suggests the same conclusion. He wears an odd outfit of "rubber slippers and a waterproof cloak with a hood," which is one of his new methods to "prevent permeation by ghosts" (103: 104). Fyodor is pained when he compares this behavior to the way he imagined that Chernyshevski viewed his dead son when he was only half insane, which suggests that Fyodor makes an important distinction between the man's more and less physical responses to manifestations from the otherworld. Concealed in this description, however, is a connection with the scene of Chernyshevski on his deathbed (324: 349). In a richly ironic passage he says that he is as certain there is no afterlife as that it is raining outside. The poignancy lies in his not realizing that what he hears is not rain but a woman watering her flowers on the floor above. Chernyshevski's waterproof outfit provides a link between the two scenes, and one concludes that his error on his deathbed may also retroactively undermine his view in the psychiatric clinic that ghosts permeate his life. In short, he was prepared for nonexistent rain in both scenes. Moreover, these associations between death and meteorological imagery recall Fyodor's father stepping into a "paradisiacal" rainbow, as well as the footprint Fyodor leaves when stepping across a puddle after a rain shower. The footstep motif's implication that Fyodor's father may have transcended death (and that Fyodor may too at the end of his life) is carefully balanced by Nabokov on the edge of ambiguity: he plants the idea in the reader's mind without actually confirming it. The footstep motif serves well, therefore, as a foil for Alexander Chernyshevski's overly concrete delusions, which have the additional function of camouflaging Fyodor's authorially sanctioned intuitions about the existence of an otherworld.

Fyodor's relatively brief comments about the problem of time, which is a central theme in many of Nabokov's other works, overlaps with his speculations about the relation of mundane existence to a transcendent dimension. In his second imaginary conversation with Koncheyev, he links man's conception of time as flowing ("an essentially phantom process" is the way he characterizes it) to the "material metamorphoses" going on within human beings, which foreshadows Nabokov's similar view in *Speak, Memory* (p. 301), as well as Humbert's in *Lolita*, and Van's in *Ada*. The perception of time is, in other words, a function of man's physicality. More importantly, however, Fyodor adds that the theory of time he finds "most tempting," despite its being "as hopeless a finite hypothesis as all the others," is that "everything is the present situated like a *radiance* outside our blindness" (italics added; 354: 384). This formulation implies a link between spiritual reality and timelessness. It also associates the idea of eternity with the passage about Delalande's "eye," and the attendant imagery of life as a house and the surrounding landscape as the otherworld, thus reinforcing the connection Fyodor implies between seeing and the otherworldly. An illustration of this formulation appeared in the first element in the footstep motif—Fyodor's clairvoyant perception in a "*radiantly* pale sky" of a boat drawn up on shore and of footsteps "filled with *bright* water" leading from it (italics added; 34: 29). Because of this motif's association with privileged insight and the transcendence of death, it can be said to illustrate Fyodor's intuition (he does not actually see the boat) that the otherworld is an immanent present. Nabokov repeats the same idea in *Strong Opinions* when he says that consciousness linked to time is what characterizes man, whereas "consciousness without time" would be characteristic of "some still higher state" than man's (p. 30).

As he also does in *Speak, Memory*, Nabokov embodies the idea that everything is the present and that time is illusory in the syntax of *The Gift*. Instances of this appear at the beginning and the end of Fyodor's recollections of Russia on the eve of his mother's arrival in Berlin. Imagining a stroll around the family estate, he comes to a group of fir trees, and, in a continuation of the same sentence, remembers how they would be covered with snow, and how the snow "used to fall straight and slow, it could fall like that for three days, five months, nine years—and already, ahead, in a clear space traversed by white specks, one glimpsed a dim yellow light approaching, which suddenly came into focus, shuddered, thickened and turned into a tramcar" on a Berlin street (92: 92). The presence of the past and the present in the same sentence draws an implicit equation between the two, thus suggesting that Fyodor's memory is capable of resurrecting the past so vividly that it acquires the immediacy of the present. (This is reinforced by Fyodor's saying when he is actually on a Berlin street that he remembered how he had approached an old reaper "here"—that is, on the family's estate, years ago—to ask him for a light [90: 90].) Nabokov validates this incident and adds to its resonance by linking it to the theme of the otherworld in the novel. As Fyodor puts it, speaking about himself in the third person, "straight from the hothouse *paradise* of the past, he *stepped* onto a Berlin tramcar." The underscored words evoke the image four pages earlier of Fyodor's father stepping into and out of a "paradisiacal" rainbow. The implication of the parallel drawn between the two scenes is that memory is also linked to the otherworldly realm that is associated with the footstep motif, which is of course borne out by Nabokov's discussion of memory in *Strong Opinions,* as well as by Fyodor's in *The Gift.* When one considers how much value artifice has in Nabokov's and Fyodor's metaphysical aesthetics, it is highly unlikely that the epithet "hothouse" could have been meant to indicate a pejorative artificiality.

The next transition between present and past in the same sentence occurs in the opposite direction, when Fyodor brushes against Christmas trees set out for sale on a Berlin street and walks out into a summer day on the estate in Russia (97: 97). Again, the memories are as intense as Fyodor's contemporaneous perceptions in Berlin. And lest the reader doubt the ontological substantiality of the events illuminated, or better perhaps to say resurrected, by memory, Nabokov has Fyodor comment that minutes after his mother arrives time collapses: "the light of the past had overtaken the present, had soaked it to the saturation point, and everything became the same as it had been in this very Berlin three years previously, as it had once been in Russia, as it had been, and would be, forever" (98–99: 99). The extensive references to light, vision, and memory in the scene of the mother's arrival function as direct connections to Fyodor's metaphor about the present being like a "radiance" outside temporally induced "blindness," which in turn evokes the complex net of associations that abuts the theme of the otherworld. (Similar "slippages" in time also appear in other contexts [60: 57, 218: 232].)

One of the most significant parallels between *The Gift* and *Speak, Memory* is the extent to which patterning in life, nature, and art function as manifestations of the otherworld. Fyodor conveys this insight in a variety of ways, including the fabric motif that suggests that his and his sister's lives were shaped by a transcendent agency. Similarly, when he reveals his love to Zina he states that he has often felt the magical strangeness of life, "as if a corner of it had been turned back for an instant and he had glimpsed its unusual lining" (195: 205). Furthermore, an unobtrusive but significant detail in the scene implies a connection between Fyodor's intuitions about fate and the metaphysical associations of the footstep motif. He and Zina are standing in a doorway, illuminated by light from the street, "while a prismatic *rainbow* lay on the wall" (italics added). The insight Fyodor has into the determined shape of their lives thus seems to be sanctioned by proximity to a phenomenon that had been defined earlier in the novel as "paradisiacal," and that has a significant link to Fyodor's father and the theme of immortality. Fyodor also echoes fabric imagery in a different way when he says that Zina was "cleverly and elegantly made to measure for him by a very painstaking fate," that the two of them formed "a single shadow, [and] were made to the measure of something not quite comprehensible, but wonderful and benevolent and continuously surrounding them" (189: 199). Later he marvels at length about the elaborate methods that fate had used to bring him and Zina together (374–76: 407–9), thus finally becoming conscious of the several missed opportunities that had been quietly alluded to in the text (e.g., 71: 69, 82: 80, 156: 162). Fyodor in effect infers the existence of a potent otherworldly dimension from the structural repetitions in his life that he then embodies in the novel he writes about it. And his sense "that he already knew a great deal about" Zina before he even met her (189: 199) also implies a fateful, "Platonic" link between them.

A similar fatidic pattern can be discerned in the way a publisher, who "happens" to resemble Alexander Chernyshevski, accepts Fyodor's book about the radical Chernyshevski through the "chance" intercession of the farcical writer Busch. Fyodor's euphoria is such that he sees "the drizzle" on the street as "a dazzling dew," and "rainbow nimbi" around street-lamps (222–23: 236–37). These details again evoke Fyodor's father in the context of the footstep motif. The fact that oblique references to him appear in connection with two highly significant events in Fyodor's life—his meeting a young woman who is a perfect match for him, and his suddenly being presented with a publisher for his book—is itself telling and implies an additional level of fateful patterning (which, however, only the reader can recognize, assuming, for lack of specific evidence to the contrary, that Fyodor in his guise as author is unaware of it). Because the metaphysics of *The Gift* include an otherworldly dimension that can be active in human affairs, the rainbows accompanying major peripeties in Fyodor's life may indicate his deceased father's influence on it in the form of a beneficent fate.

Fyodor comes to a very similar conclusion later in the novel, which

emerges from an epiphanic moment that dispels a temporary depression
caused by morbid thoughts:

> with a kind of relief—as if the responsibility for his soul belonged not to him
> but to someone who knew what it all meant—he felt that all this skein of
> random thoughts, like everything else as well—the seams and sleaziness of
> the spring day, the ruffle of the air, the coarse, variously intercrossing threads
> of confused sounds—was but the reverse side of a magnificent fabric, on the
> front of which there gradually formed and became alive images invisible to
> him. (326: 351)

An additional conclusion that can be drawn from this passage is that free
will is precluded in Fyodor's world view. This agrees with the ironic comment he makes to Zina about having successfully foiled one of fate's early
attempts to bring them together (375: 407); whatever success he has had
is clearly only temporary.

In addition to Fyodor's conception of his own life with Zina as patterned and fated, he also comments repeatedly on other aspects of the
world in which he exists as having been "made." His childhood memories
include a winter day in a park in which "the trees . . . mimed their own
ghosts [meaning, presumably, that their shapes were echoed by the snow
or frost on them] and the whole effect revealed immense talent" (31: 26).
Moving to the human realm, he thinks of the misfortunes of the Alexander Chernyshevskis—the son's suicide and the father's consequent
madness—as "a kind of mocking variation on the theme of his own hope-
suffused grief" about his father. But later Fyodor grasps "the full refinement of the corollary and all the irreproachable compositional balance
with which these collateral sounds had been included in his own life"
(104: 105; he sees a similar connection between his research about his
father and about Nikolai Chernyshevski [211: 224]). As we have seen,
Alexander Chernyshevski's preoccupation with his dead son's ghost does
in fact bear a complex parodic relationship to Fyodor's speculations
about an otherworld.

Often it is Fyodor's perception of something as beautiful that leads him
to infer the existence of a hidden maker. Near the end of the novel he sees
five nuns walking through a forest, singing, and plucking an occasional
flower, which prompts him to comment how skillfully "staged" the whole
scene was, "what a director lurked behind the pines, how well everything
was calculated" (356: 386). The impression that there is a creative consciousness behind what Fyodor sees is augmented by the fact that he mentions being struck by the swaying of a stalk of grass one of the nuns failed
to tear loose. Although Fyodor the character is puzzled about where he
had seen something similar in the past, and cannot identify the event, the
reader can. Earlier in the novel Fyodor had described the birth of a poem

as having been prompted by the sight of a street lamp swaying (66: 64). The reader who makes this connection is in the position of identifying a subtle pattern in Fyodor's life of which he is apparently unaware. The link between the two passages is confirmed by their sharing consonance of *p* and *r*.

In addition to perceptible patterning, the dominant feature of the world that leads Fyodor to conclude it has been fashioned by a higher agency is that it is filled with deceptions—or patterning that is misleading at first sight. An example is Fyodor's scathing portrait of a fellow passenger on a streetcar, whom he takes to be a quintessential German. But when the man inadvertently reveals himself to be a Russian émigré, Fyodor is not chagrined at his mistake: "That's wonderful [he thought] almost smiling with delight. How clever, how gracefully sly and how essentially good life is!" (94: 94).

The most dramatic and significant instances of deception that Nabokov presents in *The Gift* are drawn from natural history, especially from mimicry among insects. Fyodor follows his father in inferring something like a transcendent maker from "the incredible artistic wit of mimetic disguise, which was not explainable by the struggle for existence . . . was too refined for the mere deceiving of accidental predators, feathered, scaled and otherwise . . . and seemed to have been invented *by some waggish artist* precisely for the intelligent eyes of man" (italics added; 122: 126). There follow examples of remarkable instances of mimicry among butterflies that obviously derive from Nabokov's own lifelong love of lepidoptery. Fyodor also finds descriptions of analogous examples of telling artifice in the memoirs of famous explorers, such as "the mirages where nature, that exquisite cheat, achieved absolute miracles: visions of water were so clear that they reflected the *real* rocks nearby!" (132: 137). As a result, Fyodor elevates natural artifice into a fundamental principle of existence: "the most enchanting things in nature and art are based on deception" (376: 408–9). As we have seen, Nabokov would stress the same points years later in interviews collected in *Strong Opinions*: not only does mimicry transcend "the crude purpose of mere survival" (p. 153), but cunning artifice lies at the heart of nature as a whole—"all is deception in that good cheat, from the insect that mimics a leaf to the popular enticements of procreation" (p. 11).

The issue of natural deceptions inevitably raises questions about the extent to which these may be the perceiver's delusions. The perils of solipsism constitute a major theme in many of Nabokov's novels, including *Despair*, *Lolita*, and *Pale Fire*. In *The Gift* Fyodor is very careful to distinguish between true perceptions about nature and human projections onto it. He quotes his father on the importance of not letting "our reason . . . prompt us with explanations which then begin imperceptibly to influence the very course of observation and distort it: thus the shadow of the instrument falls upon the truth" (342–43: 370). In the novel's own terms, therefore, patterning and deception that are perceived in nature should be understood not as an imposition of human order onto it, but as a discovery of something that really exists in it.

Artifice of course implies an artificer, but in keeping with Nabokov's own reticence about such matters, Fyodor never gives a name to the agency or force behind the world's multifarious designs. The closest he comes to even trying is near the end of the novel when he is reveling in the pleasures of a summer morning. Using theatrical imagery that recalls *Invitation to a Beheading*, he exclaims, "there really is something, there is something!" at the "bottom of things," something is "concealed behind all this, behind the play, the sparkle, the thick, green greasepaint of the foliage." All he can say about this agent, however, is "one wants to offer thanks but there is no one to thank" (340: 368). The weight of the evidence in *The Gift* suggests this remark should be understood to mean that there is "no one" *visible* or *knowable* "to thank," and certainly not that nothing exists at all.

As the footstep motif illustrates, there are also categories of patterning that appear to be beyond even Fyodor's ken. One of the most prevalent and important of these is that of keys. Fyodor misplaces, or has stolen from him several sets of keys to the buildings and apartments in which he lodges (65: 63, 357: 387). After his landlords, the Shchyogolevs, leave Berlin, Fyodor and Zina look forward to having their apartment to themselves, and each thinks that the other has keys to it, whereas in fact neither one does (369: 401, 371: 403). On a simple level, this comic misunderstanding culminates in the reader's realization that after the novel concludes, Fyodor and Zina will not in fact be able to get into the apartment and consummate their love, something for which Fyodor yearns, as he suggests by means of a wittily erotic description of a growing thunder cloud (357–58: 388). This realization is obviously part of what Fyodor (speaking as the author in the novel's final paragraph) implies that the reader will be able to infer about events beyond the novel's conclusion. On a more profound level, the key motif articulates with several of the most serious themes in *The Gift*. The reader's inference about a future event in Fyodor's and Zina's lives constitutes a parodic parallel to Fyodor's anticipation of a future reunion with his dead father. The motif's obvious connection with door imagery justifies this conclusion, because if houses are like life, and doors—which are like death—are transitions to another form of existence, then Fyodor's being locked out of his dwelling places associates him with the otherworldly, and thus with his father. The reader's ability to "foresee" an event in Zina's and Fyodor's future also evokes the conception of time as being illusory that Fyodor quotes from Delalande. By being aware simultaneously of the characters' past, present, and (partial) future, the reader is put into the position, in the novel's own terms, of viewing their lives from an otherworldly perspective. The key motif is also directly linked to Fyodor's art: "I took away the key to [Russia]" he writes to his mother when he explains why he is certain that one day he will return to his homeland in his books (362: 393).[12]

To speak of patterning in *The Gift* that may transcend Fyodor's craftsmanship is of course not to deny that the novel also calls attention to itself as artifice on a more mundane level. By saying that he will "shuffle, twist, mix, rechew everything, add such spices of my own and impregnate things so much with myself that nothing remains of the autobiography but dust—the kind of dust, of course, which makes the most orange of skies" (376: 409), Fyodor is candidly informing Zina (and the reader) of his intention to produce an obvious artifact rather than a text masquerading as an unmediated "slice of life." Suffice it to mention that there are numerous details and passages in the work that are deceptive at first glance and that become intelligible only in retrospect, thus providing evidence for *The Gift* doubling back on itself—for being the novel Fyodor wrote as well as the story of his life. Some of the most striking instances have to do with point of view, such as the widespread and, at first, bewildering alternations between Fyodor as "he" in one sentence and "I" in the next (particularly noticeable in the English translation) that are due to Fyodor's shifts between speaking from the viewpoint of an author and that of a character. Similarly, Fyodor's movements into the minds of other characters (e.g., 47: 42), which occur without any transition or warning to the reader, as well as his dialogues with the writer Koncheyev, which suddenly prove imaginary (e.g., 84:63), also become, in retrospect, instances of deftly wrought deception. Fyodor's dream of his father is presented in the same way: it is not until we encounter references in it to flannel pants and a laprobe—the items recently stolen from Fyodor in the Grunewald—that we realize he is dreaming (364–65: 396).

Such unsignaled transitions between events that are real on the one hand, and dreamed or imagined on the other have the important ancillary effect of blurring the distinction between imagination and reality. By initially placing both on the same level in the text, and by describing what happens in his mind's eye in the same detail as what he actually perceives, Fyodor grants a mode of reality to imagined events that persists even when their true nature is revealed. Moreover, given Fyodor's intention to transfigure his autobiography in his imagination, the reader cannot know for certain which of the events that comprise *The Gift* were originally "real," and which imagined. The ultimate meaning of this feature of the work is identical to that of Fyodor's practice of "sitting in" people he knows. Rather than resulting in the creation of a fiction in the sense of a falsehood, his imaginative exercises are intuitive extrapolations from observed facts in the external world to some fuller totality of which they are an implicit part. Fyodor's comment that he knows Koncheyev well without actually knowing him (353: 382) illustrates this point by implying that he can infer the man from his works. (Nabokov comes to the same conclusion in his 1937 lecture on Pushkin, which, together with Fyodor's comment, prefigures directly V.'s claims in *The Real Life of Sebastian Knight* for intuitive spiritual union as a model for the insights one will gain after death.) And because Fyodor's free-wheeling imagination is rooted in sensory or intellectual data, and is apparently inspired by the otherworld, it emerges as analogous to cosmic synchronization.

Smaller details that serve to underscore the "madeness" of *The Gift* include Fyodor's remarks to an unnamed female persona that appear in the text prior to his meeting Zina (e.g., 65: 62, 162: 169). Upon rereading, these emerge as the authorial Fyodor's intrusions into the generally chronological story of his life. However, because the pronominal references are completely abstract before we meet Zina, they also function as expressions of Fyodor's general, unfocused anticipation of meeting a perfect soul mate, which is precisely how he refers to Zina in the passages about fate bringing them together. This may be seen as analogous to his anticipation of his future works, and implies, as does the case of Luzhin and his fiancée, that their souls may indeed have been matched in a Platonic otherworld. Finally, the numerous instances of sound repetitions in the novel, which are of course more prevalent in the Russian original (e.g., pp. 13–14, 16, 24, 224, 369), also undermine its mimetic dissimulations and, concurrently, serve as subtle links between recurrences in Fyodor's life.[13]

Seeing clearly and deeply, whether the object is one's own life, a natural phenomenon, or a work of literature is inextricably linked for Fyodor, as it is for Nabokov, with truth and beauty. Conversely, generalizations and superficial perceptions lead, at the very least, to falsehood, delusion, and pusillanimity. At worst, as in the case of Hermann in *Despair* and Humbert in *Lolita*, they lead to crime. Thus one could argue that from the point of view of Nabokov's linked aesthetic, ethical, and metaphysical criteria, the primary function of the renowned "Chernyshevski" chapter in *The Gift* is to present a negative example of what Fyodor embodies in a positive form.[14]

Other than some admiration for the famous radical's stunted spiritual élan, Fyodor's overwhelming attitude toward Nikolai Chernyshevski throughout his biography is devastating mockery. He is presented consistently as the slave of commonplaces and clichés (246: 262). He also had no understanding of real art (250: 266–67), no knowledge of various human artifacts, or of nature, which is particularly striking in a professed materialist, as Fyodor stresses. In view of Chernyshevski's ignorance of natural history, his being sent into exile in Siberia—a "bewitched, strangely luxuriant" natural setting in Fyodor's view—emerges as "an elemental, mythological punishment" (255–56: 273). Fyodor further generalizes that such ignorance of nature is widespread among "average Russian literati" (327: 353).[15]

Many others are guilty of comparable unforgivable lapses in Fyodor's eyes. "I used to feel a cloying nausea," he explains, "when I heard or read the latest drivel, vulgar and humorless drivel, about the 'symptoms of the age' and the 'tragedy of youth' " (52–53: 48–49). Similarly, when describing the three young people who constitute a bathetic romantic triangle, he remarks that "Olya studied the history of art (which, in the context of the epoch, sounds—as does the tone of the entire drama in question—like an unbearably typical *and therefore false*, note)" (italics added; 56: 53). It is significant that the italicized phrase is one that does not appear in the Russian original, which suggests that Nabokov must have added it in order to stress the connection between falsehood and generalization, a point that recurs not only throughout his own works, but with special vehemence in his prefaces to English translations of his novels. Beyond illustrating a commonplace, the function of the triangle Fyodor includes in his novel is that the varieties of tawdry love uniting the three young people emerge as grotesque parodies of his and Zina's pure and noble love (and, probably, of the *ménage à trois* in Nikolai Chernyshevski's notorious novel *What Is to Be Done?*). Fyodor treats newspaper accounts of international events with the same sarcasm that he applies to his landlord's self-deluding ordering of those events into schemes that he believes allow him effortless insight into world politics (171–72: 179). Virtually everything German is presented by Fyodor as obtuse and odious (an attitude about which Nabokov expressed some regret in the Foreword to the English translation of *The Gift*), but most Russian émigrés in Berlin are not spared either (e.g., 80: 79, 313–19: 337–44, 330–36: 356–63). The implication is everywhere that people do not see, read, or think clearly enough, or are too limited to grasp the truth. At the same time, it should be mentioned that Fyodor's extensive descriptions of what might be termed highly localized color contradict his own tastes in literature, as well as Nabokov's similar, later pronouncements against writers whose works treat eccentric national subject matter, such as Leskov.[16]

However, Nabokov's purpose in portraying purblind, and, consequently, morally tarnished characters is not only to establish a satirical contrast that makes his cognitive and aesthetic values stand out in bolder

relief. He shows a concern with broad historical issues when he describes
Fyodor's initial response to the picture of Chernyshevski in the chess magazine as a "bitter pang" about the plight of Russia under the Soviets, a
reaction that leads to his desire to understand its origins (187: 197).
Moreover, Fyodor explains that he wants everything in his biography of
the radical to be "on the very brink of parody." In an interview, Nabokov
drew a sharp distinction between parody and satire, calling the first "a
game" and the second "a lesson."[17] The implication is that parody is
more a tricky thematic or formal echoing than a value-laden caricature
whose intention is to deflate its target. Although Nabokov indicated that
his art was concerned only with parody, it is far from clear that he always
differentiates between it and satire in *The Gift*. Fyodor's ridiculing sacred
cows like Chernyshevski, especially in the context of his inquiry into the
sorry state of the Soviet Union, is less like implicitly disinterested play
than a cautionary tale with an ethical aim. Nevertheless, Fyodor's remark
about parody in the Chernyshevski biography needs to be considered seriously, even though it raises a question that he never answers directly—
what is it that will be parodied? Some indication of what this could be
may be gleaned from Fyodor's insistence that there has to be "an abyss of
seriousness" in his planned book, "and I must make my way along this
narrow ridge between my own truth and a caricature of it" (212: 225).
Presumably, Fyodor's "own truth" includes such thematic dominants in
The Gift as his intuitions about fate in his and Zina's lives, the significance of mimicry in nature, his ability via cosmic synchronization to
grasp unity in diversity, his own aesthetic principles as described and embodied in the novel, and related topics. In most abstract terms, therefore,
Fyodor's "truth" is centered on being conscious of varieties of patterning
and of their implied relation to an otherworld. If we now return to the
fact that Fyodor initially approaches Chernyshevski in the context of
Russian history, it seems reasonable to search for a parodic relationship
between the biography and other historical phenomena described or implied in the novel. Regarding this, Nabokov provides a useful hint in his
Foreword to the English translation, where he acknowledges that *The
Gift* reflects the ascendancy of the Nazi dictatorship in 1935–37, the period when he wrote the novel, rather than 1926–29, when its action takes
place (p. 10). There is hardly any mention of contemporary German politics in *The Gift*. But there are definite similarities between the Russian
nineteenth-century radicals (with their ever-present implied prefiguration
of Soviet tyranny) and the average Germans among whom Fyodor lives.
Both manifest complacency, blindness, lack of imagination, and unfastid-
iousness in Fyodor's eyes; there is, moreover, a similarity between the
rhetoric of violence among the Russians (276: 294) and the obvious potential for it among the Germans (348: 377). It has now become a com-

monplace that the Soviet and Nazi systems resembled each other in fundamental ways more than they differed, even though their relationship was, with the short-lived exception of the Molotov-Ribbentrop pact, virulently antagonistic. There are of course important differences between a small group of Russian nineteenth-century radicals—to whom Nabokov does grant a modicum of admiration for their pugnacity and reformist zeal, especially in comparison to their opponents (215: 228), and the vast numbers of German burghers for whom Fyodor feels nothing but revulsion. But Nabokov's early recognition of what could be termed the "parodic" relationship between the historical seeds of Bolshevism and the constituency of Hitler's Germany suggests more historical perspicacity than he is usually given credit for. A related series of parodic echoes, or as Fyodor puts it, "weird comparisons," links such seemingly antipodal Russian cultural phenomena as official censorship edicts in early nineteenth-century Russia and the unavowed ideological censorship of the radicals, or the toadying of the writer Bulgarin before official government ideology and the sycophancy of Turgenev before radical critics (214–15: 227–28). The addition of prerevolutionary Russian events to the parallels between Nazi Germany and the Soviet Union elevates Fyodor's observations to a general condemnation of all polities. This social-historical outlook may be one level in the "abyss of seriousness" that Fyodor wants to create in his novel. And it is hardly a surprising conclusion, given Fyodor's and Nabokov's insistence on absolute independence from any idea that is either received or widespread.

On a more personal level, however—which is unquestionably the more important one in *The Gift*—the relationship between Fyodor and Chernyshevski, as well as between those who are in each character's camp, can also be considered parodic. Thus, the vulgar Shchyogolev's casual remark "when good friends of mine die, I always think that up there they will do something to improve my destiny here" (326: 351), is a parody of the role that the spirit of Fyodor's father may play in his life. And just as Fyodor focuses on fateful patterning in his own life, he pays particular attention to identifying it in Chernyshevski's, and lists several recurring themes he has discovered—"writing exercises," "nearsightedness" and spectacles, "traveling," "angelic clarity," and Chernyshevski's Christ-like pose (226–28: 241–43). The discovery that the radical's father had once advised his son to write a light little "tale" ("skazochka"), and that years later Chernyshevski informed his wife that he wanted to compose a "good little tale," prompts Fyodor to note that this is "one of those rare correlations that constitute the researcher's pride" (300: 321). Elsewhere, Fyodor claims that "fate sorts" dates "in anticipation of the researcher's needs" (232: 247). Throughout these examples, there is an implied contrast between the use to which Fyodor puts the recurrences he recognizes

in Chernyshevski's life, and the latter's own extremely low level of awareness about what is truly significant in his existence.

On a different textual level, Fyodor's remark that Minister of Justice
Nabokov was involved in Nikolai Chernyshevski's being moved to Astra-
khan during his exile (304: 325) ties the life of *The Gift*'s real author,
whose grandfather actually was Alexander the Third's minister of justice,
to the radical. This creates an additional parodic dimension in the novel
because the fictional characters' experiences are made to echo the historical author's own search for fatidic patterning in his life. (Moreover, Fyodor's motivation in writing his novel is a desire to trace fate's patterns in
his life, which is analogous to Nabokov's avowed intention in writing
Speak, Memory.) A similar, extratextual association between the novel
and Nabokov emerges from the reference that the minor character Shirin
makes to the émigré writers Podtyagin and Ivan Luzhin (329: 355). The
former is a character in Nabokov's first novel *Mary* (*Mashen'ka*, 1926),
and the latter is the protagonist's father in *The Defense*. (Fyodor's citations from Delalande are a similar evocation of one of Nabokov's earlier
works.) These references are of course not signaled in *The Gift* in any
way. But they can be considered aspects of Nabokov's parodic design in
the novel because they are artistic constructs whose artificiality is doubly
concealed by their being mentioned in a different work from the one in
which they originated. Their resulting heightened "reality" (i.e., they
have an existence outside *The Gift*) can be seen as constituting the author's play with the idea that art derives in part from a higher reality, as
Fyodor's experiences actually demonstrate. An additional function of this
practice of self-reference, is to present the reader with the opportunity to
recognize a form of patterning that stretches across Nabokov's oeuvre. In
this guise, the concealed references are related to the entire complex of
values that he associates with enhanced consciousness.

Chernyshevski's blindness to nature also enters into the parodic relationship he has with other characters in *The Gift*. Fyodor recalls how his
father once brought back from an expedition "the *complete* vegetable
covering of a motley little mountain meadow," and imagines it as being
"rolled up in a case like a Persian carpet" (126: 130). This was a gift for
a botanist, and obviously reflects the value Fyodor's father placed on precise observation, as well as the organic unity of apprehension implied by
cosmic synchronization. Chernyshevski, by contrast, "was always ready
to embrace the rolled-up carpet of any chance subject and unfold it whole
before the reader" (246: 262), which is evidence of his reductive, unimag-
inative, and purely compilational bent of mind. (Similarly, Chernyshevski's pathetic sending of flowers that he could not identify to his son [301:
322] is a parody of the highly knowledgeable collecting carried out by
Fyodor's father.) A related image of a "rolled up . . . bundle" pertaining

to events in the life of Alexander Chernyshevski's family (349: 378) serves as a parodic link to a variety of themes and situations centering on death and an afterlife in the novel Fyodor writes (as well as to the important "fabric motif").

The parodic possibilities of having a family named Chernyshevski in a novel containing a biography of their famous namesake (whose father, as Fyodor implies, may "in fact" have baptized their ancestor [52: 48]) are further exploited in connection with the theme of death and the otherworld. One of Nikolai Chernyshevski's sons, Alexander, "was afraid of space, or more exactly, he was afraid of slipping into a different dimension" (309: 331). As we have seen, Yasha, the son of the "other" Alexander Chernyshevski in the novel, does in fact appear to his father to have slipped into a ghostly dimension, a possibility that Fyodor does not altogether discount. Another example is that the radical Chernyshevski's last words on his deathbed are parodied by those Fyodor's friend Alexander Chernyshevski utters when he is dying. The first comments "that there is not a single mention of God" in a book that Fyodor, to his regret, cannot identify through his research (312: 334). Alexander Chernyshevski cannot remember what a certain unnamed book is about (it is in fact probably Fyodor's biography of Nikolai Chernyshevski; Alexander Chernyshevski's reference to a priest in connection with the book may indicate his having confused the radical with his father, who was a priest); and he concludes, with a naive certainty that is undermined by his mistake about the weather, that there is no God (324: 349). One of Alexander Chernyshevski's final thoughts is that he will understand the ultimate mystery of existence if he can make the final, requisite mental effort (322: 347). Because of his erroneous conclusion about God in connection with the sound of falling water, this final thought emerges as a parodic echo of Fyodor's impression that he will be able to fathom the mystery of why moths fly to light if only he thinks hard enough (205: 217). Although Fyodor does not solve this particular riddle, he does have intuitions about the otherworld on the basis of various other data from natural history, whereas his friend of course does not. Alexander Chernyshevski's final thoughts also contain a parody of Fyodor's idea about the calming similarity between the darkness preceding life and that following it. By contrast, his friend thinks of "the deathly horror of birth" (323: 348).

An obvious and essential dimension of Nabokov's parodic design in *The Gift* is the extensive evocation and discussion of Russian writers and literary works, and, to a lesser extent, other aspects of Russian culture. The importance of being able to incorporate these into an understanding of the novel is marked by the fact that Nabokov frequently highlights them in the English translation by identifying authors and works for the obvious benefit of readers not familiar with Russian literature. This ranges from echoes of Pushkin, to fantasies about him had he survived his duel (which has an evident parodic relation to Fyodor's attempts to imagine what could have happened to his father), to transparent images of Russian émigré litterateurs in interwar Europe, to imitations of Turgenev's device of buttonholing his reader, of Symbolist dramatic bathos, and of Andrei Belyi's prose rhythms. By contrast, when Nabokov refers to the incidental character "X. B. Lambovski" as having something "Paschal about him" (119: 122–23), he also preserves at least one detail from the Russian that the English reader could not possibly understand. The man's surname in Russian is Baranovski, which derives from *baran*, meaning "ram," whence the related, Paschal "lamb" in English (with the difference that "baran" also implies "dolt" in Russian). But hidden in this "translation" is the fact that the man's initials, if read as Cyrillic letters, are the traditional abbreviation for the Russian Orthodox Easter greeting in Old Church Slavonic "Christ is risen" ("Khristos voskrese").

Because literary and cultural references are aspects of *The Gift* that have received considerable treatment in the criticism,[18] there is no need to catalogue them further here. It should be noted, however, that the function of these echoes in the novel emerges as threefold. Firstly, Fyodor openly censures many of the best-known writers and works, and thus presents them as a background against which his aesthetic values stand out. (It would be wrong to infer, however, that Nabokov shares all of Fyodor's views, as Koncheyev's authoritative rebuttals imply. In the Foreword to the English translation, Nabokov indicates that he gave some parts of himself to Koncheyev and the incidental character Vladimirov [p. 9].) Secondly, by praising isolated aspects of the Russian literary legacy, Fyodor implicitly includes them in his sui generis aesthetics. And thirdly, the reader (of the Russian original) is placed in the position of having to identify numerous references to Russian literature that are hidden in the text. They are thus subordinated to the novel's overarching preoccupation with Nabokov's favorite themes and structures relating to patterning, camouflage, insight, and consciousness. Nabokov's use of other primary "vehicles" than Russian literature when treating these themes in earlier and later works (chess in *The Defense*, for example, or sexual perversity in *Lolita*) indicates that Russian literature was neither specially privileged, nor of course an end in itself for him, even though literary echoes from various traditions are important constituents of all his works. As Nabokov implied in *Speak, Memory* literature is but one of several gifts that human beings have been granted.

The Real Life of Sebastian Knight

THE REAL LIFE of *Sebastian Knight* (1941) was the first novel Nabokov wrote in English.[1] It tells the story of an attempt by a Russian émigré, who refers to himself only as "V.," to learn the truth about his dead half brother, a famous English writer named Sebastian Knight, and to write his biography. What is noteworthy about V.'s quest is that it consists not only of a predictably assiduous search for facts, but of a surprising series of accidental discoveries and coincidences as well. V. also relies extensively on hunches and intuitions that go against all "commonsensical" standards of reason, "realism," and narrative reliability. However, rather than undermine the authority of V.'s narrative altogether, his practices, when seen together with other evidence in the novel, suggest that he may have been guided in his task by none other than his dead brother's spirit.[2]

Support for the seemingly unconscionable and unreliable methods that V. uses to infer information about Sebastian can be found in a remarkable lecture Nabokov gave in French in 1937 that is crucial for understanding both this novel and a number of his later works—"Pouchkine, ou le vrai et le vraisemblable" ("Pushkin, or the Real and the Plausible").[3] In the context of discussing the genre of fictionalized biography, Nabokov asks a question that is clearly relevant for V.'s quest in *The Real Life of Sebastian Knight*: "Is it possible to imagine the full reality of another's life, to relive it in one's mind and set it down intact on paper?" Nabokov's answer is "I doubt it: one even finds oneself seduced by the idea that thought itself, as it shines its beam on the story of a man's life, cannot avoid deforming it. Thus, what our mind perceives turns out to be plausible [le vraisemblable], but not true [le vrai]" (40: 367). This application of an analogue of the Heisenberg uncertainty principle to biography would seem to undermine the biographer's endeavor a priori. But Nabokov's conclusion is different: "After all, what does it matter if what we perceive is but a monstrous hoax? Let us be honest and admit that if our mind could reverse direction and worm its way into Pushkin's age, we would not recognize it. What is the difference! The joy that we derive is one that the bitterest criticism, including that which I direct at myself, cannot destroy" (40: 367). Although these remarks may seem to be a celebration of hedonistic solipsism, Nabokov is in fact implying that the intuitions, conjectures, and extrapolations that contribute to a fictionalized biography carry with them the potential for their own validation: "if I inject into them [i.e., images from Pushkin's life that may be 'false'] a bit of the same love that I feel when reading his poems, is not what I am doing with this imaginary life somehow akin to [qui ressemble à] the poet's work, if not to the poet himself?" (40: 369). In Nabokov's world view what warrants artistic intuitions such as these is of course the connection he posits between imagination and the otherworld, especially as suggested in "The Art of Literature and Commonsense." And, indeed, specific formulations in this lecture are foreshadowed by passages in the lecture on Pushkin: Nabokov asserts in the latter that "goodness and beauty retain their place of honor [in the world]"; and that if "at times life appears pretty dim to us it is because we are nearsighted" (42: 377). He also describes a series of "revelations" and "delights" in "everyday existence" that confirm his optimism, which leads him to ask "who on earth . . . can be this artist who suddenly transforms life into a small masterpiece?" The terms of this question, and the examples of theater in life that follow (42: 377–78), are familiar from Nabokov's other writings as allusions to telling artifice in nature and human existence that imply an otherworldly maker.

The practices and assumptions Nabokov outlines in the Pushkin lecture are embodied in works from different periods of his career, including his life of Chernyshevski in *The Gift*, as well as his more overtly scholarly biographies of Gogol and Abram Gannibal (who was Pushkin's African ancestor, and whose life Nabokov investigates in an appendix to his translation of *Eugene Onegin*; elements of a Pushkin biography based on the same principles are scattered throughout the Commentary to the translation).[4] Nabokov's biographical method is certainly unorthodox. But accepting or rejecting it is ultimately of lesser importance than understanding its sui generis character and the uses to which Nabokov puts it in his fictions, especially *The Real Life of Sebastian Knight* and, later, *Pale Fire*.

Although the language in which Nabokov wrote *The Real Life of Sebastian Knight* was a significant departure for him, many of the novel's themes, values, and devices were not. Indeed, Sebastian embodies a number of characteristically Nabokovian talents and interests. He may differ from Fyodor in *The Gift* by temperament, age, or degree of public success, but his conception of art and the artist makes him Fyodor's (and thus Nabokov's) first cousin.[5]

The relevance of Nabokov's metaphysical aesthetics for *The Real Life of Sebastian Knight* is implied first of all by the most striking feature of Sebastian's character—a form of consciousness that is a variant of Cincinnatus's ability to "conjoin" sensory impressions, and of Fyodor's

"multi-level thinking," in short, of Nabokov's own cosmic synchronization. As V. explains, even before Sebastian became a writer he began "to
cultivate self-consciousness as if it had been some rare talent or passion"
(p. 44). There is obvious irony at V.'s expense in this remark precisely
because Nabokov did see maximally heightened consciousness as a talent
and a passion. What this entails in Sebastian's case is his awareness "that
the rhythm of his inner being was so much richer than that of other
souls. . . . he knew that his slightest thought or sensation had always at
least one more dimension than those of his neighbors" (p. 66). V. bases
this generalization on comments Sebastian makes in his works, and the
example he quotes from one of them illustrates the characteristic blending
of sensory impressions and far-reaching mnemonic associations that are
the hallmark of cosmic synchronization:

> Most people live through the day with this or that part of their mind in a
> happy state of somnolence: . . . but in my case all the shutters and lids and
> doors of the mind would be open at once at all times of the day. . . . When
> one morning I went to see the editor of a review who, I thought, might print
> some of my Cambridge poems, a particular stammer he had, blending with a
> certain combination of angles in the pattern of roofs and chimneys, all
> slightly distorted owing to a flaw in the glass of the window pane,—this and
> a queer musty smell in the room (of roses rotting in the waste-paper basket?)
> sent my thoughts on such long and intricate errands that, instead of saying
> what I meant to say, I suddenly started telling this man whom I was seeing
> for the first time, about the literary plans of a mutual friend, who, I remem-
> bered too late, had asked me to keep them secret. . . . (P. 67–68)

The obvious parallels between this passage and Nabokov's cosmic synchronization also shed light on the related image of Sebastian as Narcissus in the novel, and illustrate again the necessity of using Nabokovian
contexts to understand his private imagery and vocabulary. A man looking at his reflection in water is in fact a good image for the heightened
consciousness that is implied by Nabokov's "monistic" epistemology, according to which whatever the subject apprehends is inevitably colored
by his mind. Thus rather than imply any kind of limitation on knowledge,
such as solipsism, in Nabokov's conception the self-consciousness of Narcissus is ultimately a vector pointing beyond the self.[6] (It is an indirect
indication of Sebastian's high standing in Nabokov's eyes that Clare
Bishop, his companion, is granted similar cognitive gifts [p. 83]. She is
thus in the same company as Luzhin's fiancée, and Zina in *The Gift*.)

The dispersion of attention that Sebastian describes at the conclusion
of the passage about his heightened consciousness has an additional bearing on his standing as a Nabokovian "hero." What might seem to tarnish
his image in the novel as a whole is his seeming coldness or vagueness

when dealing with other people. This is clearly a paradoxical trait for someone who sees himself as exceptionally attentive to everything that surrounds him. But rather than stem from egotism and, therefore, from moral failing, Sebastian's behavior is a function of his fated attachment to a higher plane of being that manifests itself in his enhanced consciousness and commitment to art. In fact, all of Nabokov's positive characters are loners in varying degrees, and are capable of acting in ways that may seem cruel at times. For example, Fyodor's father in *The Gift* abandons his wife and son for long periods when he is on his expeditions, and treats them brusquely when they try to infringe on his independence. But this clearly does not detract in the least from the aura of veneration with which Fyodor (and Nabokov, and after him, his widow and son) surrounds the image of the father. Presumably, the reasons for this are the father's behavior at other times, as well as his spiritual gifts: these motivate his actions and compensate for his lapses. Another reason that exonerates him is that he is presented as being driven by some otherworldly fateful urge, which thus removes at least part of the onus from him personally. The same considerations apply to Sebastian's treatment of V. and his mistress, Clare. He is cruel to both—in his lifelong aloofness from the first and abandonment of the second. What may be seen as compensation for Sebastian's behavior toward V. is his turning to him when he is on his deathbed, something that V. interprets precisely as recompense and reward. There is also good evidence that Sebastian's infatuation with the enigmatic woman for whom he abandons Clare is an instance of fateful cross-generational patterning in his life rather than cavalier self-indulgence. It is thus important to differentiate Sebastian's behavior from both egotistical and gratuitous cruelty and aloofness, which are moral failings he only seems to possess (e.g., pp. 16, 31).

The connection between sensory acuity and an epiphanic moment yielding the germ of a work of art is not made explicit in *The Real Life of Sebastian Knight* (as it is also not in *Invitation to a Beheading*), but it is implied. In an important passage in his last book, *The Doubtful Asphodel*, which, among other things, reads like his profession of faith in symbolic cognition, Sebastian describes a dying man's realization that the meaning of life and of the surrounding world can be read like an occult script: "it was like a traveller realising that the wild country he surveys is not an accidental assembly of natural phenomena, but the page in a book where these mountains and forests, and fields, and rivers are disposed in such a way as to form a coherent sentence; the vowel of a lake fusing with the consonant of a sibilant slope; the windings of a road writing its message in a round hand" (pp. 178–79). The connection between perception and reading a text that Sebastian's remark establishes suggests that the two are related. Next, he describes the "simple mental jerk" resulting from this act of "reading" that frees the individual's consciousness and grants it "the great understanding," as if the assemblage of natural signs suddenly became intelligible. The consequence is an equalization of the significance of all phenomena, as though they suddenly became equidistant from the perceiver, or he equally dispersed among them, and a unification of different realms of human endeavor: "science, art or religion fell out of the familiar scheme of their classification, and joining hands, were mixed and joyfully levelled" (p. 179). (This formulation recalls Nabokov's own comments about the "ridge" at which science and art meet, and the importance of factual observation in art and imagination in science.) One can infer, therefore, that the epiphanic recognition Sebastian describes in this passage may underlie the creation of texts such as *The Doubtful Asphodel*, in which it appears as the seminal insight.

Sebastian's own words confirm that he saw the recognition of a unity in the cosmos as being akin to an ultimate truth: "All things belong to the same order of things," he writes in one work, "for such is the oneness of human perception, the oneness of individuality, the oneness of matter, whatever matter may be. The only real number is one, the rest are mere repetition" (p. 105). Similar intuitions appear in *Speak, Memory* when Nabokov describes love and cosmic synchronization in the same terms— as providing a sense of transcendent unity between the self and all that exists. In fact, Sebastian anticipates this specific connection of experiences in a letter from one of his books that V. quotes in the belief that it is strongly autobiographical: "There is only one real number: One. And love, apparently, is the best exponent of this singularity" (p. 113). In the end of the novel, V. is made to experience this sense of unity firsthand when he identifies with his deceased half brother so fully that he feels he has become him. Moreover, he uses the experience to generate the hypothetical metaphysical absolute that "the soul is but a manner of being— not a constant state . . . any soul may be yours, if you find and follow its undulations. The hereafter may be the full ability of consciously living in any chosen soul, in any number of souls, all of them unconscious of their interchangeable burden" (pp. 204–5).[7]

There is also a suggestion that Sebastian has what could be called a Platonic conception of art, one, moreover, that recalls Nabokov's own. V. describes Sebastian's struggle with writing in terms of "the maddening feeling that the right words, the only words are awaiting you on the opposite bank in the misty distance," which is balanced by "the shudderings of the still unclothed thought clamouring for them on this side of the abyss" (p. 84). The implication of this image is that the "right words," and therefore the work they will constitute, somehow preexist their being set down by the writer. V.'s characterization of Sebastian's "maddening feeling" is echoed and supported by Sebastian's own description in *The*

Doubtful Asphodel of the impossibility of man's understanding what lies beyond death (which is the same idea that Fyodor quotes from Delalande in *The Gift* in the passage dealing with life as a house and death as the landscape beyond): "only one half of the notion of death can be said really to exist: *this* side of the question—the wrench, the parting, the quay of life gently moving away aflutter with handkerchiefs" (p. 177). The implied journey by water evokes mythic imagery of a transition to life after death; and even though one cannot know what is beyond the transition, something seems to be there, just as the author's words appear to preexist him.

The passages from *The Doubtful Asphodel* about reading natural phenomena like an occult script are also important because they point to the quintessential Nabokovian theme of patterning in nature and life. Sebastian concludes that "human life turns out to be *monogrammatic*, now quite clear to the inner eye disentangling the interwoven letters" (italics added; p. 179). This image of course recalls Nabokov's own references to the fatidic "watermark" that he can discern in his existence.

Nabokov implies in *Speak, Memory* that his experience of cosmic synchronization provides him intermittent escape from the prison of time. Although timelessness is not overtly associated with Sebastian's epiphanic moments, V. describes him as living as though time did not exist. Polemicizing against the fallacious assertion in the biography by Goodman that Sebastian was influenced by the historical moment in which he lived, V. asserts that "time for Sebastian was never 1914 or 1920 or 1936—it was always year 1" (p. 65). Sebastian was also unable to understand why people should be less troubled by great human catastrophes in the distant past than in the present. V. concludes from this that "time and space were to [Sebastian] measures of the same eternity, so that the very idea of his reacting in any special 'modern' way to what Mr. Goodman calls 'the atmosphere of postwar Europe' is utterly preposterous" (p. 66). It is notable that V.'s discussion of Sebastian's experience of time leads directly to his comments about his half brother's multidimensional consciousness, a juxtaposition that suggests the two are in fact connected (pp. 66–67). The same inference can be drawn from *The Doubtful Asphodel*, in which, shortly before the passage about the dying man who learns to understand the puzzle of existence, Sebastian describes time and space as "childish terms" that are "riddles invented by man *as* riddles." His reference to the entire span of the man's existence as "the kindergarten of life" further implies that after death he will enter not only into a "full-grown" state of being but one in which the "childish" earthly conception of time will no longer be relevant (pp. 178–79). One concludes, therefore, that Sebastian's "timeless" existence in life is a foreshadowing of a possible life after death, which is the same association Nabokov makes in his discursive writings. This conclusion buttresses the explanation that Sebastian's "inhuman" treatment of others is due to his being colored by an otherworldly aura.

Sebastian further resembles Nabokov in the way ethics automatically enters into his system of values in both art and life. "There was nothing of your advanced prejudice-be-damned stuff about Sebastian," V. writes. "Well did he know that to flaunt one's contempt for a moral code was but smuggled smugness and prejudice turned inside out. He usually chose the easiest ethical path (just as he chose the thorniest aesthetic one) merely because it happened to be the shortest cut to his chosen object" (p. 82). The connection between ethics and aesthetics (and by extension, with metaphysics) implied here is further reinforced by Sebastian's view that a literary cliché is "a bloated and malodorous corpse," and that "the second rate," which pretends to be better than it is, is "in an *artistic* sense, immoral" (pp. 91, 92). This is of course not to say that public morals were a direct or even significant interest of Sebastian's; for him as for Nabokov ethics is a facet of a larger whole.

Among the small-scale parallels between Nabokov and Sebastian is one that has a particular bearing on the significance of metaliterary themes and praxis in Nabokov's art. V.'s discussion of Sebastian's *Prismatic Bezel* can be read as Nabokov's veiled polemic against Khodasevich's well-known claims in the essay "On Sirin" ("O Sirine," 1937). V. speaks of the work's heroes being "methods of composition," which recalls Khodasevich's argument that Sirin's works "are populated not only with characters, but with an infinite number of devices. . . . one of his major tasks is just that—to show how the devices live and work." However, the continuation of what V. says about Sebastian's work implies he understands that it goes beyond a focus on the device. V. uses the example of a painter who seems to want to show "not the painting of a landscape, but the painting of different ways of painting a certain landscape." The crucial point, however, is that this is not an end in itself for the artist: he hopes that "the harmonious fusion" of the different methods of painting he illustrates "will disclose the landscape as I intend you to see it." There is, in other words, a core belief and a vision beneath the technical brilliance of Sebastian's art. V.'s remarks may thus be seen as directed against Khodasevich's conclusion that Sirin's theme was limited to "the life of the artist and the life of the device in the consciousness of the artist."[8]

If Sebastian bears many of his creator's signs of approval, one character in particular is made the obvious embodiment of all Nabokov reviled. This is Goodman, of course, with his blindness to specifics, and facile reliance on glib generalizations (e.g., pp. 62, 116, 117). V.'s harshly mocking treatment of his failings anticipates "The Art of Literature and

Commonsense," in which Nabokov suggests that the appropriate artistic punishment for "iniquity" is underscoring its intrinsic absurdities.⁹

The major theme on the surface of *The Real Life of Sebastian Knight* is the theoretical and practical possibility of biography, and Nabokov treats it in terms very close to those of his Pushkin lecture. V.'s warning to the reader to "remember that what you are told is really threefold: shaped by the teller, reshaped by the listener, concealed from both by the dead man of the tale" (p. 52) suggests well that Nabokov's conception of the relation between a life and a biography was both sophisticated and complex. (The sentence also provides an ambiguous hint that the dead may have influence over the quick.) Despite his own warning, however, V. uses Sebastian's belletristic writings with surprising frequency to make inferences about Sebastian's life, or to illustrate his conjectures about Sebastian's way of thinking (e.g., pp. 9, 10, 112). In short, he implies there is a connection based on truth between an artist's life and his art; the challenge lies in ascertaining what it is.

V.'s practice is explicitly supported by Sebastian's own artistic procedures, which, because they recall Nabokov's, lend weight to V.'s undertaking. After Sebastian dies, V. goes through his things and finds a series of photographs of a "Mr. H." at different ages from childhood to adulthood. An advertisement clipped from a newspaper explains that these had been solicited and bought by Sebastian for a "fictitious biography" (p. 40). Now, it may seem at first that this is a veiled authorial comment about V.'s endeavor with regard to Sebastian himself, and that V.'s biography is thus equally "fictitious" despite the bits of objective fact it may contain. Opposing this negative interpretation, according to which "fiction" is implicitly equated with "falsehood," is V.'s description of Sebastian's novel *Success*, which radically revalues the notion that fiction is untrue (and thus parallels the Pushkin lecture). This novel consists of the author's investigation of the complex causes that bring about the seemingly accidental meeting of a man and a woman who "will be happy ever after" (p. 96). V. characterizes it as "one of the most complicated researches that has ever been attempted by a writer," which is an egregiously deceptive remark because it glosses over the fact that although the novel may be about the intricate workings of fate, it treats the lives of fictional characters; there is no evidence in V.'s text that Sebastian modeled them on people who had actually existed, and the term "researches" thus proves to be especially problematic. Consistent with this is V.'s lengthy description of the novel not as skillfully wrought artifice, in which the author is responsible for fashioning the fate of his characters, but as a display of the author's ingenuity in being able to identify the events and causes that culminate in the "happy ending." There is a resemblance of course between *Success* and *The Gift* because both treat the subtle arrangements fate makes in bringing two people together. The obvious difference is that in *The Gift's* own terms, Zina's and Fyodor's fateful meeting within the text is ostensibly based on their experiences outside it. V. gives no indication that Sebastian's *Success* is similarly "autobiographical" (although he does quote a lengthy passage from it that he claims is "strangely connected with Sebastian's inner life at the time of the completing of the last chapters" [p. 98]; he does not indicate, however, what the connection is; neither is there any indication of how the passage relates to the author's investigation of fate in his characters' lives). But if V.'s remarks about *Success* are to make any sense, then we must assume that in both his and his half brother's views fictions lend themselves to investigations that one would properly carry out in life. One way of resolving this difficulty is to remember that in keeping with Nabokov's metaphysical aesthetics the implied provenance of the work of art is partially an otherworld that functions as an absolute, and partially the perceiver's apprehension of phenomena. Thus, in Nabokov's view, authentic or high art is never false, in the sense of being gratuitously unrelated to the author's experiences or the world in which he lives, even if it makes no attempt to faithfully mirror "reality" (which is both meaningless and impossible in Nabokov's conception). Another way of saying this is that imagination, which, as Nabokov explained, relies on memory as well as inspiration, yields not mere fantasy but truth (or fantasy that is "plausible" in the terms of the Pushkin lecture). This agrees with Sebastian's experience of cosmic synchronization, and also with V.'s great intuitive discovery in the end of the novel that his *imagined* emotional proximity to Sebastian is as valid as if he had really been near him on his deathbed. In light of these considerations, V.'s reading of *Success*, and inferences about Sebastian based on his other writings, suggest that the model of writing Sebastian embodied was essentially Platonic. This is also a possible implication of Sebastian's unrealized plan to write a fictitious biography of Mr. H., in which the photographs might have served as analogues for the sensory data that are often the stimuli for inspiration as Nabokov understood it in "The Art of Literature and Commonsense" and *Speak, Memory*. The validation of the imagination as the source of intuitive truth (or plausible artifice) that is implied by Sebastian's writings foreshadows Kinbote's practices and Shade's formulations in *Pale Fire*, and constitutes one of the most striking and typical, if often misunderstood features of Nabokov's art and thought (despite its obvious resonances with familiar Romantic and Symbolist aesthetics).

As we have seen throughout Nabokov's works, patterning in human life reflects fate and implies the otherworld. Thus V.'s emphasis at various points in his story on the congruences between him and Sebastian implies a fatidic link between them, one, moreover, that has a bearing on what V. learns and includes in his biography. The fact that they are half brothers of course has something to do with it, but as the spiritual parallels between Cincinnatus and his mother, or Fyodor and his father imply, the existence of "genetically" or "environmentally" determined familial traits in Nabokov's world does not necessarily preclude additional, otherworldly explanations for them as well. Nabokov's comments in *Speak, Memory* about his own character imply that he felt he had been shaped by an otherworldly influence, as do the instances of cross-generational patterning to which he refers. By contrast, the case of Luzhin and his parents demonstrates that not all members of every family in Nabokov's fiction share similar gifts or behavioral traits.

V. claims that he has "inner knowledge" of Sebastian, that he experiences a "curious" feeling of déjà vu when investigating his life, and that he shares a common "rhythm" with him: "when I imagined actions of his which I heard of only after his death, I knew for certain that in such and such a case I should have acted just as he had" (pp. 33–34; a similar admission appears on p. 36; and a comparable intuitive rhythm of understanding links Clare Bishop to Sebastian as well [p. 84]). Although it may seem odd that V. would have been sufficiently aware of his ties to Sebastian to make these remarks, but not to fully comprehend the import of what he is saying, V.'s blindness can be readily interpreted as an instance of dramatic irony that Nabokov created for the reader's benefit. After all, the artist hero of the novel is Sebastian, and V. is merely the servant of his legacy. The fitting nature of such a technique for *The Real Life of Sebastian Knight* is suggested by V.'s characterization of Sebastian's writings as "a dazzling succession of gaps" (p. 35), which implies the kind of lacunae that the reader would fill via inferences.

Although V. does not show any awareness of the extent to which major events in his quest echo Sebastian's fiction and life, he does notice such minor parallels as that they both perceived pigeons flying off a monument as "stone melting into wing" (p. 74), and that they both dislike "postal phenomena" (p. 121) or "anything made of glass or china" (p. 154). (V.'s generalization about Clare's psychological link to Sebastian is borne out by the fact that both of them see a secluded spot in the woods as an appropriate abode for a "gnome" or a "brownie" [pp. 88, 89].) A more telling parallel emerges when V. acknowledges that whenever the reasons for Sebastian's behavior prove to be mysterious, he often finds "their meaning disclosed . . . in a subconscious turn of this or that sentence put down by me" (p. 34). This remark is especially noteworthy because it points to the possibility that V.'s writing, and by extension his entire biographical enterprise, was being patterned or directed by his deceased half brother. V. expresses a similar idea when he speculates that his "unconscious cerebration" must have led him "to take the right turn in [Sebastian's] private labyrinth" (p. 183).

The theme of ghostly manifestations further supports this possibility. Its first appearance in the novel occurs in V.'s quotation from Sebastian's *Lost Property*, in which Sebastian describes a visit to what he thought was the house in which his mother had died: "Gradually I worked myself into such a state that for a moment the pink and green [of the house and a tree near it] seemed to shimmer and float as if seen through a veil of mist. My mother, a dim slight figure in a large hat, went slowly up the steps which seemed to dissolve in water" (pp. 19–20). Later, however, Sebastian discovers that his "vision" occurred in the wrong town, which inevitably raises doubts about its really having been a ghostly apparition and not a figment of his imagination. This event constitutes a carefully circumscribed instance of ambiguity in *The Real Life of Sebastian Knight*. Because the implied author does not openly provide evidence for or against an occult explanation of Sebastian's experience, it is up to the reader to muster his own. Moreover, some doubt about the validity of one's interpretation of this particular event will remain no matter what side one takes, even if one considers it in the context of other suggestive details in the text.

Supporting the reading of Sebastian's vision as an occult experience is a significant structural and thematic similarity between it and the novel's concluding scenes, which describe V.'s arrival at the hospital in St. Damier. V. does not know that Sebastian has died some hours earlier, and makes the mistake of sitting for a few minutes by another man's sickbed. During this time he draws great spiritual succor from what he believes is his proximity to his half brother, and feels that his life is changed by the experience. Even after he discovers his error, however, V. insists that the spiritual link he felt he had established with Sebastian remains valid: "Thus—I am Sebastian Knight" (p. 205). In other words, V. intuits that space and time can be overcome via something like the imaginative sympathy he had for Sebastian.

V.'s intuition about "living in any chosen soul" may seem either strikingly bizarre at first, or to lend itself to a purely metaliterary interpretation, especially in view of V.'s final remark about himself and his half brother: "perhaps we both are someone whom neither of us knows" (p. 205). Predictably, many critics have read these words either as V.'s acknowledgment that he impersonates a variety of characters in his capacity as wily author, or as his intuition that both he and all the other characters in the novel are Nabokov's creatures, or as a sign that *The Real Life of Sebastian Knight* is one of Sebastian's deceptive fictions, and that V. is his creation.[10] Upon closer examination, however, V.'s remarks reveal a similarity to Nabokov's cosmic synchronization (and his validation of imag-

ination in the Pushkin lecture). The network of links that V. believes an
individual can establish with souls separated widely by time and space
resembles the sense of cosmic unity that characterizes Nabokov's epiphanic experiences (including that of love), except that the "points" to
which the individual feels connected are psychic entities, and not physical
phenomena or memories. V.'s belief can thus be seen as hinging on a
translation of the structure of cosmic synchronization into the realm of
speculation about a transcendent spiritual reality. V.'s intuition also recalls Fyodor's practice in *The Gift* of imaginatively "sitting in" other
characters, which is related to his cosmic synchronization–like "multi-
level thinking," and to his quotations from Delalande about the all-seeing
eye as an image for the total understanding that man will achieve upon
death. Moreover, as Nabokov demonstrates in *Speak, Memory* and
dramatizes in *The Gift*, time is a function of consciousness, and timeless
moments allow free translation through space. Thus, in this light, V.
could have been near Sebastian, and the spiritual comfort he receives is,
at most, an exaggeration of Nabokov's own beliefs.

For purposes of shorthand reference, what V. undergoes in the hospital
can be characterized as communion with the spirit of one who is dead.
The significance of this experience is that it suggests that Sebastian's mistake about the place where his mother died is similar to the one V. makes
in the hospital: his error about the town may be immaterial, and may not
have invalidated his vision.[11] An additional consideration pertaining to
Sebastian's vision is that there is a curious similarity between his description of how his mother appeared to him, and V.'s description of her when
she had come to Russia during Sebastian's boyhood (p. 10). V. does not
say where he got his information about her appearance, but two sources
can be surmised. One is Sebastian's own description in *Lost Property*,
which V. could have adapted, consciously or not, despite its anachronism.
The other is Sebastian's occult influence on the wording of V.'s text, an
alternative that is strongly implied elsewhere in the novel.

Buttressing the possibility that Sebastian's vision of his mother was not
a delusion is the frequency of ghostlike apparitions V. encounters. Considered individually, each incident could be discounted as merely a striking description of something physical, as a figure of speech, or as an illusion; taken together, however, they imply an occult explanation. For
example, when V. is going through his brother's wardrobe he has "an odd
impression of Sebastian's body being stiffly multiplied in a succession of
square-shouldered forms" (p. 36). Shortly thereafter, V. seems to see "a
transparent Sebastian at his desk," although he then adds "or rather I
thought of that passage about the wrong Roquebrune [the town where
Sebastian's mother died]: perhaps he preferred doing his writing in bed?"
(p. 39). When V. visits Sebastian's old college friend at Cambridge Uni-

versity, "Sebastian's spirit seemed to hover about us with the flicker of the fire reflected in the brass knobs of the hearth" (pp. 45–46). An instance of V.'s having something like a vision in connection with a character who played a major role in Sebastian's life is his feeling of attraction to Mme Lecerf: "Dust was swarming in a slanting sunbeam; volutes of tobacco-smoke joined it and rotated softly, insinuatingly, as if they might form a live picture at any moment." V. then consolidates the impression that there may have been something like a near-apparition in this scene when he speculates that his feelings "may amuse the reader (and who knows, Sebastian's ghost too)," and when he has to make a considerable effort to shake off the effect Mme Lecerf is having on him (p. 168).

V. himself encourages an occult interpretation of Sebastian's influence on him when he speculates about where his half brother could be:"rotting peacefully in the cemetery of St. Damier. Laughingly alive in five volumes. Peering unseen over my shoulder as I write this (although I dare say he mistrusted too strongly the commonplace of eternity to believe even now in his own ghost)" (pp. 52–53). The tripartite response implies an existence after death that is distinct not only from the physical but the metaphorical as well (as in the cliché, "he *lives* in his books"). Moreover, in the light of Nabokov's later disparagement of the idea of "common-sense," V.'s reference to Sebastian's mistrust of "commonplace" ideas about life after death can be interpreted as a desire to be true to his unique experiences, rather than as his outright dismissal of the idea of a transcendent existence. Elsewhere, V. speaks of his determination to persevere with his book, and of his being "sustained by the secret knowledge that in some unobtrusive way Sebastian's *shade* is trying to be helpful" (italics added; p. 101). And finally, after describing Clare's and Sebastian's initially happy life together, V. remarks "it is hard to believe that the warmth, the tenderness, the beauty of it has not been gathered, and is not treasured somewhere, somehow, by some *immortal witness* of mortal life" (italics added; p. 87). All these remarks are in keeping with V.'s surprisingly casual reference to death as a "strange habit," which implies that it can be overcome the way bad habits are broken (p. 33).

V. also experiences a series of enigmatic promptings in his quest that are more ephemeral than the visions he has, but no less suggestive with regard to the possibility that his actions are guided from the otherworld. His decision to see Clare comes on suddenly and inexplicably; indeed, he likens it to his equally inexplicable certainty when he was rushing to Sebastian's deathbed that he "would learn something which no human being had yet learnt" (p. 76). When he actually sees Clare on the street, however, V.'s reaction is an overwhelming and "perfectly clear consciousness that I might neither talk to her nor greet her in any manner" (p. 79). He assumes that the interdiction he feels has nothing to do with his research or with Sebastian, and stems only from her "stately concentration," which is presumably due to her advanced pregnancy. Despite this disclaimer, he later acknowledges that "the spark that had kindled" his ability to capture a period in Sebastian's life "belongs in some mysterious manner to the glimpse I had of Clare Bishop walking heavily down a London street" (p. 90). It is also hardly a mere coincidence that the first thing V. pulls out of his pocket and shows Clare when he sees her on a street is the key to Sebastian's apartment (p. 80). Similarly, V. emerges once again as a plaything of forces beyond his ken when he says later that he feels he was "being given my last chance" to see Helene von Graun (p. 163), which leads to what he believes is his discovery of Sebastian's final, destructive love. Events like this confirm V.'s suspicion that he "was being led right" when attempting to write Sebastian's life (p. 137).

V.'s inklings culminate in something closer to conviction at the conclusion of the novel. He receives a letter from Sebastian asking him to come to see him, which is followed by an even more urgent summons in the form of an enigmatic dream filled with "absolute moment," but containing a phrase "which made no sense when I brought it out of my dream" (pp. 189–90). The description of this phrase (it is not quoted in the text) carries Nabokov's hallmark of what may be a message from the otherworld. It recalls such varied details as the incommensurability of Luzhin's chess genius with his mundane existence in *The Defense*, the "*nonnons*" in *Invitation to a Beheading*, and Delalande's distinction in *The Gift* between the house and the landscape in his allegory about life after death. All reflect Nabokov's sense that the otherworld is fundamentally unknowable in earthly terms.

A variant of the idea that V. is being guided is his discovery of a preexisting pattern into which the facts he unearths appear to fit. He speaks of this in terms of his quest having "developed its own magic and logic" (p. 137). An example is his conclusion that "there seems to have been a law of some strange harmony in the placing of a meeting relating to Sebastian's first adolescent romance in such close proximity to the echoes of his last dark love" (p. 137). Since he was led to his meeting with "Rosanov's sister"—the "adolescent romance" in question—by a chance remark Helene Grinstein made, the "harmony" V. discovers and sets down in his text is not of his own making. He can be seen instead as stumbling across a pattern, or as being led to fashion one, which, in either case, implies that his actions are not free but determined.

Given these implications regarding V.'s quest, and the fact that Sebastian is a writer, it seems plausible within Nabokov's world that Sebastian's endeavors should also be under the guidance of, or in contact with an otherworldly dimension. Indeed, this is implied by V.'s image of how the words Sebastian will use await investment by his thought. It is also suggested by his friend Sheldon's idea that "the world of the last book [Sebastian] was to write several years later (*The Doubtful Asphodel*) *was already casting its shadow* on all things surrounding him and that his novels and stories were but bright masks, sly tempters under the pretense of artistic adventure *leading him unerringly towards a certain imminent goal*" (italics added; p. 104). As we know from V.'s description of it, *The Doubtful Asphodel* produces the teasing impression that its author has uncovered the secret of "all questions of life and death" (p. 104). Since there are various intimations about death not being final in *The Real Life of Sebastian Knight* that support V.'s interpretation of Sebastian's last work, Sheldon's comment raises the possibility that Sebastian's insight into the otherworld led to his being guided by it throughout his entire artistic career.

As in all of Nabokov's works, seeming coincidences play a decisive role in *The Real Life of Sebastian Knight* and imply that an otherworldly fate rules over characters' lives. For example, it is "by a very grim coincidence," as V. puts it, that Sebastian's father hears on two consecutive days from two different people about his former wife's (and Sebastian's mother's) checkered past (pp. 11–12). He challenges the man who spread these rumors and dies of complications following the duel that results. As Fyodor in *The Gift* might have phrased it, this begins the theme of entanglements with destructive women in Sebastian's family that includes his own involvement with his "last dark love." The continuity of this theme across generations resembles the cross-generational patterns Nabokov identifies in *Speak, Memory*.

V.'s unraveling of the Nina de Rechnoy, Helene von Graun, Mme Lecerf tangle of identities (if he in fact does unravel it) is also based on a network of seemingly chance coincidences that is further complicated by a series of ambiguous hints. Since the entire complex is central to the novel and to Nabokov's method, it deserves to be traced in some detail. A logical starting point is the little Russian language test V. conducts that leads him to conclude Mme Lecerf is Nina de Rechnoy when she happens to mention that she once kissed a man who could write his name upside down (pp. 171–73). This reminds V. of "Uncle Black" at "Pahl Pahlich" Rechnoy's apartment in Paris, who could do the same trick (pp. 142–44). Moreover, V.'s language test hinges on his deceiving Mme Lecerf about there being a spider on her neck. This detail is obviously important because Carswell's portrait of Sebastian peering into water, in which the painter "wanted to hint at a woman somewhere behind him or over him," includes "a very slight ripple on the hollow cheek, owing to the presence of a water-spider," which suggests a link with Mme Lecerf (p. 119). An additional element in the receding chain of coincidences, but one of which V. does not appear to be aware, is that Mme Lecerf admits kissing the

man after V. scrawls lines on the ground with a cane he had happened to
find on a bench at her country place (pp. 170, 171). This inevitably reminds the reader of Mme Lecerf's retelling what she claims is Helene von
Graun's description of how a man (who V. believes may have been Sebastian) used to visit her with a cane (p. 160). There is no way to ascertain
of course if the cane V. uses is Sebastian's, or indeed, if he ever actually
carried one; in any event, V. never mentions his doing so. Nevertheless,
the detail remains as one of several planted by Nabokov in V.'s text to
hint ambiguously that Mme Lecerf may have been Sebastian's last mistress. (The detail also functions well as an illustration of the way in which
Nabokov's reader is made to enact the kind of retrospective discovery of
patterning in the text that Nabokov describes with regard to his own life.)
Another example of controlled, suggestive ambiguity related to the search
for the woman is the scene from Sebastian's youth when a girl ("Rosanov's sister") tells him that she loves someone else by writing the word
yes on the earth with a stick (p. 139). This indirectly associates Sebastian
with both the cane and Mme Lecerf via the scene between her and V. We
also have Mme Lecerf's chance remark about what she says is Helene von
Graun's "sens quasi-religieux des phénomènes de la vie" (p. 161), which
may be related to what Paul Rechnoy refers to as Nina's "talk of death
and the Nirvana or something—she had a weakness for Lhassa" (p. 147).
This echo between the two descriptions can be interpreted as implying
that Nina and Helene are one and the same; but it is not proof of their
identity. By the same token, Mme Lecerf's expression of shock at "the
way he spoke of religion" (p. 160), by which she means the man with
whom she says Helene von Graun was involved, reminds the reader of
how Sebastian's old friend at Cambridge remembers being annoyed by
his "obscurely immoral statements, related to Life, Death or God" (p.
48). From this point of view it is thus possible that "Helene"'s unhappy
lover and Sebastian were one and the same. Another bit of evidence the
reader must decipher is that Nina's surname before it became Rechnoy
was Toorovetz (Nina Rechnoy also recalls Nina Zarechnaia in Chekhov's
The Seagull, allusions to which appear elsewhere in the novel). "Toora"
or "tura" in Russian means the chess piece "castle" or "rook," which
together with Clare Bishop's surname, and St. Damier ("Saint Checker-
board"), the name of the hospital in which Sebastian dies, establishes a
network of concealed references to chess that resonates in obvious harmony with Sebastian's last name. These connections may be additional
hints by Nabokov, over V.'s, or any other character's head, that Nina was
indeed Sebastian's fateful love.

If Mme Lecerf is Nina de Rechnoy, another strikingly unlikely coincidence is that V. discovers her by accident after deciding that he should
"drop the Rechnoy clue altogether" and focus his attention on Helene

von Graun instead (p. 163). (A similar coincidence is his meeting "Rosanov's sister" after a chance comment by Helene Grinstein [p. 136]; moreover, Natasha Rosanov and Nina Rechnoy have the same initials.) But despite V.'s apparent conviction about Mme Lecerf's identity, it does not seem possible to resolve unequivocally whether or not V. found the right woman, even though many readers follow him in assuming that he has.[12] Various mutually exclusive permutations of possibilities are supported by details in the novel to differing degrees. Rather than see this textual fact as a frustrating dead end, however, or as evidence for the novel being about the arbitrariness of fiction or artifice, one can take as a guide V.'s conclusion about Sebastian's last work: "it is not the parts that matter, it is their combinations" (p. 176). The odd but suggestive resemblance between Raul Rechnoy's description of his former wife and Mme Lecerf's story of her friend's love affair constitutes a pattern, and it is the discovery of patterning in any aspect of existence (so long as it is not a character's obvious projection, as in *Despair*) that betrays the workings of the otherworld in Nabokov's world. Thus even if the two women had no relation to each other, the fact that V. would have come across two stories that seem to have much in common is telling enough in itself. This is close to the kind of significant patterning that we will find developed at length in *Pale Fire*. Moreover, the fact that a series of improbable coincidences leads V. to the discovery of parallel tales heightens the impression that his own quest does not so much reflect his volition as conform to a design that transcends his awareness.

Another category of patterning in the novel, of which V. is unaware, consists of pairs of details from opposite ends of the time sequence he embraces in his text. At one point he describes the scene of Sebastian's parting from a girl in his youth (pp. 139–40) without remembering or realizing what the reader has in fact already inferred—that V. had glimpsed the same girl's picture many years before while examining the contents of Sebastian's secret drawer in their boyhood home (p. 17). The resulting irony is that because V. cannot imagine what the girl must have looked like in her youth he paints a very abstract picture of her when he describes the poignant scene of her telling Sebastian she loves another: "the seated girl's shape remains blank except for the arm and a thin brown hand toying with a bicycle pump" (p. 139). When V. is looking for Nina he arrives at Paul Rechnoy's, who greets him while holding "a black knight" in his hand (p. 142). Not only does this obviously evoke Sebastian's surname, and therefore imply that V. may be on the right track in pursuing the Nina de Rechnoy lead, it also reminds the reader, but apparently not V., of the drawing of a black knight chessman that Sebastian placed as a signature under the poems he wrote when a youth (p. 17).[13] A related "sign" that V. may be being "led right" is the way he discovers the name of the hospital in which Sebastian is dying. V. struggles in vain to remember it all night on the train to Paris, and then fails to reach the doctor who could tell him. After he hangs up the telephone, however, he idly scans the graffiti on the wall of the booth and notices that "some anonymous artist had begun blocking squares—a chess board, *ein Schachbrett, un damier.* . . . There was a flash in my brain and the word settled on my tongue: St. Damier!" (pp. 197–98). Similarly, despite his assiduous research into Sebastian's life, V. does not appear to realize that the theme of the "destructive woman" links his half brother to their father. This is all the more notable given the similarities in the physical appearance of Mme Lecerf, who is "small, slight, pale faced" and wears black (p. 150), and Virginia Knight—"a slim, slightly angular woman, with a small quivering face under a huge black hat" (p. 10). Another curious parallel links Sebastian to his mother (in addition to the fact that they both die from heart ailments [pp. 11, 186]). Some time after abandoning Clare, he happens to meet Helen Pratt near a London bookshop into which she had just accompanied Clare. Instead of alluding to his past with Clare he tells Miss Pratt "an elaborate story about a couple of men who had attempted to swindle him at a game of poker the night before" (p. 184). This recalls the second incident in the novel in which an errant lover comes close to meeting the injured "other party." As V. describes it, Virginia Knight arrived unexpectedly in Russia one winter and sent a note asking to see her son. In what must have been a fortuitous coincidence, her former husband was away, which prevented their meeting, and which is comparable to Sebastian's not going into the bookstore where Clare was. Instead, V.'s mother took Sebastian to see Virginia, who anticipated her son's behavior many years later in an analogous situation (but with genders reversed) by telling yet another tale of petty crime—"a pointless and quite irrelevant story about a Polish woman who had attempted to steal her vanity-bag in the dining-car" (p. 10). The stories mother and son tell are non sequiturs only with regard to their immediate contexts; their "relevance" as thematic echoes of each other emerges through time. A related detail is Paul Rechnoy's reference to Nina's making a row in a hotel about some change that a maid had supposedly stolen (p. 146), which links her to the theme of errant lovers in the novel and thus to Sebastian's life. (A similar link, as Fromberg has suggested, is that Paul Rechnoy's slurred patronymic Pahlich [for Pavlovich] is close in sound to Palchin, the name of the man who wounded Sebastian's father in a duel.)[14] A long thread throughout V.'s text that ties him to his half brother is the "violet" motif, and references to the flower and the color appear in the most varied contexts (pp. 10, 17, 19, 37, 83). It is also most noteworthy that V. describes Mme Lecerf's dark eyelids as "violet" (p. 171). She is thus associated with the entire motif, which, because of its extent, takes on a typically Nabokovian significance. Moreover, Mme Lecerf's violet eyelids associate her specifically with Virginia's physical appearance, which is also hinted at in other ways. This in turn raises the intriguing possibility that Sebastian's "inexplicable" attraction to Nina de Rechnoy (assuming that this is in fact Mme Lecerf's former name, and that she was Sebastian's lover) was due to two interrelated reasons—a fateful recapitulation of his father's past with his mother (another instance of cross-generational patterning), and the physical resemblance of the young woman to his mother. Finally, V. describes a "violet-blue night-lamp" reflected in the window of the train he takes to Paris. It is tempting to speculate that Nabokov mentions the color at this point not as a random "realistic" detail, but as a portent. One wonders if this could be the moment when Sebastian dies in St. Damier? Moreover, as Stuart suggests, the fact that the last two references to the color violet—the nightlamp and Mme Lecerf's eyelids—are linked to V.'s perceptions, rather than to Sebastian's, can be read as adumbrating V.'s sense at the novel's conclusion that he has become Sebastian.[15]

Even when V. does notice a significant pattern, a large part of it still appears to be aimed over his head at the reader. A case in point is his remark about the year in which Sebastian dies, 1936. He states that as he looks at the figure, he "cannot help thinking that there is an occult resemblance between a man and the date of his death. . . . This date to me seems the reflection of that name in a pool of rippling water. There is something about the curves of the last three numerals that recalls the sinuous outlines of Sebastian's personality" (p. 183). V.'s intuition is borne out by the reader's realization that Sebastian had lived at 36 Oak Park Gardens (p. 36), occupied room 36 in the hospital at St. Damier (p. 201), and was thirty-six years old when he died (p. 129); similarly, "61–93," the telephone number of the doctor from whom V. learns where Sebastian is dying (p. 196), unscrambles to the year of Sebastian's death. The reference to a "reflection" in a "pool of rippling water" of course recalls Carswell's portrait of Sebastian, and the themes of perception and fate associated with it; while the "curves" echoing "the sinuous outlines of Sebastian's personality" evoke V.'s sense that his rhythms match Sebastian's.

The most dazzling and original pattern in *The Real Life of Sebastian Knight* suggesting that V. is caught in a fatidic web is that he experiences situations and meets characters from Sebastian's fictions. These have the additional function of implying that his quest and life are being directed by a consciousness other than his own. Because V. is unaware of these remarkable coincidences, they can be seen as constituting another category of patterning directed at the reader that is not filtered through any characters' exegeses. Fiction coming to life is also another indication that what Sebastian writes is not arbitrary, even if it may have been fanciful, and that, as Nabokov implies about art in general, it is grounded in an absolute reality transcending the mundane.

As virtually all commentators have noted, the most dramatic instance of V.'s life imitating Sebastian's art is his encounter with a character from the short story "The Back of the Moon." Unaware of the significance of what he is saying when he is describing the story, V. characterizes this "Mr. Siller" as "the most alive of Sebastian's creatures and . . . the final representative of the 'research theme,' which appears in others of Sebastian's works." V. goes on to make the even more striking remark that "it is as though a certain idea steadily growing through two books has now burst into real physical existence, and so Mr. Siller makes his bow" (p. 104). Some pages later these words emerge as unwittingly prophetic when "Mr. Siller" appears before V. as "Mr. Silbermann." His function in V.'s life is of course precisely what it had been in Sebastian's story: to help V.'s research by providing what V. fails to obtain at Blauberg—the names of four women who had stayed there at the same time as Sebastian, any-one of whom could have become his last mistress (Silbermann even provides the notebook in which V. will write the story). Among other details that signal Mr. Silbermann's relation to Sebastian's Mr. Siller is their physical resemblance: the latter is "little," bald, has "bushy eyebrows," brown eyes, a "modest moustache," a prominent Adam's apple, and a "big strong nose" (pp. 103–4); the former is also "little," bald, has "bushy eyebrows," a "small moustache," a mobile Adam's apple, brown eyes, and a "big shiny nose" (pp. 126–27, 132). Sebastian's character helps three train travelers in different ways, and V. meets Silbermann in a train compartment. While trying to persuade V. of the futility of his quest, Silbermann goes so far as to name in passing the story in which he had appeared: "You cant see de odder side of de moon" (p. 132). Another particularly intriguing detail is that among the few Russian words and phrases Silbermann happens to know and repeat for V. is "*Braht, millee braht*," "brother, dear brother," which sounds uncannily like a veiled appeal or greeting to V. from Sebastian (p. 128). This possibility is supported by the character of Silbermann's spoken English, which apparently bears some resemblance to Sebastian's, who also makes "queer mistakes" and rolls his *r*'s (p. 48).

The possibility that Nabokov may have had a particular occult teaching in mind when describing Silbermann's behavior is implied by his enigmatic calculation of what V. owes him for his services. Quite apart from the absurdly low sum he names, what is notable about the fee is that he deducts from it the cost of the notebook he gave V., and then returns to V. the entire remaining sum as well (p. 133). In other words, Silbermann carries out the mirror image of the expected action by returning what he should have taken. It is as if he were not another entity in relation to V. but a part of him, or an emanation from him, which is how he can be thought of if we assume that he is Sebastian's (i.e., his half brother's) emissary.[16] In any event, Silbermann's behavior is in keeping with Nabokov's own conception of the antithetical relationship between mundane and otherworldly realms.

Smaller, but no less significant instances of V.'s reliving elements from Sebastian's books also occur in the novel. When V. is visiting Mme Lecerf at her dreary country place, he notices some earth that had been dug up in the garden and recalls "for some odd reason," as he puts it, which cannot but pique the reader's curiosity, "a murder that had happened lately, a murderer who had buried his victim in just such a garden as this" (p. 169). This may be an oblique evocation of Sebastian's novel *The Prismatic Bezel*, in one part of which a seeming murder occurs in a country house (pp. 94–95). The parallel between V.'s experience at Mme Lecerf's country house and *The Prismatic Bezel* is strengthened by the possibility that she may be playing a role for V.'s benefit, which is similar to the revelation in Sebastian's novel that the murder was feigned and that the ostensible victim had disguised himself as someone else.

It has struck most readers of the novel that events in V.'s life also appear to be modeled on a cluster of details from Sebastian's last work *The Doubtful Asphodel*. These include "the gentle old chess player Schwarz" (p. 175), who of course recalls "Uncle Black" in Paul Rechnoy's apartment, and the nephew he entertains (pp. 142–44). The "fat Bohemian woman with that grey streak showing in the fast colour of her cheaply dyed hair" is a clear evocation of the minor character Lydia Bohemsky, whom V. briefly investigates in an amusing scene (p. 153). Other examples include women stepping into puddles (pp. 170, 175), the murder and suicide of Swiss couples (pp. 124, 175), and the mourning young women (pp. 135, 175).[17] Thus the list Siller/Silbermann provides leads V. to avatars of images from Sebastian's book. Even a rejected draft of Sebastian's, in which a character is apparently afraid of "missing tomorrow's . . . train" (p. 39), may be read as foreshadowing V.'s rush by train to Sebastian's deathbed in the end of the novel.[18] In the context of such hints about V.'s being under his dead half brother's occult influence, his wondering whether or not Sebastian had been aware that he had ever read his works (p. 33) emerges as an instance of poignant irony.

Equally, if not more, significant, is that V.'s rush to Sebastian's deathbed, and his expectation that he will hear something of utmost importance from Sebastian's lips, parallels the impression that V. forms of the narrative shape of *The Doubtful Asphodel*, which seems to be moving toward an answer to the riddles of human life and death (p. 179). Moreover, as Fromberg argues, V.'s repeated hesitations about going to Sebastian's side lead to his failing to reach him while he is still alive, and thus learn the ultimate secret. This parallels the author's hesitation in *The Doubtful Asphodel* about revealing his secret, as a result of which he dies before he can utter it. Fromberg goes on to suggest that V.'s conclusion about being Sebastian, and his speculation about the interchangeability of souls as a model for the hereafter, is in fact borne out by the narrative that V. creates during his quest, which is apparently guided everywhere by Sebastian's occult influence and shows V.'s gradual merging with Sebastian. V. is not aware of the true import of what he has written, however, which means that the secret meaning of his text is like that which was never articulated by the dying author of *The Doubtful Asphodel*—it is "intertwined with other words whose familiar guise" deceived V. But this secret meaning *is* accessible to the reader of *The Real Life of Sebastian Knight*.[19]

Another major reason for seeing V. as the otherworld's agent is the incommensurability of his conception of his own literary and linguistic skills with the beauty, fluency, and novelistic artfulness of the text he produces. If one accepts as true what he says about his command of English being completely inadequate to the task of writing Sebastian's life (p. 101), then he could not have written such deftly crafted passages as the ones about the old don at Cambridge (pp. 51–52), or Goodman with his mask (pp. 56–57, 59, 60), without significant help from someone else. To suggest this conclusion is the most likely function of the passage in which V. describes the "be-an-author" correspondence course he took. That V. actually marvels at the story his instructor sent him to demonstrate "what his pupils could do and sell" confirms V.'s low opinion of his own resources. The story is clearly a pastiche of hoary clichés from popular fiction, and contains "among other things a wicked Chinaman who snarled, a brave girl with hazel eyes and a big quiet fellow whose knuckles turned white when someone really annoyed him" (p. 35). V.'s opinion that this is a "perfect glory," as he puts it without any apparent irony, strikes a distinctly dissonant note in the context of his evaluations and descriptions of Sebastian's works, or even of Goodman's trashy biography. V. appears to be an unusually perceptive judge of both of the latter, an impression that is augmented by the complete harmony between what he says and the aesthetic values and interests Nabokov expresses in his discursive and other belletristic writings. Thus, V.'s blindness with regard to the story from the writing course might be due to its not having anything to do with Sebastian's life or creations; and when V. is "on his own" with the story, his true abilities are revealed. Conversely, his insight into Sebastian's works may stem from his spiritual kinship with the latter, or from Sebastian's spiritual influence on him, which may be the same thing, according to the novel's concluding paragraph.

As we have seen, *The Real Life of Sebastian Knight* is like all of Nabokov's novels in omitting crucial information that the reader must infer. It is noteworthy, however, that V. identifies such omissions as a characteristic feature of Sebastian's writings, which he says are "a dazzling succession of gaps" that he could never imitate (p. 35). In truth, however, V.'s own narrative is filled with them: among the numerous examples are his failing to give the name of the man for whom Virginia left his and Sebastian's father, a name, however, that the reader can deduce (pp. 9, 11, 13), his omitting what it was that the old linguist had inferred about Sebastian (p. 51), or what story Uncle Black told the little boy (p. 148). Thus, because V.'s narrative is also characterized by what is defined in the world of *The Real Life of Sebastian Knight* as the distinctive feature of Sebastian's writing, and because V. claims he is incapable of imitating this feature of his half brother's craft, we are again left with the impression that Sebastian may be behind what V. sets down. In terms of writing, therefore, V.'s situation recalls Cincinnatus's in *Invitation to a Beheading*. Cincinnatus's doubts about his ability to write in the way that he wanted to were belied by the beauty of his language; but it is possible to infer that this may have been the product of the spiritual side of his being, which was shown to be linked to the otherworld. It should be noted that neither character's blindness to the relation between his writing and otherworldly influence raises any substantive questions about his testimonies being unreliable; at most, what they say is incomplete, but in a manner that induces the reader to infer the missing connection.

Lolita

THE REMARKABLE reception *Lolita* received after it was published in 1955—celebration, outrage, best-sellerdom—prompted
Nabokov to come to its defense in an unusual afterword, "On a
Book Entitled Lolita."[1] He explained that part of the reason the
novel was widely misunderstood was that "none of my American friends
have read my Russian books and thus every appraisal on the strength of
my English ones is bound to be out of focus" (p. 318). This is an important admission by Nabokov about the continuity between the Russian
and English parts of his oeuvre. Indeed, *Lolita* can best be seen as an
ingenious variation on the themes and artistic practices that characterize
all of his earlier works. In terms of the development of Nabokov's art,
what is perhaps most striking about *Lolita* is the sudden increase in the
distance between its surface features and its deeper concerns. Rather than
portray an eccentric chess genius, or a gnostic captive, or a brilliant ex-
patriate writer, Nabokov created a character obsessed with sexual perversity to explore love, passion, art, perception, fate, morality, and their
ties to the otherworld.

Nabokov's own pronouncements support this inference. In the afterword, the eloquent justification he provides for any truly artistic novel's
existence is also undoubtedly a statement about *Lolita*: "a work of fiction
exists only insofar as it affords me what I shall bluntly call aesthetic bliss,
that is a sense of being somehow, somewhere, connected with other states
of being where art (curiosity, tenderness, kindness, ecstasy) is the norm"
(pp. 316–17). References to "other states of being" and "ecstasy" in relation to art, as well as the ethical resonances of the words *tenderness* and
kindness, evoke the implications of Nabokov's "otherworldly" theme.[2]
Although Nabokov denies in the afterword that *Lolita* has any didactic
intent (p. 316)—which clearly it does not, in the limited sense of being
concerned with pointing an accusatory finger at sexual perversion in the
United States, or at "modern man's" moral failing in general—in his private correspondence with Edmund Wilson he insisted that the novel is a
"pure and austere work" and "a highly moral affair."[3] In an interview,
he made this point equally strongly: "I don't think *Lolita* is a religious
book, but I do think it is a moral one. And I do think that Humbert Humbert in his last stage is a moral man because he realizes that he loves *Lolita*

[*sic*] like any woman should be loved. But it is too late, he has destroyed her childhood. There is certainly this kind of morality in it."⁴ On other occasions he referred to *Lolita* as "the purest of all, the most abstract and carefully contrived" of his works; and "as my most difficult book—the book that treated of a theme which was so distant, so remote, from my own emotional life that it gave me a special pleasure to use my combinational talent to make it real."⁵ The notoriety that in some quarters is still attached to *Lolita*, and which ironically led to its original popular success, results largely from misunderstandings caused by the deceptive surface features of the story.

Another source of confusion, particularly with regard to the central question of whether or not Humbert undergoes an authentic moral awakening (which Nabokov believed he did) is the double point of view that is inherent in a memoir, and is thus a function of the genre. Critics have claimed that Humbert's expressions of contrition, and professions of love for the married Lolita are undermined by passages in which he allows his passion for her to eclipse all other feelings. It is essential to realize, however, that this feature of the text is not Nabokov's attempt to confuse or complicate the issue of ethics in the novel, but an inevitable consequence of the fact that Humbert's recollections of Lolita are both a record of his experiences as they happened, and the way he views them later, when he is recording them in prison. Separating the two points of view and the two time frames is a fundamental change in Humbert's attitude toward Lolita that occurs during the "friendly abyss" scene following her escape from him, and that Humbert includes near the end of his text (p. 309). Nabokov carefully plots this change in the novel's chronology, with the result that Humbert's guilt and purified love for Lolita emerge as a final, reconsidered view of her. But since his purpose is truth about his past—which he wants to explain to others and understand himself—he preserves as well his contemporaneous states of mind in all their sweep and mad passion without adulterating them through retroactive projection. Thus, whatever moral equivocation Humbert records is confined solely to his contemporaneous experiences with Lolita. A related, double point of view informs the image of Charlotte that Humbert creates. Even though she remains forever a philistine in his mind, his expressions of contrition are his final, and dominant attitude toward her.⁶

Although it would be misleading simply to translate Humbert's passion for little girls—what he calls "nympholepsy"—into the terms of Nabokov's aesthetics, art is intimately connected with Humbert's pursuits and thus with what lies at the novel's core.⁷ On the obvious level that most readers have noted Humbert refers to himself as a "poet" (e.g., pp. 90, 133), both in relation to his perceptions of Lolita and of the world around

him, and his attempts to render these in words in the long confession that
constitutes the body of the novel (as well as in a number of interpolated
smaller pieces, including verse). Humbert also raises implicit questions
about the nature of his artistic gift by making a typically Nabokovian
connection between it and ethics when he asserts "poets never kill" (p.
90), which, it should be noted, he writes *after* he murders Quilty. However, the fact that Nabokov grants his character's document a range of
cunning narrative strategies, and numerous passages of great beauty, pathos, and humor (in addition to some of bathetically purple prose) suggests that Humbert's presumptions about his talent cannot be altogether
dismissed.[8] In other words, Nabokov can be understood as having intentionally shared part of his own genius as a writer with a first-person narrator who in most other respects is deplorable.[9] This results in a fictional
world that presents unusual complexities from the point of view of differ-
entiating between truth and falsehood, right and wrong, parody and what
can be taken literally.

One path through this tangle is provided by Humbert's attempt to define nymphets, which clearly lies at the heart of his compulsion to explain
his life to himself as well as his readers. What has not been realized by
commentators is that his formulations recall the specific terms of Nabokov's descriptions of cosmic synchronization and artistic inspiration in
his earlier novels, in the "The Art of Literature and Commonsense," and
in chapter 11 of *Speak, Memory*, which he wrote at approximately the
same time as his early stages of work on *Lolita*.[10] The effect of this overlap between Nabokov's aesthetic concepts and Humbert's erotically
charged speculations about nymphets is that the latter emerge as aestheticized—as a sort of potential artistic medium, subject, or construct about
which Humbert thinks and with which he attempts to work. Humbert's
theories confront pragmatics when he meets Lolita; and as his experiences with her prove, there are disastrous consequences to confusing love
and erotics with aesthetics when the object of one's attention is an independent being and refuses to be malleable. Put more simply, Humbert's
desire "to fix once for all the perilous magic of nymphets" (p. 136) proves
to be realizable in words, but not in the flesh.[11]

The central, albeit abstract, instance of Humbert's aestheticization of
love and passion is his description of the fundamental difference between
nymphets and normal girls. He claims the latter "are incomparably more
dependent on the *spatial world of synchronous phenomena* than on that
intangible island of entranced time where Lolita plays with her likes"
(italics added; p. 19). To speak of timelessness in connection with intense
love or passion is of course a commonplace in writing on the subject from
all times. But the synchronization of phenomena in space, especially when
contrasted with a privileged moment in time, recalls nothing so much as

Nabokov's discussions of "cosmic synchronization" or "inspiration." There are two crucial differences, however. The first is of course that Nabokov's subject is the provenance of verbal art, not the nature of nymphets or other human beings (although it is important to recall that he describes love in *Speak, Memory* in terms very similar to those he uses for cosmic synchronization). And the second is that Humbert severs into two incompatible realms what Nabokov describes as phases in a causal sequence or continuum: it is precisely the artist's recognition of linkages, or synchronization, among widely separated phenomena, that, when combined with memories, leads to a timeless, epiphanic moment of inspiration. Because of Humbert's distortions, the relationship between his formulations and Nabokov's ideas can be understood as *parodic*. Humbert's conception of nymphets thus illustrates what Nabokov once described in an interview as his practice of giving characters ideas that are "deliberately flawed."[12]

This inference is supported by other details in Humbert's analysis. His explanation that one has to be "an artist and a madman . . . to discern at once, by ineffable signs" a nymphet among other little girls (p. 19) parallels Nabokov's insistence on the importance of sensory data for the creation of art. (In practice, Humbert of course betrays this requirement.) When Humbert first meets Lolita, and recognizes in her, as he believes, his long lost Annabel, he experiences a timeless moment that is very like Nabokov's descriptions of the disappearance of time under the impact of memory or during artistic inspiration: "The twenty-five years I had lived . . . tapered to a palpitating point, and vanished"; "I find it most difficult to express with adequate force that flash, that shiver, that impact of passionate recognition" (p. 41). The result of Humbert's privileged perception of nymphets is a kind of insight into a transcendent realm that resembles the Nabokovian artistic epiphany. Humbert claims that in contrast to the sexual experiences of normal men with "terrestrial" women he had "caught glimpses of an incomparably more poignant bliss" (p. 20), one that is "*hors concours* . . . belongs to another class, another plane of sensitivity" (p. 168). He also speaks of the nymphets he encounters as if they were indelibly colored for him by the timelessness of epiphanic perceptions: he wants the young prostitute Monique to remain forever in his consciousness as she was "for a minute or two" (p. 25), and yearns for "the eternal Lolita as reflected in my blood," even when he realizes she will change with time (p. 67).

In the context of Nabokov's descriptions of cosmic synchronization, Humbert's severing the realm of normal little girls (a "spatial world of synchronous phenomena") from that of nymphets (an "island of entranced time") constitutes an implicit claim regarding his ability to achieve a form of transcendence without going through the preliminary step that anchors the experience in the material world. In short, Humbert is actually speaking of what is, in Nabokov's terms, an unwarranted leap into an empyrean. This is one of the most important conclusions to be drawn from the famous "couch scene," during which Humbert believes he transcends the quotidian plane of being—but only by solipsizing Lolita, that is, by *not* seeing her for what she is.

The fundamental error in Humbert's conceptual segregation of "nymphets" from little girls is amply confirmed by his own experiences. In one of the most important passages in the novel, when he finally and unequivocally acknowledges that his relations with Lolita were profoundly immoral, Humbert is standing on a cliff edge, looking out over a vast valley containing a town, and listening to children at play in the distance. The passage is filled with sound repetitions, and Humbert's perceptions are dominated by a sense of harmony and synaesthetic linkages between sights and sounds. In other words, we have the ingredients implied by the idea of a "spatial world of synchronous phenomena." And it is in this setting that Humbert comes to his momentous conclusion that the "hopelessly poignant thing" was not that Lolita had run away from him with Quilty but that her voice was missing from "that concord" rising from the valley floor (pp. 309–310). The entire proto-epiphanic image is thus an implicit rebuttal of Humbert's original idea that nymphets occupy a special realm of frozen time different from that of other girl children. But the implications of the passage reach even further, because by erasing the difference between Lolita and other girls Humbert is in effect abandoning the entire category of "nymphet," which, in retrospect, appears to have been nothing more than his aberrant fantasy. It is noteworthy that in his afterword to *Lolita* Nabokov includes this scene in his short list of the "nerves . . . secret points, the subliminal co-ordinates by means of which the book is plotted" (p. 318).

The privileged nature of Humbert's experience above the "friendly abyss" is also underscored by its position at the intersection of several important motifs in the novel. One of these is Humbert's constant concern with ethical questions, which is resolved in the scene; another involves his varying, but repeated impression of being on the edge of a figurative abyss during his travels with Lolita. A third and less obvious motif consists of scenes that are structured as antitheses to the feeling of harmony and unity he experiences on the cliff edge; in fact, what characterizes them is a striking disunity among their constituent elements. Humbert calls attention to this himself in a passage that is particularly important because it also includes something like an occult message that he does not appear to understand. While waiting for Lolita at a gasoline station, he describes the various unrelated objects he sees, and comments that the rhythm of the radio music coming out the door "was *not syn-*

chronized with the heave and the flutter and other gestures of wind-animated vegetation"; then he adds: "The sound of Charlotte's last sob *incongruously* vibrated through me as, with her dress *athwart* the rhythm, Lolita *veered* from a totally *unexpected* direction" (italics added; pp. 213–14). On a simple level, Lolita had presumably again eluded Humbert's watchful eye for a few moments in order to communicate with Quilty, thus prefiguring her permanent escape shortly thereafter. But the reference to the incongruity of Charlotte's "last sob" in connection with the "unexpectedness" of Lolita's appearance can be read as Nabokov's allusion to Charlotte's final words to Humbert shortly before she is killed about how he will never see Lolita again (p. 98). The "sob" thus foreshadows Humbert's imminent loss of Lolita, and is "incongruous" only because he is unaware of what is in store for him (which contrasts with the true Nabokovian epiphany). The association of the sob with Humbert's fragmented perception suggests that the latter may be a fateful predisposition on his part—one that is intimately connected not only with his loss of Lolita, but also with how he perceives her. This interpretation is supported by the link between Humbert's holistic perception in the scene on the cliff edge (from which Lolita is absent) and his view of her as his victim. The "sob" also fits the pattern of other clairvoyant visions of Charlotte in or near death, which literally haunt Humbert during his life with Lolita.

Another passage suggesting that Humbert's experiences are parodies of cosmic synchronization is a diary entry he makes soon after meeting Lolita. He quotes her request to be taken swimming, which she delivers in a "voluptuous whisper," and then enumerates the following details: "The reflection of the afternoon sun, a dazzling white diamond with innumerable iridescent spikes quivered on the round back of a parked car. The leafage of a voluminous elm played its mellow shadows upon the clapboard wall of the house. Two poplars shivered and shook. You could make out the formless sounds of remote traffic; a child calling 'Nancy, Nan-cy!' In the house, Lolita had put on her favorite 'Little Carmen' record which I used to call 'Dwarf Conductors,' making her snort with mock derision at my mock wit" (p. 47). These details stand out in effective relief, but it is odd (in the context of Nabokov's style) that potential linkages among them, which clearly lie just beneath the surface, are never realized by Humbert: the quivering of the sun's reflection on the car is not unlike the play of shadows on the wall or the shivering of poplars; and these motions, in turn, have something of the randomness of the traffic sounds and a child's cries (which of course foreshadow the children's voices in the scene on the cliff edge, and which Humbert perceives altogether differently). Moreover, the reference to the record establishes obvious links with the orgasmic couch scene during which Humbert garbles the song in question. One would also think that the entire brief diary entry would be associated with the effect that Lolita's voluptuous whisper had on Humbert. However, the listed details are not erotically charged, and are free of timelessness or synchronization; in fact, time's passage is implied by the gap between Lolita's whisper and the record she plays. Given Humbert's still selfish, and therefore limited view of Lolita at this point in his story, it is possible to conclude that his method of seeing the rest of the world is similarly flawed. The importance of this conclusion is that it points to his particular limitation as an artist in terms of Nabokov's values. This also has a bearing on the nature of the memoir he produces, which on a textual level is filled with numerous linkages that he does not notice (in addition to those for which he does claim responsibility).

The ethical implications of perception in Nabokov's terms are underscored in a scene that relates the effect Lolita's appearance has on Humbert to the way he perceives details. He is on the verge of seeing her again after a month's lapse, and wants to capture the moment "in all its trivial and fateful detail." The reader inevitably expects Humbert to be in a state of erotico-aesthetic inspiration. But the description that follows is strikingly unpoetic, and shows nothing of Humbert's conception of nymphets: "hag Holmes writing out a receipt, scratching her head, pulling a drawer out of her desk . . . photographs of girl-children." Moreover, among the various items he notices in the camp office is "some gaudy moth or butterfly, still alive, safely pinned to the wall" (p. 112); in Nabokov's world, Humbert's uncertainty about the two major subdivisions of the order Lepidoptera is an obvious encoded sign of blindness. The anti-epiphanic description of the setting continues even after Lolita arrives, when "for a second" Humbert is struck by the impression that she is "less pretty than the mental imprint I had cherished for more than a month" (p. 113). (Humbert makes similar, "prosaic" observations about Lolita's adolescent philistinism and grubbiness later in the novel as well [e.g., pp. 150, 206].) In other words, Humbert at first sees her as something other than his quintessential nymphet, which, therefore, again puts into question whether or not nymphets exist outside his imagination, and only during aberrant moments at that. This is reinforced by Humbert's acknowledgment that his impression regarding Lolita's looks carries with it a distinct sense of moral obligation to give this "orphan" a "healthy and happy childhood" (p. 113). Seeing Lolita for what she is thus elicits a "normal" human reaction from Humbert. This state lasts a very short time, however, before the "angelic line of conduct" is "erased," and Humbert sees her as "my Lolita again" (p. 113), which indicates that a secondary projection has obscured the initial perception. An additional element in this sequence that underscores the difference between Humbert's perception of Lolita and his conception of nymphets is his remark when the ethical imperative disappears that "time moves ahead of our fancies." This suggests that, paradoxically, Humbert sees Lolita as an *orphan* during a timeless fancy (what he also calls "a very narrow human interval between two tiger heartbeats"), which counters the notion of Lolita being a *nymphet* on an island of entranced time. In turn, this moment anticipates the scene on the cliff edge when Humbert acknowledges his guilt during a proto-epiphanic moment.

But what of Humbert's claims throughout his text regarding his unerring ability to discern a nymphet by means of subtle physical indices? Although in theory this resembles Nabokov's elevation of perceptual acuity to a primary aesthetic principle, Humbert's claims are in fact undermined by the varieties of flagrant blindness that he manifests, most notably with regard to Lolita's emotional and psychological constitution during the years of their travels. His claims are also undermined by another fundamental principle in his conception of how a nymphet can be perceived, which, moreover, appears to be yet another parodic evocation of Nabokov's aesthetics in *Speak, Memory*. Humbert's discussion of the conditions necessary to perceive a nymphet hinges on the issue of time, which he says "plays such a magic part in the matter." His point is that there must be a significant difference in age "between maiden and man to enable the latter to come under a nymphet's spell. It is a question of focal adjustment, of a certain distance that the inner eye thrills to surmount" (p. 19). Humbert's translation of time into space ("a certain distance") is a curious echo of his announcement at the outset of this entire discussion of nymphets that he has chosen to "substitute time terms for spatial ones" (p. 18). In fact, he does the opposite, because he refers to the ages of "nine" and "fourteen" in spatial terms: "as the boundaries—the mirrory beaches and rosy rocks—of an enchanted island haunted by those nymphets of mine." The result of this confusion is that time and space become interchangeable in Humbert's discussions of nymphets, with the unintentionally ironic consequence that his emphasis on temporal *difference* begins to sound like spatial *distance*. (This also further undermines his distinction between girls occupying a "spatial world" and nymphets who live on an "island of entranced time.") And distance cannot help but raise questions about the accuracy of perception. Indeed, there are several descriptive passages later in the novel that resemble dramatizations of Humbert's original formulation, and that suggest his distanced cognitive stance is an inducement to projection rather than accurate perception. In one he states: "it may well be that the very attraction immaturity has for me lies not so much in the limpidity of pure young forbidden fairy child beauty as in the security of a situation where infinite perfections fill the gap between the little given and the great promised"; and he goes on to admit that "I sometimes won the race between my fancy and nature's reality" (p. 266). In another passage about how he slowly and stealthily approaches Lolita before trying to touch her, Humbert states that he seems "to see her through the wrong end of a telescope" (p. 56), which means, of course, that she appears to be more distant than she in fact is, and that he is actively resisting seeing her as she is.

A discussion of related issues also appears in *Speak, Memory*, and develops out of Nabokov's marveling at such things as the beauty of magic lantern slides when not projected but held up to the light, and, conversely, the beauty of slides under the microscope. He concludes: "There is, it would seem, in the dimensional scale of the world a kind of delicate meeting place between imagination and knowledge, a point, arrived at by diminishing large things and enlarging small ones, that is intrinsically artistic" (pp. 166–67). The implication of this passage is that imagination, and, by extension, art can be valid only if rooted in precise knowledge, and that the blending of knowledge and imagination, or the transition between them, is not arbitrary but a function of specific circumstances. Thus knowledge and imagination are not only not incompatible, but are necessary complements for each other, which is an idea that Nabokov repeated often in other discursive writings as well. In these terms, Humbert's error is that he has not respected the "delicate meeting place" between fact and fancy in his perceptions of Lolita or other "nymphets" (Annabel was another matter because she was Humbert's coeval and loved him). A remark of Humbert's following his epochal visit to Lolita after she has become Mrs. Schiller confirms this inference and shows that he has come to understand his error in the same terms: "I reviewed my case. With the utmost simplicity and clarity I now saw myself and my love. Previous attempts seemed *out of focus* by comparison" (italics added; p. 284). In *Lolita*, Nabokov can thus be understood as having chosen to dramatize the failure of a character to respect the crucial dividing line between insight and solipsism, or sensory data and imagination, that other characters, such as Fyodor in *The Gift* or Sebastian Knight, succeed in maintaining.

Parody is not the only link between Humbert's and Nabokov's ideas; there are also some topics on which they simply agree. Two of the more obvious instances are their keen eye for varieties of American "poshlost'," including psychoanalysis, and their similar admiration for American scenic beauties. A more complicated link between them hinges on another aspect of time. Humbert describes an essay he had once published entitled "Mimir and Memory" that presents "a theory of perceptual time based on the circulation of the blood and conceptually depending . . . on the mind's being conscious not only of matter but also its own self, thus creating a continuous spanning of two points (the storable future and the stored past)" (p. 262). What Humbert seems to mean by this is that the sense of time is a function of being alive (i.e., of the "circulation of the blood"), and thus is not a fact independent of human existence; moreover, both the individual's perceptions and his apprehension of time may be relative because both depend on the individual's consciousness.

The first thing to say about this is that Humbert's perceptions of Lolita (as well as other, earlier nymphets) flagrantly contradict his theory in the essay. Prior to his moral awakening on the cliff edge, Humbert's relations with Lolita hinge on his attempts to ignore or deny her individuality: as a nymphet she purportedly exists out of time, but Humbert in fact worries intermittently about what he will do once she outgrows this state. Thus, in the case of his relations with the most important person in his life, Humbert is not fully aware of what lies outside him and focuses primarily on what is within his consciousness. In short, no "continuous spanning of two points" actually takes place with regard to Lolita. Instead, Humbert recalls the specific "circulatory" imagery of the essay when he speaks of the "*eternal* Lolita as reflected in my *blood*" (italics added; p. 67). This immutability contradicts the process implied in his "theory of perceptual time."

Although Humbert's linking of time to the circulatory system might seem at first to be a joke or a pseudoprofundity, intended perhaps as a sign of his eccentricity, it is most interesting that Nabokov makes the same connection in *Speak, Memory* when he speaks of his little son's fondness for all fast, wheeled things, especially railway trains. (The deeply emotional tone of the entire chapter in which this description appears precludes any possibility that he may have been joking.) This leads to Nabokov's implication that time is a human projection onto the world, and that the child's love for velocity may be an adumbration of cosmic synchronization, since the outermost limit of the desire to maximize spatial enjoyment is omnipresence or omniscience in a moment of time. (Fyodor in *The Gift* comes to very similar conclusions [354: 384].)

Humbert's "Mimir and Memory" can thus be seen as a reasonably faithful variation on Nabokov's own ideas. What significance does this have for understanding *Lolita*? Firstly, it adds weight to the conclusion that Humbert is not simply a madman, and thus implies that other hidden "Nabokovian" themes, ideas, and practices in his long confession might have to be taken seriously when making sense of the novel as a whole. Secondly, Humbert's essay also has a bearing on how we can understand the status of Lolita in his life. Although the theory of perception in "Mimir and Memory" and Humbert's actual perception of Lolita as a nymphet are contradictory and incommensurable, she remains a central fact of his existence; another way of saying this is that she has an intrusive relationship to it, and is discordant within it. This may seem a paradoxical claim, given that Humbert spends much of his life anticipating or searching for Lolita following his abortive love for Annabel. But in fact, seeing Lolita as alien to at least a part of Humbert's consciousness underscores her fateful role in his life. He is, as can be demonstrated, driven toward her by forces that largely transcend his ken.

Another instance of Humbert's being given a distinctive Nabokovian trait is the narrative strategy he claims to have used in telling his story. When he finally extracts Quilty's name from Lolita, Humbert does not actually reveal it to the reader; instead, he makes an oblique allusion to a moment several years before when Jean Farlow almost spoke Quilty's name out loud. Humbert explains that his purpose in doing this is to let the reader experience the same kind of realization that he had when he heard the name: "Quietly the fusion took place, and everything fell into order, into the pattern of branches that I have woven throughout this memoir with the express and perverse purpose of rendering . . . that golden and monstrous peace through the satisfaction of logical recognition, which my most inimical reader should experience now" (p. 274). Nabokov has thus granted Humbert a form of artistic control that is modeled on his own (the importance of which is signaled at the conclusion of *Speak, Memory* by the reference to the game "Find What the Sailor Has Hidden"). The crucial difference between the two, however, is that Nabokov's formal method parallels the structure of cosmic synchronization. By contrast, the "golden and monstrous peace" to which Humbert refers in connection with his aesthetic structure recalls the conclusion of his falsely epiphanic ecstasy with Lolita in the couch scene ("that state of absolute security, confidence and reliance not found elsewhere in conscious life" [p. 62]) which, rather than being expansive and oriented toward making connections between the self and what lies outside it, is narrowly (indeed solipsistically) focused on what lies within the self.

Humbert's experience in the couch scene is a major thematic and structural node in the novel that is characterized by a hybridization of aesthetics and erotics: as he puts it, he feels "suspended on the brink of [a] voluptuous abyss (a nicety of physiological equipoise comparable to certain techniques in the arts)" (p. 62). (This image of the "abyss" has an obvious antiphonal relationship to the scene on the cliff edge when Humbert experiences his moral awakening, a fact of which he is of course unaware.) The result of this synthesis, as he freely admits, is that "what I had madly possessed was not she, but my creation, another, fanciful Lolita—perhaps, more real than Lolita; overlapping, encasing her; floating between me and her, and having no will, no consciousness—indeed, no life of her own" (p. 64). It is a measure of Humbert's occasional perspicacity that he is sufficiently aware of what he is doing to say that "Lolita had been safely solipsized"; the Russian translation makes the point even more bluntly: "Real'nost' Lolity byla blagopoluchno otmenena," which means, literally, "Lolita's reality was successfully canceled" (pp. 62: 49). There is thus considerable authorial irony implied by Humbert's assertion that because Lolita was supposedly unaware of what he was doing he "had stolen the honey of a spasm without impairing the morals of a minor" (p. 64). That Humbert would be concerned with ethical considerations is to his credit in Nabokov's terms, but his actual blindness with regard to Lolita in this and numerous other scenes is a clear sign of his moral failing. Indeed, Humbert's congratulating himself because Lolita had noticed nothing is itself undermined by how he describes her during the act and immediately afterward: "a sudden shrill note in her voice," "she wiggled and squirmed, and threw her head back, and her teeth rested on her glistening underlip as she half-turned away," "she stood and blinked, cheeks aflame, hair awry" (p. 63). Later in the novel, in what may be a reference to the same scene, Lolita accuses Humbert of trying to violate her when he was still her mother's roomer (p. 207). Humbert's misperception of Lolita even betrays his love for Annabel, which, as he admits, is the mainspring of his life and all his subsequent passion. The distinctive feature of the "frenzy of mutual possession" that he experienced with Annabel is that it "might have been assuaged only by our actually imbibing and assimilating every particle of each other's soul and flesh" (p. 14). With Lolita, by contrast, there is neither mutual attraction, nor any concern on Humbert's part with anything like her soul.

The scene on the couch also contains several details the sole purpose of which appears to be to call into question Humbert's entire theory of nymphets. For example, at the outset, Lolita and Humbert grab an apple and a magazine out of each other's hands, which leads him to comment: "pity no film had recorded the curious pattern, the monogrammatic linkage of our simultaneous or overlapping moves" (p. 60). Humbert's emphasis on the patterning and simultaneity of their actions recalls what he had said earlier about normal girls being dependent on the world of synchronous phenomena in contrast to nymphets (and constitutes a sharp contrast to Quilty's pornographic film project that Lolita rejects). Thus the implication of Humbert's perception of Lolita in terms of spatial synchronization is either that Lolita is a normal girl, or that nymphets do not exist. The other detail with a comparable function is that Humbert enters into an isolated, timeless state of bliss when Lolita is on his lap. Since she is unaware of his state, his generalization about nymphets and islands of timelessness seems more a remark about his own peculiar consciousness and solipsistic projections than about Lolita or other hypothetical nymphets.

In order to grasp fully the nature of Nabokov's deceptive complication of ethics in the novel, it is important to realize that a number of Humbert's perceptions of Lolita transcend his habitual purblindness. The most striking illustration is his celebration of her playing tennis in Colorado. He does not see her as a nymphet at this point, but as a participant in a game comparable to the theatrical exercises she also enjoys. In Humbert's view, her form is so perfect he has "the teasing delirious feeling of teetering on the very brink of unearthly order and splendor" (p. 232). Although this image might seem to be yet another variant of his specious claims about nymphets and the realm they inhabit, the reference to the "brink" suggests a veiled connection with the cliff edge where Humbert undergoes his moral epiphany. In fact, on an abstract level, the two passages share the same cardinal feature—Humbert's acknowledgment of the difference between what Lolita actually is, and his own view of her as a nymphet or other aestheticized being: "Her tennis was the highest point to which *I can imagine* a young creature bringing the art of make-believe, although I daresay, *for her it was* the very geometry of basic reality" (italics added; p. 233). The scene is also distinguished by the fact that Humbert pays close attention to all the specifics of Lolita's gestures and behavior during the game, rather than allowing projections to intervene (pp. 232–36). Humbert even unwittingly registers a typically Nabokovian authorial intrusion into the entire sequence, which sanctions it as being especially noteworthy, when he comments: "An inquisitive butterfly passed, dipping, between us" (p. 236).

A more intriguing imprimatur for Humbert's sensation that he is close to something literally "unearthly" is that the description of Lolita's game is followed by the fulfillment of a prophetic vision he had some time earlier. He is called away from Lolita's side on the tennis court by a telephone call that proves to be a ruse. When he returns, he sees her playing with three other people—Quilty and two of his friends, as the reader, but not Humbert, concludes. This incident is noteworthy not only because it provides additional evidence for Quilty's shadowing Humbert and Lolita prior to spiriting her away, but also because Humbert actually foresaw a variant of the scene during one of Lolita's previous tennis games in Arizona. He was returning with drinks he had brought for her and another girl with whom she had been playing (which is itself part of a fatidic pattern, since it foreshadows his return to the tennis court in the episode with Quilty), and feels "a sudden void" in his chest when he sees that the court is empty:

> I stooped to set down the glasses on a bench and for some reason, with a kind of icy vividness, saw Charlotte's face in death, and I glanced around, and noticed Lo in white shorts receding . . . in the company of a tall man who carried two tennis rackets. I sprang after them, but as I was crashing through the shrubbery, I saw, in an alternate vision, as if life's course constantly

branched, Lo, in slacks, and her companion, in shorts . . . beating bushes
with their rackets in listless search for their last lost ball. (P. 165)

As a number of commentators have noted, Humbert's vision of a man
with Lolita is of course a prefiguration of Quilty.[13] But it should be noted
that the image of "Charlotte's face in death" can also be linked directly
to Humbert's imminent loss because of her warning to him before she
died that he would never see Lolita again (p. 98). Charlotte's prediction
is borne out not only by Lolita's eventual escape, but also by the fact that
Lolita the nymphet no longer exists either in Humbert's imagination or
in reality when he finally meets her again as Mrs. Richard Schiller. The
prophetic character of Humbert's vision is also confirmed by the detail
that he foresees Lolita leaving in "white shorts," whereas in actuality she
is wearing "slacks" while playing with her friend in Arizona (p. 165).
When Quilty intrudes into the tennis game in Colorado, Lolita is indeed
wearing "white wide little-boy shorts" (pp. 232–33).

The significance of the links between the two passages dealing with
tennis is twofold. Humbert emerges as being caught in a sequence of
events of which he is only partially aware, and of which Quilty is a function rather than a cause. The second tennis scene's role as a confirmation of a clairvoyant vision makes it stand out in the novel and suggests that its other implications are also especially important. And in
contrast to his problematic segregation of nymphets on a timeless island,
Humbert does manage to glimpse Lolita as transcending his habitual reality—but only when he focuses on her, and temporarily eschews the category of nymphet. Humbert's experience in this instance thus approaches
an unadulterated Nabokovian moment of inspiration.

In his afterword to *Lolita*, Nabokov describes the "initial shiver of inspiration" that eventually became the novel as having been "somehow
prompted by a newspaper story about an ape in the Jardin des Plantes,
who, after months of coaxing by a scientist, produced the first drawing
ever charcoaled by an animal: the sketch showed the bars of the poor
creature's cage" (p. 313). Whether or not this is a faithful account of the
origin of the novel is less important than the clear hint the anecdote provides about the novel's central problem, which can be put into the form
of a question: what can an imprisoned creature see other than the means
of its imprisonment?[14] This is, in effect, a formulation of the problem that
preoccupied Nabokov throughout his oeuvre. It is surely no mere coincidence that Humbert suggests the most obvious parallel between the anecdote and the novel when he refers to his "aging ape eyes" at the moment
he first sees Lolita (p. 41; later, Quilty calls Humbert "you ape, you," p.
300). In part, this is of course an allusion to the "bestial" nature of his

passion, and thus reflects his ambivalence toward it. But because the context for the phrase is the link between his memories of Annabel's nudity and what he imagines is concealed beneath the garment Lolita is wearing when he first sees her, the reader concludes that Humbert's perceptions of Lolita and Annabel are inextricably tied. This point is also amply and overtly confirmed as early as the novel's eighth line—"there might have been no Lolita at all had I not loved . . . a certain initial girl-child"—and by Humbert's references to Lolita as "my Riviera love" and "the same child" (p. 41). Thus, Annabel emerges as an analogue to the bars on the ape's cage in the anecdote, and Humbert's perception of Lolita is like the ape's drawing of the bars of its cage. In other words, Humbert cannot help perceiving the nymphets who constitute the world in which he is trapped because of Annabel.

It is another sign of Humbert's intermittent perspicacity that he invokes the concept of fate when he ponders his fixation on nymphets in general and Lolita in particular. He raises a crucial question for understanding the novel when he asks if it was during the summer with Annabel "that the rift in my life began; or was my excessive desire for that child only the first evidence of an inherent singularity?" (p. 15). Neither he, nor the novel can answer his question unequivocally. But a comparison of Humbert's short-lived affair with Annabel to analogous moments in Nabokov's earlier works suggests that their meeting was somehow foreordained. Firstly, all of Humbert's descriptions stress that the attraction between them was not only physical but also spiritual (e.g., pp. 14, 16). Secondly, the details he provides to prove this point imply that their spiritual link was underlain by experiences that touched upon the otherworldly: "Long after her death I felt her thoughts floating through mine. Long before we met we had the same dreams. We compared notes. We found strange affinities. The same June of the same year (1919) a stray canary had fluttered into her house and mine, in two widely separated countries" (p. 16). These are precisely the kinds of seminal details that a purely metaliterary reading of the novel cannot explain (except by stressing metaliterary patterning beyond all credibility), and which, therefore, militate against it. (A different but not unrelated textual detail that adds to the slight flavor of the extramundane in aspects of Humbert's childhood is that his aunt, appropriately named Sybil, predicted correctly that she would die soon after his sixteenth birthday [p. 12].)

The Platonic conception of love implied in Humbert's description of his tie to Annabel can be found in Nabokov's early poetry, in the case of Luzhin and his fiancée, Cincinnatus and his idealized image of a soul mate, and Fyodor and Zina. The sense of spiritual affinity that Humbert has with Annabel after her death is also like V.'s with Sebastian after his death. And the seemingly trivial detail about the canaries that Humbert mentions is actually no different in kind from what Nabokov describes when he speaks of fateful patterning in *Speak, Memory*, whose significance is unrelated to its content. All this lends weight to the argument in favor of taking what Humbert says about his love for Annabel at face value—as an extraordinary experience that literally marked him for life: "We loved each other with a premature love, marked by a fierceness that so often destroys adult lives. I was a strong lad and survived; but the poison was in the wound" (p. 20). In terms of the hierarchy of values Humbert establishes in the novel, his love for Annabel raises him to her level—to "that same enchanted island of time" she occupies. Humbert's search for nymphets is thus a (futile) attempt to reexperience what he knew through Annabel, which appears to have been an authentic spiritual affinity for a specific girl, marked by a plane of being transcending the earthly.

This larger context for Humbert's existence is not limited to his child-hood. From the start, the word *fate*, and what it implies, is a leitmotif of his narrative about Lolita (e.g., pp. 16, 23, 52, 68, 105, 118, 175); he goes to the extent of personifying it as "Aubrey McFate" (p. 58), and invoking "angels" as the agents behind it (p. 169). Moreover, Humbert's conception of "destiny" is like Nabokov's in that it is essentially backward- rather than forward-looking: Humbert understands that memory can use "certain obscure indications" to discern patterns in the past, and that these should not be read as foreshadowings of the future (p. 213). He is also aware of the limitations to which memory and interpretation are subject: "It is just possible that had I gone to a strong hypnotist he might have extracted from me and arrayed in a logical pattern certain chance memories that I have threaded through my book with considerably more ostentation than they present themselves with to my mind even now when I know what to seek in the past" (p. 257). This admission cannot but prompt the reader to search for the connections and meanings that elude Humbert.

Humbert's own hermeneutic efforts yield both insight and varying degrees of error or uncertainty regarding events that appear to have been portentous. On the one hand, he marvels at the coincidence of finding a book in his prison library that contains a series of references to people and events in his life (pp. 33–34). On the other, there is no indication that he ever recognizes the significance of Lolita's saying during a thunderstorm, "I am not a lady and do not like lightning" (pp. 222: 201), which parodies the title of one of Quilty's plays that is mentioned in the book: "*The Lady Who Loved Lightning.*" Moreover, Lolita's remark is also an echo of the accidental death of Humbert's mother, which he laconically summarizes as "picnic, lightning" (p. 12). It is worth noting that Nabokov made a significant change in this scene when he translated the novel into Russian: he added Humbert's comment that Lolita "stranno vyrazi-las' " when she utters her phrase about lightning, which means, literally, "expressed herself in a strange manner," or "put it oddly." This inevitably calls the reader's attention to the hidden meaning of her words in a way that the English original does not, and at the same time implies that Humbert could not have noticed it.

Humbert also wonders at the coincidence that Lolita is in fact on a hike at her camp after he had asserted that she was, for the benefit of the Farlows (pp. 102, 108). This event is accompanied by the additional curious detail that the pay telephone he uses to call the camp returns all the coins he had deposited, causing him to wonder if this is not a signal from McFate (p. 109). The reader familiar with *The Real Life of Sebastian Knight* may be tempted to answer this question on the basis of the similarity between the telephone's returning Humbert's money and Silbermann's returning V.'s. In both instances, the sudden gifts are contrary to expected norms, and can be correlated with the hints that both recipients' quests are touched by the otherworld.

Humbert seems to be at least partially aware of the rather fantastic series of coincidences that leads to his landing at Charlotte's and eventually becoming Lolita's guardian: the McCoo house, in which he had been planning to stay, burns down upon his arrival in Ramsdale (p. 37), and he has to be put up somewhere else. (In the Russian translation of the scene where Lolita is telling Humbert about her life after she had run away from him and how Quilty's ranch burned down, Nabokov adds the following remark to Humbert's lines: "Chto zh, u Mak-Ku bylo tozhe pokhozhee imia, i tozhe sgorel dom" [p. 257], which means, "Well, McCoo had a similar name, and his house also burned down." This enlarges the network of patterning in the novel by exploiting the echo between Quilty's nickname in the Russian version, "Ku" as in "Koo," and the McCoos, and between the latter and Humbert's personified "McFate." Similarly, Boyd has pointed out that Nabokov strove to augment the theme of fate in Humbert's life when he wrote his screenplay of *Lolita* "as compensation for the loss of Humbert's reflections on the theme— which only shows how essential Nabokov felt it to be to any treatment of the *Lolita* story—or to make explicit the motivation implicit in the novel.")[15] Humbert is thus handed over to Charlotte as a boarder, but the only reason he manages to marry her, and stay near Lolita, is that the old spinster Miss Phalen, who was supposed to take care of Humbert and Lolita while Charlotte sought employment in a city, happens to fall and break her hip "on the very day" Humbert arrives (p. 58). Charlotte's death is also multifariously fatidic: it saves Humbert from having to leave Lolita because his passion for her has been discovered; it is a realization of the murder that he himself contemplates; and it is caused by the neighbor's dog that he mentions as attacking his car when he is first being driven to Charlotte's house (p. 38).

What prevents these overt coincidences from becoming merely a metaliterary parody of fate is that they are anchored to the "reality" of *Lolita*'s fictional world by the much subtler patterning in Humbert's life of which he is *unaware*. An important example is Humbert's observation that his pursuer left clues that were "tuned" to his "mind and manner." Humbert goes so far as to conclude that "the tone" of Quilty's brain "had affinities with my own" (p. 251). What Humbert does not appear to notice, however, is that this is a trait he also shared with Annabel, whose thoughts he "felt," and with whom he had other "strange affinities" (p. 16). This coincidence adds to the portentousness of Quilty's role in helping Lolita escape Humbert, which can be seen as a variation on Humbert's loss of Annabel, and a foreshadowing of his permanent loss of Lolita when she becomes Mrs. Richard Schiller. In light of this, Humbert's calling Quilty his "brother" (p. 249) is much more ironic than might have seemed at first. Commentators tend to interpret this reference in terms of the Romantic literary theme of "the double," a concept whose relevance to Nabokov's works is questionable, and which he rejected in interviews. Humbert's use of the word can actually be explained more simply—as an instance of his ironic play with Quilty's claim about being Lolita's "uncle" when he signs her out of the hospital (p. 248). Since Humbert on occasion thinks of Lolita as his daughter, her "uncle" is potentially his "brother." The hint of a covert tie based on unspecified "affinities" linking Annabel, Humbert, and Quilty is more intriguing than the obvious connections among Humbert, Quilty, and Lolita because it points to a misperception on Humbert's part about the nature of the mesh in which he is caught. (The two triangles cannot be equated because the nature of Humbert's tie to Annabel is fundamentally different from that to Lolita.) Humbert understands that Lolita's illness "was somehow the development of a theme—that it had the same taste and tone as the series of linked impressions which had puzzled and tormented me during our journey; I imagined that secret agent, or secret lover, or prankster, or hallucination, or whatever he was, prowling around the hospital" (p. 243). What he does not recognize, however, is that Quilty (although not exclusively a "nympholept") is not a random pursuer but a significant part of the same pattern that begins with Annabel and centers on her. Quilty's connection to Humbert's fate is further strengthened by the fact that he connives with Lolita at the very time when she is sufficiently ill to require hospitalization; he becomes, as it were, part of the illness that wrests Lolita from Humbert. And although Lolita recovers, her escape from Humbert via the hospital is as permanent as his loss of Annabel, who "died of *typhus* in Corfu" (italics added, p. 15).

Many other details fall into patterns which Humbert does not recognize either during the time frame of his experiences, or when he is setting them down in prison. An important example is the scene at Hourglass Lake when Charlotte says "waterproof," and Jean Farlow mentions that she once saw "two children, male and female, at sunset, right here, making love. Their shadows were giants" (p. 91). Humbert's sole concern as narrator at this point is to preserve the "reality" of the scene by not supplying Quilty's name after Jean almost mentions it. But the reader cannot help noticing the symbolic significance of what Jean describes: that the shadow of Humbert and Annabel—the novel's original children on a beach—in fact falls across Humbert's entire narrative; that the shadow's association with what Charlotte likes to think of as her private beach anticipates the recapitulatory nature of Humbert's involvement with Lolita; and that the shadow's contiguity with an allusion to Quilty once again links him to Annabel as much as to Lolita.

Before going on to other important hidden patterns in *Lolita*, it is worth pausing on the question of the relation between them and the reliability of parts of Humbert's narrative. Despite his claims about his prodigious memory, it may seem implausible that he could have remembered so many details, but did not openly integrate them into his story. A related consideration is that Humbert admits to intentionally hiding networks of details in his narrative on occasion, as in the case of the word *waterproof*. It is thus possible to conclude, as many readers have, that Nabokov made Humbert an untrustworthy narrator in order to foreground the fictionality of his memoir, and by extension of all literature and life stories. Given that the bulk of *Lolita* is told in the first person, there is no way of totally disproving Humbert's supposed untrustworthiness. But there are compelling arguments that can be made against it. A dominant theme in the novel is Humbert's blindness about what is most important to him—Lolita. If he can fail to comprehend what he is doing to her for much of his narrative, he can certainly fail to notice subtle patterns that suggest he is trapped in a course of action that is not of his own devising. Nabokov has Humbert acknowledge as much when he says that a hypnotist could have extracted significant patterns from his memory, which suggests that Humbert realizes that he has seen and remembered details whose significance he cannot fathom. There is also the pressure of the context of Nabokov's other writings. Although his earlier and later novels cannot dictate a specific reading of *Lolita*, they can help to buttress a choice between alternative readings that are suggested by the text of the novel itself.

One of the most important hidden networks of recurring details in Humbert's life consists of two strands linking Lolita and her mother that center on meteorological and water imagery. Early in the novel, he de-

scribes Charlotte's eyes as "sea green" (p. 39). This association is resurrected when he briefly falls asleep near Lolita in The Enchanted Hunters
and dreams that "Charlotte was a mermaid in a greenish tank" (p. 134).
What could have motivated Nabokov to plant this connection in the
novel? A possible answer is the significance of water and beaches in Humbert's life: on the one hand, he met and loved Annabel on the Riviera; on
the other, he contemplated drowning Charlotte in Hourglass Lake in order to possess Lolita. Charlotte's association with the sea and a mermaid
can thus be read in several ways: as ironic, because Humbert describes
her in the scene at the lake as "a very mediocre mermaid" (p. 88), and as
a "clumsy seal" (p. 89); as Charlotte's being linked to the theme of Annabel, which she clearly is through her daughter; and, what is most intriguing, as a suggestion that Charlotte may be at home in water, or, in
other words, that she might not have died had Humbert actually tried to
drown her (and not because Jean Farlow was concealed nearby, or because someone else might have come to the rescue), and, therefore, that
her death in the car accident might not have been final.

There are in fact hints in *Lolita* that Humbert is accompanied by Charlotte's occult presence after she dies.[16] These first appear in connection
with the thunderclap that reverberates immediately after Jean Farlow tells
Humbert, "kiss your daughter for me" (p. 106). On a "realistic" level,
the thunder derives from the "black thunderhead" Humbert had just described as looming over the town (p. 105).[17] But on a symbolic level,
given the words Jean utters, the thunder is a melodramatically portentous
sign that recalls the striking of the midnight hour when little Luzhin first
demonstrates his chess prowess openly: the thunder marks a turning
point in Humbert's life similar to Luzhin's by underscoring the falsehood
he told Jean, which is instrumental in his obtaining control over Lolita.
The fact that the sign is obvious tends to camouflage its true import, because one is tempted to dismiss it as a mere gothic flourish on Humbert's
(or Nabokov's) part. However, another, subtler manifestation of the approaching storm enters into this network of associations together with
Charlotte. Humbert looks at her house before leaving it, and notes the
following details: "The shades—thrifty, practical bamboo shades—were
already down. On porches or in the house their rich textures lend modern
drama. The house of heaven must seem pretty bare after that. A raindrop
fell on my knuckles" (pp. 105: 91). Nabokov's Russian translation makes
it clear that the second sentence in this passage is a quotation from an
advertisement on which Charlotte had relied while decorating. Thus,
Humbert's reference to "the house of heaven" can be taken as a clear
allusion to the different circumstances in which Charlotte finds herself
after death. What changes this from being merely a turn of phrase on
Humbert's part is the sentence about the "raindrop" that falls on his

hand. On one level, this is still a manifestation of the same thunder cloud. But the detail has greater significance that emerges from an additional complex of associations scattered across the early parts of the novel. The first of these is revealed when Humbert is registering at The Enchanted Hunters with Lolita. After receiving the key with the obviously significant number "342," he happens to notice that Lolita is leaving a dog that she had stopped to pet in the lobby, which he interprets as a foreshadowing of how she will eventually leave him (and which is part of the novel's concealed "dog motif.") He then writes: "a raindrop fell on Charlotte's grave" (p. 120). In its immediate context this is an odd detail to mention, even though it recalls the raindrop that falls onto Humbert's hand earlier in the novel. The incongruity of the raindrop's appearance while Humbert is registering militates against its being his subtle way of signaling that his guilty conscience does not allow him to forget Charlotte; after all, he is quite willing to express contrition openly on a number of occasions. The necessary explanation for the raindrop is suggested by the scene of Humbert buying clothing for Lolita prior to going to her camp: "I moved about fish-like, in a glaucous aquarium. I sensed strange thoughts form in the minds of the languid ladies that escorted me from counter to counter, from rock ledge to seaweed, and the belts and the bracelets I chose seemed to fall from siren hands [in Russian, 'iz rusaloch'ikh ruk,' 'from mermaid hands'] into transparent water" (pp. 110: 95). Thus Lolita (and Humbert) become associated with marine imagery that had been used for her mother, a link that is further augmented by the substitution of "mermaid" for "siren" in the Russian translation. (Later, Humbert describes Lolita's approach to the gifts he bought her as "the lentor of one walking under water or in a flight dream" [p. 122]; he also speaks of her as "a little curved fish" in her mother's stomach [p. 78], buys *The Little Mermaid* for her [p. 176], and himself sheds "merman tears" [p. 257]. Moreover, Annabel is evoked in this context by Humbert's reference to being able to sense the salesclerks' "thought forms.") But Charlotte herself is not forgotten, because a few lines later Humbert remarks that "somehow, in connection with that quiet poetical afternoon of fastidious shopping, I recalled the hotel or inn with the seductive name of The Enchanted Hunters which Charlotte happened to mention shortly before my liberation" (p. 110). As a result of this remark, the raindrop that inexplicably falls on Charlotte's grave is revealed to be part of a network of allusions that subtly remind the reader of her and her prophecy at crucial points in Humbert's affair with Lolita. It is of course at The Enchanted Hunters that Humbert's loss of Lolita begins because that is where Quilty sees her. Thus Charlotte's spirit appears to abet this event by prompting Humbert to go to that hotel. In the context of *The Gift* and *The Real Life of Sebastian Knight*, where there are hints that the dead may attend the quick, as well as in keeping with the otherworldly aura established by Humbert's description of the spiritual links between him and Annabel, the series of rain and water images can be interpreted as hints that Charlotte's spirit is a constituent element of Humbert's fate.[18] (Similar hints appear when Humbert rings Mrs. Richard Schiller's door-bell and hears a dog barking [p. 271], which recalls the moment of Charlotte's death and her prophecy [pp. 99, 100]; when Lolita lights a cigarette, and Charlotte appears to rise from her grave [p. 277]; and when Humbert murders Quilty, which makes him think of Charlotte "sick in bed" [p. 306].)

Some chains of details in Humbert's narrative recur so often, and change so little, that they become leitmotifs. One such strand is that of sunglasses, which first appear "lost" by somebody on the beach where Humbert tries to possess Annabel (p. 15), and then reappear as "dark glasses" on one of the men in the procuress's apartment that Humbert visits in search of a nymphet (p. 26; they also appear on pp. 41, 56, 85). The most obvious meaning of this motif, in addition to its import as a formal recurrence in Humbert's life, is of course that dark glasses obscure vision, which is obviously related to Humbert's blindness when pursuing nymphets. (Sunglasses have a similar function in Nabokov's short story "Sovershenstvo," "Perfection.")

Another leitmotif in the novel is centered on the color red and colors related to it. In a note to Appel, Nabokov objected to the latter's tracing "red" imagery in the novel because the practice tended to make the color symbolic and thus to substitute "a dead general idea for a live specific impression"; moreover, Nabokov explained, distinctions between "visual shades" ("a ruby" and "a pink rose") are as important for him as differences between colors.[19] Nabokov's warning is entirely unexceptionable when understood as his annoyance with readers who do not pay due attention to details, or who approach works in terms of preconceived ideas. His remarks are thus not directed against the possibility that systems of correspondences could be identified in a particular work that derive from the specific associations that colors are given in the work. This is in fact what we find in *Lolita*. For example, Humbert and Annabel have their last tryst "in the violet shadow of some red rocks ['rozovykh skal,' literally 'rose cliffs' in Nabokov's translation]" (pp. 15: 5); and Humbert imagines nymphets on an island whose boundaries include "rosy rocks" ("aleiushchie skaly," which in Russian denotes cliffs of a color related to bright red; pp. 18: 8). It is clear that Humbert's nymphets begin with Annabel, and the related setting and colors simply confirm this on another level. Nabokov's modifications of colors in his translation actually serve to increase the correspondence. Similarly, it would be a mistake not to note that a wind blows out Charlotte's "red" candles when Humbert is sitting with her on the veranda (p. 67), because Quilty's first concealed appearance is in the "rubious convertible" that makes room for Humbert and Lolita when they arrive at The Enchanted Hunters (p. 119), because Quilty says "sleep is a rose" to Humbert when the latter unwittingly sits next to him on the hotel porch (p. 129), and because Quilty strikes "a light" in the same scene that fails to illuminate his face, probably because the wind blows it out (p. 129). It is possible "the dark-red private plane" that flies over Hourglass Lake when Humbert is there with Charlotte (p. 88) is also an evocation of Quilty's role in the novel (although not necessarily of his presence in the sky), especially since Humbert will eventually murder him rather than drown Charlotte. (On the other hand, Nabokov removed the color description of the plane from this scene in his screenplay of the novel, which suggests either that he may not have intended it to be an allusion to Quilty, or that he made a concession to black-and-white cinematography. Nabokov also changed the scene by having Humbert refer to the plane as a "guardian angel," and by indicating in the scenic directions that "a butterfly passes in shorebound flight." These details serve to underscore the moral dimension of Humbert's contemplated crime.)[20] Nabokov in fact increases the significance of the family of colors related to "red" and associated with Quilty by adding a phrase to the Russian translation of the scene when Lolita plays tennis with Quilty about how his tennis balls have "domodel'nye otmetiny krovavogo tsveta" (literally: "homemade, blood-colored marks") on them, a detail that is absent altogether from the English original (pp. 237: 216). And finally, when Humbert is on his way to kill Quilty, he notices an "airplane . . . gemmed by Rubinov" (p. 284). Nabokov does not translate the jeweler's surname in either the original or the Russian version of the novel. In fact, the name can be read as a genitive formation from the Russian word for "ruby" ("rubin"), a gloss that is probably not entirely over the heads of readers without Russian. Thus this detail establishes a neat, and fateful symmetry with the red plane above Hourglass Lake when Humbert is thinking of murdering Charlotte.[21]

Given the numbers of readers who view *Lolita* as an immoral or amoral work, it is indeed ironic that Nabokov allows Humbert to make one of the most overt connections among ethics, aesthetics, and metaphysics that can be found in any of his novels. This is the entire content of a page-long chapter in which Humbert describes how he had once gone to a Catholic priest because he "hoped to deduce from my sense of sin the existence of a Supreme Being" (p. 284). Humbert's ethics turn out to be much more severe than those of the Church: he states that "I was unable to transcend the simple human fact that whatever spiritual solace I might find, whatever lithophanic eternities might be provided for me, nothing could make my Lolita forget the foul lust I had inflicted upon her." Thus Humbert rejects personal salvation because he is convinced that there can be no forgiveness for his crime. All he can allow himself as "treatment of my misery" is "the melancholy and very local palliative of articulate art."

The ethical stance to which Humbert subscribes is encapsulated in a quotation from an unnamed "old poet" (whom Nabokov invented, as the Russian translation implies): "The moral sense of mortals is the duty / We have to pay on mortal sense of beauty" (pp. 285: 263). In other words, an individual's perception of something or someone as beautiful automatically awakens an ethical faculty in that person; this emerges as a function of being alive, or "mortal."[22] It is significant in terms of the novel's development that Humbert makes this point shortly after he describes his meeting with Lolita in her avatar as Mrs. Schiller. She is no longer a nymphet, and by his previous standards, Humbert should have lost all interest in her. Instead, he abandons his entire erotico-aesthetic set of criteria: "I insist the world know how much I loved my Lolita, *this* Lolita, pale and polluted, and big with another's child, but still grey-eyed, still sooty-lashed, still auburn and almond, still Carmencita, still mine" (p. 280). The fact that he says he loves her now more than "anything I had seen or imagined on earth" (p. 279) is an additional sign that he has abandoned "nymphet" as a category. In other words, when he sees Lolita as she really is, he finds her more beautiful than when he perceived her solipsistically; and a full awareness of her physical and spiritual constitution during the present moment makes him realize his crime toward her in the past. The importance of this kind of network of connections among perception, beauty, and ethics for understanding *Lolita* is that it is identical to Nabokov's own as he describes it in "The Art of Literature and Commonsense." Moreover, Humbert's twice repeated emphasis on "mortal" experience in the couplet he quotes evokes the metaphysical task he had set himself—of deducing "the existence of a Supreme Being ['Vysshego Sudii,' literally, 'Supreme Judge']" from his "sense of sin." He does not indicate directly whether or not he succeeded in arriving at the faith he sought. But his intuition that it does matter "in the infinite run" (p. 285) that he sinned against Lolita anchors his ethical stance in something beyond the mortal realm.[23] (Humbert thus stops short of rejecting God or His world because of the unjustifiable suffering of an innocent child. In this he differs from Ivan in Dostoevsky's *The Brothers Karamazov*, whose concern with comparable issues inevitably comes to mind in connection with *Lolita*.) We thus return to the theme of Humbert's existence being colored by experiences that transcend the earthly, which was first sounded in connection with Annabel, and then repeated in the form of fatidic patterning that fills his life. The vagueness of Humbert's intuitions, which do not extend as far as a literal belief in God, does not betray Nabokov's own intimations about the role of the "other-world" in his existence.

This short chapter, together with the scene of Humbert's moral epiphany on the cliff edge, defines a crucial change in Humbert's existence and the entire novel's direction. But it is important to remember that the ethical stance Humbert assumes in it is clearly foreshadowed throughout the earlier parts of his narrative, and is intimately interwoven with them. Humbert refers to Lolita as "my sin, my soul" in the novel's first line, thus raising the theme of ethics, as well as weaving it into the rhythmical and alliterative texture of the novel. Elsewhere, ambivalence is the hallmark of Humbert's view of what he has been doing to Lolita. His passion and lust for her are on the surface throughout. But concurrently, and showing through them, we find that he was consistently, if intermittently, filled with an acute awareness of his sin. Representative examples include his reference to "the cesspoolful of rotting monsters" behind his smile (p. 46), his intention to "protect the purity of that twelve-year-old child" (p. 65), and his moment of hesitation before entering the room where Lolita is asleep in The Enchanted Hunters, when he says, before inserting the key into the lock, "one could still—" (pp. 129: 113; the Russian version is even more explicit: "Mozhno bylo eshche spastis'," literally, "One could still save oneself"). As Humbert indicates himself, blindness explains his behavior toward Lolita. In an especially revealing passage, he describes how Lolita is weeping in his arms after "the operation was over." Her reason is that he "had just retracted some silly promise she had forced me to make in a moment of blind impatient passion, and there she was sprawling and sobbing, and pinching my caressing hand, and I was laughing happily, and the atrocious, unbelievable, unbearable, and, I suspect, eternal horror that I know *now* was still but a dot of blackness in the blue of my bliss" (p. 171; similar moments appear on pp. 137, 139, 142).

Humbert's blindness also underlies an ethically based generalization about nymphets that he uses a number of times in the novel. He says that their "true nature" is "demoniac" (p. 18), that a nymphet is a "little deadly demon" (p. 19), or a "demon child" (p. 22), and that "nymphean evil breath[ed] through every pore" of Lolita (p. 127), who is actually "some immortal daemon disguised as a female child" (p. 141), and that a "devil" was behind his initial dealings with Lolita when he was still a roomer in her mother's house (pp. 57, 58). How can Humbert's allusion to one of the commonest religious explanations for the existence of evil be reconciled with the novel? Or is it simply Humbert's turn of phrase? The answer is suggested retroactively, when, after making some purchases, Humbert returns to the motel where he had stopped with Lolita, and notices "a red hood [that] protruded in somewhat codpiece fashion" from one of the garages (p. 215). Humbert does not recognize that this is of course Quilty's car, as both the color and the sexual connotation of its description indicate. When he enters the room, however, Humbert sees Lolita "dreamily brim[ming] with a diabolical glow that had no relation to me whatever" (p. 216). The reader concludes that Lolita has just been left by Quilty, and even Humbert suspects "her infidelity," although he does not know with whom (p. 217). Lolita has a similar mien later in the novel when she is recovering in the hospital. Humbert has unwittingly just seen an envelope that must have contained a letter from Quilty, and it is presumably under its influence that Lolita is lying in bed, as Humbert puts it, "innocently beaming at me or nothing" (p. 245). These two passages contain a nexus of details implying that Humbert's conception of nymphets as diabolical is yet another function of his blindness, and is thus a solipsistic projection rather than a true perception. It is Lolita's *indifference* to him, her being caught up in concerns that are totally unrelated to him, that Humbert perceives as "nymphean evil." Humbert's abandoning the category of nymphet as a specious fiction of course also supports the view that his "demons" are nonexistent. The conception of evil that emerges from *Lolita* is thus comparable to that described in "The Art of Literature and Commonsense"—it is the absence of good, even in the limited sense of empathy or attentive sympathy, rather than a "noxious presence."

At the conclusion of the novel, Humbert addresses Lolita rhetorically and explains that his reason for wanting to live a few months longer than Quilty is "to make you live in the minds of later generations. I am thinking of aurochs and angels, the secret of durable pigments, prophetic sonnets, the refuge of art. And this is the only immortality you and I may share, my Lolita" (p. 310). His implicit inclusion of his narrative in the category of "art" (which is in keeping with his earlier references to himself as a "poet"), together with his mentioning "angels" and "immortality," inevitably evokes his couplet about the "moral sense in mortals" being "the duty" they "have to pay on mortal sense of beauty." This connection implies that ethics have a textual dimension, because if Humbert's narrative is art, and therefore beautiful (the attempt to capture Lolita's beauty in language) there is a "moral sense" attached to it. This bridge implies another—that memory has an ethical dimension as well, which follows from the fact that the mode of existence of art ("durable pigments," "prophetic sonnets"), as well as other things both "real" and not ("aurochs," which are extinct, and "angels," who belong to imagination or metaphysics), is to "live in the minds of . . . generations." This conclusion inevitably draws the reader into the novel's, and Nabokov's, value system: if beauty is a function of accurate perception, then the careless reader is immoral. The final implication of the novel's conclusion has to do with metaphysics. Humbert speaks of the "refuge of art" being the "only immortality" that he can share with Lolita. This does not mean, however, that art is the only immortality that exists. Humbert's couplet in fact suggests that his ethical sense is a sign of some absolute that validates human behavior. In these terms, therefore, the emphasis in the novel's concluding sentence can be seen as falling on the *kind* of immortality that the *sinner* can share with his *victim*, which leaves open the possibility that Lolita occupies another space altogether.

Pale Fire

FOLLOWING his achievement of international celebrity with *Lolita*, Nabokov had increasingly numerous opportunities to discuss his own works in interviews and occasional pieces. His remarks about *Pale Fire* (1962) are especially valuable because they suggest a way to situate the novel in his oeuvre even though it is startlingly innovative in formal terms. Shortly after *Pale Fire* was published, Nabokov acknowledged that "some of my more responsible characters are given some of my own ideas. There is John Shade in *Pale Fire*, the poet. He does borrow some of my own opinions." Nabokov then quotes a list of the things Shade loathes, which includes cruelty, philistinism, Freud, Marx, and other targets of Nabokov's scorn familiar from both belletristic and discursive writings.[1] Even more revealing, however, is that in his seminal article "Inspiration" Nabokov quotes at some length Shade's description of how he composes his verse, without signaling, however, either that Shade is a character in one of his novels, or that the quotation is a passage from Shade's poem that has been reprinted as prose.[2]

These acknowledged parallels constitute only a fraction of Shade's debt to Nabokov. The poem *Pale Fire*, a moving and skillfully wrought stylization of Pope and Wordsworth that has not been sufficiently appreciated on its own terms,[3] is a virtual pastiche of Nabokov's most important themes from fictional and discursive works of his Russian and English periods. Indeed, Shade is second only to Fyodor in *The Gift* in the extent to which he embodies Nabokov's own views about such topics as memory, writing, fateful patterning in life and art, the correlation of disparate and seemingly unrelated phenomena, intuitions about a transcendent otherworld, nature and artifice, perceptual acuity, perspicacity, and their relation to good and evil.[4] Because these topics are also clearly central to Kinbote's parts of the novel, Shade and his poem actually provide an exegetic anchor for *Pale Fire* as a whole. This is not to say that there is a simple key to the text that suddenly resolves all its mysteries. More than any of Nabokov's works that preceded it, *Pale Fire* incorporates ambiguity on every level and as an integral part of its themes and form. But at the same time, the ambiguity is circumscribed by the beliefs that Shade shares with Nabokov, and is thus included in a coherent world view that is not in itself irresolvably ambiguous.

Before turning to Shade's Nabokovian outlook on life, it will be instructive to examine the ways in which various forms of uncertainty are
built into the novel. Their primary source is of course Kinbote—the ostensible author of the Foreword, Commentary, and index. Kinbote's very
funny and egregious misreadings of Shade's poem, which are intertwined
with his homosexual and possibly insane fantasies and projections, are
quite obvious and have been examined in detail in the criticism. The resulting apparent hiatus between Shade's poem and what purports to be a
critical apparatus attached to it is the major structural problem in the
novel. Some readers have attempted to unite the two by championing either Shade or Kinbote (or even an inferred third character) as the wily,
and concealed author of the whole thing.⁵ But these arguments oversim-
plify the actual situation in *Pale Fire* because it is inevitably possible to
find passages counterbalancing the textual details that are invoked in support of any unitary author. For example, Kinbote's remark that "it is the
underside of the [poem's] weave that entrances the beholder and only
begetter" might seem to be his inadvertent admission that he is the poem's
author, a conclusion that is appealing in light of his probable fabrications
elsewhere in the text.⁶ But it is difficult to reconcile this possibility with
Kinbote's admission later that he "can imitate any prose in the world (but
singularly enough not verse—I am a miserable rhymester)" (p. 289), a
remark that seems designed (and placed in the novel) precisely to undermine, but not to negate conclusively, a reading that takes him to be the
author of the poem. An example of a possible argument in favor of Shade
being the author of the whole hinges on the appearance of the second
person pronoun at two different points in the novel: in the Foreword:
"Canto Two, your favorite" (p. 13), and in the poem, "You went on /
Translating into French Marvell and Donne" (ll. 677–78; p. 58). The former implied addressee remains unidentified until we encounter the latter,
who, as the context makes clear, is Shade's wife Sybil. Thus it might seem
that the pronoun in the Foreword refers to her as well, and that it was in
fact written by Shade masquerading as Kinbote.⁷ Although this possibility
cannot be disproven unequivocally, many other textual details can be
mustered against it. One is Shade's "reasonable" certainty about awakening on 22 July (ll. 980–81; p. 69), which stems from his important (and
recognizably Nabokovian) metaphysical speculations, and which is seemingly vitiated by his being killed on 21 July. Since this fact is reported
several times by the commentator and editor (e.g., pp. 13, 295), it follows
that Kinbote cannot be a mask for Shade, at least on the basis of the detail
in question.⁸

This sort of debate about a unified author in fact begs the larger question of narrative reliability in *Pale Fire*. Shade's poem, if considered apart
from its context, does not contain any discrepancies or other indices sig-

naling that its author is prevaricating. But as all readers of the novel have noted, Kinbote's texts are an entirely different matter. They contain numerous indications that suggest, but do not prove, that he may be a madman who has invented Zembla, his life and adventures there as King Charles Xavier Vseslav the Beloved, and the regicidal plot involving Gradus. There are also details in Kinbote's text that can be read as supporting the story Jack Grey supposedly tells after shooting Shade—that he is a criminal who escaped from an asylum in order to avenge himself on Judge Goldsworth, the man who had sentenced him (p. 299). For example, early in the novel, Kinbote mentions seeing a picture of a "homicidal maniac" sentenced by the Judge who resembles Gradus (p. 83). The reader is provided with several characters' remarks that allow him to conclude that Shade in fact may resemble the Judge (p. 267). In this possible scenario, therefore, which could be called the "realistic" one, Jack Grey shoots Shade by mistake because he mistakes him for Judge Goldsworth. Who, then, is Kinbote? Perhaps, as some readers have argued, he is deluded Professor Botkin, who is described in the index as "American scholar of Russian descent" (p. 306). The nearly anagrammatic relation between his and Kinbote's names of course supports this possibility. Sybil Shade's references to Kinbote as "a king-sized botfly; a macaco worm" (p. 172) also echoes the anagrammatic pair of names, as well as the additional information in the index under Botkin that the "king-bot" is the "maggot of [an] extinct fly" (p. 306). The possibility that Kinbote is Botkin may also motivate the otherwise inexplicable comment that "happily" Professor Botkin "was not subordinated to" Professor Pnin (p. 155; a detail that is clearly significant from the point of view of Nabokov's allusions to his own works as well).[9]

Support for the "realistic" reading of Kinbote's tale comes from the fact that Gradus, as Kinbote describes and characterizes him, could not have been capable of fabricating the story that the killer told the police for the simple reason that Gradus could not have known anything about Judge Goldsworth. Nothing in what Kinbote says to explain why his version of the events differs from Grey's can adequately account for this discrepancy. Kinbote further undermines his own story by relating details from Gradus's journey that he could not have gleaned from either Gradus himself, or any other sources to which he alludes. One of these, among many others, is that "Izumrudov," Gradus's superior, successfully hides himself from Gradus in Nice (p. 251). Because Gradus's main characteristics according to Kinbote are stupidity and pathological purblindness, there is no reason to suspect that Gradus could have seen through the stratagem Izumrudov uses to conceal his identity from an underling.

Finding such chinks in Kinbote's narrative involves the reader in a highly enjoyable task that is clearly an inherent part of *Pale Fire*'s overall artistic design. Because the reader appears to be inferring conclusions on his own, he feels rewarded with a sense of superiority to the flawed narrator and with the belief that he is privy to a hidden level of meaning in the text. Rather than continue to catalogue additional instances of this sort, however, many of which have been identified in the criticism, it would be instructive to indicate how Kinbote's narrative resists being reduced to a simple allegory in which one layer of meaning is implied by another. Kinbote makes what can be seen as a preemptive move against the alternative, "realistic" reading of the events outlined above when he speculates about how he might "cook up a stage play, an old-fashioned melodrama with three principles: a lunatic who intends to kill an imaginary king, another lunatic who imagines himself to be that king, and a distinguished old poet who stumbles by chance into the line of fire" (p. 301). One could argue that Kinbote's awareness of this alternative suggests a level of perspicacity about himself that militates against his being simply insane, with a madman's monomania and blind spots. Of course, the statement could also be read as an indication that madmen are capable of great cunning.

A seeming slip of the tongue that adds to the irresolvable ambiguity of Kinbote's version is his remark at one point: "had I been a northern king—or rather had I still been a king (exile becomes a bad habit)" (p. 292). This statement both teases the reader with the possibility that it is an unintentional revelation, and provides its own cancellation of this possibility through a plausible explanation. The Zemblan language, like the invented names of states and other geographic place names in the novel (e.g., "Utana," p. 29—is this Kinbote's delusion, or Nabokov's fictional geography?), also lends itself to conflicting interpretations. On the one hand, "Onhava" is the name of the Zemblan capital (pp. 75, 311), on the other, the phrase "onhava-onhava" that Gradus utters is translated by Kinbote as "far, far away" (p. 255). There is no way of deciding whether the city's name has the meaning Kinbote gives, or whether he simply forgot that the word he translates is one he had already used for another purpose. Similarly, no definite conclusion can be made about the significance of Kinbote's remark that a doctor he and Shade both consulted "once confused neuralgia with cerebral sclerosis" (p. 250). This can be taken either as evidence of the doctor's incompetence, or as applying to Kinbote, and as indicating therefore that the doctor diagnosed him as being mentally impaired. If this is the same doctor who happened to be present when Shade collapsed during his talk on poetry, then his insightfulness has already been implicitly tarnished in the novel by his attempt to deny the validity of what Shade took to be an authentic clairvoyant experience with far-reaching implications for his world view (ll. 722–28; p. 60).

On another level, the "realistic" reading of Kinbote's story is counter-balanced by the sheer weight of Kinbote's version—both in terms of the quality, quantity, and continuity among the details he provides, and the vividly baroque language in which he embodies them, all of which contrast with the sparse and inconclusive details that argue for the more "realistic" reading. Gradus's command of English is a case in point. Kinbote's numerous descriptions and quotations consistently reveal it to be accented and flawed (pp. 199, 201, 215, 283). On the one hand, there is no evidence that anyone notices anything unusual in the killer's English after the police arrive (p. 295), which could be construed as indicating that his English was a familiar American version, and that he could not be the foreigner Gradus. On the other hand, apart from the Anglo-Saxon sounding name of the man, there is no reason to assume that Jack Grey would have had an American accent.

In the end, the reason why many of the ambiguities in Kinbote's texts cannot be resolved is of course that the reader has no criteria outside the novel by which he can gauge the referential accuracy of what Kinbote says. We do not even know for certain if the variants he cites for Shade's poem are really derived from it or not. A vaguely Baltic or Scandinavian land called Zembla, with a revolution and an exiled king, is a plausible fictional construct that has a number of analogues in "real" twentieth-century European history. Similarly, assassins, sexual deviation, small town academic life—these are all familiar aspects of the contemporary scene. Kinbote's tale thus cannot be readily faulted on the level of the kind of general experience of life (admittedly, a vague, even if unavoidable concept) that a reader inevitably brings to a text—the kind of experience that would brand as implausible (but certainly not meaningless) a man turning into a beetle, or a bronze statue coming to life. Except for the text of Shade's poem itself, which sounds entirely different from any of Kinbote's utterances (though there are crucial parallels between it and his Commentary), everything else in the novel is filtered through Kinbote's consciousness. All that the reader's experience can provide is a sense that Kinbote obviously misreads Shade's words on a number of occasions (judging by the context in which these occur), which makes all his other claims suspect. In this, Kinbote differs markedly from a character such as Fyodor in *The Gift*, who also filters what we see of his world, but whose unreliability is not a theme in the novel. There is also a difference between Kinbote and the first-person narrators of *The Real Life of Sebastian Knight* and *Lolita*. V.'s only instance of unreliability that the reader can verify is his praise for the story he receives from his mail-order writing teacher. V.'s heavy reliance on intuition in his investigation is a different matter, and cannot be proven false even if any given reader of the novel does not share V.'s faith in intuition. And with the exception of "nymphets," Humbert's world is much less fanciful and eccentric than Kinbote's. Thus what Kinbote says might be largely true, entirely false, or somewhere in between, and attempts to weigh the accuracy of his reporting about an implied, external "reality" become a futile pursuit.

This does not mean, however, contrary to what some readers have thought, that *everything* Kinbote says is merely an elaborate, and otherwise meaningless verbal game in which Nabokov indulges. As Shade argues in his poem, and as Nabokov insists in other writings, the highest forms of signification are not simply equal to referential accuracy.[10] Before turning to this question in more detail, it is worth recalling some of Nabokov's remarks about the genesis of *Pale Fire*, because these are germane to the problem of what Kinbote is about. In a short preface to the English translations of the stories "Ultima Thule" and "Solus Rex," Nabokov explains that they are the first two chapters of his unfinished, last Russian novel on which he worked during the winter of 1939–40, and that they are echoed in *Bend Sinister*, "and, especially, *Pale Fire*." In summarizing what he remembers of his intentions for the novel, Nabokov alludes to the question of whether or not the character Adam Falter truly understands the ultimate mysteries of existence, and then turns to a description of the relation between the "mundane" existence of the narrator, whose name is Sineusov, and an imaginary country he invents and embodies in his art. At first, Sineusov's fantasy merely helps him deal with the grief his wife's death causes him. But then, Nabokov explains, the fantasy "grew into a self-contained artistic obsession" and began to "develop its own reality" to the extent that Sineusov moves into it physically—specifically, "into a bleak palace on a remote northern island." Moreover, his art allows him to resurrect his wife in another guise as "Queen Belinda," albeit only temporarily, since she perishes during an attempted coup.[11] Although Nabokov's summary is elliptical and laconic, it does suggest clear parallels with Kinbote's story about the misadventures of King Charles the Beloved. It also suggests that even if Kinbote's story is some sort of elaborate compensation for profound unhappiness in his mundane existence, the artistic nature of his fantastic construct grants it a form of validity that is far from negligible. What exactly it is in his fantasy that gives it this significance can be gleaned from John Shade's related concerns in his poem.

Shade's interests, values, and beliefs are especially close to those Nabokov describes in *Speak, Memory*. One of the first that should be mentioned is Shade's unusual visual acuity and sensitivity to color, which, among other things, allows him to discern the colors of shadows (l. 55; p. 35), and which parallels Nabokov's famed sharpness of eye. (Nabokov grants a similar ability to Victor Wind in *Pnin*, who, for this and related reasons, is a distinctly positive Nabokovian personage, as well as part of

a network of links between *Pnin* and *Pale Fire*.) Moreover, Shade's visual
acuity, like Nabokov's, is causally linked to his fondness for, and deep
knowledge of, natural history: Shade feels nature "glued" to him; loves
its "Half-fish, half-honey" taste (ll. 102–4; p. 36); never tires of pointing
out to a somewhat exasperated Kinbote how faunal and floral zones are
mixed in the area in which they live (p. 169); and likes the company of
an old farmer who "knows the names of things" in the local woods and
fields (p. 185). However, natural history is but one particular focus for
Shade's attentive eye. All phenomena, from "The claret taillight of that
dwindling plane / Off Hesperus," to "this good ink" with which he pens
his poem, are so dear to him that he says he will "turn down eternity"
unless they can be also "found in Heaven by the newlydead" (ll. 528–29,
532, 534; p. 53).

Paralleling Nabokov's description of the "spherical" "prison of time"
in *Speak, Memory*, Shade speaks of "The painted parchment papering
our cage," and asserts that "we are most artistically caged" in the phenomenal world (ll. 106, 114; pp. 36, 37). Like Nabokov, Shade also invokes deception and mimicry as evidence for the telling artificiality of
nature: "In life, the mind / Of any man is quick to recognize / Natural
shams, and then before his eyes / The reed becomes a bird" (ll. 710–13;
p. 59). The fact that Shade would establish in the continuation of this
passage a parallel between mimicry in nature and his otherworldly vision
of a white fountain implies that he sees a hidden meaning in mimetic behavior comparable to that which he infers from his vision. The metaphysical implications of artifice in nature are, of course, a recurrent theme in
Nabokov's writings. (By contrast, Kinbote is given a parodic version of
Nabokov's generalization about natural artifice [p. 252].)

It is most important to recognize that central to Shade's preoccupation
with death, both during his life and in his poem, is a series of epiphanic
experiences he had while still a boy that resemble nothing so much as
repeated moments of cosmic synchronization. The first occurrence is
linked to a toy with which he is playing, and which prefigures the most
important fatidic pattern in Shade's life. He describes the experience as
"a sudden sunburst in my head. / And then black night. That blackness
was sublime. / I felt distributed through space and time: / One foot upon
a mountaintop, one hand / Under the pebbles of a panting strand, / One
ear in Italy, one eye in Spain" (ll. 146–51; p. 38). The image of his body
as the unifying agent for phenomena widely scattered in space and time
is structurally congruent with the "organism of events" that Nabokov
describes forming around him during his epiphanic experiences (*Speak,
Memory*, p. 218). Moreover, because Shade's image of his expanded body
serves to unify the past, the present, and the future, the linearity of time
is eliminated in a way that is also comparable to cosmic synchronization:

"There were dull throbs in my Triassic [the distant past]; green / Optical spots in Upper Pleistocene [the present], / An icy shiver down my Age of Stone [the more recent past], / And all tomorrows in my funnybone [the future]" (ll. 153–56; p. 38). To some extent, because Shade's epiphany is associated with illness and death, it also recalls the incident of Nabokov's boyhood clairvoyance while he was recuperating from pneumonia. Shade explains that "A thread of subtle pain, / Tugged at by playful death, released again, / But always present, ran through me"; he also makes a direct correlation between the end of the experiences and an improvement in his health (ll. 139–41; 160; p. 38). This of course suggests that Shade's epiphany is at most a fictional composite or variant of several of Nabokov's experiences, rather than a direct transcription of any one of them.

The resemblance between Shade and Nabokov is further enhanced by the centrality of their preoccupations with death. At the beginning of Canto Two, Shade describes how he felt for a time that he was alone in not knowing the truth about life after death, and how he thought that mankind could not be sane if it could remain in the same state of ignorance. All this leads him to want to devote his entire life "to this / One task," namely—to "explore and fight / The foul, the inadmissible abyss" (ll. 167–81; p. 39). Nabokov sounds the same thematic dominant on the opening pages of *Speak, Memory* when he speaks about the "cradle rock[ing] above an abyss," the "young chronophobiac," and his own "colossal efforts to distinguish the faintest of glimmers in the impersonal darkness on both sides of my life" (pp. 19–20).

What could be termed Shade's near-death experience following a heart attack also bears significant structural similarities to cosmic synchronization, even if in its specifics it is unlike anything that Nabokov describes in his autobiographical writings. Shade's experience clearly implies a distinction between the physical and spiritual components of his being: "Everything I loved was lost / But no aorta could report regret." What he glimpsed when he "crossed / The border" between this world and the next could be characterized as an image of great unity in multiplicity, which is of course the most salient characteristic of cosmic synchronization: "blood-black nothingness began to spin / A system of cells interlinked within / Cells interlinked within cells interlinked / Within one stem." It is against this background that Shade sees "a tall white fountain," something that will become the object of much speculation on his part (ll. 699–708; p. 59). He concludes that the fountain stands in relation to otherworldly truth as the mimic does to its model in nature, and that neither he nor other mortals are capable of fathoming the otherworldly vision's true significance. As we have seen, this radical separation of mundane existence from the otherworld is one of the constants of Nabokov's own beliefs as they emerge from both autobiographical and belletristic works.

Although Shade realizes that the ultimate significance of the fountain is unknowable, he is nonetheless able to glean a momentous meaning from it. Following his vision, Shade reads about a woman who apparently also saw a fountain during a near-death experience. His excitement over this seeming coincidence is undermined, however, when he discovers that what the woman actually saw was a mountain, not a fountain. "Life Everlasting—based on a misprint!" he exclaims ironically, and contemplates giving up his attempts to fathom the mystery of death. Instead he is struck by an intuitive realization that is not only his most important insight into existence, but also one of the two major keys in his poem for understanding *Pale Fire* as a whole. What Shade discovers is Nabokovian patterning. It dawns on him that the "real point" of the incident with "fountain-mountain" is its "contrapuntal theme." Signification thus lies not in the congruence of specific details, but in abstract patterns that can be inferred on their basis—on the common elements that unite them: "not text, but texture; not the dream / But topsy-turvical coincidence, / Not flimsy nonsense, but a web of sense. / Yes! It sufficed that I in life could find / Some kind of link-and-bobolink, some kind / Of correlated pattern in the game, / Plexed artistry, and something of the same / Pleasure in it as they who played it found" (ll. 808–15; p. 63). This idea is so comforting that Shade does not rail against the impossibility of knowing who "they" are who "play" with mortals and terrestrial events both great and small. It is sufficient for him to know that they coordinate "Events and objects with remote events / And vanished objects," and that they are responsible for "Making ornaments / Of accidents and possibilities." And this realization is enough for him to have "Faint hope" in an afterlife (ll. 816–29, 834; p. 63).

Shade further resembles Nabokov in that his metaphysics are linked directly to his aesthetics. Following his conclusion about the meaning of patterning, Shade asserts that "Now I shall spy on beauty as none has / Spied on it yet" (ll. 835–36; p. 64), implying that an awareness of fate (and thereby the otherworld) empowers the perception and creation of beauty. In the context of his poem this means two additional interrelated things. The first is suggested by Shade's imagining that he is being led to a wall to be shot. The details in this scene are entirely congruent with the passage about Gumilev facing execution in "The Art of Literature and Commonsense," and with Fyodor's father in the same situation in *The Gift*. Like these victims, Shade, who also has the gifts of perspicacity and visual acuity, feels infinitely superior to the "dedicated imbeciles" who would destroy him: "We'll think of matters only known to us— / Empires of rhyme, Indies of calculus; / Listen to distant cocks crow, and discern /

Upon the rough gray wall a rare wall fern" (ll. 597–608; p. 55). The ability to notice and identify a detail like a rare fern during the moment before one's death is the quintessential mark of the Nabokovian artist hero. Moreover, the redundancy in the last line is precisely the kind of patterning to which Shade refers when he speaks of "plexed artistry" in life: there is a coincidence—both predictable and hidden at the same time—in being able to correlate the fern with its locus. Thus, Shade's alertness to the metaphysical implications of patterning among phenomena, for which one needs a good eye, is clearly linked to his ability to "spy on beauty."

But Shade is a poet—a creator of beauty as well, and he implies that his being armed with an awareness of patterning's significance is linked directly to his artistic skill: "Now I shall cry out as / None has cried out. Now I shall try what none / Has tried. Now I shall do what none has done" (ll. 835–88; p. 64). This leads him to make the following explicit connection between aesthetics and metaphysics, which can also be taken as programmatic for Nabokov's art:

> Maybe my sensual love for the *consonne*
> *D'appui*, Echo's fey child, is based upon
> A feeling of fantastically planned,
> Richly rhymed life.
> > I feel I understand
> Existence, or at least a minute part
> Of my existence, only through my art,
> In terms of combinational delight;
> And if my private universe scans right,
> So does the verse of galaxies divine
> Which I suspect is an iambic line.
>
> > > (ll. 967–77; pp. 68–69)

In short, patterning in art is a microcosmic reflection of a macrocosmic order. And although patterning lies in the eye of the beholder, it is nonetheless a valid, if darkling reflection of a transcendent truth, and not a solipsistic projection.

Shade's sui generis variant of the theological "argument from design" (which recalls not only Pope's *An Essay on Man*, but the popularity of the argument throughout the eighteenth century) obviously needs to be borne in mind when making sense of the relation of Kinbote's Commentary to his poem. It is important, therefore, that Shade makes several observations about the metaphysical significance of patterning that have such an obvious relation to Kinbote's endeavor that they read like hermeneutic guides to the entire novel; at the heart of each is the fundamental Nabokovian transvaluation of the terms *natural* and *artificial*: for example, after describing various attempts that human beings have made to fathom the relation of this life to the next, Shade presents the following concise credo: "*Life is a message scribbled in the dark.* / Anonymous" (ll. 235–36; p. 41). The immediate context, as well as the rest of the poem, clearly sheds light on the meaning of this phrase: human life has meaning—it is a communication that some consciousness has composed, but human beings are constitutionally incapable of grasping more than glimmers of it. Immediately after this aphorism, Shade provides an image that constitutes an attempt to gloss the "message" contained in human life. Recalling the day his Aunt Maude died, Shade remembers that he saw "An empty emerald case, squat and frog-eyed, / Hugging the trunk; and its companion piece / A gum-logged ant" (ll. 238–40; p. 41). The symbolism is clear—the cicada, or other insect with a comparable life cycle, has undergone a metamorphosis into another form of being and flown away, while the ant is entombed in a future bit of amber. The lesson Shade draws from this is a correction of the famous fable: "Lafontaine was wrong: / Dead is the mandible, alive the song" (ll. 243–44; p. 42). In other words, "the song," or art, is linked to transcendence, while utilitarian efforts are not. Through textual contiguity, this conclusion suggests that Aunt Maude may also have shifted into another dimension of being, because, as we are told, she was an artist. Finally, the "coincidental" similarity of the French fabulist's name, which is now associated with an image of transcendence, to "the fountain" that Shade saw during his near-death experience reinforces Shade's point about the intimations of immortality that can be gleaned from patterning, which is also the message contained in human life.

The other guide to interpretation in Shade's poem is his statement: "*Man's life as commentary to abstruse* / *Unfinished poem.* Note for further use" (ll. 939–40; p. 67). Because this is a strikingly polysemous remark, it can be seen as betraying the viewpoint of an implied author. First of all, it is an obvious allusion to Kinbote's Commentary, and could be interpreted as evidence for Shade's authorship of it. But it could also be read as indicating that Kinbote's Commentary is not totally invalid, because it reflects the interpretive strategies used by Shade himself. Lastly, this aphoristic formulation is close to "*Life is a message scribbled in the dark.* / Anonymous." Both statements conceive of human life as a system of signs dependent on some higher order of meaning that remains ultimately unattainable. In this light, Shade's aesthetics and metaphysics again merge, because patterning in life—which follows the lead, as it were, of some cosmic poem that transcends it—takes on the implications he ascribes to patterning in poetry.

The passages in Shade's poem in which he ridicules the attempts of the "Institute of Preparation for the Hereafter" to make sense of what is inherently incomprehensible are an obvious parallel to Nabokov's view that the otherworld must remain a mystery (ll. 501–644; pp. 52–57). According to Shade, the "trouble" with all such speculations is that "we do not make it [i. e., the realm beyond death] seem / Sufficiently unlikely; for the most / We can think up is a domestic ghost" (ll. 228–30; p. 41). This also recalls the early pages in *Speak, Memory* in which Nabokov describes all the different occult methods "short of suicide" that he had tried when attempting to penetrate into "the darkness on both sides of my life." At the same time, Shade's conviction after Hazel dies that no communication from the otherworld is possible (ll. 647–52; p. 57) is put into question by seemingly occult events that do occur in the novel, thereby echoing Nabokov's occasional intuitions, and, concurrently, reinforcing ambiguity as an inalienable dimension of the novel's thematics.

Memory and the view that time is illusory are two additional topics in Shade's poem that are also of central importance for Nabokov. Shade calls himself a "preterist" (l. 79; p. 35), which denotes someone with an interest in a timeless past. This designation is easy to correlate with another passage in the poem in which Shade states that "Time means growth, / And growth means nothing in Elysian life" (ll. 572–73; p. 54). The sense of these remarks—that time is an illusion because it is a function of the organic and psychological processes constituting life—is familiar from *Speak, Memory* (the passages in which Nabokov speaks of his son's fondness for trains), from interviews in which Nabokov admits that he does not believe in time, and from fictional variants of this idea in *The Gift, Lolita,* and other works.

The parallels between Shade's and Nabokov's views also bear on the unity of *Pale Fire.* There are a number of instances in which Kinbote in his Commentary quotes or paraphrases pronouncements of Shade's that are also well-known views of Nabokov's. As a result, Kinbote's text acquires a certain patina of validity and authority because not everything he reports is farcically wrong or distorted if we judge it by the values of Nabokov's known world outside the novel. For example, we learn from the Commentary about Shade's insistence that in order to study Shakespeare properly in college "the freshman" should be trained "to dismiss ideas, and social background," and, instead, "to shiver, to get drunk on the poetry . . . to read with his spine and not his skull." Shade also follows Nabokov when he objects violently to symbol hunting by students, and to their use of "simple" and "sincere" as terms of praise (pp. 155–56; other examples include Shade's loathing for "Vulgarity and Brutality" [p. 217], his idea that man is innately good [p. 225], and that cross-generational patterning may explain Hazel's behavior [p. 166]).

Even more important for understanding the unity of *Pale Fire* are the parallels between Kinbote's own ideas and Nabokov's. In this regard,

Kinbote recalls Humbert, who also embodies some of Nabokov's beliefs, a fact that prohibits simply dismissing him as a madman or a pervert. Kinbote's conception of art is a case in point because it is thoroughly Nabokovian. Kinbote's description of how Shade perceives the world around him prior to writing—"re-combining its elements in the very process of storing them up so as to produce at some unspecified date an organic miracle, a fusion of image and music, a line of verse"—is virtually identical to what we find in "The Art of Literature and Commonsense." Kinbote's blending this image of poetic creation with that of a "conjurer" he had seen when a boy (pp. 27–28) implies the idea of art as deception that we find everywhere in Nabokov. The special significance of this idea for *Pale Fire* is that it implies the necessity of judging Kinbote's text by other criteria than simple "realism." This is also suggested by Kinbote's description of a trompe l'oeil painter's works in his Commentary, where he makes the following typically Nabokovian remark about the nature of "reality": it is "neither the subject nor the object of true art which creates its own special reality having nothing to do with the average 'reality' perceived by the communal eye" (p. 130). The similarity between this generalization and Kinbote's actual practice again returns us to the possibility that verisimilitude of verbal artifacts based on empirical events is not the only, or not even the most important, measure of signification in *Pale Fire*.

A common denominator among Nabokov, Kinbote, and Shade is their faith in the existence of an otherworld that is involved in human affairs. Kinbote differs from Shade and Nabokov in the anthropomorphic and overtly religious terminology he uses when discussing his beliefs. But if this reservation is borne in mind, then the nature of most, although not all of what Kinbote believes is very close to Nabokov. This includes a respect for precise knowledge and a concomitant reveling in the ultimately mysterious nature of existence: "the scientific and the supernatural, the miracle of the muscle and the miracle of the mind, are *both* inexplicable as are all the ways of Our Lord" (p. 167). Kinbote's advocacy of suicide as a means of reaching God's world of course has no parallel in Nabokov's published discursive writings. But Kinbote's imagery when describing God's role in human life in the passage that follows does: "when [the soul] distinguishes His sign at every turn of the trail, painted on the boulder and notched in the fir trunk, when every page in the book of one's personal fate bears His watermark, how can one doubt that He will also preserve us through all eternity?" (pp. 221–22). Especially noteworthy is the reference to the divine "watermark" Kinbote discerns in his fate, since this is a direct reflection of Nabokov's implying that the fatidic "intricate watermark" in his life is explainable only by reference to the otherworld (*Speak, Memory*, p. 25). Kinbote's quotation from St. Augustine in support of the idea that one should not "demand too clear an image of what is unimaginable" because "one can know what God is not, one cannot know what He is," paraphrases Nabokov's conceptions of the otherworld throughout his fictions (p. 227).

If we now turn to ethics in *Pale Fire*, we find that Kinbote's sarcastic depiction of Gradus is a typically Nabokovian view of moral failing as he describes it at length in "The Art of Literature and Commonsense" and elsewhere. Gradus "worshiped general ideas" and felt nothing but animosity toward any form of specialized knowledge, which leads directly to his support of the farcical Zemblan revolution (pp. 152–53). In turn, mental dullness is inextricably linked to his inattention to details and lack of imagination. We have, in other words, the familiar image of evil as a banal and petty phenomenon, and as the absence of good (be it knowledge, sight, or consciousness), rather than as a potent presence.

Finally, we have the matter of Kinbote's art. Whatever reservations one may have about the accuracy of his ostensible glosses and reportage, there is much extremely funny, as well as beautifully written prose in his story—such as any part of Gradus's journey, or the highly Nabokovian description of the Red Admirable (p. 290). In other words, Kinbote is a wonderful stylist, and although his frequently baroque manner is different from Shade's (reflecting, as it does, his quirks and proclivities), it falls within the tonal range that we find in Nabokov's oeuvre. This stylistic proximity between Kinbote and Nabokov inevitably contributes to throwing the reader off balance with regard to the novel's import, and could even mislead the unwary into seeing a greater similarity between author and character than actually exists. One is tempted to conclude that Nabokov granted some of his own opinions to Kinbote, a character who is flagrantly unlike him in most other respects, because of the appeal that irony has for him in general. The teasing uncertainty that irony engenders on this level of the text is a means of engrossing the reader, as well as of augmenting the impression of the work's suggestive ambiguity.

It is hardly necessary to dwell on the ways in which Kinbote betrays his avowed task of demonstrating correlations between his story and Shade's poem. At the same time, it is worth recalling that after actually reading Shade's text Kinbote does not in fact claim that the poem is a poeticized transcript of his story of Zembla, but only that it contains faint echoes of it (pp. 81, 297). It should also be stressed that Kinbote's misreadings actually serve to camouflage the fact that his entire exegetic endeavor is a variant of Shade's world view. One of the ways this is expressed is via Kinbote's equating both Gradus and the form of Shade's poem with fate: "The force propelling [Gradus] is the magic action of Shade's poem itself, the very mechanism and sweep of verse, the powerful iambic motor. Never before has the inexorable advance of fate received such a sensuous form" (p. 136). On an abstract level, this is not altogether different from Shade's conclusion that his life and his poem both embody patterns related to an otherworldly order.

It is clearly of the greatest significance for understanding *Pale Fire* that despite Kinbote's obvious projections onto the poem there are in fact a large number of subtle parallels between it and his story, many of which, moreover, he does not appear to notice. Kinbote's seemingly insane exegetic program thus emerges not only as a parallel to Shade's, but also as a skewed variant of Fyodor's wish in *The Gift* to correlate the life of his friend Alexander Chernyshevski with his own, and of V.'s unwitting repetition in his life of events from Sebastian's fictions.

The importance of "chance" parallels for understanding the deeper mechanics and meaning of *Pale Fire* is signaled by Shade's discussion of patterning in his poem, especially by his emphasis on correlations based on "texture" and not "text." He illustrates what he means by this when he links his description of his daughter's ill-fated double date and subsequent suicide to his and his wife's activities at home—his work in his study, and the television programs they watch (ll. 404–77; pp. 47–50). Indeed, were it not for Shade's conclusion about the significance of "texture," his correlation of the two series of activities might seem as arbitrary as Kinbote's yoking the story of Charles the Beloved to the poem. But in light of Shade's conclusion the section of the poem leading up to Hazel's death resembles a guide intended to illuminate the relation of Kinbote's Commentary to the poem, even though Kinbote criticizes the principle behind Shade's practice at the same time that he deploys an egregious variant of it (p. 196). Shade's poem even contains what could be understood as "built-in" validations of the correlative method, which appear after he says that "time forked" (l. 404; p. 47). For example, the travelogue he watches with his wife shows a place they visited "Nine month before her [Hazel's] birth" (l. 435; p. 48). The number of months of course implies that Hazel may have been engendered there, and the coincidence that the place would be shown on television shortly before her death creates a poignant symmetry that appears highly significant "texturally." (Could it also be Nabokov's hint that her death was not final? Similar juxtapositions appear on the first page of *Speak, Memory*, and in *Invitation to a Beheading*.) However, the coincidence seems considerably less startling and portentous when we realize that the place in question is the French Riviera, which is hardly a rare locale in televised travelogues. A similar example of a coincidence concealed within what appears to be an arbitrary correlation, but that nonetheless seems to be significant, is that the film the Shades watch, *Remorse*, is transparently related to Hazel's romantic fantasies (ll. 450–57; p. 49). However, the latter are so universally human that, under closer scrutiny, the import of the coincidence tends to evaporate. The same can be said about the moment when the television is turned off, which Shade appears to coordinate with Hazel's death (ll. 471–74; p. 50). The unfortunately prosaic question of how could Shade have known the precise moment of Hazel's death remains unanswerable. Thus, despite the suggestive structural character of Shade's poem, how is the reader to tell the difference between Shade's correlations and Kinbote's when both seem equally arbitrary? The answer has to be sought in Shade's metaphysical aesthetics, which are modeled on Nabokov's. The crucial element in both is an intuitive faith in the otherworldly sanction for artistic imagination. Thus Shade's choosing to yoke together two independent sequences of events that coexist in time, and his embodying them in poetically structured language, contains its *own* validation of the correlation; this is because Shade has the physical and spiritual gifts of sensory acuity, intelligence, and intuition that Nabokov posits as prerequisites for true artists. In the end, one can either accept or reject Shade's (and Nabokov's) beliefs; there is no "proof" for them that can be rooted in any authority outside them (except, perhaps, comparable experiences).

A sign of the importance of this conception of art for *Pale Fire* is the number of times it recurs in different guises. One cluster appears in the rejected variants from Shade's poem that Kinbote cites. If these are real, they recall parts of the King's story, and thus constitute a link between Shade and the Commentary. But more interesting than the possibility that Shade actually registered something of what Kinbote pressed upon him, which is all that Kinbote cares about of course, is the apparent use to which Shade seemed to be putting Kinbote's tale, which illustrates the hermeneutic principles that he embraces. Thus in a passage that appears to summarize the King's escape across the mountains, Shade is actually more interested not in the escape itself, but in how it underscores an important paradigm: "There are events, strange happenings, that strike / The mind as emblematic. They are like / Lost similes adrift without a string, / Attached to nothing" (p. 99). In other words, Shade is struck not by the content of Kinbote's story but by its being like something else—by its congruence with, or reference to, something that he does not or cannot name. The same kind of suspended simile appears in another variant that Kinbote quotes, this one possibly dealing with the closet hiding a secret tunnel in the palace through which the King eventually escapes: "As children playing in a castle find / In some old closet full of toys, behind / The animals and masks, a sliding door / [four words heavily crossed out] a secret corridor—" (p. 118). What unites the variants is that they first posit the same underlying interpretive principle, and then present the reader with a lacuna. Kinbote's glimpse of their significance is only partial, and cannot help the reader to decide with any certainty how Shade intended to resolve his suspended similes. But given the central importance he ascribes to patterning and coincidence in his life and art, it is certainly possible to infer that he may have recognized in Kinbote's seemingly fantastic story a corollary to his own. This constitutes a sort of "synchronizing" or yoking together of meanings that mirrors what Kinbote carries out with regard to Shade's poem, with the result that their readings of each other are mutually, albeit only partially, complementary.

That Shade actually could have approved of such tactics in reading is suggested by another passage rife with implications for the novel's interpretive strategies. At a party, Kinbote happens to overhear Shade make a remark that might seem at first to be the key to the entire Zemblan story in the Commentary: "That is the wrong word," Shade responds to an interlocutor whose words we do not hear, "one should not apply it to a person who deliberately peels off a drab and unhappy past and replaces it with a brilliant invention. That's merely turning a new leaf with the left hand" (p. 238). By this point in the novel, the reader is tempted to infer that Shade was responding to an interlocutor who had called Kinbote "insane," all the more so because Shade looks at Kinbote with "glazed eyes" when, immediately after the remark about the "left hand," Kinbote appears before him. The poet's look could be interpreted as the shock of a polite person who is unexpectedly confronted by the object of his analysis. However, the continuation of the scene undermines the plausibility of this interpretation. Without a hitch, or any sign of confusion (which may of course be simply evidence of a quick wit and well-developed social graces), Shade's heretofore implied interlocutor, "Mrs. H[urley]," turns to Kinbote for his opinion about the actions of an old man at the local railway station "who thought he was God and began redirecting the trains." She thinks he is "a loony" and explains that Shade "calls him a fellow poet." Kinbote's response is "we all are, in a sense, poets." Thus Kinbote confirms Mrs. H.'s reading of Shade's remark, which, it is significant to note, Shade does not retract. If the conversation between Shade and Mrs. H. had been about Kinbote and not some railway worker, the relevance of Shade's remarks to Kinbote would only have been augmented. This is assuming, of course, that Kinbote's story of the King is a deliberate invention designed to replace an unhappy past, which it may not be. In any event, the dominant feature of Shade's formulations is that any truly artistic construct retains its validity and signification even if it is not referentially accurate. This conclusion is a variant of Nabokov's conception of reality as relative, and of art as only partially based on it, and echoes his views about the meaningful patterning that memory and imagination can impose on, and discover in, disparate events from the past. Shade's insight thus counters the opinion widespread among critics that

Nabokov's purpose in *Pale Fire* is to dramatize only the pure relativity of artistic constructs in life and art.[12]

Kinbote's Commentary contains a mix of both suggestive and specious parallels with Shade's poem. Shade's overt preoccupation with death is echoed by Kinbote's with the approach of the death-dealing assassin, although it is not clear that he is aware of the similarity. Ironically, the difference between the two preoccupations is decreased not through Kinbote's conscious effort to find resemblances between his story and Shade's poem, but as a result of his comments about Gradus. These have the effect of making the assassin's reality more ambiguous, and at the same time of augmenting his symbolic significance, all of which strengthens the parallels between him and Shade's theme of death. For example, when Kinbote speaks of his fears for his life, he admits that "at times I thought that only by self-destruction could I hope to cheat the relentlessly advancing assassins who were in me, in my eardrums, in my pulse, in my skull, rather than on that constant highway looping up over me and around my heart" (p. 97). This implicit equation between "Zemblan assassins" and processes within Kinbote's own body transforms the former into a figure for the destruction wrought by time, or by life itself (a point reminiscent of Nabokov's linking man's sense of time to the fact of being alive). A similar translation of the Zemblan assassin into a figure of human fate occurs in the last lines of Kinbote's Commentary. Even though Gradus has been arrested, Kinbote expresses his conviction that "a bigger, more respectable, more competent Gradus" will inevitably come to ring at his door (p. 301). Gradus is in fact made into an agent of fate when he inadvertently and unwittingly suggests to his cohorts that they will be able to find information about the King's whereabouts at the Villa Disa (pp. 216, 255). This proves true, and allows Gradus to resume his fateful journey. In this context, Kinbote's expressions of faith in God and an afterlife emerge as even closer to Shade's than if Gradus were simply a "real" Zemblan assassin.

The theme of love provides an entire fabric of ties between Shade's poem and Kinbote's Commentary. The most obvious strand is suggested by Kinbote himself when he claims that there is a striking resemblance between Charles the Beloved's wife, Queen Disa, and the image of Shade's wife, Sybil, in the poem. Kinbote reacts to this ostensible resemblance in a way that evokes Shade's conclusions based on fatidic coincidence: "I trust the reader appreciates the strangeness of this, because if he does not, there is no sense in writing poems, or notes to poems, or anything at all" (p. 207). Although the reader usually has no way of verifying Kinbote's assertions (to the extent that it is uncertain if Disa even exists outside Kinbote's mind), there is some textual evidence suggesting that his claim may not be entirely specious. An example is his passing reference to Sybil's "close-fitting brown trousers" that remind him of those his wife used to wear (p. 86). The casual nature of the observation suggests its plausibility (or the consistency of his imagination). The same can be said about Kinbote's indication that the Shades were married "exactly three decades before King Charles wed Disa" (p. 173). More noteworthy perhaps is Kinbote's discussion of Shade's reference in his poem to Sybil as "My dark Vanessa," which leads him to mention that the butterfly in question appears "in the escutcheon of the Dukes of Payn" (l. 270; p. 172). Because in this passage Kinbote seems to have forgotten that Disa is the Duchess of Payn (a point he does make elsewhere, pp. 173, 306 [where he accurately and humorously calls her Duchess of "Great Payne and Mone"]), and because the two women are linked by means of a butterfly that has an obviously portentous role in the novel (it appears moments before Shade is shot), one concludes that there may in fact be a concealed, authorially sanctioned link between Disa and Sybil. This possibility should not be allowed to obscure the obvious difference between Shade's relation to Sybil, and the King's to Disa. Shade's poem is a moving record of his deep and long devotion to his wife. By contrast, the King's attitude toward Disa is curiously forked: in waking life, his homosexuality rules over his relations with her; while in his dreams he feels both great love for her and contrition for his waking behavior (pp. 209, 210, 214). The latter point can in fact be seen as another concealed link between Kinbote's story and Shade's poem. The constant guilt that the King feels toward Disa when he dreams of her recalls the lines in Shade's poem in which he speaks of dreaming about the dead: "For as we know from dreams it is so hard / To speak to our dear dead! They disregard / Our apprehension, queaziness and shame" (ll. 589–91; p. 55). Fyodor expresses a similar sentiment in *The Gift*, as does Nabokov himself in *Speak, Memory* (p. 50). The parallel between the King's dream guilt and Shade's comparable feelings may thus be a hint that Disa is dead. This interpretation would be more far-fetched were it not for its resemblance to Nabokov's description of the unfinished novel *Solus Rex* that he said is echoed in *Pale Fire*. In this light, Kinbote can be seen as a variant of Sineusov, whose wife died, and who, as a consequence, enters an imaginary world that he invented. Something of this possibility can be discerned in Kinbote's urging Shade to retell in poetic form the story of the King and Disa, because "once transmuted by you into poetry, the stuff *will* be true, and the people *will* come alive" (p. 214). There is obvious irony of course in the fact that the story of the King and Disa is transformed into art by virtue of its central place in Kinbote's rather than Shade's text. Kinbote indirectly (and perhaps unwittingly) supports this inference when he imagines a series of different fates for Disa, one of which is "that she had become a character in a novel" (p. 212). This observation underlies another unsignaled parallel between Sybil and Disa: the former's stylized image is central to Shade's poem, just as the latter's is to the Commentary.

The theme of love in Shade's poem is also connected with the pathetic story of his daughter's suicide, and there are several intriguing links between it and Kinbote's tale. Kinbote shows partial awareness of this himself when he says that "it is . . . true that Hazel Shade resembled me in certain respects." His immediate reason for this generalization is his belief that he is the source of several "mirror words," or palindromes, that Shade uses in his poem and ascribes to his daughter (p. 193). Kinbote claims to remember "the poet's expression of stupefaction" when he mentioned these words to him, and implies that Shade's reaction resulted from his being struck by the reversibility of "spider" and "redips." It is equally possible, however, that Shade's amazement, if real, was due to another reason entirely—the coincidence that Kinbote used the same examples of palindromes that Hazel had, and this is a coincidence of which Kinbote is unaware. Although this possibility is suggested by Shade's general preoccupation with, and alertness to, significant patterning in life, the question of who is the true originator of the palindromes remains, in the end, ambiguous. On the one hand, Kinbote appears to use them spontaneously (e.g., p. 162); on the other, he writes his Commentary after he reads Shade's poem, which means that it could have been his source.

A more certain parallel between Kinbote and Hazel is that both are unhappy in love. Encountering the phrase "Would never come for her" in Shade's poem, Kinbote ignores its obvious reference to the young men who would never court Hazel, and, instead, provides a typical inversion of it by noting how he used to wait for "a ping-pong friend, or for old John Shade" (p. 184). Suicide is another bond between Hazel and Kinbote, as he realizes. She takes her life because of unhappiness in love, and Kinbote is drawn to suicide both out of a sense of the ugliness and unhappiness of life (p. 312), which appears to be a reflection of his ambivalence toward his treatment of Disa and related matters, and, perversely, but logically given his premises, out of a love for God (p. 221). (The theme of his relation to Disa, which was prefigured by his treatment of Fleur, suggests that on another level Kinbote's and Hazel's problems stand in a parodic relationship to one another: he is the breaker of women's hearts, while she is a victim.) It might seem that Kinbote's hope that God would help him shed his desire to follow Hazel and Gradus in actually committing suicide (p. 300) is a countervailing argument against linking the pair too closely. However, it is worth noting that in Nabokov's imagination, as he indicated in an interview after *Pale Fire* was published, Kinbote "certainly did [commit suicide] after putting the last touches to his edition of the poem" (*Strong Opinions*, p. 74).

Shade's description of Hazel in his poem suggests that her unhappiness in love was a consequence of her being physically unattractive. But Nabokov may have concealed an additional explanation that, if accepted, draws Hazel significantly closer to Kinbote and his problems. There is a faint, albeit discernible chain of connections among Hazel, her great aunt Maude, and homosexuality. This possibility is suggested by Kinbote's description of the sexually ambiguous couple that comes to Shade's birthday party and that is associated with Maude (assuming, as always, that Kinbote is not projecting what he claims he sees): "I saw, ensconced in their tiny Pulex, *manned* by her *boy-handsome* tousle-haired *girl friend*, the patroness of the arts who had sponsored Aunt Maude's last exhibition" (italics added; p. 160). The name of their car is Latin for "flea," which, through its denotation of small size, parasitism, and quickness, adds a comic touch at the same time that it connotes tight quarters. Although this is, admittedly, only a tenuous possibility, the car's name may also be a Nabokovian allusion to John Donne's famous poem "The Flea," and a hint, thereby, regarding the relations between the two women (with the obvious difference that Donne's sonnet is about a heterosexual seduction). Donne is relevant for *Pale Fire* because he is mentioned several times in connection with Sybil's translations into French (ll. 677–78; pp. 58, 240–42). One of Donne's poems that Kinbote discusses is "Death be not proud," which bears some thematic resemblance to the kinds of baroque subjects Maude chose for her poetry and paintings: "realistic objects interlaced / With grotesque growths and images of doom" (ll. 85–89; p. 36). Moreover, Kinbote had also observed that "Aunt Maude was far from spinsterish, and the extravagant and sardonic turn of her mind must have shocked sometimes the genteel dames of New Wye" (p. 113). Although he does not elaborate on this remark, it implies that her "life of the heart" was as unconventional as her art. Kinbote himself suggests a link between Hazel and Maude on the basis of the "psychokinetic" manifestations that appear shortly after the aunt dies (pp. 165–67). This thematic association between the two women is augmented by Kinbote's mentioning that Shade uses his aunt's favorite cane when he examines the site where a "haunted barn" had stood, a building in which Hazel had experienced what appears to have been an occult communication with a ghost (ll. 345–47; pp. 186–93). A faint, but insistent association of the cane with the theme of homosexuality, and, in turn, of the latter with the occult can also be traced through the novel: the cane is first mentioned in connection with a photograph taken by "a young roomer" of Kinbote's (p. 26); and Hazel's transcript of the occult message she receives in the barn is paralleled by the rigged-up seance that King Charles attends in

Zembla, during which he receives a message designed to persuade him to "renounce sodomy" (p. 109). The presence of occult messages in Kinbote's story and Shade's poem is of course also important as a textural pattern uniting them.

Numerous other small bridges link Kinbote's story and Shade's poem. These include Shade's description of how to behave after one has become a ghost (l. 555; p. 54), which is embodied in Kinbote's narrative point of view when describing Gradus aboard an airplane (p. 278). Similarly, Kinbote's fear of a Zemblan firing squad (p. 96) has its parallel in a description of Shade's (ll. 597–608; p. 55), which, in turn, recalls Nabokov's portrayal of Gumilev in "The Art of Literature and Commonsense." The bizarre incident of Shade's having an out-of-body experience, or seeing his own double (ll. 872–84; p. 65), has its visual equivalent in the King's seeing a false reflection, or a double, during his escape from Zembla (p. 143). It is also echoed in Kinbote's remark in the Foreword that "our shadows still walk without us" (p. 15), which remains enigmatic until one recognizes that the reference to "shadows" in connection with the theme of doubling evokes the poem's initial image—the "shadow" of the slain waxwing that lives on after its death, and thus implies transcendence (all of which resurrects the theme of the spiritual "double" in *Invitation to a Beheading*). The significance of Kinbote's conclusion that Shade was divinely inspired when composing his poem, which is camouflaged by Kinbote's assertion that Shade is an agnostic who would have tried to deny this conclusion (p. 89), is in fact a correlate of Shade's views on the metaphysical implications of art (ll. 975–76; p. 69). Finally, it is hardly a coincidence that the King's mother dies on the same date as Shade, 21 July (p. 104), that Kinbote, Shade and Gradus all have the same birthday, 5 July, and, as Kinbote himself may recognize, that he and Gradus are exactly the same age (pp. 13, 173, 275).

As in all of Nabokov's works, the most telling connections in *Pale Fire* are hidden below the surface. They appear on a level, and are of a nature that cannot be ascribed to either Shade or Kinbote (provided one assumes they are independent characters, and that Kinbote's silence regarding a correlation is evidence of his being unaware of it). The only agency that can be invoked to explain the presence of such details—which connect to form a pattern of meaning that is obviously linked to the novel's overt themes, and which testify to its essential unity—is an otherworldly fate impersonated by Nabokov's artistic consciousness.

One of the most important of these "textural" patterns or coincidences in the novel, which not only lends great weight to Shade's hermeneutic principles but also links Kinbote's story to the poem, is Shade's "clockwork toy— / A tin wheelbarrow pushed by a tin boy" that is associated with his childhood epiphanic spells (l. 144; p. 38). In Nabokov's world, this fact of association is meaningful all by itself. What augments its sig-nificance, however, is the ocurrence of a scene reminiscent of the toy just before Shade is killed. In the last lines of his poem, he mentions "Some neighbor's gardener . . . / Trundling an empty barrow up the lane" (ll. 998–99; p. 69). Kinbote comments on this image, and reveals that the gar-dener in question is a black man (pp. 217, 291–92), which confirms his resemblance to Shade's toy "little Negro of painted tin" (p. 137). (At the same time, Gradus, whom Kinbote repeatedly describes as if he were a mechanical man [e.g., pp. 152, 279], and whom he makes into a figure for fate, is also evoked by the toy, and is thus implicated in the scene of Shade's murder even before he appears; through the link with the toy, Gradus is as much a part of Shade's fate as Kinbote's.) Moreover, Shade's poem mentions, and Kinbote's Commentary repeats, that a butterfly flies near the gardener just prior to the murder. Apart from the significance of butterflies for Nabokov in general, Shade evokes a butterfly-like meta-morphosis of another insect as an emblem of transcendence in the passage alluding to La Fontaine's fable. (Black butterflies, a "black-winged fate," and a related "batlike moth" clearly constitute a leitmotif in the novel [pp. 15, 123, 142, 182, 202, 314] culminating in the Red Admirable that appears just before Shade's death; this butterfly had a specifically pro-phetic association for Nabokov [*Strong Opinions*, p. 170].) The transcen-dence associated with metamorphosis is in harmony with Shade's epiph-anies, during which he has the sensation that he is transcending time and space; the epiphanies are also evoked at the moment of Shade's death through the association of the clockwork toy with the gardener and his wheelbarrow. (Shade himself links his heart attack and the impression that he crossed into the otherworld to his epiphanies [ll. 691–92, p. 58].) In short, there are a number of hints in the text that Shade's death may not be final. This possibility adds a typically Nabokovian ironic twist to the novel. It turns out that despite his being shot, Shade is correct in sus-pecting, as he puts it in his poem, that he would awaken on the following day and even survive death. The irony is heightened all the more by the fact that his murder would seem to have disproven his inferences about survival, which he made on the basis of his ability to create art that "scans right" (l. 974; p. 69). The theme of immortality is also evoked in the scene of Shade's murder via Kinbote's description of the poet lying with "open dead eyes directed up at the sunny evening azure" (p. 295). This of course evokes the image in the beginning lines of the poem, in which the wax-wing was "slain / By the false azure in the windowpane" while Shade himself "Lived on, flew on, in the reflected sky" (ll. 1–4; p. 33). The fact that Kinbote searches actively for patterns linking his experiences to Shade's, but does not notice this nexus surrounding Shade's death, suggests that it would be wrong to ascribe it to his desire to force connections.

Another major instance of meaning directed over Kinbote's head is presented in the novel as an overtly occult message. Hazel recorded a series of letter groups that were "dictated" to her by what she took to be a spirit in the haunted barn she visits. Kinbote tries to decipher these and fails to find "the least allusion to the poor girl's fate." Nevertheless, it is quite clear that the letters do contain a message, albeit one apparently meant for her father and not to her: the cluster "not ogo old wart" can be read as "not to go Goldsworth," which refers to the name of the owner of the house where Shade is killed (pp. 188–89).[13] This reading is confirmed by Vera Nabokov's Russian translation of the letter clusters, which includes "nedi ogol varta"; this sequence can be deciphered as "ne idi o[kolo] goldsvorta," which, although not grammatically correct Russian, is obviously the equivalent of the English warning not to go to Judge Goldsworth's house (p. 179). There is a precedent in Nabokov's oeuvre for seeing this as an occult message, because comparable encoding appears in the stories "Ultima Thule" and "The Vane Sisters" (1959). In the former, the narrator does not appear to notice that Falter, who claims to have plumbed the ultimate mysteries of existence, repeats a list of things the narrator's deceased wife had said she loved, thus implying that she may be communicating with her husband from beyond the grave via Falter. In the second story, the comparable device is that the narrator does not notice that the two dead sisters have planted an acrostic-like message in the final paragraph of his tale.

Because commentators have identified a large number of other patterns in the novel, there is no point in describing any more in detail here. Suffice it to mention such complexes as the hidden parallels between Gerald Emerald and Izumrudov ("izumrud" means "emerald" in Russian), and the possibility that Kinbote was involved with the former (pp. 24, 97, 98, 251, 255, 256, 267, 283, 310); the palindromic relations among the names of characters such as Jacob Gradus and Sudarg of Bokay (pp. 77, 111, 150, 310, 311); and the whole matter of Kinbote's being unaware of the source of Shade's title for his poem, despite the subtextual omnipresence of references to *Timon of Athens*, including a Zemblan translation, throughout his text (e.g., pp. 15, 132, 240, 285, etc.).[14]

A different level of patterning in *Pale Fire* is accessible only to readers who know Russian. In this case, the identification of a pattern or a texture depends on recognizing that the true meaning of a Russian word that appears in the text has what might be termed a punning relationship to the meaning that is given. Thus we are told by Kinbote that the whole of Gradus's clan, whose name may derive from "the Russian word for 'grape,' *vinograd*, to which a Latin suffix had adhered," "seems to have been in the liquor business," "except" for his father, and an uncle named "Roman Tselovalnikov" (p. 77). The joke here is that "tseloval'nik" is obsolete Russian for "innkeeper" or "publican," and Roman is, of course, a Russian first name derived from the civilization whose language was Latin. The resulting reduction to the absurd of the preposition *except*, which occupies a syntactical space implying logical categorization, is also a veiled evocation of a comparable maneuver in Gogol's "The Overcoat," with its play on "shoe," "boot" and the protagonist's surname Bashmachkin ("bashmak" means "shoe" in Russian). Another example of concealed Russian in the text is Fleur's "three mousepits," which, although they may in fact be "Zemblan anatomy" (p. 110), are also a playful variant of the Russian "myshki," which means both "little mice" and "armpits." Although such jokes and puns operate on another level of the text than the patterns linking Shade's poem and Kinbote's Commentary, their significance for the novel as a whole is the same: they fall within the purview of Shade's fundamental hermeneutic principle of textural coincidence.

Yet another level of concealed signification in the novel consists of allusions to Nabokov's other works. The charming, pathetic, and pedantic Professor Timofey Pavlovich Pnin is not only resurrected from *Pnin*, but is also provided with satisfying job security as "Head of the bloated Russian Department" at Wordsmith University, something he lacked in the earlier novel (p. 155; even his little dog is reborn into a peaceful and plump existence, p. 282). But Pnin's relevance to *Pale Fire* goes beyond an author's desire to give a character a happier fictional fate than seemed likely at the conclusion of the earlier novel. In fact, there are many important thematic links between the two works. For example, Pnin, like Shade, experiences repeated seizures during which time collapses, and that are comparable to epiphanies. Like Kinbote, Pnin is also a lonely exile from a distant northern land that may seem quite unreal to his readers and colleagues. In connection with this, it is worth mentioning that Victor Wind's fantasy in chapter 4 of *Pnin* about a King's escape by water is a clear foreshadowing of Charles the Beloved's flight from Zembla. In similar fashion, the obvious allusion to *Lolita* in Shade's poem (l. 680; p. 58) is more than a playful self-indulgence on Nabokov's part. He gives it to Kinbote to echo a key idea from the afterword to *Lolita* when in a dialogue with Shade he speaks of the limitations of a "personality consisting mainly of the shadows of its own prison bars" (pp. 226–27). This epistemological problem is also central to *Pale Fire*, of course, as is the theme of sexual deviance. Nabokov even alludes to the unfinished novel *Solus Rex* twice (pp. 118–19, 306), which appears to be motivated more by the thematic relevance of that work as Nabokov himself describes it than by the relatively minor role of chess in *Pale Fire*. In another vein, one can find details in the novel that anticipate Nabokov's later English works. These range from the transparency of Gradus and the airplane in which he is traveling, which will become the dominant point of view of the otherworldly narrator who moves freely through time in *Transparent Things*, to the erotically charged, fanciful world of *Ada*, which, despite its seemingly frivolous and baroque surface is focused on issues related to Nabokov's otherworld. These prospective and retrospective glances, which extend the patterning in *Pale Fire* into the textual dimension of Nabokov's oeuvre, not only constitute one of the warrants for a contextual approach to the novel, but also serve as a justification for the kinds of correlations of seemingly unrelated worlds of experience and life lines that Shade and Kinbote carry out.

Nabokov and the Silver Age of
Russian Culture

WERE the émigré critics who described Nabokov's art as "un-Russian" right? Are there in fact no antecedents for it in Russian literature and culture?

Nabokov spoke candidly of his few strong sympathies, and his numerous and equally strong antipathies, in his interviews, prefaces, and lectures. He also echoed, parodied, and satirized many Russian, and non-Russian, writers in his fictions. But as far as I know, other than occasionally making a laconic and ambiguous acknowledgment of Pushkin's and Gogol's importance for him, Nabokov systematically objected to virtually all suggestions that any other writer had ever influenced him.[1] This stance was part of his public persona.

The mask slips, however, in a private document—a letter to Edmund Wilson from 1949—in which Nabokov objects to the latter's singularly uninformed remark that Russian literature underwent a decadence after 1905: "The 'decline' of Russian literature in 1905–1917 is a Soviet invention," Nabokov explains, because "Blok, Bely, Bunin and others wrote their best stuff in those days. And never was poetry so popular, not even in Pushkin's days. *I am a product of that period, I was bred in that atmosphere*" (italics added).[2] This is a highly revealing admission, for it indicates that Nabokov saw his own artistic origins in the so-called Silver Age of Russian culture.[3] But in what specific aspects of this variegated period did they lie? It is certainly noteworthy that Nabokov mentions two Symbolists—Blok and Belyi. But he also includes Bunin on his short list, who is usually, and very loosely, classified as a "realist" (although it is known that Nabokov valued his verse more than his prose),[4] and he implies that there are other figures, presumably belonging to other classificational categories, who were important for him as well. With all due respect to Nabokov's contempt for generalizations—particularly for academic categories that end in "ism"—I would like to suggest that the Russian literary movements during the period 1905–1917 whose theories and practices are closest to Nabokov are Symbolism and Acmeism, with, perhaps, a tilt toward the former. Specifically, Blok, Belyi, and Gumilev appear to have influenced aspects of his artistic development. (Another significant influence on Nabokov is the poetry of Vladislav Khodasevich, which is also a product of the Silver Age; this promising topic still awaits its investigator.) Added to this is the possibility that one of Nabokov's most productive ideas—the artificiality of nature—may have been derived from, or influenced by two individuals who were contemporaries of the well-known writers of the Silver Age and shared some traits with the Symbolists—the occultist Petr Uspenskii (1878–1947; known as "P. D. Ouspensky" in English) and the playwright, director, historian, and theoretician of the theater Nikolai Evreinov (1879–1953).

The relation of Nabokov to all five of these individuals, as well as their contemporaries, is a large and complicated topic that deserves its own book-length study, and that I will be able to treat only cursorily. Moreover, my focus on each one will be highly selective, and is designed to illustrate but not to exhaust the kinds of connections that can be drawn between them and Nabokov. A useful sense of the complexity of such an endeavor can be found in Nabokov's own description of the "mechanism" of literary influence as he conceived it in 1930:

> [It] is a dark and unclear thing. One may imagine, for example, two writers, A and B, completely different but both under a certain very subjective Proustian influence; this influence goes unnoticed by reader C inasmuch as each of the three (A, B, and C) has understood Proust in his own way. It happens that a writer has an oblique influence through another writer, or that some sort of complex blending of influences takes place, and so on. One may not foresee anything in this regard.[5]

With the above statement as a necessary caveat, I would like to begin by characterizing briefly what links Nabokov to the Silver Age in general. Paramount is the dominance of lyric poetry at the turn of the century, a point Nabokov underscores in his letter to Wilson. This is reflected not only in the fact that Nabokov began as a poet, and that he continued to write poetry all his life, but most importantly in the poetization of his prose fiction, which relies heavily on sound repetition and rhythm, and even contains passages written in meter. It is quite possible that Andrei Belyi's poeticized prose was a specific, intermediate model in this regard. As far as Aleksei Remizov is concerned, Nabokov is reported to have thought little of him as a writer.[6] (Nabokov's opinion would of course not have been affected by the fact that Remizov is a forerunner of the "ornamental prose" style, which, although normally used to characterize certain Soviet works of the early 1920s, bears some resemblance to Nabokov's style.) The "addition" of rhythm and sound orchestration to prose results in qualitative, and not merely quantitative changes in its density and complexity. This can be related to another feature of Nabokov's novels and stories that may also be traceable to the influence of poetry—their reflexive structure, which is akin to what Frank has termed "spatial form" in modern literature. Nabokov's belletristic prose is fashioned in accordance with the structure of cosmic synchronization, as a result of which the reader can understand certain crucial levels of meaning in a work only by grasping simultaneously the connections among word groups that are scattered throughout the text and embedded in contexts that conceal the words' true import. Thus Nabokov's prose fiction, like much modernist literature with roots in late nineteenth- and twentieth-century poetry according to Frank, requires the reader to suspend temporarily the process of identifying signs in the text with referents outside it, "until the entire pattern of internal references can be apprehended as a unity."[7]

I invoke Symbolism and Acmeism as antecedents for Nabokov because two other dominant features of his art can be correlated with these movements. It is in Acmeism that we find the kind of celebration of sensual details and of perceptual acuity that is one of Nabokov's hallmarks (as he signals via his image of Gumilev in "The Art of Literature and Commonsense"). And it is Symbolism that cultivated the kind of metaphysical dualism—or division between visible phenomena and a "higher" spiritual reality—that underlies Nabokov's depictions of phenomena in this world. Nabokov's art thus constitutes a unique fusion of distinctive features from both these movements, and belies the superficial conception of them as simply and inevitably antithetical.

Any examination of Nabokov's connection with Russian Symbolism should begin with his debt to the poet Aleksandr Blok (1880–1921). Nabokov made a number of remarks over the course of several decades that show he saw him as a teacher. In a letter to Wilson from 1942, Nabokov explains that he had been "trained on the verse of Blok, Annensky, Bely and others who revolutionized the old ideas about Russian versification" (p. 72). The following year Nabokov describes Blok to Wilson as "one of those poets that get into one's system ... I, as most Russians, went through that stage some twenty-five years ago" (p. 94). In his notes to his translation of *Eugene Onegin* (1964) Nabokov refers to Blok as "by far the greatest poet of the first two decades of this century."[8] In 1966 Nabokov tells an interviewer that ever since his boyhood he has "remained passionately fond of Blok's lyrics." And in an interview from 1970, Nabokov admits that during his youth he saw himself as a poet "of the Blokian era," and chose to associate himself with it via the pseudonym "Sirin," which is a mythical creature that appears in Blok's verse, as well as the name of a publishing house linked to Symbolism.[9]

Nabokov's admiration for Blok is clearly reflected in his own verse.

First of all, he dedicated poems to him, such as the short cycle entitled "Na smert' Bloka" ("On the Death of Blok") in the early collection *Grozd'* (1923).[10] One poem is a variation on Blok's best known themes—most notably that of the "prekrasnaia dama" ("beautiful lady"); and the other has the shades of Pushkin, Lermontov, Tiutchev, and Fet gathering in paradise to welcome Blok's soul into their midst. Secondly, Blok's collection *Stikhi o prekrasnoi dame* and the poem "Neznakomka" ("The Stranger") become dominant subtexts in Nabokov's poems from the early 1920s, and contribute imagery, themes, lexicon, and rhythms to them. Some examples include the poem beginning "Mechtal ia o tebe tak chasto, tak davno, / za mnogo let do nashei vstrechi" ("I dreamed of you so often, so long ago, many years before our meeting"; *Grozd'*, p. 27; *Stikhi*, p. 50, dated 6.7.21; this poem also contains the line "Ia zval tebia, ia zhdal. Shli gody. Ia brodil" ["I called you, I waited. Years passed. I wandered"], recalling Blok's famous "O doblestiakh, o podvigakh, o slave" from *Vozmezdie*); "Storozhevye kiparisy" (*Gornii put'*, p. 45), which contains such lines as "I ch'ia-to ten' iz-za ogrady / uporno smotrit na menia" ("And someone's shade from behind the fence intently looks at me"), and "A tam,—glaza Shekherezady / v moi zvezdnyi i zveniashchii sad / iz-za beleeiushchei ogrady, / prodolgovatye gliadiat" ("And there, Scheherazade's elongated eyes peer from behind the whitish fence into my stellar and ringing garden"); "M. W." (*Gornii put'*, pp. 76–77), beginning "Chasy na bashne raspevali / nad zyb'iu rtutnoiu reki, / i v bezdnakh ulits voznikali, kak kapli krovi, ogon'ki" ("The clock sang on the tower above the quicksilver rippling of the river, and in the abysses of the streets appeared lights like drops of blood"), and including such lines as "i na kolesakh korabli, zrachkami krasnymi vrashchaia, v tumane s grokhotom polzli" ("and ships on wheels, revolving their red pupils, crawled thunderously in the fog"), and "i vstala barkhatnaia taina / v tvoikh iazycheskikh glazakh" ("and a velvet secret arose in your pagan eyes"; for other examples see *Stikhi*, pp. 89, 106–7).

These and related poems (a number of which clearly belong to Nabokov's juvenilia) are imitations of the Blokian lyric persona's impression that the woman he encounters is somehow mystically familiar, and fatidically tied to him. It should be noted, however, that Nabokov eschews the apocalyptic undertones derived from Vladimir Soloviev that underlie Blok's verse. Neither is there the mood of mystical despair or abandonment that appears in Blok; by contrast, Nabokov's poems are filled with hope.

Thus the overarching theme Nabokov borrows from Blok is a variant of the Platonic idea that via love, which is the vehicle for regaining a transcendent unity of being, human souls strive to reunite with their mates from whom they were separated upon incarnation. The continuing importance of this idea for Nabokov is suggested by the fact that he included several poems about it that he had written half a century or more earlier in the collection of verse he had prepared just prior to his death in 1977. In one, beginning "V khrustal'nyi shar zakliucheny my byli" (*Stikhi*, p. 11, dated 1918), he has the speaker say to his soul mate that he will be able to recognize her "po etoi pyli zvezdnoi, / ostavsheisia na konchikakh resnits" ("by that stellar dust that is left on the tips of your eyelashes") deriving from their celestial origins.

This mystically colored conception of love also survives Nabokov's youthful poetry. It loses its sometimes naive pathos and becomes more subtle, but continues to appear in most of his major novels during the following decades. We find it in *The Defense* in Luzhin's sense that there is something a priori familiar about the unnamed woman who will become his wife, even though he had apparently never seen her before their first meeting.[11] Cincinnatus in *Invitation to a Beheading* yearns for his soul's counterpart, who together with him will constitute one completed design.[12] Fyodor in *The Gift* sees Zina as part of a transcendent pattern into which he also fits.[13] The theme is sounded strongly throughout *Bend Sinister* and *Ada*. And it appears in *Speak, Memory* as a fact of Nabokov's own experience when he describes his love for members of his family in terms identical to "cosmic synchronization" (pp. 296–97).

Lolita can be seen as constituting yet another variation on this theme. The entire novel hinges on the inexplicable physical and spiritual harmony between Humbert and his childhood love Annabel, which predates their first meeting, and which Humbert then erroneously tries to rediscover in Lolita. Indeed, Humbert's conception of the "nymphet" as a creature touched by otherworldly magic, and one whose significance only he can perceive, resembles a parodic treatment of Blok's themes of the "beautiful lady" or "the stranger."[14] This can be illustrated by Humbert's description of the effect that seeing Lolita's name on her class list has on him (pp. 54–55: 42). The details congruent with Blok's "Neznakomka" that appear in this passage include the mystery, the secret recognition through privileged vision, the veil, and the sound repetitions in the exotic word *charshaf*, which recall the sibilants and hushing sounds in the Russian poem. Although Humbert is speaking about Lolita, it is noteworthy that none of these details is appropriate for her or the kind of clothing she wears. On the other hand, virtually all the elements of Humbert's reverie can also be found in the poems that Nabokov wrote in the twenties under Blok's influence. One of the changes Nabokov made when he translated *Lolita* into Russian was to introduce Blok's name into it by changing the name of Quilty's anagrammatic collaborator from "Vivian Darkbloom" to "Vivian Damor-Blok" (33: 22).

The legacy of Andrei Belyi (1880–1934) is more varied than Blok's, and different aspects of it attracted Nabokov during much of his life. His very high regard for Belyi's *Petersburg* as one of the four greatest works of twentieth-century prose is well known.[15] Nabokov also paid tribute to Belyi's insights about Gogol in his own study of the author.[16] On a number of occasions, Nabokov singled out Belyi's approach to Russian versification (embodied in several essays in the volume *Simvolizm* [1910]) for special praise. In a letter to Wilson from 1942, Nabokov refers to these as "probably the greatest work on verse in any language" (p. 78). In his Commentary to his translation of *Eugene Onegin* (vol. 3, p. 459) Nabokov acknowledges that he became greatly fascinated with Belyi's essays during his youth. And in a letter to his sister from 1950 Nabokov reveals that the utility of Belyi's ideas on versification has still not paled for him with the passing years when he mentions that in his teaching at Wellesley he uses tables based on Belyi's system that he had fashioned with her in the Crimea in 1919.[17]

It is probably the quasi-scientific descriptive force of Belyi's work on versification that elicited Nabokov's praise for it. But what are the reasons for his admiration for *Petersburg*? As far as I am aware, there are no published comments by Nabokov about Belyi's masterpiece, or Belyi in general, that shed any light on this question. If we consider Nabokov's broadest aesthetic criteria, however—criteria about which he was very clear and insistent on many occasions—we can infer that he must have valued *Petersburg* as a skillfully wrought artifact quite unlike anything that Russian, or, indeed, European literature had ever seen. But there must have been more to it than that. Belyi's manner is inseparable from his matter and Nabokov surely recognized this. Thus it is hard to believe that he would have ignored Belyi's frankly metaphysical thematics in *Petersburg* and elsewhere and focused exclusively on the novel's linguistic, stylistic, and formal features.

I am encouraged in this supposition by two things: first, the general congruence between Belyi's and Nabokov's aesthetics as they defined them in theoretical writings, and second, the fact that several of Nabokov's novels contain evocations of key moments, motifs, or ideas from both Belyi's fictional and discursive writings that point to his metaphysics.

There are at least four points of contact between Belyi's and Nabokov's aesthetics.[18] (1) Both see a causal connection between the perceiver-artist's cognitive act and the resulting work of art; but whereas in Belyi's theory there is an implied mimetic relationship between the symbolic perception and the work, in Nabokov's case the symbolic perception acts as a catalyst for the "germ" of the future work, which does not necessarily have a connection with the sensory or other data that gave rise to it (although it may, as Nabokov describes in *Speak, Memory*, p. 217). (2) Nabokov's seminal concept "cosmic synchronization" bears a strong resemblance to Belyi's symbolic cognition; indeed, in *The Gift*, this form of privileged perception is described as "a supersensory insight into the world accompanied by our inner participation" (322: 347), which could serve as an encapsulation of Belyi's ideas. (3) For Belyi and Nabokov individual cognitive acts are relative in the sense that each cognizing subject is unique and therefore infuses an aspect of the world outside himself with an aspect of that uniqueness (another way of saying this is that the world each subject perceives is unique). In fact, in two separate interviews, Nabokov virtually echoes Belyi when he claims that the existence of anything outside the individual perceiver is a function of that individual's cognitive act. Nabokov also goes so far as to claim that so-called "average reality begins to rot and stink" when individual creative perception ceases;[19] this recalls Belyi's very similar point in the major essay "*Magiia slov*" ("The Magic of Words," 1909) about words that have lost their creative, poetic character being "a foul-smelling, decaying corpse ['zlovonnyi, razlagaiushchiisia trup']."[20] (4) For both Belyi and Nabokov the source of the work of art lies at least partially in a transcendent realm: in Belyi's case the Absolute acts through the perceiver-artist when he focuses on something outside himself; and in Nabokov's, an otherworld yields the seed of the work of art to the artist-perceiver during the timeless moment of cosmic synchronization that is also initiated when he focuses on something outside himself.[21] In both cases, it is the role of the transcendent during the creative process that saves individual perceptions from being mere projections. (It is of course evident that the roots of these conceptions lie in German Idealism and ultimately in Plato.)

If we move now to the level of general aesthetic tactics, we find a fundamental parallel between the value that both Belyi and Nabokov place on deception in art. Fyodor in *The Gift* clearly echoes Nabokov when he says about chess: "Every creator is a plotter; and all the pieces impersonating his ideas on the board were here as conspirators and sorcerers. Only in the final instant was their secret spectacularly revealed" (184: 193). Belyi proclaims a very similar principle in *Zapiski chudaka* (*Notes of an Eccentric*): "Tak—vsiakii roman: igra v priatki s chitatelem on; a znachenie arkhitektoniki, frazy—v odnom: otvesti glaz chitatelia ot sviashchennogo punkta: rozhdeniia mifa" ("Thus every novel is a game of hide and seek with the reader; and the aim of the architectonics, the phrase is exclusively to lead the reader's eye away from the sacred point: the birth of myth," vol. 1, p. 63). The praxis of both writers is of course precisely to conceal what is most important, and to make the reader work to discover it.

A major difference between Nabokov's and Belyi's metaphysical aesthetics is that Nabokov describes his beliefs in terms of intuitions and intimations, whereas Belyi tends to pedantic certainty—whether in passages pretending to rigorous philosophical analysis or oracular solemnity. This underlies a number of radically different stylistic and formal characteristics of the two authors' novels.

A number of notable Belyi echoes appear in *The Gift*. Fyodor refers openly to Belyi's theories about rhythmic structures in poetry, and calls attention to his parody of Belyi's rhythmicized prose from the late novels (163: 170, 169: 177). More interesting, however, is Nabokov's unmarked evocation of elements from Belyi's works that imply man's dependence on a transcendent realm. An example is Fyodor's description of how he tries to infer the "law of composition" according to which shops are arranged on Berlin streets. When he does not find the expected sequence where he lives, he speculates that the proper "rhythmic swarming had not yet established itself" ("roenie ritma tut eshche ne nastalo," 17: 11). The two words "roi" ("swarm") and "ritm" ("rhythm") are among the most important and insistently repeated leitmotifs in Belyi's *Kotik Letaev*, where they refer to the fundamental causative principle by which the world of spirit shapes the protagonist's material world.[22] Nabokov appears to be alluding to the same kind of spiritual significance, because Fyodor's search for a pattern among shops is but one particular, and in this case lighthearted, instance of his search for patterning throughout the novel. And, as we have seen, he finds it wherever he looks—in his material world, in his relations with Zina and other characters, and in nature.

There are several intriguing evocations of details from *Petersburg* in *The Gift* as well. On the novel's second page a thought occurs to Fyodor about a future work he would like to write, which is presumably the novel *The Gift* itself: "[eto] podumalos' mel'kom s bespechnoi ironiei—sovershenno, vprochem, izlishneiu, potomu-chto kto-to vnutri nego, za nego, pomimo nego, vse eto uzhe prinial, zapisal i pripriatal" (because of differences between the languages, the English translation does not convey the passive nature of this experience quite as strikingly as the Russian: "The fleeting thought was touched with a careless irony; an irony, however, that was quite unnecessary, because somebody within him, on his behalf, independently from him, had absorbed all this, recorded it, and filed it away," 16: 10). The reflexive verb form, "podumalos' " (literally "it thought itself") augments the description of Fyodor as being split between a passive, mundane self, and a hidden, active, artistic self. Nabokov's point here, as elsewhere in the novel, is to hint that there is a spiritual side to Fyodor that acts as the receptor for the otherworldly "germ" of the work of art. A related sort of thinking occurs in *Petersburg* as well. The verbal cluster "podumalos' " "s bespechnoi" or "izlishneiu" "ironiei" (literally: "it thought itself" "with careless" or "unnecessary"

"irony") recalls the phrases "dumy dumalis' sami" ("meditations medi-
tated themselves"), "mysli myslilis' sami" ("thoughts thought themselves"), and "prazdnaia [or 'nekomu nenuzhnaia'] mozgovaia igra"
("idle [or, literally, 'unnecessary to anyone'] cerebral play") that appear
in many of the most important scenes in *Petersburg*.[23] The significance of
these phrases, which Belyi seems to use as interchangeable synonyms, is
that they describe or imply the intrusion of occult forces into the minds
of different personages—forces whose effect is to *create* aspects of those
personages' worlds. It is most significant for understanding *Petersburg*
that the narrator-author claims that he too is subject to these forces and
that his book results from them. This is yet another parallel with Fyodor's
passive thought about a future work that turns out to be the novel *The
Gift*.

A similar evocation of *Petersburg* can be discerned in Fyodor's childhood dream about an expedition into Asia, in which he sees himself as a
tortured horse screaming "in a Mongolian voice" ("mongol'skim golo-
som") and has the sensation that "someone would unstitch me from top
to bottom, after which an agile hand would slip inside me and powerfully
squeeze my heart" ("rasparyval menia sverkhu do nizu, posle chego pro-
vornaia ladon' pronikala v menia i sil'no szhimala serdtse," 29: 23). We
find a related scene in *Petersburg* when Apollon Apollonovich almost
freezes to death in the countryside and feels someone's cold fingers thrust
into his chest and stroke his heart; the same hand then proceeds to lead
him up the steps of his career (vol. 1, pp. 104–5: pp. 52–53; this image
has additional antecedents in Soloviev's "Brief Tale about the Antichrist,"
Ivan's encounter with the devil in *The Brothers Karamazov*, and, possibly, in Pushkin's poem "The Prophet"). This passage is one of many that
show Apollon Apollonovich to be the agent of malevolent, reactionary,
and ossifying forces that are associated with the so-called pan-Mongolian
phase of Soloviev's eschatology. Fyodor's dream also implies that his destiny is shaped by an otherworldly force, which follows from the fact that
references to Asia in *The Gift* are linked to hints that the spirit of Fyodor's
father, who conducted expeditions into Asia, has been subtly guiding
Fyodor's life. (At the same time, it must be stressed that there are major
differences between Belyi's and Nabokov's uses of Asia in their novels,
and that they cannot be simply equated.)

The Real Life of Sebastian Knight contains a number of additional evocations of *Petersburg* and other aspects of Belyi's legacy. V.'s reference
to the "unconscious cerebration"[24] that he believes has led him correctly
throughout his attempt to reconstruct the life and psychology of his deceased half brother resembles the "self-thinking thoughts" and "idle cerebral play" that punctuate major moments of characters' lives in *Petersburg*. Belyi's radical claim at the end of the first chapter of *Petersburg*

that his fictions will henceforth be as real for the reader as the reader's own world is taken a step further in *The Real Life of Sebastian Knight* when Mr. Siller, one of Sebastian's fictional characters, comes to life as the salesman and detective Mr. Silbermann. In his aesthetics and his belletristic works Sebastian Knight recalls Nabokov himself. For this reason Sebastian's description in his final novel of a traveler reading a landscape as if various parts of it were an alphabet is especially intriguing (pp. 178–79). The symbolistic cognitive stance this implies is very similar to Belyi's description of his journey from Switzerland to Russia in *Zapiski chudaka* as constituting an occult script.[25] (Behind both Nabokov's description and Belyi's memoir may lie Baudelaire's "Correspondances," in which nature sometimes utters "confuses paroles.") Tammi has also pointed out similar formulations about the relation between art and an otherworld in Nabokov's and Belyi's studies of Gogol.[26] (Some other possible ties between Belyi and Nabokov include echoes of *Petersburg* in *The Defense* and in *Invitation to a Beheading*, which, like some of Nabokov's poems, also contains possible echoes of *Kotik Letaev*.)

Finally, there is a basic structural parallel between Belyi's and Nabokov's novels that derives from their comparable reliance on "Romantic irony." At the conclusion of *Petersburg*'s first chapter, the author steps forward to discuss how his characters appeared before him and how he has displayed "pictures of illusions" before the reader. Many of Nabokov's works contain a similar intrusive authorial consciousness. "Romantic irony" has of course been an important feature of the novel since Cervantes. But what distinguishes Belyi's and Nabokov's use of it is that both ultimately treat "Romantic irony" *ironically*. In *Petersburg*, Belyi goes on to reveal that what may seem to be merely "pictures of illusions" are in fact manifestations of creative occult forces acting through him; and he concludes by claiming that his fiction is thus as real as the reader's own world. Similarly, in Nabokov's novels the authorial intrusions function as analogues on the level of the text of what characters perceive to be fateful patterning on the level of their fictional worlds. Thus what may appear to be Nabokov's purely metaliterary device is in fact a model of the metaphysical tie between man and the otherworld. Moreover, since in Nabokov's novels (as in his aesthetics) it is repeatedly suggested that the source of art lies in the otherworld, the effect of authorial intrusions is to sanction the validity and verisimilitude of the text that they appear to disrupt. Nabokov actually signaled this himself when he explained in the Introduction to *Bend Sinister* that the author appearing in the novel's conclusion was "an anthropomorphic deity impersonated by me."

However suggestive the similarities between Nabokov and aspects of Belyi's thought and art may be, they should not be allowed to obscure the obvious stylistic and formal differences between *Petersburg* and most of

Nabokov's fictions. Belyi's novel is characterized by a frenzied surface texture of events occurring on various terrestrial and spiritual planes of being, which reflects Belyi's complex, multiplanar world view. This is quite unlike the generally more placid and cohesive-looking surfaces of Nabokov's works, beneath which are hidden subtle and ambiguous signs of otherworldly influence on human existence.

Of all the Acmeists, Nikolai Gumilev (1886–1921) plays the most obvious, and possibly the most interesting, role in Nabokov's oeuvre. The nature of his influence differs from that of Belyi and Blok, however, because it includes not only literary themes and style, but also the poet's persona.

Among Nabokov's earliest published references to Gumilev is the heartfelt but somewhat awkward panegyric "Pamiati Gumileva" ("To the Memory of Gumilev"): "Gordo i iasno ty umer, umer, kak Muza uchila. / Nyne, v tishy Eliseiskoi, s toboi govorit o letiashchem / mednom Petre i o dikikh vetrakh afrikanskikh—Pushkin" ("You died proudly and brilliantly, you died as the Muse taught. Now in Elysian quiet, there converses with you about the flying bronze Peter and about the wild African winds—Pushkin"; *Stikhi*, p. 95, dated 19.3.23).

Some fifty years later, Nabokov again wrote a poem about Gumilev: "Kak liubil ia stikhi Gumileva! / perechityvat' ikh ne mogu, / no sledy, naprimer, vot takogo / perebora ostalis' v mozgu: / " . . . I umru ia ne v letnei besedke / ot obzhorstva i ot zhary, / a s nebesnoi babochkoi v setke / na vershine dikoi gory" ("How I loved Gumilev's poems! I cannot reread them, but traces, for example, of this kind of strum have remained in my brain: '. . . And I will die not in a summer-house, from gluttony and hot weather, but with a celestial butterfly in my net on the top of a wild mountain' "; *Stikhi*, p. 297, dated 22.7.72). Thus, although Nabokov's admiration for much of Gumilev's poetry had faded since the time he placed him in Pushkin's exalted company, the existential stance Gumilev assumes in his verse continued to retain its charm for Nabokov.

Gumilev's heroism, adventurousness, cult of artistic craftsmanship, poetic achievement, and, of course, tragic end at the hands of the Bolsheviks are all part of his legacy. Because Nabokov makes this image central to "The Art of Literature and Commonsense," I would like to concentrate on it, and to pass over the interesting matter of Gumilev's influence on Nabokov's own verse (reflected in such poems as "Iasnookii, kak rytsar' iz rati Khristovoi" [*Stikhi*, p. 68, dated 1. 12. 22], "Avtobus" [*Stikhi*, pp. 120–21, dated 5. 10. 23], and "Ia Indiiei nevidimoi vladeiu" [*Stikhi*, p. 125, 7. 12. 23]).[27]

Gumilev appears in "The Art of Literature and Commonsense" as the embodiment of all the virtues that Nabokov values: "One of the main reasons why the very gallant Russian poet Gumilev was put to death by Lenin's ruffians thirty odd years ago was that during the whole ordeal, in the prosecutor's dim office, in the torture house, in the winding corridors that led to the truck, in the truck that took him to the place of execution, and at that place itself, full of the shuffling feet of the clumsy and gloomy shooting squad, the poet kept smiling" (pp. 376–77). Far from being frivolous bravado, Gumilev's smile is a sure sign that in a moral sense he is unassailably superior to those who would destroy him. Moreover, since the smile denotes that Gumilev possesses the heightened consciousness that is a prerequisite for cosmic synchronization (what Nabokov calls "inspiration" in the lecture), he emerges as an artist-hero graced by contact with the otherworld, and with all that this implies for Nabokov about the immortality of the soul.

Perhaps the most significant evocation of a Gumilev-like personage in Nabokov's oeuvre appears in *The Gift*, when Fyodor speculates about how his father might have died after capture by the Reds. The telling details in the passage are the father's "smile of disdain" at the firing squad, and his following with a glance of encouragement a whitish moth just before the Bolsheviks open fire (149: 155). This last detail is the quintessential Nabokovian privileged perception, as he makes clear in "The Art of Literature and Commonsense." In connection with this, it is worth recalling that in her "Preface" to her husband's posthumous collection of poems Nabokov's widow singled out the image of the father in *The Gift* as an excellent illustration of what the otherworld meant for Nabokov himself.

The heroic spirit of Gumilev can also be found in Nabokov's *Glory* (*Podvig*, 1932). Although the poet is not named in the novel, the qualities that Nabokov associated with him are the main inspiration behind Martin's heroic fantasies (e.g., 16: 23), including how he imagines he might be executed at dawn (182: 209). It is also possible that there are specific Gumilev subtexts in the novel. One of the minor characters is the writer Bubnov, whom the narrator presents as being highly talented and appealingly eccentric. He is in the process of writing "a book" about Christopher Columbus, or more precisely about a Russian "d'iak" ("scribe" or "clerk") who miraculously joins the crew of one of his ships (140: 162). Since this constitutes a sort of "Russification" of the epoch-making voyage, it may be worth recalling that a Russian narrative poem about Columbus, entitled *Otkrytie Ameriki* ("The Discovery of America"), had already been published by Gumilev in 1910.[28] The references to "Muza Dal'nikh Stranstvii" ("The Muse of Distant Wanderings") in *Otkrytie Ameriki*—which constitute an implicit equation between artistic creation and voyaging—is relevant for Martin throughout *Podvig*, even though he is an artist only with regard to his own life, in particular when he crosses the border into "Zoorland" at the end of the novel. (It is relevant as well for Fyodor in *The Gift*, where part of the description of his creative process is rendered in terms of travel imagery—specifically, his father's expeditions through Central Asia.) Martin's seemingly pointless act is intertwined with the theme of his thwarted love for Sonia, and recalls the image of gratuitous heroic ecstasy in the conclusion of Gumilev's poem "Devushke" (1912): "I vam chuzhd tot bezumnyi okhotnik, / Chto, vzoidia na krutuiu skalu, / V p'ianom schast'e, v toske bezotchetnoi / Priamo v solntse puskaet strelu" ("And alien to you is that mad hunter, who, having climbed a steep cliff, in drunken joy, in inexplicable anguish, sends an arrow straight into the sun"; vol. 1, p. 156). The connection between this poem and Nabokov's celebration of romantic heroism is buttressed by the very similar sentiment he expressed in a newspaper article from 1921, in which he tries to distinguish between Russians and Englishmen (there is something of the traditional conception of English reserve in the image of the "Turgenev heroine"–like girl in Gumilev's poem): the latter "do not know that whirlwind of inspiration, pulsation, radiance, that furious dance, that malevolence and tenderness, which transport us [Russians] into God-only-knows-what heavens and abysses; we have moments when the clouds are about our shoulders and the sea about our knees—go free, my soul! For an Englishman this is incomprehensible, unheard of, yes, and alluring."[29] Even later, in his 1937 lecture on Pushkin, Nabokov continued to find the existential stance of Gumilev's hunter attractive: "in reality the mountain wind is as thrilling as ever, and to die pursuing high adventure remains forever an axiom of human pride."[30]

The theme of dangerous adventure constitutes a textual echo between one of Gumilev's travel pieces and the conclusion of *Invitation to a Beheading*. In the last paragraph of "An African Hunt: From a Travel Diary" ("Afrikanskaia okhota: Iz putevogo dnevnika," 1916) Gumilev asks himself why he is not troubled by killing one animal after another for entertainment, and why his blood tie to the world is only strengthened by it. He then concludes with the following sentence, which provides an implicit answer to these questions by suggesting that he too will die, and that death is not final: "And at night I dreamed that for participating in some sort of Abyssinian palace revolt my head was chopped off, and that, bleeding profusely, I am applauding the executioner's skill and rejoicing in how simple, good, and completely painless it all is" ("A noch'iu mne prisnilos', chto za uchastie v kakom-to abissinskom dvortsovom perevorote mne otrubili golovu, i ia, istekaia krov'iu, aplodiruiu umen'iu palacha i raduius', kak vse eto prosto, khorosho i sovsem ne bol'no"; vol. 4, p. 152). The reference to a dream, the method of execution, the devaluation of death, and the victim's implied transcendence all recall Cincinnatus's experiences, reactions, and behavior. Nabokov would presumably not have approved of Gumilev's celebration of hunting because of its inherent cruelty. But because Gumilev was executed by the Bolsheviks for complicity in an antigovernmental plot (a sort of "palace revolt"), it is possible that Nabokov saw the passage in question as literally prophetic. Moreover, given the implications of immortality surrounding the image of Gumilev in "The Art of Literature and Commonsense," it is quite possible that Nabokov would have shared as well the most far-reaching aspect of Gumilev's prophetic dream.

The views that Gumilev expressed in his own writings on literature are perfectly in harmony with the image Nabokov made him play in "The Art of Literature and Commonsense." Indeed, Gumilev's discursive writings function as "subtexts" for several of the lecture's most important points. In a review from 1910 in which he speaks of satire, Gumilev provides virtually the same definition of "zdravyi smysl" ("common sense") as Nabokov elaborated for "commonsense": "dlia menia nesomnenno, chto dlia khoroshego satirika neobkhodima izvestnaia tupost' vospriiatii i ogranichennost' krugozora, to est' to, chto v obshchezhitii nazyvaetsia zdravym smyslom" ("It is completely clear to me that a good satirist absolutely needs *a certain dullness of perception and limitation to his range of interests, that is, what in daily life is called common sense*"; vol. 4, p. 239; italics added). A further parallel with Nabokov's lecture can be found in Gumilev's essay "Chitatel'" (first published in Berlin in 1923, where Nabokov was then living), in which he describes poetic creation via imagery that is very close to Nabokov's: the moment of inspiration is "sovsem osobennoe chuvstvo, inogda napolniaiushchee takim trepetom, chto ono meshalo by govorit', esli by ne soputstvuiushchee emu chuvstvo pobednosti, soznanie togo, chto tvorish' sovershennye sochetaniia slov, podobnye tem, kotorye nekogda voskreshali mertvykh, razrushali steny" ("an entirely special feeling, which sometimes fills one with such trembling that it would hamper speech were it not accompanied by a victorious feeling, by an awareness that you are creating perfect combinations of words, comparable to those *that once resurrected the dead*, that destroyed walls"; vol. 4, p. 178; italics mine). Nabokov's description of the epiphanic moment in his lecture is "you experience a shuddering sensation of wild magic, of *some inner resurrection, as if a dead man were revived* by a sparkling drug which has been rapidly mixed in your presence" (p. 378; italics added). Gumilev also speaks of the elasticity of time that poets can experience during epiphanic moments in a way that recalls Nabokov's description of cosmic synchronization: "vechnost' i mig—eto uzhe ne vremennye poniatiia i poetomu mogut vosprinimat'sia v liuboi promezhutok vremeni; vse zavisit ot sintezuiushchego pod"ema sozertsaniia" ("Eternity and the moment—these are already not temporal concepts, and for this reason can be perceived during any interval of time;

everything depends on *the synthesizing ascent of contemplation*"; vol. 4, p. 335; italics added). The fact that this conclusion follows Gumilev's celebration of the variety of earthly existence brings the idea even closer to Nabokov's.

The belief in a transcendent that Gumilev reveals in his discursive writings, and especially vividly in his later poetry, is particularly close to Nabokov's. Indeed, the following passage from Gumilev's programmatic piece "Nasledie Simvolizma i Akmeizm" ("The Legacy of Symbolism and Acmeism," 1913) could serve as a perfect description of Nabokov's faith, as he expressed it in "The Art of Literature and Commonsense," *Speak, Memory*, and his novels: "Vsegda pomnit' o nepoznavaemom, no ne oskorbliat' svoei mysli o nem bolee ili menee veroiatnymi dogad-kami—vot printsip akmeizma. Eto ne znachit, chtoby on otvergal dlia sebia pravo izobrazhat' dushu v te momenty, kogda ona drozhit, pribli-zhaias' k inomu; no togda ona dolzhna tol'ko sodrogat'sia" ("To always remember the unknowable, but not to offend one's thought about it with more or less probable conjectures—this is the principle of Acmeism. This does not mean that [Acmeism] rejects the right to depict the soul during those moments when it approaches that which is other; but then [the soul] must only shudder"; vol. 4, p. 175). These views of Gumilev's are integrated into his specifically aesthetic ideals in a way that again recalls Nabokov's works. In "Nasledie Simvolizma i Akmeizm" Gumilev advocates "svetlaia ironiia, ne podryvaiushchaia kornei nashei very" ("a bright irony that does not undermine the roots of our faith") and states that one of Acmeism's principles is "vsegda idti po linii naibol'shego so-protivleniia" ("to always follow the path of greatest resistance"; vol. 4, p. 173). Both statements can serve as capsule summaries of Nabokov's artistic praxis.

The connection between Nabokov and Uspenskii and Evreinov is specu-lative for one primary reason: he left no published testimony suggesting they were important for him. What warrants speaking of a possible influ-ence, however, is that Nabokov shared with them several unusual ideas, including the seminal redefinition of "artifice" and "nature" as synonyms for each other on the basis of mimicry among insects. The high degree of congruence between Nabokov's formulations and those of Uspenskii and Evreinov is what suggests that his thinking about mimicry may have been derived from, or at least influenced by them. To the best of my knowl-edge, the specific arguments Uspenskii and Evreinov made are unique (al-though related to each other), and had not appeared previously in the history of speculation about mimicry in nature.[31]

As he acknowledges in *Speak, Memory* and elsewhere, Nabokov was passionately interested in lepidoptera ever since he was a boy; he collected and studied them throughout his life, and read voraciously about them. It is thus inevitable that he would have encountered Darwinian explanations of mimicry because the phenomenon was discovered by naturalists studying butterflies shortly after the publication of *The Origin of Species* in 1859. They immediately enlisted their findings in support of Darwin's views, with the result that, despite various elaborations over the years, survival of the fittest has remained a commonplace of scientific writing about butterflies ever since.[32] Darwin's theory of evolution was also attacked as soon as it appeared by those who saw it as undermining the view that all existence is a product of divine creative will, an attitude that also survives to the present day.[33] Because Nabokov must have been familiar with these polemics, it is important to acknowledge the possibility that he could have developed his views about the metaphysical implications of mimicry entirely on his own.

Petr Uspenskii's place in the history of culture is as a thinker whose ideas influenced a surprisingly wide range of major figures in Russia and Europe during and after the First World War.[34] In simplest terms, Uspenskii's ideas can be seen as part of the broad stream of syncretic mysticism that appeared in Europe during the last quarter of the nineteenth century with the "theosophy" of Elena Petrovna Blavatskaia ("Madame Blavatsky"). This fed into the revival of religious, philosophical, and mystical speculation in Russia around the turn of the century, where it left a profound influence on many major writers, artists, and musicians of the day—including Belyi, Vasilii Kandinskii, Kazimir Malevich, Aleksei Kruchenykh, Aleksandr Scriabin, and others (the influence was also great outside Russia of course, among the Surrealists, for example, and on Yeats). Uspenskii's ideas, like all branches of this broad trend, centered on the nature of the relationship between the material world and "higher dimensions" of being, and the consequence this has, or should have, for man's life. More specifically, Uspenskii argued that man's normal existence consists of mechanical responses to various random events. But by cultivating a higher form of consciousness that gives insight into the "fourth dimension," man can transcend his state and thereby also serve a realm higher than his own.[35] In contrast to such movements as theosophy and anthroposophy, Uspenskii's system does not include staggeringly detailed descriptions of otherworldly realms, and is in general much more restrained in its speculations about them. This feature of Uspenskii's ideas might have appealed to Nabokov, and not jarred too strongly with his own tentative intuitions about the otherworld.

Uspenskii's discussion of mimicry appears in the first chapter of one of his major treatises, *A New Model of the Universe* (1931, 1934), and constitutes his fundamental illustration of the proposition that many natural phenomena have never been properly understood by science.[36] He begins by describing instances of spectacular mimetic disguise among insects, including butterflies "whose folded wings represent a large, dry leaf," and dwells in some detail on examples that he observed himself during his travels. He then turns to the attempt that science has made to explain the phenomenon by invoking the principle of the survival of the fittest, and rejects it because of the implausibility that the perfection of the mimic's imitation of a model could have been arrived at by "thousands, perhaps even tens of thousands of repeated accidents."[37] Although Uspenskii's critique of Darwinian explanations of mimicry is more detailed than Nabokov's, he comes to the same conclusion: "The principle of utilitarianism ha[s] to be abandoned" (p. 44). And like Nabokov, Uspenskii makes it axiomatic that artistic deception operates throughout nature: "the general tendency of Nature [is] toward decorativeness, 'theatricalness,' the tendency to be or to appear different from what she really is at a given time and place." This applies to butterflies and other insects as well, all of whom "are dressed up and disguised; they all wear masks and fancy dresses. Their whole life is passed on the stage. The tendency of their life is not to be themselves, but to resemble something else, a green leaf, a bit of moss, a shiny stone" (p. 44). Darwin's idea of the survival of the fittest thus cannot be Nature's direct aim, and "is attained only by the way, only casually"; what is "permanent and intentional is the tendency towards decorativeness, the endless disguise, the endless masquerade, by which Nature lives."

For Uspenskii, the phenomenon of mimicry is ultimately "a miracle" that implies a transcendent "plan, intention and aim" in nature (p. 45). Although this abstract formulation comes very close to Nabokov's views, it is important to note that the details of what Uspenskii means by "plan, intention and aim," to say nothing of his discussions of organized insect life on the pages that follow, go far beyond anything that Nabokov would probably have been willing to entertain. Uspenskii interprets mimicry among insects as pointing to the "fourth dimension" (which is a concept that he did not invent, and which has a long and complex history in turn-of-the-century thought), and as evidence for an impulse in the cosmos whose aim is to produce a being capable of achieving transcendence. By contrast, when Nabokov speculates about higher forms of consciousness than man's, he typically does no more than sketch possibilities, as when he condenses them into the following laconic form: "Time without consciousness—lower animal world; time with consciousness—man; consciousness without time—some still higher state."[38] There is also no question that Nabokov's knowledge of the details of mimicry among lepidoptera far exceeds Uspenskii's more casual observations.[39]

Other parallels between Nabokov and Uspenskii include their ideas about consciousness in relation to motion, space, and time. In *Speak,*

Memory, Nabokov suggests that the processes constituting life are the source of man's experience of time, and that through cosmic synchronization the true artist can enter atemporal space, transcend time, and catch a glimmer of what may lie beyond death. This resembles Uspenskii's description of the relation of the "fourth dimension" to time and motion: "Motion, growth, 'becoming,' which go on in the world around us are no more real than the movement of the house as we drive by, or the movement of trees and fields past the window of a fast-moving railway carriage. . . . Movement goes on inside us, and it produces the illusion of movement around us. . . . if a man were able at once to embrace with his mind all that ever entered his perception and all that is never clearly illumined by thought . . . then a man might perhaps find himself in the midst of a *motionless universe*, containing simultaneously all that usually lies for a man in the remote depths of memory, in the past; all that lies at a great distance from him; all that lies in the future." The last part of this formulation recalls especially clearly Delalande's "all-seeing eye" in *The Gift*. Nabokov's opening image in *Speak, Memory* of the "commonsensical" view that human "existence is but a brief crack of light between two eternities of darkness" is very close to one that Uspenskii uses when explaining that "the sensation of motion in time (and there is no motion that is not in time) arises in us because we look at the world through a narrow slit, as it were. . . . This incomplete sensation of time (of the fourth dimension)—sensation through a slit—gives us the sensation of motion, i.e., creates an illusion of motion, which is not actually there, and instead of which, in reality, there is only an *extension* in a direction we are unable to imagine." Finally, Uspenskii's speculations about *"extension in time"* being "extension into an unknown *space*," as a result of which time is the *"fourth dimension of space,"* recall Nabokov's idea about the possible relations among time, space, thought, and higher dimensions of being: "if, in the spiral unwinding of things, space warps into something akin to time, and time, in its turn, warps into something akin to thought, then surely, another dimension follows—a special Space maybe, not the old one, we trust, unless spirals become vicious circles again" (*Speak, Memory*, p. 301).[40]

It is most intriguing that Uspenskii himself suggests a connection between his ideas about artifice in nature and Nikolai Evreinov's conception of theater. A footnote in *A New Model of the Universe* calls attention to the fact that "this tendency not to be oneself and the tendency to theatricalness (in human life) are interestingly described in N. N. Evreinov's book, *The Theatre in Life*" (p. 45).[41] Indeed, perhaps the best-known aspect of Evreinov's legacy is his idea that the world of nature is filled with "artificial" theatricality, which underlies his iconoclastic view of the theater as a completely natural institution. The examples he adduces include such phenomena as a cat playing with a mouse, and the mouse's feigning death in order to escape (p. 7), desert flowers that look like stones (p. 11), elaborate dances performed by birds in areas they specially prepare for that purpose (p. 15), and the like. Virtually all forms of human behavior are also characterized by playacting: the inevitable hypocrisy of social intercourse (p. 65), the stratagems of courtship and carnal desire (p. 79), and the prescribed forms of behavior in religious life (p. 103).

Evreinov also refers specifically to mimicry among butterflies as further proof of his claim that theater exists in nature: "You see a little protruding spot on the trunk of a tree; but no sooner do your fingers touch it than it separates from the trunk and flies away sparkling with bright colours of its lower wings which have been concealed beneath the dark-grey, cork-like upper wings" (p. 11). Like Nabokov and Uspenskii, Evreinov interprets the phenomenon in his own, antiscientific way (although without reference to Darwin, which is an important difference): "mimicry may be not only a special case of convergence, as naturalists claim, but a special stage of theatrical development as well. This assertion is pregnant with inferences [sic] of the highest import to the philosopher, including the revaluation of the very concept of 'naturalness' " (p. 14).

There are also resemblances between Nabokov's and Evreinov's conceptions of the origins of art. For Evreinov the fact that children play at make believe of their own accord "proves that nature herself has planted in the human being a sort of 'will to the theatre' " (p. 36); the child's "independent, individual, wholly arbitrary creation of a new reality from the material furnished by the outside world is a form of creative energy to which no other adjective than 'theatrical' can be applied" (p. 37). Nabokov expressed a similar view when he spoke about the causal relationship between universal deception in nature and the birth of poetry: "Do you know how poetry started? I always think that it started when a cave boy came running back to the cave, through the tall grass, shouting as he ran, 'Wolf, wolf,' and there was no wolf."[42]

Moreover, in his 1937 lecture on Pushkin, Nabokov provides a description of theater in everyday life that sounds exactly like Evreinov. "Who on earth," he asks, "can be this artist who suddenly transforms life into a small masterpiece?" And then he goes on to describe "how many times, in a city street, I have been dazzled by this miniature theater that unpredictably materializes and then vanishes. . . . I have watched comedies staged by some invisible genius, such as the day when . . . I saw a massive Berlin postman dozing on a bench, and two other postmen tiptoeing . . . to stick some tobacco up his nose. I have seen dramas. . . . Not a day goes by that this force, this itinerant inspiration, does not create here or there some instantaneous performance. . . . One would therefore like to think that what we call art is, essentially, but the picturesque side of reality."[43]

Evreinov's conception of natural theatricality leads him in a direction similar to Nabokov's and Uspenskii's—a belief in a transcendent spiritual reality that is the cause of the multifarious forms of artifice on earth. "The name of my God is Theatrarch," Evreinov proclaims; "My intuitive premonitions and my philosophic knowledge tell me that man in his spiritual being is immortal and cannot disappear like a bubble. For my face and body are but masks and garments in which the heavenly Father has clothed my ego, sending it to the stage of this world where it is destined to play a certain role." Evreinov goes on to express faith in metempsychosis, and in his God as "the aboriginal source of everlasting transformation of all things living" (p. 128). The end result of the millions of reincarnations that Evreinov believes are his destiny is that he will "get close to Him, my Stage Manager, until, perfectly trained in the cosmic series, I shall become His inseparable and worthy associate" (p. 131).

The implicit parallel that Evreinov draws between his God and himself as creators in this passage (a parallel he makes explicitly elsewhere: "It is in the theatre, if anywhere, that man . . . becomes a Creator" [p. 8]), together with Evreinov's opposition to realistic theater in favor of underscored artificiality on the stage, are especially relevant for Nabokov, who often underscores the fictiveness of his novels. But the close resemblance between their ideas should not be allowed to obscure the fact that conceptions of the artist as a rival of God, and of man's artistic creations as analogues to God's natural world, have a venerable tradition in European culture, especially among the Romantics (and their heirs the Symbolists, who, it should be remembered, were active in Russia concurrently with Uspenskii and Evreinov). Thus Novalis could state that "it is idle chatter to seek to distinguish between nature and art" because "art is nature" and "nature possesses an artistic instinct." Schelling makes the same point in terms of the Romantic metaphor about the organic character of art: "If we are interested in pursuing as far as possible the construction, the internal disposition, the relations and entanglements of a plant or, generally speaking, of any organic being, how much more strongly ought we to be attracted by the recognition of these same entanglements and relations in that plant, so much more highly organized and bound up in itself, that is called a work of art." The reason why this parallelism should exist, as Friedrich Ast, a disciple of Friedrich Schlegel and Schelling, puts it, is that "artistic production" and "divine production" "are one, and God is revealed in the poet as he produces corporally in the visible universe."[44] The idea of life being a stage is of course even older than the Romantics. It receives its most famous expression in Shakespeare's *As*

You Like It (act 2, scene 7), and, as Evreinov himself points out, can also be found in Erasmus and Marcus Aurelius.[45]

Such parallels suggest that Nabokov's ideas about artifice in nature can be seen as part of a general trend in Western thought to which Uspenskii and Evreinov also belong (and which is ultimately a variant of the ancient theological "argument from design"). This obviously complicates the issue of determining influence. The only real evidence for the possibility that Nabokov derived ideas directly from either one remains the closeness of some of their central formulations, but, as we have seen, even here there are significant divergences. An additional complication is of course the possibility that Uspenskii and Evreinov could have influenced each other as well (beyond what is implied by Uspenskii's footnote about Evreinov). Both were well-known figures in St. Petersburg before and during the First World War, Uspenskii as a popular lecturer and writer, and Evreinov as an avant-garde theatrical figure with many publications to his credit. Because they had friends in common, and visited the famous artistic cabaret "The Stray Dog" at the same time, it is even possible that they met.[46] There were thus ample opportunities for them to become acquainted with each other's ideas.

But what was the chance that Nabokov knew about them? He could have heard something of Uspenskii's beliefs before leaving Russia in 1919 because Uspenskii lectured in St. Petersburg from approximately 1909 to 1913, and again in 1915; by this time Nabokov was already passionate about lepidoptera.[47] Nabokov could also have heard about him in the Crimea, where he sought refuge from the Bolsheviks with his family during the Civil War, and where he apparently evinced some interest in mysticism.[48] Most easily, of course, Nabokov simply could have read Uspenskii's *A New Model of the Universe* after it was published in English in 1931 and again in 1934.

Nabokov's contacts with Evreinov are less speculative. It is altogether remarkable that in 1925 at an émigré ball in Berlin Nabokov acted the role of Evreinov himself in a mock trial of his play *The Chief Thing* (*Samoe glavnoe*, 1921) that was then enjoying a great success throughout Europe. Nabokov is reported to have been made up to look like Evreinov, and defended the play's message that happiness can be achieved when life is transformed into theater.[49] Nabokov's willingness to take on this role necessarily suggests some familiarity with Evreinov's ideas, as well as at least a degree of sympathy with them. (At the same time, it is noteworthy that the existential act of theatricalizing life in Evreinov's sense is not a theme in Nabokov's fictions, or an aspect of his world view in his discursive writings.) Nabokov also apparently met Evreinov once, and lived near him for a while in Paris in 1939.[50] But as in the case of Nabokov and Uspenskii, the most important consideration is that Evreinov's writings and ideas were widely available and known throughout Europe at the very time Nabokov was maturing as a writer.

The ultimate significance of the parallels among Nabokov's, Uspenskii's, and Evreinov's ideas about artifice in nature, and of the connections among Nabokov, Belyi, Blok, and Gumilev, is not that they reveal heretofore unseen aspects of Nabokov's art, but that they buttress a reading of his works that firmly integrates their characteristic themes and formal features with his belief in a transcendent "otherworld." An additional consequence is that Nabokov emerges as somewhat less "foreign" than many of his Russian émigré critics had thought. It is all a matter of what periods and aspects of Russian culture you choose as representative. It would of course be a great mistake to suggest that Nabokov's unique genius should be downplayed in favor of making him the passive point of intersection of influences and impersonal literary forces. But there are many less promising conceptions of him than as the heir of the fascinatingly varied, complex, and brilliant avant-garde culture that flowered in Russia during the first two decades of this century.

Notes

INTRODUCTION

1. Critics who argue for a metaliterary Nabokov are legion. A representative sampling includes: Alter, *Partial Magic*, 180–217; Appel, "Introduction," in *The Annotated Lolita*, xv–lxxi; Bader; Paul Bruss, 33–97; Couturier; Field, *Nabokov: His Life in Art*; Grabes; Khodasevich, "On Sirin"; Lee; Maddox; Packman; George Steiner. Useful overviews of criticism are *Vladimir Nabokov: A Reference Guide*, and *Nabokov: The Critical Heritage*. Bibliographies of criticism can also be found in Tammi, 365–82, and Rampton, 213–30. A short survey is provided by Parker.

2. Struve, 282. By contrast, Rampton, 1–2, cites reviews by prominent émigrés that praise Nabokov's fiction for its comments on contemporary life. Overviews of Russian émigré reactions to Nabokov appear in: Struve, 278–90; Foster, "Nabokov in Russian Émigré Criticism"; Grayson, 2–3, 232–37; Tammi, 10–15.

3. See, for example, Appel's "Introduction," *The Annotated Lolita*, xviii–xxi, xxxiii; or the anonymous obituary of 5 July 1977 in *The [London] Times*, reprinted in *Nabokov: The Critical Heritage*, 241; or George Steiner. Rampton, 2–3, identifies the same trend and also disagrees with it, but for reasons different from mine.

4. Vera Nabokova, 3. An English translation of her remarks appears in Dmitri Nabokov's "Translating with Nabokov," 174–75. See also Dmitri Nabokov's brief discussion of his father's beliefs as manifested in *The Gift*, *Pale Fire* and other works in "Nabokov and the Theatre," 16–18.

5. *Lectures on Literature*, 371–80.

6. For example, Rampton, 99, cites Vera Nabokov's remarks about the otherworld, accepts uncritically Rowe's *Nabokov's Spectral Dimension* (which, although concerned with an aspect of Nabokov's metaphysics, should be seen as an encouragement for further study), and concludes that Nabokov's "secret has little to do with some mysterious knowledge of an ineffable beyond," and is, instead, a reference to his powerful imagination that can play with reality at will. A similar, recent denial by a Russian émigré is Bakhrakh's.

7. Boyd's article "Nabokov's Philosophical World" is an essential outline of the subject (subsequently incorporated into his *Nabokov's Ada*). Other important studies include De Jonge; Johnson, *Worlds in Regression*, 1–4, 185–223; Pifer, "Shades of Love"; Setschkareff (Setchkarev); Sisson; and Toker, 1–20. Quite a few other critics include isolated passing remarks about Nabokov's otherworldly beliefs, while several focus on these specifically in individual works: e. g., Davydov, *Teksty Matreški*, 100–182; Davydov, "Dostoevsky and Nabokov," 169; Field, *VN*, 30–31; Foster, "Nabokov's Gnostic Turpitude," 119; Fowler, 102; Karlinsky, "Vladimir Nabokov," 162; McCarthy, 78–79, 82; Moynahan, *Vladi-*

mir Nabokov, 11, 14; Schaeffer; Stuart, 178–80; Tammi, 22–25; Varshavsky, 215, 233; Edmund White, 22–25.

8. *Strong Opinions*, 45; *Lectures on Literature*, 377.

9. Boyd's *Nabokov's Ada* is the best and fullest treatment of the interrelations among metaphysics, ethics, and aesthetics in *Ada*, and his discussion of Nabokov's "philosophy," 49–88, which collates passages from discursive and belletristic writings, supports many of my own conclusions. Fowler, 42, stresses the connection of ethics and aesthetics in Nabokov's art, but without a grounding in the otherworld. A detailed defense of Nabokov as an ethical humanist is Pifer's *Nabokov and the Novel*.

10. *Nikolai Gogol*, 141.

11. See Sisson, 25–39, and intermittently throughout his brilliant dissertation, for another discussion of Nabokov's epiphanies and their function in his works.

12. *Nabokov's Ada*, 26; see also 24–27 for a discussion of this aspect of Nabokov's style in *Ada*.

13. I borrow these terms from de Man, xvii.

14. *Nabokov and the Novel*, 159–65.

15. *Nikolai Gogol*, 145.

16. Iser, 282. Interaction between the reader and Nabokov's texts is Packman's focus, though both his general and specific conclusions are different from my own. A good discussion of how Nabokov involves his readers in creating the meaning in *Pnin* and in the short story "Signs and Symbols" can be found in Carroll.

17. Relevant here is Riffaterre's discussion of the "superreader," 203–4.

18. Todorov, *Symbolism and Interpretation*, 9–11. For a related discussion, see Packman, 10–13.

19. *Nikolai Gogol*, 144.

20. *Nikolai Gogol*, 45.

21. *Strong Opinions*, 179. It is ironic that this passage ends with what is probably a misprint: "utmost truthfulness and perception [should it not have been 'precision'?]." Lubin provides an insightful analysis and defense of Nabokov's style.

22. "Pushkin, or the Real and the Plausible," 41; "Pouchkine, ou le vrai et le vraisemblable," 372.

23. *Problems of Nabokov's Poetics*, 25 n. 65. For a representative example of the view that *Lolita* and Nabokov's other works are part of an endless web of allusions without a "final signified," see Packman, 42.

24. See Tammi's table summarizing connections among Nabokov's works, 359.

25. *Strong Opinions*, 95.

26. "Kickshaws and Motley," 193–96. Rowe, "The Honesty of Nabokovian Deception," describes Nabokov's style from the point of view of its subtly controlled deceptions. For a study of butterflies in Nabokov's oeuvre, see Karges.

27. A similar point, but to a different end, is made by Maddox, 1–3, 9, and by Packman, 27–32ff.

28. See, for example, Todorov, "Reading as Construction," Schor, Prince, and

Ong. Tammi, 241–72, discusses discriminatingly the ways in which Nabokov's texts imply and condition specific kinds of readers and readings.

29. Sisson, 1, 10–24, makes a similar point.

30. *A Poetics of Composition*, 128; *Poetika kompozitsii*, 169.

31. *Nabokov and the Novel*, 171.

32. Tammi, 232–35, provides an excellent overview of Nabokov's use of details from his life in his fictions. See also Grayson, 166.

33. See Rabinowitz's discussion of a related issue, 252. De Jonge's overview of the metaphysical implications of patterning in Nabokov's novels is excellent.

34. Tammi, 320–41, surveys in detail this and related authorial intrusions and markers in Nabokov's novels.

35. *Strong Opinions*, 11. The importance of this point for Nabokov is also stressed by Shloss.

36. Bader, 14–15; Alter, *Partial Magic*, 182.

37. *Lectures on Russian Literature*, 106.

38. Rabinowitz, 263.

39. A famous discussion of this problem is Jakobson's "O khudozhestvennom realizme" ("On Realism in Art," 1921).

40. Pifer, *Nabokov and the Novel*, 126, comes to a similar conclusion from a different direction.

41. *Strong Opinions*, 158. Tammi, 238, also calls attention to this passage, as well as to Nabokov's reference to "the person I usually impersonate in Montreux" (*Strong Opinions*, 298). Tammi is also correct to interpret Nabokov's famous insistence on writing his responses to interviewer's questions as additional evidence for his concern with creating a public persona that is in fact an aesthetic object.

42. *Strong Opinions*, 115.

43. Quoted by Field, *Nabokov: His Life in Art*, 375.

44. Quoted by Breit.

45. *Nabokov's Ada*.

CHAPTER ONE

1. *Speak, Memory*, 19. Hereafter, all page references will be given in the text.

2. *Conclusive Evidence*, 1; *Drugie berega*, 9. The versions have been compared by Grayson, 139–66. For an ingenious discussion of temporal indices in the three versions, see Tammi, 168–72.

3. *Lectures on Literature*, 371–80. Updike states in his Introduction, xxii, that the lecture dates from 1941, which is obviously a misleading reference to the *first* publication of a variant of the lecture as "The Creative Writer." Nabokov's reference in the body of the lecture to "the very gallant Russian poet Gumilev [who] was put to death by Lenin's ruffians *thirty odd years ago*" (italics added, 376; in "The Creative Writer" Nabokov has "twenty years," 25), indicates that the lecture must have been redelivered around 1951 since Gumilev is known to have been executed on 24 August 1921. All subsequent page references to this lecture, which is of inestimable worth in understanding Nabokov, will be given in the text.

4. *Strong Opinions*, 141.

5. *Strong Opinions*, 30.

6. *Strong Opinions*, 85, 124; *Nikolai Gogol*, 119. Rampton, 44, misinterprets Nabokov's use of "monism" and confuses what is in fact Nabokov's conception of the relation between the mind and what it apprehends with the duality of body and spirit in many of his works.

7. *Strong Opinions*, 142. Cosmic synchronization and its implications are the focus of Sisson's dissertation, which is an intelligent discussion of the subject, and with much of which I agree.

8. A brief discussion of the term can be found in Abrams, 52–53. See Hirsch for an illuminating discussion of epiphanies in prose fiction, which, however, differ markedly from Nabokov's.

9. *Lectures on Literature*, 226, 211.

10. Sisson, 28–29. Tammi, 16–17 n. 43, also cites a similar formulation by T. S. Eliot (whom, as Tammi is aware, Nabokov did not like). See also Sisson's discussion, 66–68, of Jung's theory of "synchronicity" and Paul Kammerer's earlier, similar theory in connection with the issue of synchronizations and coincidences in Nabokov's works and thought. A contrasting, metaliterary reading of cosmic synchronization is Appel's in his "Introduction" to *The Annotated Lolita*, xxvi.

11. Tammi, 16, also points out this parallel, and correctly concludes that the experience "lies at the very core of the author's literary system," 16–17.

12. *Strong Opinions*, 309; see 55 and 310 for Nabokov's fascinating recollections of the "first real pang" of *Pale Fire*, and the "first throb" of *Ada*. In his Foreword to *The Defense*, 7, Nabokov describes the specific physical setting, which he remembers with "special limpidity," where "the main thematic idea of the book first came to me." Compare with Pasternak's similar description of Zhivago's inspiration in *Doktor Zhivago*, 448 (a novel which Nabokov held in contempt).

13. Quoted in English by Field, *His Life in Part*, 192.

14. *Strong Opinions*, 69.

15. "Prof. Woodbridge in an Essay on Nature," 15.

16. *Lectures on Don Quixote*, 157; *Strong Opinions*, 70. In a letter to Wilson, Nabokov mentions Plato in connection with his loathing for "all Perfect States": *The Nabokov-Wilson Letters*, 159.

17. *Strong Opinions*, 78. In his lecture on *In Search of Lost Time* Nabokov quotes approvingly a similar comment made by Marcel: "all these materials for literary work. . . . I had stored them up without foreseeing their final purpose or even their survival, any more than does the seed when it lays by all the sustenance that is going to nourish the seedling" (*Lectures on Literature*, 249).

18. *Chudesnaia zhizn'*, 9.

19. See also *Strong Opinions*, 16–17, 32.

20. However, in response to a question about whether or not butterfly hunting and writing were in any way comparable, Nabokov answered "No, they belong to quite different types of enjoyment," *Strong Opinions*, 32. This remark does not necessarily vitiate the similarities between "cosmic synchronization" and moments of blossoming awareness induced by seeing butterflies in their habitats.

Perhaps Nabokov's response to the interviewer was determined by the latter's reference to "hunting." It is interesting to note that Nabokov's description of the pleasures of lepidopterology in this interview includes something like the hunter's "forefeeling" the possibility of capturing "the first specimen of a species unknown to science."

21. "The Poem" (1944), in *Poems and Problems*, 157.

22. See, for example, Updike's "Introduction" to *Lectures on Literature*, which contains the following conclusions: "in any decade Nabokov's approach would have seemed radical in the degree of severance between reality and art that it supposes"; and "in his aesthetic, small heed is paid to the *lowly delight of recognition*, and the blunt virtue of verity" (xxv–xxvi; italics added). Rampton's main purpose is to argue against this widespread view. However, he approaches and criticizes Nabokov from the vantage point of his own epistemological and ontological assumptions about reality, which betray and distort Nabokov's fundamental position—that the world in which an individual exists is inevitably a function of the interaction of that individual's mind with what exists outside it (the interaction Nabokov calls "monism"), and, implicitly, that different individuals' worlds may overlap to varying degrees but are not congruent.

23. *Strong Opinions*, 79, 10, 32; "Inspiration," 312 (similar formulations appear in "L'Envoi," 382). This general idea provides an obvious bridge between Nabokov's lepidoptery and fictions.

24. *Strong Opinions*, 330.

25. *Strong Opinions*, 10–11.

26. *Strong Opinions*, 154.

27. *Strong Opinions*, 118; "The Creative Writer," 26. By contrast, Boyd, *Nabokov's Ada*, 5off., argues that for Nabokov "reality is elusive not because it is doubtful whether it exists outside the mind, but because it exists out there so resolutely, so far beyond human modes of perception and explanation in its endlessly detailed complexity." See also Sisson, 99, for a discussion of parallels among Nabokov's conception of cognition, Werner Heisenberg's "Principle of Indeterminacy," and Niels Bohr's "Principle of Complementarity," especially in connection with "Terra Incognita."

28. "Pouchkine, ou le vrai et le vraisemblable," 369; "Pushkin, or the Real and the Plausible," 40.

29. *Strong Opinions*, 160, 39.

30. Field, *His Life in Part*, 87–88, discusses these and additional "otherworldly" parallels between Nabokov and his mother. Field also quotes Nabokov as having once told him that all his novels "have an air—'not quite of this world, don't you think?'."

31. *Strong Opinions*, 40.

32. Poulet's description of a reader experiencing fully the consciousness of the work's author resembles in some respects the conception of reading postulated by Nabokov.

33. *Lectures on Russian Literature*, 105.

34. *Nikolai Gogol*, 41.

35. Stuart, 180, also notes the interrelations of poetic inspiration, chess, butter-flies, and love in Nabokov's hierarchy of values.

36. Although the text of *Speak, Memory*, 290, reads that the really interesting and significant "clashes" in works of fiction always take place between the author and "the world," and not between the characters, Nabokov apparently meant that the "clashes" actually occur between the author and the reader; see *Strong Opinions*, 183.

37. *Poems and Problems*, 15.

38. Roth, 57, 44.

39. Andrei Belyi, aspects of whose legacy Nabokov admired, embodies a spiral conception of time in several of his works that resembles what one finds in *Speak, Memory*. See my *Andrei Bely*, 49–52, 61–62, 87–88, 147–48, 190.

40. Rowe, "Nabokovian Superimposed and Alternative Realities," 59–66, dis-cusses various instances of this narrative practice in Nabokov's oeuvre, and con-cludes that these "may be seen as suggestive attempts to transcend the limitations of time and space," 65. Sisson, 147, discusses the possible origin of the "folded carpet" metaphor in H. G. Wells's "The Remarkable Case of Davidson's Eyes."

41. *Strong Opinions*, 327.

42. "Parizhskaia poema" ("The Paris Poem"), in *Poems and Problems*, 122–23.

43. *Lectures on Literature*, 249.

44. *Strong Opinions*, 95, 75 (see also 177). However, on another occasion (ibid., 117), when asked to "explain the role of fate" in his novels, Nabokov responded that "I can't find any so-called main ideas, such as that of fate, in my novels." It is significant, however, that Nabokov did not dismiss the relevance of the idea of fate so much as inadequate generalizations about his art.

45. "The Tragedy of Tragedy," 326, 341. Boyd argues in *Nabokov's Ada*, 56, that in addition to fate Nabokov also believed in free will, and quotes from an unpublished document in which Nabokov refers to "the miserable idea of deter-minism, the prison regulation of cause and effect. We know from real life that however obediently we may follow the paths of causation, some queer and beau-tiful force, which we call free will from want of a better expression, allows or at least appears to allow us to escape again and again from the laws of cause and effect." However, the quotation suggests that Nabokov's view of free will was ambivalent, since he appears willing to entertain the possibility that it is illusory ("at least *appears* to allow us to escape" [italics added]). Boyd recognizes that there is a problematic relationship between Nabokov's insistence on freedom and the fatidic patterning in his novels. In general, however, I agree with Boyd's per-ceptive discussion (67–88) of Nabokov's conception of consciousness, patterning, and what may lie beyond the phenomenal world.

46. "Smert' " (1924), in *Stikhi*, 130. For a typically metaliterary and "secular" reading of the image of the watermark in *Speak, Memory* see Eakin, 278.

47. *Strong Opinions*, 186–87, 143.

48. Elizabeth Bruss, *Autobiographical Acts*, 127–62, goes too far in stressing the dependence of Nabokov's autobiographical self-conception on the act of writ-

ing as the only source of truth—a critical view that is linked to traditional, rather than Nabokovian conceptions of "nature" and "artifice."

49. "L'Envoi," 381.

50. *Strong Opinions*, 11, 153.

51. *Strong Opinions*, 77.

52. "Spatial Form in Modern Literature." Tammi, 16–17 n. 43, also notes the relevance of Frank's analysis, as well as Yurii Lotman's in *Struktura khudozhes-tvennogo teksta*. For additional illustrations of this feature of Nabokov's art, but without mention of Frank, see Fleischauer.

53. The following discussion is based on my unpublished paper "Epiphanic Structures in Nabokov."

54. Quoted in English translation by Field, *His Life in Part*, 181–82. See also Nabokov's poem "Vecher na pustyre" (1932, "Evening on a vacant lot"), *Poems and Problems*, 68–73, which is dedicated to the memory of "V. D. N." (the initials of Nabokov's father), and which concludes with: "And in the twilight toward me a man / comes, calls. I recognize / your energetic stride. You haven't changed much since you died," 72–73.

55. "On Hodasevich," 227.

56. Tammi, 25 n. 64, cites the following passage from Nabokov's 1922 piece on Rupert Brooke: "Ni odin poet tak chasto, s takoi muchitel'noi i tvorcheskoi zorkost'iu ne vgliadyvalsia v sumrak potustoronnosti [I have corrected Tammi's mistakes in the transliterated Russian]" ("No poet has so frequently and with such painful astuteness looked into the dimness of the otherworld").

57. Johnson, *Worlds in Regression*, 10–27, identifies a series of different ingenious correlations of motifs and details in *Speak, Memory*, as does Stuart, 165–91. See also Stuart, 187–91, and Bruss, *Autobiographical Acts*, 153–54, for discussions of concealed patterns of allusions within the autobiography's index.

58. See Boyd, *Nabokov's Ada*, 53–56, for an overview of other aspects of Nabokov's conception of time, especially his disbelief in the future.

59. *Nikolai Gogol*, 149.

60. *Strong Opinions*, 93.

61. *Strong Opinions*, 193.

62. *Strong Opinions*, 19. It is interesting to compare Nabokov's image with his description of the relation between Dr. Jekyll and Mr. Hyde in Stevenson's novel: *Lectures on Literature*, 182–84.

63. *Lectures on Literature*, 287, and *Lectures on Don Quixote*, especially "Cruelty and Mystification," 51–74.

64. Quoted in English by Field, *His Life in Part*, 181.

65. *Strong Opinions*, 3.

66. *Strong Opinions*, 100–101. Nabokov's first, and most famous discussion of "poshlost' " in English appears in *Nikolai Gogol*, 63–74.

67. Levy, 29.

68. *Strong Opinions*, 119.

69. Nabokov's 1931 "hilarious send-up of Freud" is mentioned by Grayson, 116. The reluctance of Freudians simply to accept Nabokov's rejection of Freud

is illustrated well by Green, 78, who writes: "it is as if Nabokov had a need to create Freud."

70. *Strong Opinions*, 116.

71. *Poems and Problems*, 133, note to line 52 of the poem "O praviteliakh" ("On rulers").

72. *Lectures on Literature*, 372–73. Henceforth, all page references will be given in the text.

73. Nabokov made these remarks in his lecture on Kafka's "The Metamorphosis," *Lectures on Literature*, 255, in the context of objecting to religious and Freudian readings of Kafka's art and personality. Nabokov's quarrel here (as elsewhere) is with generalizations that reduce art to ideas.

74. *Strong Opinions*, 58.

75. Quoted by Field, *His Life in Art*, 375.

76. "The Creative Writer," 25. A reference to Venus occurs on p. 26 of the conclusion of a fascinating passage that is missing from "The Art of Literature and Commonsense," and that may have been collated by mistake with the paragraph in question.

CHAPTER TWO

1. Hereafter, all page references will be given in the text in the form (English: Russian).

2. Clancy, who is disturbed by Nabokov's supposed inability to identify "the true nature of the malady that possesses Luzhin," provides an especially shallow reading of the novel, 36–37

3. *Speak, Memory*, 290. Hereafter, all page references will be given in the text.

4. *Strong Opinions*, 35. Tammi, 135, gives an excellent overview of other parallels that Nabokov drew between chess and music, as well as between chess and literature. Tammi also argues convincingly against searching Nabokov's texts for "specific parallels between Nabokovian prose style and given properties of the game," and suggests instead an analogical relationship between chess moves and compositional devices (pp. 135–36).

5. There appears to be a curious slip in the novel at this point. Luzhin is described as unrolling "an oilcloth board" when he insists on playing chess with his aunt (45: 53), but there is no indication where he got it from, or that he even knew that playing chess requires a board. Could this be another of Nabokov's tricky, surreptitious indications of Luzhin's prophetic precocity?

6. Collected in the anthology *Sogliadatai*, 185–207; English translation in *Nabokov's Dozen*, 95–111.

7. See, for example, Campbell, 77–89.

8. See Jonas, 57, 68, 73.

9. Ibid., 55–56.

10. A possible related detail is the "gyratory" ("vertliavyi," 139: 159) voice that calls Luzhin away from the true chess world into the unreal phantom world of things. There are at least two other references to the devil in *The Defense* (157: 167, 158: 168). Irena and Omry Ronen, 371–86, discuss some additional appearances of devils in Nabokov's works.

11. Jonas, 57.

12. *Worlds in Regression,* 80.

13. Identified by Appel, *Nabokov's Dark Cinema,* 161, 165. A good overview of recurrences and patterns in the novel is provided by Tammi, 138–42.

14. *Strong Opinions,* 184, 185.

15. Quoted by Field, *VN,* 132. Nabokov was also quite capable of treating the theme of "climbing" to transcendence in a humorous and parodic vein; see his poem "The Ballad of Longwood Glen" (1957) in *Poems and Problems,* 177–79, in which "Art Longwood" climbs a tree, is greeted by "delirious celestial crowds . . . in the snow of the clouds," and never returns to earth.

CHAPTER THREE

1. Hereafter, all page references will be given in the text in the form (English: Russian). The allegorical character of the novel was noted by Bitsilli, as soon as it appeared in an émigré journal.

2. Moynahan, "Predislovie," "A Russian Preface"; Davydov, *Teksty Matreški,* 100–182. See also Sisson, 140–41, for a discussion of the novel as an "elaboration of the themes of H. G. Wells's 'The Country of the Blind' "; however, Sisson does not claim any parallels based on otherworldly thematics. Shapiro tries to argue that the novel is based on Christian motifs and imagery.

3. More criticism has been published on *Invitation to a Beheading* than on any of Nabokov's Russian novels. The earliest and most famous reading of the novel as a quintessentially metaliterary work is Khodasevich's essay "On Sirin" (1937). (A rare disagreement with Khodasevich's influential views from within the emigration is Varshavsky, 215, 223.) For a recent variant, see Connolly. The reluctance of critics to accept the novel's metaphysical dimension is well illustrated by Penner, 33, who concludes that the novel is "a classic work of absurdist literature." Similarly, Boegeman, 112, denies the novel any "spiritual" or "ethical" concern, and labors to present it as Nabokov's exhortation to himself to switch to English, 118–207. Field, *VN,* 150, sees the novel as "triumphant solipsism." Peterson recognizes that the novel supports a metaphysical reading, but returns to a view of Nabokov as a metaliterary writer opposed to "realism." Rampton, 40–41, sees Cincinnatus as finding himself "in a fallen world." Alter, "*Invitation to a Beheading,*" 55, speaks of Nabokov's "esthetic" as leading back "to a metaphysic, and one with ultimately moral implications," but means something quite different by these terms than I do: he concludes that the novel is concerned with dramatizing that the "inevitability of [the artist's] partial failure spur[s] him to attempt again and again the impossible magic of comprehending life in art," 58.

4. Davydov, *"Teksty-Matreški,"* 112–14, 117–23, 128–32, 133–40. Motifs congruent with Gnostic myth, but not necessarily derived from it, can also be found in Nabokov's poetry of the 1920s. See, for example, "O, kak ty rvesh'sia v put' krylatyi" (1923, "Oh how you strain to be on [your] winged way"), in which the lyric persona addresses his "insane soul," speaks of its "shirt of flesh," and concludes "smert' gromykhnet tugim zasovom / i v vechnost' vypustit tebia" ("death will bang its tight bolt / and release you into eternity"), *Stikhi,* 103. As

Nabokov himself indicated in his "Introduction" to *Bend Sinister*, vi, there are strong parallels between it and *Invitation to a Beheading*.

5. For example, Bitsilli, 116; and Alter, "*Invitation*," 58.

6. The theatrical theme has been noted by virtually all readers of the novel: see, for example, Stuart, 58–66. Pifer, *Nabokov and the Novel*, 49–67, argues that the function of artifice in *Invitation to a Beheading*, and throughout Nabokov's oeuvre, is as a foil for the select individual's heightened consciousness, which is the only source of value in the world because it validates the individual's reality as true and authentic. Although an important step in the right direction, this view still does not do full justice to Nabokov's transvaluation of the terms *natural* and *artificial*, or to the otherworldly roots of his beliefs.

7. Stuart, 61–62, discusses other interchangeable characters.

8. Stuart, 71, makes a similar point but to a radically different end, namely that imagination can triumph over limitations placed on it.

9. The symbolic function of the moth in this novel is not vitiated by the assertion Nabokov made in an interview: "That in some cases [i. e., paintings by Old Masters] the butterfly symbolizes something (*e. g.*, Psyche) lies utterly outside my area of interest" (*Strong Opinions*, 168). Nabokov uses a large moth as an overt symbol of a dead boy's immortal soul in the short story "Rozhdestvo" (1925), translated as "Christmas."

10. *Lectures on Literature*, 378.

11. Johnson, *Worlds in Regression*, 28–32, discusses various motifs related to letters of the alphabet; see also 157–64 for an analysis of the novel's "two world" theme.

12. *"Teksty-Matreški,"* 150–51.

13. Van Veen discusses the nature of time, and his disbelief in the future, at length in *Ada*, 535–63. In *Strong Opinions*, 185, Nabokov suggests that he shares some of Van's essential views on the subject.

14. *Strong Opinions*, 76; Rampton, 59–60, makes a simlar point. By contrast, Klemtner, 436, argues that Cecilia C.'s lesson to her son is that he "can be reborn if he will abandon fixed space for a fluid, moving angle of vision."

15. See my discussion of the latter, *Andrei Bely*, 153–82.

16. Sologub, 106

CHAPTER FOUR

1. *Strong Opinions*, 13, 52; *Speak, Memory*, 280. Nabokov also states that he has "the greatest esteem" for *Invitation to a Beheading* (*Strong Opinions*, 92). Henceforth, all page references to *Strong Opinions*, *Speak, Memory*, "The Art of Literature and Commonsense," and *The Gift* (in the form English: Russian) will be given in the text.

2. Johnson, *Worlds in Regression*, 17–18, discusses the connections between Nabokov's colored hearing in *Speak, Memory* and *The Gift*. Rampton, 70–71, provides a useful list of critics who have claimed (in general terms, and without considering the idea of the otherworld) that Fyodor repeats many of Nabokov's views, a conclusion with which Rampton agrees. Levin, 206–7, analyzes insightfully the narrative devices used by Fyodor that also appear in *Drugie berega*—the

second, Russian version of Nabokov's autobiography. See also my article "The 'Otherworld.' "

3. Vera Nabokova, "Predislovie," 3–4; Dmitri Nabokov, "Translating with Nabokov," 176.

4. Quoted by Grayson, 140.

5. Rowe, *Nabokov's Spectral Dimension*, 31–39, also traces the rainbow motif, and others related to it, such as butterflies, in the context of his discussion of the influence that the spirit of Fyodor's father may be exerting on his son's life.

6. Quoted in English translation by Field, *His Life in Part*, 181–82.

7. Given Nabokov's attention to fatidic dates, the fact that he stresses the precise time and date when Fyodor emerges onto shore is probably significant. If 28 June is taken to be in the "Old Style," then Fyodor climbs onto shore on 11 July in the New Style. There is only one day's difference between this date and Fyodor's birthday, which is given as 12 July 1900 (assuming it is in the New Style; 24: 19). It may not be a coincidence that Fyodor's emerging out of water—a familiar image for rebirth—is nearly coordinated with his birthday. It is of course no mere chance that Fyodor's birthday falls on the same date as Nikolai Chernyshevski's, 12 July (312: 334); but the fact that Chernyshevski's is in the Old Style, while Fyodor's is probably in the New, makes the relation between them a *parodic* one. Similarly, it is no mere chance that Fyodor's father's birthday is 8 July 1860 (115: 118), while Nabokov's father was born on 20 July 1870 New Style, or 8 July Old Style (*Speak, Memory*, 173). There are undoubtedly other patterns to the numerous dates mentioned in *The Gift*. Nabokov discusses aspects of the novel's chronology in his preface to the English translation of the story "Krug" (1936): "The Circle," 254.

8. For a discussion of the narrative structure of *The Gift* as a "Möbius strip" that closes in upon itself, see Irena and Omry Ronen, 378; Davydov, *"Teksty-Matreški,"* 196–97; and Levin, 203.

9. Jonas, 254–55.

10. Rowe, *Nabokov's Spectral Dimension*, p. 35, shows how Delalande's image of the all-seeing eye enters into a network of motifs implying that the spirit of Fyodor's father may have influenced his son's life. Rowe's certainty needs to be tempered, however, by Nabokov's sense that the otherworld is ultimately unknowable.

11. Delalande's "free eye" recalls a famous passage in Ralph Waldo Emerson's proto-symbolistic essay "Nature" (1836), where he describes the effect that an immersion in a natural setting has on him: "I become a transparent eyeball; I am nothing; I see all; the currents of the Universal Being circulate through me; I am part or parcel of God," 24. See also Sisson, 328–29, for a discussion of intriguing parallels between Nabokov and Thoreau, especially in connection with *Transparent Things*.

12. Johnson, *Worlds in Regression*, 93–106, provides an insightful survey of the key motif.

13. Levin, 206, discusses the "slips" in Fyodor's memory pertaining to the length of the poems in his collection, and the name of one of his landladies. Fyodor also seems to make mistakes about the color of his book of poems (18: 13,

21: 15, 67: 65, 167: 174, 191: 201). These details may augment the verisimilitude of his character and "autobiographical" book on the principle that to err is human. The narrator's unreliability is not a significant theme in *The Gift*.

14. See Davydov, "Nabokov's Aesthetic Exorcism," 357–74, for an investigation of several aspects of the Chernyshevski biography.

15. Rampton, 64–100, attempts to defend Chernyshevski (and a number of other targets of Fyodor's attacks) because he finds aspects of his views, conclusions, and claims to knowledge both moving and convincing. By contrast, White argues correctly for the importance of both empirical reality and an implied transcendent in the novel's world view.

16. See, for example, Nabokov's "Postskriptum k russkomu izdaniiu," *Lolita*, 299.

17. *Strong Opinions*, 75.

18. In addition to Davydov, "Nabokov's Esthetic Exorcism," and Rampton, see Karlinsky, "Nabokov's Novel *Dar*."

CHAPTER FIVE

1. All page references to the novel will be given in the text. Nabokov wrote the novel in English in Paris in 1938, in anticipation of emigration to England or the United States.

2. Fromberg comes to the same conclusion in her illuminating study. Rowe, *Nabokov's Spectral Dimension*, 21–25, also has a comparable view of the novel, although in a number of instances he stretches the evidence.

3. All page references will be given in the text in the form (English: French).

4. "Appendix One: Abram Gannibal."

5. Stuart, 16–17 n. 5, among others, discusses the parallels between Sebastian's life and Nabokov's.

6. By contrast, Stuart, 24–25, 28, concludes that Sebastian shares "Narcissus' curse" of "self-consciousness."

7. Bader, 14–15, suggests we "read 'art' for 'the hereafter' " in this passage, which is part of her conscious strategy of interpreting Nabokov in exclusively metaliterary terms, even when he seems to be pointing elsewhere. Olcott, 113, demonstrates how V. and Sebastian "exchange" their national identities in a way that foreshadows V.'s claims about having become Sebastian.

8. Khodasevich, 97, 100.

9. This counters Stuart's arguments, 38–45, 51, that there is not much difference between V.'s and Goodman's biographies of Sebastian, and that the novel dramatizes the untrustworthiness of memory.

10. For example, Field, *His Life in Art*, 27–28.

11. One of the few published comments that Nabokov made about the novel appears in *Speak, Memory*, 257, where he refers in passing to its "self-mate combinations." (Another, unusually harsh, judgment appears in the preface to *Drugie berega*, 8, where he speaks of the novel's "nevynosimye nedostatki" ["unbearable weaknesses"].) "Self-mate," or "suimate" as it is also known, is a checkmate

forced by the side that is checkmated. The term can thus be understood as desig-
nating a victory achieved at the moment that one is defeated. In this it recalls V.'s
conclusion that although he may not have succeeded in reaching Sebastian in time
and sat by the wrong bed in the hospital, he still experienced a comforting proximity to him.

12. For example, Stuart, 4.

13. Stuart, 14–15, also traces chess imagery in the novel, and provides an ingenious reading of the detail of Paul Rechnoy's throwing his black chess knight
onto a table so that its head falls off, only to have his opponent, "Uncle Black,"
screw it back on: Sebastian loses his head over Nina, and Uncle Black is the character who provides V. with the clue he needs to identify her.

14. Fromberg, 440. Her observation is valuable even if she is wrong to refer to
"Palich" as a "middle name," and to claim that one can arrive at "Palchin" simply
by rearranging the patronymic's letters; one is obviously missing.

15. Stuart, 8; he also discusses the parallels among Sebastian's mother, Nina
Rechnoy, and Natasha Rosanov.

16. Occult systems such as anthroposophy teach that aspects of the spiritual
realm have a mirror-image relation to this world; see, for example, Rudolf
Steiner, 146. For a comparable occult manifestation in Belyi's *Petersburg*, see my
study *Andrei Bely*, 118–19.

17. Maddox, 45–46, suggests that Mme Lecerf's other guest at her country
house resembles the conjuror from *Success*. Among those who also provide overviews of parallels between V.'s quest and Sebastian's books are Nicol, 88–94;
Stuart, 23; and Olcott, 112.

18. Stuart, 20–22, discusses other instances of train imagery, including the way
that V.'s journey to Sebastian's deathbed echoes the latter's fondness for express
trains, which he inherited from his mother.

19. Fromberg, 436–39. She also concludes that V.'s text should be understood
as Sebastian's final work, and among other insights, provides a gloss for the odd
assemblage of titles on Sebastian's shelf.

CHAPTER SIX

1. All page references are to *The Annotated Lolita* and will be given in the text.
Where given, references to Nabokov's Russian translation of the novel will be in
the form (English: Russian). Some of the changes Nabokov made when translating the novel are discussed by Grayson, 255, and by Barabtarlo.

2. Maddox, 74–78, makes a similar point and draws parallels with Proust,
Keats, and Poe, all of whom are alluded to in the novel.

3. *The Nabokov-Wilson Letters*, 296, 298. Rampton, 103–7, argues against
seeing *Lolita* as pornographic, and provides an excellent analysis of Nabokov's
style from this point of view.

4. Quoted by Rampton, 202 n. 34.

5. *Strong Opinions*, 47, 15; see ibid., 23, for Nabokov's sympathy for Lolita.
Nabokov's remark in his afterword to the novel (316) that "*Lolita* has no moral

in tow" should clearly be read as a denial that there is anything in the work that is not fully integrated into its themes and form. It is also noteworthy that Nabokov saw Humbert as someone who had partially redeemed himself ("Foreword" to *Despair*, 9).

6. Rampton, 107–9, 115, discusses the issue of the reader's ethical response to the work, but sees it as more equivocal than I do. A good, brief overview of trends in criticism of *Lolita* is in Tammi, 276–79. Tammi also stresses the importance of distinguishing between Humbert as character and Humbert as self-conscious narrator of his experiences (281–86). However, not all features of Humbert's narrative can be ascribed to him; a higher agency of which he is not fully aware is also implied in the novel. For a discussion of the novel's subtle rhetoric, see Tamir-Ghez.

7. A related argument has been advanced by Fowler, 162; and Appel, "Introduction," *The Annotated Lolita*, lvi. Tammi, 275, concludes after an ingenious examination of the evidence about the audience for whom Humbert intends his narrative, that he comes close to seeing it "as a literary work in its own right."

8. Tammi, 279ff., argues convincingly that Humbert's own narrative strategies derive from detective fiction, and that he is not, therefore, as unselfconscious a narrator as some critics have thought.

9. Fowler, 148–51, clearly overstates the case when he claims that Humbert is one of Nabokov's "favorites." This assessment is due in part to Fowler's misreading the scene at Hourglass Lake when Humbert contemplates drowning Charlotte: since Jean Farlow is concealed nearby, Humbert is hardly presented with the opportunity for a "perfect crime." On the other hand, Fowler is correct to stress the role of fate in Humbert's existence, and the important effect it has on limiting his guilt.

10. "The Art of Literature and Commonsense" was delivered around 1951 (see above, chapter 1, note 3). Chapter 11 of *Speak, Memory*, which deals with "cosmic synchronization" and related matters, was first published in the September 1949 issue of *Partisan Review* (see *Speak, Memory*, 10). Nabokov states that he began to compose *Lolita* in approximately 1949 (after writing a related story in Russian some ten years earlier, which was published posthumously in English translation as *The Enchanter*) and completed the manuscript in 1954 (see "On a Book Entitled *Lolita*," *The Annotated Lolita*, 314).

11. A similar conclusion has been reached by a number of readers: see, for example, Bell, and Levine, who also discusses the related issue of the impossibility for Humbert to live in a timeless world with Lolita. *Laughter in the Dark* (1938) resembles *Lolita* in the way the villain Axel Rex views and treats all other human beings in terms of aesthetic criteria. However, the omniscient narrative structure of this novel allows Nabokov to condemn Rex overtly.

12. *Strong Opinions*, 147.

13. For example, Appel, *The Annotated Lolita*, 409 n. 237/2; other patterning related to tennis is described by Appel in *Nabokov's Dark Cinema*, 150.

14. Field, *VN*, 316–17, reports that he found no such story in French newspapers of the day, and concludes it was probably "one of Nabokov's false trails."

He also discusses the story in *His Life in Art*, 323–24. Appel traces prison imagery in his introduction and notes to *The Annotated Lolita*, xx–xxi, lii, 438.

15. Boyd, *Nabokov's Ada*, 238 n. 14. Boyd assumes (57) that free will as well as chance plays a role in Humbert's life, and gives such examples as "had not Humbert been tempted by the thought of lodging with Ginny McCoo, he would never have come to Ramsdale," and "had not Humbert by chance spotted Lolita, he would not have stayed at 342 Lawn Street." However, given that Humbert wonders if he is not predisposed toward nymphets, it is inevitable that he would be tempted to investigate a little girl in the person of Ginny (whose surname echoes Quilty's nickname, moreover, and thus acquires additional resonance). And the fact that Humbert spots Lolita sunning herself in a scene that is clearly a parodic evocation of Annabel by the sea, makes the "chance" nature of the sighting more than suspect. In general, the dominance of fate and patterning in Nabokov's fictions makes it virtually impossible to prove the absence of determinism from any concatenation of events.

16. Rowe, *Nabokov's Spectral Dimension*, 67–73, also investigates this possibility, and traces some of the related meteorological imagery.

17. Proffer, 127, points out that the thunderhead is also linked to the church that Charlotte attended during Humbert's couch scene with Lolita, which increases its portent.

18. Boyd, *Nabokov's Ada*, 182–83, 187, 192, 194, 227, points out that aquatic and mermaid imagery in *Ada* suggests that Lucette's spirit may have influenced Van and Ada after she commits suicide.

19. Quoted by Appel, *The Annotated Lolita*, 362 n. 58/1.

20. *Lolita: A Screenplay*, 81.

21. Another dimension of concealed patterning is literary allusions; useful studies that identify these include Appel's annotations in *The Annotated Lolita*, and Proffer, *Keys to Lolita*, 3–53.

22. Tammi, 286, reads this passage in the light of his basically metaliterary view that Nabokov is often concerned with demonstrating "the superiority of literary structuring [to private illusion] as the dominant theme of [his] novels."

23. The novel's ethics are thus less nihilistic than a number of interpreters have claimed: for example, Martin Green.

CHAPTER SEVEN

1. *Strong Opinions*, 18. Hereafter, all page references will be given in the text.

2. "Inspiration," 311. That Nabokov took Shade's poem seriously can also be inferred from his description of it as "the hardest stuff I ever had to compose," and his designation of Shade as "by far the greatest of *invented* poets" (ibid., 55, 59). Moreover, Nabokov's tone of voice when reading the part of the poem dealing with Hazel's ill-fated date and suicide shows clearly that he did not treat either the poem or her story as comic; he does not read even the final lines of Canto Two, with the rhymes "bank" "sank," for laughs. This is in obvious contrast to

Nabokov's comic reading of part of Kinbote's Foreword (Reading at Harvard University, tape recording).

3. McCarthy identifies Pope (as does Alter, *Partial Magic*, 198, 201–3) and Wordsworth as precursors of the poem's themes in the context of an illuminating discussion of the novel's devices and major systems of motifs. Field, *His Life in Art*, 106–12 passim, also discusses the poem's relation to Wordsworth.

4. A few of these parallels have been noted in passing by Fowler, 100, 102.

5. Tammi, 201–4, provides a concise overview of critical arguments regarding the unified authorship of the novel. See also Sisson, 190–207, for another survey of critical interpretations. Among those who argue for the necessity of keeping Kinbote distinct from Shade is Pifer, *Nabokov and the Novel*, 117–18.

6. *Pale Fire*, 17. Hereafter, all line and page references to Shade's poem, and page references to the rest of the novel, will be given in the text.

7. Berberova, 152, argues that Kinbote's phrase "we may concede, Doctor" (*Pale Fire*, 279) implies that the first address ("your favorite") refers to this unspecified Doctor as well, and is thus evidence for Kinbote's being mad and under medical care. Although this is an intriguing possibility, its effectiveness for interpreting the novel lies precisely in the fact that it cannot be proven.

8. That the two pronouns should not be read as referring to the same addressee—and are therefore not uttered by the same person—is supported by Vera Nabokov's Russian translation of the novel. She renders "Your favorite" as "Vasha liubimaia," *Blednyi ogon'*, 9, using the Russian second person plural, or polite pronominal form, and gives "Ty prodolzhala," ibid., 54, or the single, familiar form, for "You went on / Translating." Hereafter, and wherever necessary, all page references to the Russian translation of the novel will be given in the text.

9. Johnson, *Worlds in Regression*, 60–73, defends Botkin's authorship in the context of other ingenious decipherings of the novel.

10. Packman, 68–89, reduces the novel to the dramatization of a modernist model of reading. By contrast, Sisson, 217–53, argues for maintaining in suspension, and without resolving, the mutually exclusive "alternative realities" in the novel. Sisson also suggests, 228–29, a fascinating connection between *Pale Fire* and, of all things, Anthony Hope Hawkins's *The Prisoner of Zenda* (1894).

11. *A Russian Beauty*, 147–48. For discussions of the unfinished novel and its relation to Nabokov's oeuvre see Johnson, *Worlds in Regression*, 206–19; Field, *His Life in Art*, 292–97, 305–8, 310; and Sisson, 185–88.

12. See, for example, Maddox, 14–34.

13. Tammi, 217, among others, provides additional possible decipherings of the letter clusters. For example, following the reference to Goldsworth's house, he finds the phrase "a tale of a far-away land is being told." If accepted, this could conceivably be interpreted as an occult imprimatur for Kinbote's story. However, the Russian translation of the letter clusters in question does not support Tammi's reading (but we should bear in mind that Nabokov's widow admitted in her short translator's note, *Blednyi ogon'*, 1, that she is not certain that she has grasped all the hidden dimensions in the text). On the other hand, Tammi's suggestion, 337 n. 92, that the letter clusters "ata lane" refer to the butterfly *Vanessa atalanta* is

quite plausible. Tammi also provides an excellent overview of various hidden parallels between Kinbote's and Shade's texts (207–16).

14. Other important motifs include bird imagery (33, 35, 37, 48, 65, 95, 121, 127, etc.), electricity (see Rowe, *Spectral Dimension*, 26–32), and glass and mirrors (Alter, *Partial Magic*, 187–208 passim).

CONCLUSION

1. In *Strong Opinions*, 103, Nabokov admits to a certain influence by Pushkin, "no more than, say, Tolstoy or Turgenev were influenced by the pride and purity of Pushkin's art." He also states (ibid., 151) that "every Russian owes something to Gogol, Pushkin, and Shakespeare."

2. *The Nabokov-Wilson Letters*, 220. Hereafter, all page references to Nabokov's letters to Wilson will be given in the text. Among the more convincing arguments for Nabokov's possible debts to, or parallels with, other writers, see Karlinsky, "Nabokov and Chekhov," "Nabokov's Novel *Dar*," and "Vladimir Nabokov," 164–65. For suggestive parallels between Nabokov and H. G. Wells (aspects of whose legacy Nabokov is known to have admired) see Sisson, chapter 5, "Alternative Realities in Alternative Fictions."

3. On the basis of the same letter, Johnson concludes that Symbolism was important for Nabokov: *Worlds in Regression*, 2–3. Others who have remarked on Nabokov's ties to this period include Struve, 284, who speaks of Nabokov's debt to Belyi; and Karlinsky, "Introduction," in *The Nabokov-Wilson Letters*, 20. By contrast, Field, *His Life in Part*, 95, claims that except for Blok "there is absolutely no influence upon Nabokov by the artists of the Silver Age." Field also states that in an (unspecified) interview Nabokov "denied the influence of the Russian Symbolists," even though he admitted to digesting the "entire population" of the Silver Age. At the same time, Field claims that Belyi's influence begins after 1917.

4. *Speak, Memory*, 285. Hereafter, all page references will be given in the text.

5. Quoted by Field, *His Life in Art*, 265.

6. Field, *VN*, 188.

7. Frank, 13. Sisson, 3, makes a similar point.

8. *Eugene Onegin*, vol. 3, p. 525. Hereafter, all page references to this edition of the translation will be given in the text in the form (volume, page). For Nabokov's parallels with Blok, Belyi, and Gumilev, see also my article "Nabokov's Metaphysical Esthetics."

9. *Strong Opinions*, 97, 161.

10. *Grozd'*, 19–21. The other collection of Nabokov's poetry published in the same year, 1923, is *Gornii put'*. Selected poems from all periods of Nabokov's life were collected in his posthumous *Stikhi*. Hereafter, all page references to these three collections, and dates of composition, will be given in the text. (For corrections to dates of poems included in *Stikhi*, see Boyd, "Nabokov's Russian Poems," 13–28.) All translations are my own, and include only those lines and phrases that could be of interest to the reader who does not know Russian.

11. *The Defense*, 98–99; *Zashchita Luzhina*, 108. Hereafter, all page references will be given in the text (English: Russian).

12. *Invitation to a Beheading*, 60; *Priglashenie na kazn'*, 69. Hereafter, all page references will be given in the text (English: Russian).

13. *The Gift*, 199; *Dar*, 189. Hereafter, all page references will be given in the text (English: Russian).

14. Rampton, 117, makes a similar point. Page references to *Lolita* will be given in the text (English: Russian).

15. *Strong Opinions*, 57.

16. *Nikolai Gogol*, 76, 91.

17. *Perepiska s sestroi*, 62. Field, *VN*, 55, reports on Nabokov's contacts with Belyi's ideas during the period 1917-1919. Fyodor in *The Gift* attempts to write poetry in accordance with Belyi's theories (163: 170). A useful survey of parallels between Nabokov and Belyi is Johnson's "Belyj and Nabokov."

18. The analysis of Belyi's ideas is derived from my book *Andrei Bely*, 103–6.

19. *Strong Opinions*, 10–11, 118.

20. Belyi, *Simvolizm*, 436. English translation from *Selected Essays by Andrey Bely*, 100.

21. Nabokov's conception of the process that yields the work of art can also be summarized as a form of movement *a realibus ad realiora* (from the real to the more real), which is the epitome of Viacheslav Ivanov's Symbolist aesthetics; see the essay "O granitsakh iskusstva" (1913). It is of course also important to note that in addition to similarities there are major, indeed irreconcilable differences between the aesthetic platforms, beliefs, and artistic practices of Ivanov and Nabokov.

22. Alexandrov, *Andrei Bely*, 161–62.

23. Belyi, *Peterburg*, vol. 1, 42; vol. 2, 143; *Petersburg*, 18, 218. Hereafter, all page references will be given in the text in the form (Russian: English). For more on "self-thinking thoughts" see my *Andrei Bely*, 116–18.

24. *The Real Life of Sebastian Knight*, 183.

25. *Zapiski chudaka*, vol. 1, 155–58.

26. Tammi, 24, 24 n. 63. This is part of Tammi's thorough, but inconclusive, survey of references to the otherworld in Nabokov.

27. Field, *His Life in Part*, 29, quotes Nabokov as saying that he "may have been influenced" in his youthful literary reviews by "the spirit of cruel criticism of the sort that Gumilyov wrote." Nabokov adds, however, that this critical style "was also current in English journals of the time when I was young." Irena and Omry Ronen, 372, note an allusion to Gumilev's poem "Zabludivshiisia tramvai" in Nabokov's last novel *Look at the Harlequins!*, 246.

28. *Sobranie sochinenii*, vol. 1, 199–208. Hereafter, all volume and page references will be given in the text.

29. Quoted in English by Field, *His Life in Art*, 63–64.

30. "Pushkin, or the Real and the Plausible," 42; "Pouchkine, ou le vrai et le vraisemblable," 378.

31. Sisson, 138–40, in the context of a discussion of Nabokov's parallels with H. G. Wells, points out a resemblance between Nabokov's ideas about mimicry and "the apparent conflict between Darwinian natural selection and the sense of

beauty" as expressed by the eponymous protagonist in Wells's novel *Ann Veronica, A Modern Love Story* (1909).

32. Carpenter and Ford, 5, explain that the first Darwinian explanation of mimicry was given in 1862 on the example of butterflies from the Amazon River valley. See also Portmann, 70–74, and Wickler, 7–8.

33. Futuyma defends evolutionary theory, and summarizes contemporary American "creationist" arguments against Darwinian evolution. Simpson, who was Professor of Natural Science at New College in Edinburgh at the beginning of this century, provides a better informed and subtler "creationist" argument for natural phenomena. Although he does not discuss mimicry, he comes close to speaking of natural phenomena in terms of aesthetic categories when he concludes that "purely mechanical" explanations for them are inadequate (21–22) because "Nature is the orderly guise of the ultimate Spiritual Causality" (248). In general, this view is a variant of the theological "argument from design" that can be found in the Bible (Romans 1:20), and that has been especially popular from the eighteenth century to the present. It is interesting to note that Gould, 20–21, criticizes using "ideal design" in nature to support evolution because this "mimics the postulated action of an omnipotent creator. Odd arrangements and funny solutions are the proof of evolution—paths that a sensible God would never tread." It is of course unclear why Gould would believe that he knows "God's mind."

34. A brief overview of Uspenskii's life and works can be found in the brochure *Remembering Pyotr Demianovich Ouspensky*; Reyner's is a more detailed study by an ardent admirer.

35. Reyner, 2.

36. *A New Model of the Universe*, 42–43; the first edition was published in English in 1931. According to *Remembering Pyotr Demianovich Ouspensky*, 18, Uspenskii completed the book that was to become known in English as *A New Model of the Universe* prior to meeting Gurdjieff (another influential occultist) in 1915, and strove to keep the latter's ideas out of it when he was revising it for translation into English (the Russian text was never published). Hereafter, all page references to the second edition of the English translation will be given in the text.

37. When Uspenskii's book was first published, evolutionary biologists did not in fact invoke such large numbers of genetic mutations (what he calls "repeated accidents") to account for close resemblances between mimics and models (Carpenter and Ford, 106); and scientists still maintain that major differences can be effected by a change in a single gene. Uspenskii's versions of other Darwinian arguments are also inaccurate by the standards of contemporary evolutionary biology, but this topic is beyond the scope of the present study. It is worth noting that Nabokov consciously opposed his own ideas to reigning evolutionary theory when in *Speak, Memory*, 301, he spoke of acquired characteristics in Lamarckian terms.

38. *Strong Opinions*, 30.

39. Karges, e.g., 17, 30, recognizes that butterflies are connected with the tran-

scendent in Nabokov's oeuvre, but does not pursue the implications of this conclusion.

40. *Tertium Organum*, 171–72, 32 (this is probably Uspenskii's best-known and most influential work, and was published in Russia in 1912, and in 1916; the first two English translations appeared in 1920). Some of the other tantalizing parallels between Uspenskii's ideas and Nabokov's include art as a vehicle for understanding the noumenal world via phenomena (131), the occult implications of electricity (116), and the possible perspective of a higher dimensional being onto a lower world (chapters 9 and 10), which is relevant for *Laughter in the Dark* and *Transparent Things*.

41. In his note, Uspenskii indicates that Evreinov's *The Theatre in Life* was originally published in St. Petersburg in 1915, and in translation in London by G. G. Harrap & Co. (no date given). However, none of the books Evreinov published in Russian has the expected title "*Teatr v zhizne*," and nothing resembling it appeared in 1915; see the detailed bibliography in Golub, 275–76ff. *The Theatre in Life* does exist in English; however, as its editor indicates (xi) this is a compendium of chapters taken or revised from a number of earlier books that had appeared originally in Russian. Given that *The Theatre in Life* is akin to an anthology of Evreinov's thought, and that Uspenskii appears to have actually consulted it, I will use it to illustrate Evreinov's ideas; page references will be given in the text.

42. *Strong Opinions*, 11. Evreinov and Nabokov share another parallel in their conceptions of the link between ethics and imagination. In "The Art of Literature and Commonsense," Nabokov speaks of criminals as those who lack the imagination to picture the consequences of their crimes. Similarly, Evreinov discusses Raskolnikov from Dostoevsky's *Crime and Punishment* as someone who would not have needed to kill the old pawnbroker if he had been a better "actor for himself" (120–21).

43. "Pushkin, or the Real and the Plausible," 42; "Pouchkine, ou le vrai et le vraisemblable," 377-78.

44. Novalis, Schelling, and Ast are quoted by Todorov, *Theories of the Symbol*, 168–69. For another overview of this idea, see Wellek, 17, 47, 76, 136. It is known that Novalis and other Romantics were important for Evreinov (Golub, 70). Given Uspenskii's wide reading in idealist philosophy it is more than likely that he knew them as well. For a discussion of Belyi's comparable ideas, see my book *Andrei Bely*, 109–18, 120–22.

45. *The Theatre in Life*, 46–47.

46. For an indication of Uspenskii's considerable influence on various leading cultural figures of the day, especially through his best-known book *Tertium Organum*, see the index entries under "Ouspensky, P. D." in *The Spiritual in Art*, 433. For friends Uspenskii and Evreinov had in common, and for their visits to "The Stray Dog," see John E. Bowlt, "Esoteric Culture and Russian Society," in *The Spiritual in Art*, 172-73.

47. I have not been able to ascertain the specific subjects of all of Uspenskii's lectures; thus it is not certain that he mentioned butterflies in St. Petersburg before the Revolution. In *A New Model of the Universe*, 60, Uspenskii indicates that he

wrote the chapter in which he discusses mimicry between 1912 and 1929. Nabokov mentions that he became interested in butterflies at the "age of seven," which would mean in 1906 (*Speak, Memory*, 119).

48. Field, *VN*, 53, quotes from Vladimir Pohl's published account describing how he tried to guide the young Nabokov's thoughts toward mysticism. That Nabokov read various occult teachings (without, of course, necessarily accepting them) is obvious from *Speak, Memory*, 20, his parodies of them in *Sogliadatai* (*The Eye*, 1930), and his utilization of Gnostic topoi in *Invitation to a Beheading* and other works.

49. A brief note about this incident was published by "A. A.," together with a blurred reproduction of a photograph purportedly showing Nabokov and the other actors. (A clearer reproduction of this photograph appears in *Evreinov: Foto-biografiia*, 47; Nabokov, although not specifically identified, is recognizable in the front row on the left.) See also Golub, *Evreinov*, 267 n. 41, for another account of this incident. Field, *VN*, 129, states that "on the basis of the Evreinov trial it is fair to place Evreinov behind Nabokov as a major Russian influence"; this is because Nabokov defended the protagonist's desire in *The Chief Thing* "to make reality over into a transcendent illusion," which "is a central idea that we can follow in Nabokov from *The Eye* and *Glory* through *Pale Fire* and *Look at the Harlequins!*" This conclusion is debatable, and it is worth remembering that Nabokov's unequivocally positive personages such as Fyodor in *The Gift* (to say nothing of Nabokov himself in *Speak, Memory*) are concerned with perceiving their own unique realities clearly; indeed, it is Nabokov's negative and blind characters who make solipsistic projections onto the world. Evreinov's possible influence on Nabokov is also suggested by "A. A.," and by Slonim.

50. Field, *VN*, 129, 188; Golub, 266 n. 41.

Works Cited

In the footnotes, an item listed here is referred to only by the author's name unless further data are needed to distinguish the publication from others by the same author.

WORKS BY VLADIMIR NABOKOV

Ada. New York: McGraw-Hill, 1969.

The Annotated Lolita. Edited, with a preface, introduction, and notes by Alfred Appel, Jr. New York: McGraw-Hill, 1970.

"Appendix One: Abram Gannibal." In *Eugene Onegin*, by Aleksandr Pushkin. Revised edition. Translated with a commentary by Vladimir Nabokov. Four volumes. Princeton: Princeton University Press, 1975. Vol. 3, 387–447.

Bend Sinister. 1947. Reprint. New York: McGraw-Hill, 1974.

Blednyi ogon'. Translated by Vera Nabokov. Ann Arbor: Ardis, 1983.

"Christmas." In his *Details of a Sunset and Other Stories.* New York: McGraw-Hill, 1976. 151–62.

"The Circle." In his *A Russian Beauty and Other Stories.* New York: McGraw-Hill, 1973. 253–68.

Conclusive Evidence: A Memoir. New York: Harper and Row, 1951.

"The Creative Writer," *Bulletin of the New England Modern Language Association* 4, no. 1 (1942): 21–29.

Dar. 1952. Reprint. Ann Arbor: Ardis, 1975.

The Defense. Translated by Michael Scammell in collaboration with the author. 1964. Reprint. New York: Capricorn, 1970.

Drugie berega. 1954. Reprint. Ann Arbor: Ardis, 1978.

The Enchanter. Translated by Dmitri Nabokov. New York: Putnam's, 1986.

"L'Envoi." In his *Lectures on Literature.* Edited by Fredson Bowers. New York: Harcourt Brace Jovanovich/Bruccoli Clark, 1980. 381–82.

"Foreword." In his *Despair.* New York: Putnam's, 1965. 7–10.

The Gift. Translated by Michael Scammell in collaboration with the author. 1963. Reprint. New York: Wideview/Perigee, n.d.

Glory. Translated by Dmitri Nabokov in collaboration with the author. New York: McGraw-Hill, 1971.

Gornii put'. [Under pseudonym Vladimir Sirin]. Berlin: Grani, 1923.

Grozd'. [Under pseudonym Vladimir Sirin]. Berlin: Gamaiun, 1923.

"Inspiration." In his *Strong Opinions.* New York: McGraw-Hill, 1973. 308–14.

Invitation to a Beheading. Translated by Dmitri Nabokov in collaboration with the author. 1959. Reprint. New York: Capricorn, 1965.

Laughter in the Dark. 2d ed. New York: New Directions, 1960.

Lectures on Don Quixote. Edited by Fredson Bowers. New York: Harcourt Brace Jovanovich/Bruccoli Clark, 1983.

Lectures on Literature. Edited by Fredson Bowers. New York: Harcourt Brace Jovanovich/Bruccoli Clark, 1980.

Lectures on Russian Literature. Edited by Fredson Bowers. New York: Harcourt Brace Jovanovich/Bruccoli Clark, 1981.

Lolita. Translated by Vladimir Nabokov. New York: Phaedra, 1967.

Lolita: A Screenplay. New York: McGraw-Hill, 1974.

Look at the Harlequins! New York: McGraw-Hill, 1974.

Nabokov's Dozen. 1958. Reprint. Garden City, N. Y.: Anchor, 1984.

The Nabokov-Wilson Letters: Correspondence between Vladimir Nabokov and Edmund Wilson, 1940–1971. Edited, annotated, and introduced by Simon Karlinsky. New York: Harper and Row, 1979.

Nikolai Gogol. New York: New Directions, 1944.

"On Hodasevich." In his *Strong Opinions.* New York: McGraw-Hill, 1973. 223–27.

Pale Fire. 1962. Reprint. New York: Wideview/Perigee, 1980.

Perepiska s sestroi. Ann Arbor: Ardis, 1985.

"Pil'gram." In his *Sogliadatai.* 1938. Reprint. Ann Arbor: Ardis, 1978. 185–207.

Pnin. 1957. Reprint. New York: Avon, 1969.

Podvig. 1932. Reprint. Ann Arbor: Ardis; New York: McGraw-Hill, 1974.

Poems and Problems. New York: McGraw-Hill, 1970.

"Postskriptum k russkomu izdaniiu." In his *Lolita.* New York: Phaedra, 1967. 296–99.

"Pouchkine, ou le vrai et le vraisemblable." [by Vladimir Nabokoff-Sirine]. *La Nouvelle revue française* 48 (1937): 362–78.

Priglashenie na kazn'. 1938. Reprint. Paris: Editions Victor, n. d.

"Prof. Woodbridge in an Essay on Nature Postulates the Reality of the World." *New York Sun,* 10 December 1940, 15.

"Pushkin, or the Real and the Plausible." Translated by Dmitri Nabokov. *New York Review of Books,* 31 March 1988, 38–42.

Reading at Harvard University on 10 April, 1964. Tape recording. Poetry Room, Lamont Library, Harvard University.

The Real Life of Sebastian Knight. New York: New Directions, 1959.

"Rozhdestvo." In his *Vozvrashchenie Chorba.* 1929. Reprint. Ann Arbor: Ardis, 1976. 67–75.

"Solus Rex." In his *A Russian Beauty and Other Stories.* New York: McGraw-Hill, 1973. 183–218.

"Sovershenstvo." In his *Sogliadatai.* 1938. Reprint. Ann Arbor: Ardis, 1978. 208–24.

Speak, Memory: An Autobiography Revisited. New York: Putnam's, 1966.

Stikhi. Ann Arbor: Ardis, 1979.

Strong Opinions. New York: McGraw-Hill, 1973.

"The Tragedy of Tragedy." In his *The Man From the U.S.S.R. and Other Plays.* Edited by Dmitri Nabokov. New York: Harcourt Brace Jovanovich/Bruccoli Clark, 1984. 323–42.

"Ultima Thule." In his *A Russian Beauty and Other Stories.* New York: McGraw-Hill, 1973. 145–82.

"The Vane Sisters." In his *Nabokov's Quartet*. New York: Phaedra, 1966. 73–90.

Zashchita Luzhina. 1930. Reprint. Paris: Editions de la Seine, n.d.

OTHER WORKS

"A. A." [Note about Nabokov and Evreinov]. *Russkaia mysl'*, no. 3184, 29 December 1977, 10.

Abrams, M. H. *A Glossary of Literary Terms*. 3d ed. New York: Holt, Rinehart and Winston, 1971.

Alexandrov, Vladimir E. *Andrei Bely: The Major Symbolist Fiction*. Cambridge: Harvard University Press, 1985.

———. "Epiphanic Structures in Nabokov." Conference on The Legacy of Vladimir Nabokov: Commemorating the 10th Anniversary of His Death, Yale University, 14 February 1987.

———. "Nabokov's Metaphysical Esthetics in the Context of the Silver Age." Article MS (forthcoming).

———. "Nabokov's Metaphysics of Artifice: Uspenskij's 'Fourth Dimension,' and Evreinov's 'Theatrarch.' " *Rossiia/Russia* 6, nos. 1 and 2 (1988): 131–43.

———. "The 'Otherworld' in Nabokov's *The Gift*." In *Studies in Russian Literature in Honor of Vsevolod Setchkarev*, edited by Julian W. Connolly and Sonia I. Ketchian. Columbus, Ohio: Slavica, 1987. 15–33.

Alter, Robert. "*Invitation to a Beheading*: Nabokov and the Art of Politics." In *Nabokov: Criticism, Reminiscences, Translations, and Tributes*, edited by Alfred Appel, Jr., and Charles Newman. Evanston: Northwestern University Press, 1970. 41–59.

———. *Partial Magic: The Novel as a Self-Conscious Genre*. Berkeley: University of California Press, 1975.

Appel, Alfred, Jr. "Introduction." In *The Annotated Lolita*, by Vladimir Nabokov, edited and annotated by Alfred Appel, Jr. New York: McGraw-Hill, 1970. xv–lxxi.

———. *Nabokov's Dark Cinema*. New York: Oxford University Press, 1979.

Bader, Julia. *Crystal Land: Artifice in Nabokov's English Novels*. Berkeley: University of California Press, 1972.

Bakhrakh, Aleksandr. "Brat i sestra." *Novoe russkoe slovo*, 11 August 1985, 4.

Barabtarlo, Gennady. "Onus Probandi: On the Russian *Lolita*." *Russian Review* 47, no. 3 (1988): 237–52.

Bell, Michael. "*Lolita* and Pure Art." *Essays in Criticism* 24, no. 2 (1974): 169–84.

Belyi, Andrei. *Kotik Letaev*. 1922. Reprint. Munich: Eidos, 1964.

———. *Peterburg*. 1928. Reprint. Munich: Fink, 1967.

———. *Petersburg*. Translated, annotated and introduced by Robert A. Maguire and John E. Malmstad. Bloomington: Indiana University Press, 1978.

———. *Selected Essays of Andrey Bely*. Edited and translated by Steven Cassedy. Berkeley: University of California Press, 1985.

———. *Simvolizm*. 1910. Reprint. Munich: Fink, 1969.

Belyi, Andrei. *Zapiski chudaka.* 2 vols. 1922. Reprint. Lausanne: Editions l'age d'homme, 1973.

Berberova, Nina. "The Mechanics of *Pale Fire*." In *Nabokov: Criticism, Reminiscences, Translations, and Tributes,* edited by Alfred Appel, Jr., and Charles Newman, 147–59. Evanston: Northwestern University Press, 1970.

Bitsilli, Petr. "The Revival of Allegory." In *Nabokov: Criticism, Reminiscenses, Translations, and Tributes,* edited by Alfred Appel, Jr., and Charles Newman, 102–18. Evanston: Northwestern University Press, 1970.

Boegeman, Margaret Byrd. "*Invitation to a Beheading* and the Many Shades of Kafka." In *Nabokov's Fifth Arc,* edited by J. E. Rivers and Charles Nicol, 105–21. Austin: University of Texas Press, 1982.

Boyd, Brian. *Nabokov's Ada: The Place of Consciousness.* Ann Arbor: Ardis, 1985.

––––––. "Nabokov's Philosophical World." *Southern Review* 14, no. 3 (1981): 260–301.

––––––. "Nabokov's Russian Poems: A Chronology." *The Nabokovian,* no. 21 (1988): 13–28.

Breit, Harvey. "Talk with Mr. Nabokov." [Interview]. *New York Times Book Review,* 1 July 1951, 17.

Brown, Clarence F. "Nabokov's Pushkin and Nabokov's Nabokov." In *Nabokov: The Man and His Work,* edited by L. S. Dembo, 195–208. Madison: University of Wisconsin Press, 1967.

Bruss, Elizabeth W. *Autobiographical Acts: The Changing Situation of a Literary Genre.* Baltimore: Johns Hopkins University Press, 1976.

Bruss, Paul. *Victims: Textual Strategies in Recent American Fiction.* Lewisburg, Pa. Bucknell University Press/Associated University Presses, 1981.

Campbell, Joseph. *The Hero With a Thousand Faces.* 2d ed. Princeton: Princeton University Press, 1968.

Carpenter, G. D. Hale, and E. B. Ford. *Mimicry.* London: Methuen, 1933.

Carroll, William. "Nabokov's Signs and Symbols." In *A Book of Things about Vladimir Nabokov,* edited by Carl Proffer, 203–17. Ann Arbor: Ardis, 1974.

Clancy, Laurie. *The Novels of Vladimir Nabokov.* London: Macmillan, 1984.

Connolly, Julian W. "Nabokov's 'Terra Incognita' and 'Invitation to a Beheading': The Struggle for Imaginative Freedom." *Wiener Slawistischer Almanach,* no. 12 (1983): 55–70.

Couturier, Maurice. *Nabokov.* Lausanne: L'Age d'homme, 1979.

Davydov, Sergej. "Dostoevsky and Nabokov: The Morality of Structure in *Crime and Punishment* and *Despair*." *Dostoevsky Studies* 3 (1982): 157–70.

––––––. *Teksty Matreški Vladimira Nabokova.* Munich: Otto Sagner, 1982.

––––––. "*The Gift*: Nabokov's Aesthetic Exorcism of Chernyshevski." *Canadian-American Slavic Studies* 19, no. 3 (1985): 357–74.

De Jonge, Alex. "Nabokov's Uses of Pattern." In *Vladimir Nabokov: A Tribute,* edited by Peter Quennell, 59–72. London: Weidenfeld and Nicolson, 1979.

de Man, Paul. "Introduction." In *Toward an Aesthetic of Reception,* by Hans Robert Jauss, vii–xxv. Minneapolis: University of Minnesota Press, 1982.

Eakin, Paul John. *Fictions in Autobiography: Studies in the Art of Self-Invention.* Princeton: Princeton University Press, 1985.

Emerson, Ralph Waldo. "Nature." In *Selections from Ralph Waldo Emerson*, edited by Stephen A. Whicher, 12–56. Boston: Houghton Mifflin, 1957.

Evreinoff, Nicolas. *The Theatre in Life.* Translated and edited by Alexander I. Nazaroff. 1927. Reprint. New York: Benjamin Blom, 1970.

Evreinov: Foto-biografiia / Evreinov: A Pictorial Biography. Edited by Ellendea Proffer from materials collected by Anna Evreinova. Ann Arbor: Ardis, 1981.

Field, Andrew. *Nabokov: His Life in Art.* Boston: Little, Brown, 1967.

———. *Nabokov: His Life in Part.* New York: Viking, 1977.

———. *VN: The Art and Life of Vladimir Nabokov.* New York: Crown, 1986.

Fleischauer, John F. "Simultaneity in Nabokov's Prose Style." *Style* 5, no. 1 (1971): 57–69.

Foster, Ludmila A. "Nabokov's Gnostic Turpitude: The Surrealistic Vision of Reality in *Priglašenie na kazn*.'" In *Mnemozina: Studia Litteraria Russica in Honorem Vsevolod Setchkarev*, edited by Joachim T. Baehr and Norman W. Ingham, 117–29. Munich: Fink, 1974.

———. "Nabokov in Russian Emigre Criticism." In *A Book of Things about Vladimir Nabokov*, edited by Carl R. Proffer, 42–53. Ann Arbor: Ardis, 1974.

Fowler, Douglas. *Reading Nabokov.* Ithaca: Cornell University Press, 1974.

Frank, Joseph. "Spatial Form in Modern Literature." In his *The Widening Gyre: Crisis and Mastery in Modern Literature*, 3–62. 1963. Reprint. Bloomington: Indiana University Press, 1968.

Fromberg, Susan. "The Unwritten Chapters in *The Real Life of Sebastian Knight*." *Modern Fiction Studies* 13, no. 4 (1967–68): 427–42.

Futuyma, Douglas J. *Science on Trial: The Case for Evolution.* New York: Pantheon, 1983.

Golub, Spencer. *Evreinov: The Theatre of Paradox and Transformation.* Ann Arbor: UMI Research Press, 1984.

Gould, Stephen Jay. *The Panda's Thumb: More Reflections on Natural History.* New York: Norton, 1980.

Grabes, Herbert. *Erfundene Biographien: Vladimir Nabokovs englische Romane.* Tübingen: Max Niemeyer, 1975.

Grayson, Jane. *Nabokov Translated.* Oxford: Oxford University Press, 1977.

Green, Geoffrey. *Freud and Nabokov.* Lincoln: University of Nebraska Press, 1988.

Green, Martin. "Tolstoy and Nabokov: The Morality of *Lolita*." In *Vladimir Nabokov's Lolita*, edited by Harold Bloom, 13–33. New York: Chelsea House, 1987.

Gumilev, Nikolai. *Sobranie sochinenii.* 4 vols. Edited by Gleb P. Struve and Boris A. Filippov. Washington, D. C.: Victor Kamkin, 1962–1968.

Hirsch, Edward. "A War Between the Orders: Yeats's Fiction and the Transcendental Moment." *Novel* 17, no. 1 (Fall 1983): 52–66.

Iser, Wolfgang. *The Implied Reader: Patterns of Communication in Prose Fiction from Bunyan to Beckett.* Baltimore: Johns Hopkins University Press, 1974.

Ivanov, Viacheslav. "O granitsakh iskusstva [1913]." In his *Sobranie Sochinenii*. Brussels: Foyer Oriental Chrétien, 1974. Vol. 2, 627–51.

Jakobson, Roman. "O khudozhestvennom realizme." In *Readings in Russian Poetics, No. 2*, edited by L. Matejka et al., 29–36. Ann Arbor: University of Michigan, Department of Slavic Languages and Literatures, 1962.

Johnson, D. Barton. "Belyj and Nabokov: A Comparative Overview." *Russian Literature* 9, no. 4 (1981): 379–402.

———. *Worlds in Regression: Some Novels of Vladimir Nabokov*. Ann Arbor: Ardis, 1985.

Jonas, Hans. *The Gnostic Religion: The Message of the Alien God and the Beginnings of Christianity*. 2d ed. Boston: Beacon Press, 1963.

Karges, Joann. *Nabokov's Lepidoptera: Genres and Genera*. Ann Arbor: Ardis, 1985.

Karlinsky, Simon. "Nabokov and Chekhov: The Lesser Russian Tradition." In *Nabokov: Criticism, Reminiscences, Translations and Tributes*, edited by Alfred Appel, Jr., and Charles Newman, 7–16. Evanston: Northwestern University Press, 1970.

———. "Nabokov's Novel *Dar* as a Work of Literary Criticism: A Structural Analysis." *The Slavic and East European Journal* 7 (1963): 284–90.

———. "Vladimir Nabokov (1899–1977)." In *Histoire de la littérature russe. Le XXème siècle. La Révolution et les années vingt*, edited by Efim Etkind et al., 153–73, 868–71. Paris: Fayard, 1988.

Khodasevich, Vladislav. "On Sirin." Partial translation by Michael H. Walker, edited by Simon Karlinsky and Robert P. Hughes. In *Nabokov: Criticism, Reminiscences, Translations and Tributes*, edited by Alfred Appel, Jr., and Charles Newman, 96–101. Evanston: Northwestern University Press, 1970.

Klemtner, Susan Strehle. "To 'Special Space': Transformation in *Invitation to a Beheading*." *Modern Fiction Studies* 25, no. 1 (1979–80): 427–38.

Kuzmin, Mikhail. "Vvedenie." In his *Chudesnaia zhizn' Iosifa Bal'zamo, grafa Kaliostro*, 7–10. Petrograd, 1919. Reprint. New York: Russica, 1982.

Lee, L. L. *Vladimir Nabokov*. Boston: Twayne, 1976.

Levin, Iu. V. "Ob osobennostiakh povestvovatel'noi struktury i obraznogo stroia romana V. Nabokova 'Dar.' " *Russian Literature* 9, no. 2 (1981): 191–229.

Levine, Robert T. " 'My ultraviolet darling': The Loss of Lolita's Childhood." *Modern Fiction Studies* 25, no. 3 (1979): 471–79.

Levy, Alan. *Vladimir Nabokov: The Velvet Butterfly*. Sag Harbor, N. Y.: The Permanent Press, 1984.

Lubin, Peter. "Kickshaws and Motley." In *Nabokov: Criticism, Reminiscences, Translations and Tributes*, edited by Alfred Appel, Jr., and Charles Newman, 187–208. Evanston: Northwestern University Press, 1970.

Maddox, Lucy. *Nabokov's Novels in English*. Athens: University of Georgia Press, 1983.

McCarthy, Mary. "Vladimir Nabokov's 'Pale Fire.' " *Encounter* 19, no. 4 (1962): 71–84.

Moynahan, Julian. "Predislovie." *Priglashenie na kazn'*. 1938. Reprint. Paris: Editions Victor, n. d. 13–17.

————. "A Russian Preface for Nabokov's *Beheading*." *Novel*, no. 1 (1967): 12–18.

————. *Vladimir Nabokov*. University of Minnesota Pamphlets on American Writers, no. 96. Minneapolis: University of Minnesota, 1971.

Nabokov, Dmitri. "Nabokov and the Theatre." In *The Man from the U.S.S.R. and Other Plays*, by Vladimir Nabokov translated and introduced by Dmitri Nabokov, 3–26. New York: Bruccoli Clark/Harvest, 1984.

————. "Translating with Nabokov." In *The Achievements of Vladimir Nabokov*, edited by George Gibian and Stephen Jan Parker, 145–77. Ithaca: Center for International Studies, Cornell University, 1984.

Nabokov: The Critical Heritage. Edited by Norman Page. London: Routledge & Kegan Paul, 1982.

Nabokova, Vera. "Predislovie." In *Stikhi*, by Vladimir Nabokov, 3–4. Ann Arbor: Ardis, 1979.

Nicol, Charles. "The Mirrors of Sebastian Knight." In *Nabokov: The Man and His Work*, edited by L. S. Dembo, 88–94. Madison: University of Wisconsin Press, 1967.

Olcott, Anthony. "The Author's Special Intention: A Study of *The Real Life of Sebastian Knight*." In *A Book of Things about Vladimir Nabokov*, edited by Carl R. Proffer, 104–21. Ann Arbor: Ardis, 1974.

Ong, Walter J., S.J., "The Writer's Audience is Always a Fiction," *PMLA* 90, no. 1 (1975): 9–21.

Ouspensky, P. D. *A New Model of the Universe: Principles of the Psychological Method in Its Application to Problems of Science, Religion, and Art.* 2d ed. 1934. Reprint. New York: Knopf, 1943.

————, *Tertium Organum: The Third Canon of Thought, A Key to the Enigmas of the World.* Revised translation by E. Kadloubovsky and the Author. 1922. New York: Vintage, 1982.

Packman, David. *Vladimir Nabokov: The Structure of Literary Desire*. Columbia: University of Missouri Press, 1982.

Parker, Stephen Jan. "Nabokov Studies: The State of the Art." In *The Achievements of Vladimir Nabokov*, edited by George Gibian and Stephen Jan Parker, 81–97. Ithaca: Center for International Studies, Cornell University, 1984.

Pasternak, Boris. *Doktor Zhivago*. Ann Arbor: The University of Michigan Press, 1958.

Penner, Dick. "*Invitation to a Beheading*: Nabokov's Absurdist Initiation." *Critique: Studies in Modern Fiction* 20, no. 3 (1979): 27–39.

Peterson, Dale E. "Nabokov's *Invitation*: Literature as Execution." *PMLA* 96, no. 5 (1978): 824–36.

Pifer, Ellen. *Nabokov and the Novel*. Cambridge: Harvard University Press, 1980.

————. "Shades of Love: Nabokov's Intimations of Immortality." *Kenyon Review* 11, no. 2 (Spring 1989): 75–86.

Portmann, Adolf. *Animal Camouflage*. Translated by A. J. Pomerans. Ann Arbor: University of Michigan Press, 1959.

Poulet, Georges. "Criticism and the Experience of Interiority." In *The Structur-*

alist Controversy: The Languages of Criticism and the Sciences of Man, edited by Richard Macksey and Eugenio Donato, 56–72. Baltimore: Johns Hopkins University Press, 1972.

Prince, Gerald. "Notes on the Text as Reader." In *The Reader in the Text*, edited by Susan R. Suleiman and Inge Crosman, 225–40. Princeton: Princeton University Press, 1980.

Proffer, Carl R. *Keys to Lolita*. Bloomington: Indiana University Press, 1968.

Rabinowitz, Peter J. " 'What's Hecuba to Us?' The Audience's Experience of Literary Borrowing." In *The Reader in the Text*, edited by Susan R. Suleiman and Inge Crosman, 241–63. Princeton: Princeton University Press, 1980.

Rampton, David. *Vladimir Nabokov: A Critical Study of the Novels*. Cambridge: Cambridge University Press, 1984.

Remembering Pyotr Demianovich Ouspensky. Edited by Merrily E. Taylor. New Haven: Yale University Library, 1978.

Reyner, J. H. *Ouspensky, the Unsung Genius*. Boston: G. Allen & Unwin, 1981.

Riffaterre, Michael. "Describing Poetic Structures: Two Approaches to Baudelaire's *Les Chats*." In *Structuralism*, edited by Jacques Ehrmann, 188–230. New York: Anchor, 1970.

Ronen, Irena, and Omry Ronen. "Diabolically Evocative: An Inquiry into the Meaning of Metaphor." *Slavica Hierosolymitana* 5–6 (1981): 371–86.

Roth, Phyllis A. "Toward the Man behind the Mystification." In *Nabokov's Fifth Arc*, edited by J. E. Rivers and Charles Nicol, 43–59. Austin: University of Texas Press, 1982.

Rowe, W. W. "The Honesty of Nabokovian Deception." In *A Book of Things about Vladimir Nabokov*, edited by Carl Proffer, 171–81. Ann Arbor: Ardis, 1974.

———. "Nabokovian Superimposed and Alternative Realities." *Russian Literature Triquarterly*, no. 14 (1976): 59–66.

———. *Nabokov's Spectral Dimension*. Ann Arbor: Ardis, 1981.

Schaeffer, Susan Fromberg. "*Bend Sinister* and the Novelist as Anthropomorphic Deity." *Centennial Review* 27, no. 2 (1973): 115–51.

Schor, Naomi. "Fiction as Interpretation / Interpretation as Fiction." In *The Reader in the Text*, edited by Susan R. Suleiman and Inge Crosman, 165–82. Princeton: Princeton University Press, 1980.

Setschkareff, Vsevolod. "*Zur Thematik der Dichtung Vladimir Nabokovs: Aus Anlass des Erscheinens seiner gesammelten Gedichte*." *Die Welt der Slaven* 25, no. 1 (1980): 68–97.

Shapiro, Gavriel. "*Khristianskie motivy, ikh ikonografiia i simvolika, v romane Vladimira Nabokova 'Priglashenie na kazn.*' " *Russian Language Journal* 33, no. 116 (1979): 144–62.

Shloss, Carol. "*Speak, Memory*: The Aristocracy of Art." In *Nabokov's Fifth Arc*, edited by J. E. Rivers and Charles Nicol, 224–29. Austin: University of Texas Press, 1982.

Simpson, James Y. *The Spiritual Interpretation of Nature*. 3d ed. London: Hodder and Stoughton, 1923.

Sisson, Jonathan Borden. "Cosmic Synchronization and Other Worlds in the Work of Vladimir Nabokov." Diss., University of Minnesota 1979.

Slonim, Mark. [Review of *Look at the Harlequins!* by Vladimir Nabokov]. *Russkaia mysl'*, no. 3026, 21 November 1974, 9.

Sologub, Fedor. *Melkii bes*. St. Petersburg: Shipovnik, 1907.

The Spiritual in Art: Abstract Painting, 1890–1985. Edited by Maurice Tuchman et al. New York: Abbeville Press; Los Angeles: Los Angeles County Museum of Art, 1986.

Steiner, George. "Extraterritorial." In *Nabokov: Criticism, Reminiscences, Translations and Tributes*, edited by Alfred Appel, Jr., and Charles Newman, 119–27. Evanston: Northwestern University Press, 1970.

Steiner, Rudolf. *Knowledge of the Higher Worlds and its Attainment*. Translated by G. Metaxa. Edited by Harry Collison. New York: Anthroposophic Press, n. d.

Struve, Gleb. *Russkaia literatura v izgnanii*. 2d ed. Paris: YMCA-Press, 1984.

Stuart, Dabney. *Nabokov: The Dimensions of Parody*. Baton Rouge: Louisiana State University Press, 1978.

Tamir-Ghez, Nomi. "The Art of Persuasion in Nabokov's *Lolita*." *Poetics Today* 1, nos. 1–2 (1979): 65–84.

Tammi, Pekka. *Problems of Nabokov's Poetics: A Narratological Analysis*. Helsinki: Suomalainen Tiedeakatemia, 1985.

Tekiner, Christina. "Time in *Lolita*." *Modern Fiction Studies* 25, no. 3 (1979): 463–69.

Todorov, Tzvetan. "Reading as Construction." In *The Reader in the Text*, edited by Susan R. Suleiman and Inge Crosman, 67–82. Princeton: Princeton University Press, 1980.

———. *Symbolism and Interpretation*. Translated by Catherine Porter. Ithaca: Cornell University Press, 1982.

———. *Theories of the Symbol*. Translated by Catherine Porter. Ithaca: Cornell University Press, 1982.

Toker, Leona. *Nabokov: The Mystery of Literary Structures*. Ithaca: Cornell University Press, 1989.

Updike, John. "Introduction." In *Lectures on Literature*, by Vladimir Nabokov, edited by Fredson Bowers, xvii–xxvii. New York: Harcourt Brace Jovanovich/Bruccoli Clark, 1980.

Uspenskii, Boris. *Poetika kompozitsii*. Moscow: Iskusstvo, 1970.

Uspensky, Boris. *A Poetics of Composition*. Translated by Valentina Zavarin and Susan Wittig. Berkeley: University of California Press, 1973.

Varshavskii, Vladimir. *Nezamechennoe pokolenie*. New York: Chekhov, 1956.

Vladimir Nabokov: A Reference Guide. Edited by Samuel Schuman. Boston: G. K. Hall, 1979.

Wellek, René. *A History of Criticism: 1750–1950. Volume II: The Romantic Age*. New Haven: Yale University Press, 1955.

White, Duffield. "Radical Aestheticism and Metaphysical Realism in Nabokov's *The Gift*." In *Russian Literature and American Critics: In Honor of Deming*

Brown, edited by Kenneth N. Brostrom, 273–91. Ann Arbor: Department of Slavic Languages and Literatures, University of Michigan, 1984.

White, Edmund. "Nabokov: Beyond Parody." In *The Achievements of Vladimir Nabokov*, edited by George Gibian and Stephen Jan Parker, 5–28. Ithaca: Center for International Studies, Cornell University, 1984.

Wickler, Wolfgang. *Mimicry in Plants and Animals*. Translated by R. D. Martin. New York: McGraw-Hill, 1968.

Index